CONCEPT OF ISLAMIC LAW

CONCEPT OF ISLAMIC LAW

Editor

Arif Ali Khan

Co-editor

M.H. Syed

PENTAGON PRESS

CONCEPT OF ISLAMIC LAW

First Published 2007

ISBN 81-8274-220-X

Published by

PENTAGON PRESS
A-38, Hauz Khas, New Delhi-110016 (India)
Phones: 011-41656996/7/8, 41517091
Telefax: 011-41656997
email: pentagonpress@airtelbroadband.net

Sales Office:
Flat # 105-106, 4262, St. # 3
Ansari Road, Darya Ganj, New Delhi-110002
Phones: 011-41563901/2, 23287705
Website: www.pentagon-press.com

Printed at New Elegant Printers, New Delhi.

CONTENTS

PREFACE

The concept, various characteristic features and merits of Islamic law are strongly rooted in different sources in origin. These sources are the divine books, especially Holy Quran, Tradition or the sayings of the Holy Prophet, customs, traditions and cultural heritage, acquired by Muslim community, over a long period of time. A consensus-based approach was also adopted to bring new legislation in the society.

Like personal laws of other religious communities and the mainstream law of the modern society, the concept of Islamic law is very clear. It implies that it consists of, and advocates for, all those features, which strongly ensure the collective conscience, Quranic ethos, the cultural heritage of Islam, tradition, customs and folkways etc. of the Muslim community. For example, the observance of fast during the month of Ramadan is equally applicable to all the adherents of Islam, irrespective of Shias and Sunnis and different Muslim caste groups. However, they separately follow their own chosen codes of conduct. There are variations over approaches and provisions in different codes of conduct, but the basic ethos and tenets remain the same. The worship of Allah, moral values, sense of humanism, rationality, positive thinking, mutual cooperation, peace and harmony in society and other social measures have been incorporated into various features and aspects of the Islamic law.

The notion of Islamic law is also oriented at eliminating all forms of inequality and exploitation from the society and to establish a just and harmonious social system. The principles of democracy have been adopted in the formulation of principles of law and it has been expressed through many codes and regulations in the Shariah. The Islamic law also provides guidelines on; how one can earn one's livelihood. It promotes good deeds and hard work, devoted to Allah. It does not prescribe any unjust practice for earning livelihood. Another major feature of Islamic law is the concept of spirituality or metaphysical thinking. It is the abstract thinking for searching the realities of this mundane world. It reveals the correlation of an individual human soul with the super-power of God or Allah. All ceremonies and rites from birth to death are clearly guided by sacred laws and any deviation from these is considered a sin, or at least a shameful act.

The Islamic society is based on equality and homogeneity and the operating laws are, to some extent, common. Thus, there are no ideological and practical hurdles on the path of conformity to law. The caste system is a taboo in Islam. The different practices and rituals of different distinct groups, if any, are supposed to create contradictions in society.

The present book titled: 'Concept of Islamic Law', presents a reasonable description of the background, sources, religious foundations and the concept of Islamic law. It has incorporated the genesis, objectives, application and different latent concepts of Islamic law. Hopefully the book would definitely assist the student community, professionals, especially lawyers, academicians, administrators and intellectuals in our society and many more. All reasonable suggestions from enlightened readers are awaited.

Arif Ali Khan

Concepts of Islamic Law

1

INTRODUCTION

The purpose of studying the *hukm shari* is to understand the conceptual part of Islamic law. This study provides the framework within which the meaning of Islamic law is understood, the nature of its rules is grasped, and the operation of the legal system is seen.

Hukm Shari : The *hukm shari* in its literal sense conveys the meaning of a rule of Islamic law. It comes into being through the operation of its three elements *(arkan)*. These elements are:

1. The true source from which the *hukm* originates. The original source for Islamic law is the *Hakim* or the Lawgiver, that is, Allah Almighty;
2. The *mahkum fih* or the act on which the *hukm* operates—also called the *mahkum bih;* and
3. The *mahkum alayh* or the subject (legal person) for whose conduct the *hukm* is stipulated.

A discussion of the meaning of the *hukm shari* in Islamic law amounts to asking the question: what is Islamic law? The response deals with Islamic law as a system as well as with individual rules. The study of the *hukm shari,* when it deals with the nature of rules, reveals the types of legal obligation created by the rule. It tells us that all the rules may not create an obligation and that some rules are laid down by the Lawgiver to facilitate the operation of other rules. A classification of the various type of rule or *ahkam* becomes necessary to grasp these meanings.

The first of the three *arkan* (elements) of the *hukm shari* mentioned above is the Lawgiver (the *Hakim).* In the study of this element, it is shown that Allah is the Ultimate and True Source of all laws in Islam. Further, the implication of this statement is examined, that is, what do we mean by saying that Allah is the source of all laws?

The second element deals with the act on which the *hukm* operates and the legal rights that are affected. The third element deals with the types of subjects who are affected by a *hukm,* that is, those who possess full legal capacity and those who do not. It also deals with cases in which the legal capacity of the subject is restricted or becomes defective.

The Meaning of the Hukm Shari or the Meaning of Islamic Law : The Arabic word *hukm* (pl. *ahkam)* in its literal sense means a command. In its technical sense it means a "rule" This may be a rule of any kind. Thus, it may be a rational rule, like 2 + 2 = 4, or the rule that the whole is greater than its parts. It may be a rule perceived by the senses, like fire burns.

Again, it may be based upon experience or experiment, like aspirin is good for headache. Here, however, we are concerned with the legal rule, which is called the *hukm shari*[1].

The Muslim jurists give us a definition of the *hukm shari* when they attempt to answer the question: What is Islamic law? They define it as:

> A communication from Allah, the Exalted, related to the acts of the subjects through a demand or option or through a declaration.

This Definition Highlights the Following Important Points

1. The *hukm* or a rule of law (to be referred to as *hukm* from now on) is *a communication from Allah.* This means that it is not treated merely as a command. It also means that a communication from anyone else cannot be considered as a *hukm,* be he a ruler or someone else in authority.
2. *The Communication is Related to the Acts of the Subjects:* The communication invariably gives rise to a rule of some kind and enables the jurist to understand whether the requirement is for the commission of an act or its omission, or whether a choice has been granted for the commission or omission of such act. Thus, the words of Allah, "Do not go near unlawful sexual intercourse *(zina)"* [Quran 17 : 32] contain a *hukm* that requires omission and affects conduct. Some jurists divide the *khitab* into two types: *khitab jinai* and the *khitab* of *muamalat* (criminal and civil liability).

3. *The Hukm may be Expressed Through a Demand:* The demand in this case may be for the commission of an act or its omission. In each case, the demand may be expressed in binding terms or otherwise. When the demand is expressed in binding terms and requires the commission of an act, the *hukm* creates an obligation *(ijab).* When the terms used are not binding or absolute, the *hukm* gives rise to a recommendation *(nadb)* for the commission of the act. The jurists use various rules to decide when a demand has been expressed in binding terms.

   When the demand in the *hukm* is for abstention from or omission of an act and is expressed in binding or absolute terms, the *hukm* conveys a prohibition *(tahrim).* If the demand, for omission, is not expressed in binding terms the act is looked down upon and conveys disapproval *(karaha).*

   Al-Ghazzali[2] describing the division of commission and omission and the resulting *rules,* says: When there is a demand for the commission of an act, we conclude that there is a command *amr,* but when this command is accompanied by additional evidence about a consequential penalty for omission the act is obligatory *wajib.* In case we do not find such evidence, the act is recommended. In the case of a demand for the omission of an act, if there is accompanying evidence entailing punishment for the omission, the act is *haram;* if not, the act is *makruh.*

   In any case, we have four categories of obligations arising from a demand: obligation, recommendation, disapproval, and prohibition. These obligations are mostly associated with sanctions. When the obligations relate to ritual or worship the sanctions pertain to the hereafter or to censure through public opinion, and when the obligations relate to mundane affairs they invoke sanctions in the form of punishment in this world.

4. *The Hukm may Grant a Choice or Option to the Subject for the Commission or Omission of an Act :* If a text tells the subject to "eat and drink," a choice is offered to him that he may exercise when he likes. In other words, the subject is free to perform the act at his discretion. The bulk of the Islamic laws fall under this category and include all kinds of contracts and transactions. The Lawgiver, it is sometimes said, is indifferent to the performance of such acts.

5. *The Communication may be Expressed Through a Declaration:* In this case, the communication declares or determines the relationship of an act, or set of facts, with the *hukm.* The communication, therefore, declares that an act or set of facts is the cause *(sabab),* condition *(shart),* or an

impediment *(mani)* for the application of the *hukm*. For example, in the *hukm* of the payment of *Zakat* (obligatory religious contribution), the possession of a minimum amount of wealth *(nisab)* is the cause for the application of the *hukm,* having retained this wealth for a year *(hawl)* is a condition for the *hukm,* and the existence of debts against the subject may be the impediment or obstacle in the way of fixing liability for *Zakat*[3]. The declaratory communication explains the relationship of all these categories.

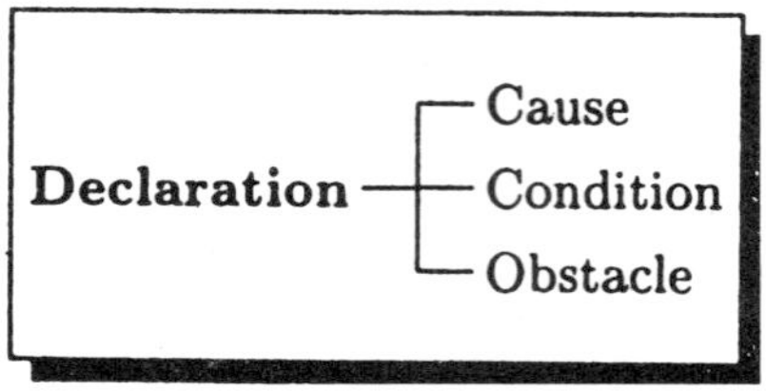

If we separate demands and choices from declaratory communications, we have two main categories for the *hukm*. The first is called the *hukm taklifi* or the obligation-creating *hukm*. The second category is called the *hukm wadi* or the declaratory *hukm*. We shall first, take up the discussion of the obligation creating rule or the *hukm taklifi*.

The Hukm Taklifi—Obligations and Duties : The *hukm taklifi* or the obligation-creating rule is viewed from two perspectives in Islamic law. It is viewed from the point of view of the *usuli,* who is a specialist in *usul ul-fiqh*[4], and from the point of view of the *faqih,* who is a specialist in *fiqh* or the substantive law. It is possible, though, that one jurist may be performing both functions. The definition of the obligation-creating rule from the point of view of the *usuli* is: "The demand of the Lawgiver requiring the subject, to perform or omit an act or to have a choice between commission and omission." The definition from the point of view of the *faqih* is: "The legal attribute of the acts of the subject after the demand of the Lawgiver requiring its commission or omission or to His granting a choice between commission and omission."

It is obvious that the earlier jurists were not providing different, definitions to satisfy the requirements of their individual perspectives. There is a legal basis for the two views. When we look at these categories from the point of view of the jurist who is concerned with derivation of the *hukm* (that is, the *usuli),* we call them obligations. The *usuli* is concerned with the question as to whether the *hukm* has created an obligation. On the other hand, the *fuqih* is more concerned with the performance of the acts and he, therefore, looks at the duties that are created. The two perspectives are, thus, complementary. The *usuli* is looking at the obligations that are created by the *hukm shari,* while the *faqih* is looking at the corresponding duties that arise;. A similar distinction is made with respect to the *hukm wadi* as well.

These two perspectives have an effect on the terminology employed in *usul ul-fiqh.* Let us list the different categories from both perspectives to see the difference in the terminology.

The Hukm Taklifi from the Perspective of the Usuli : The *usuli,* who is emphasising the obligations created by the *hukm,* uses the following terminology for the five categories:

1. Obligation *(ijab)*
2. Recommendation *(nadb)*
3. Disapproval *(karaha)*
4. Prohibition *(tahrim)*
5. Permissibility *(ibaha)*

The *usuli* is saying that the *hukm* to be derived from the texts is creating an obligation, or a recommendation and so on.

The Hukm Taklifi from the Perspective of the Faqih

The faqih, who is emphasising the performance of duties created by the hukm, states the five categories in the following terminology:

1. Obligatory (*Wajib*)
2. Recommended *(Mandub)*
3. Reprehensible, Disapproved (*Makruh*)
4. Prohibited *(Haram)*
5. Permissible *(Mubah)*

The *faqih* is saying that the *act* to which the derived *hukm* is related is obligatory, recommended and so on. He will be focusing on duties and their performance all the time.

The Hukm Taklifi According to the Hanafis : These five categories of obligations and duties emerge from the operation of laws in the opinion of the majority of the Sunni schools. The Hanafis[5] derive seven categories from the same definition. Let us view the categories derived by the Hanafis in terms of duties, that is, from the perspective of the *faqih,* who is concerned more about the performance of duties.

1. *Fard:* (Obligatory) This duty arises from an evidence or source that is definitive with respect to the authenticity of its transmission.

2. *Wajib:* (Obligatory) This duty is slightly weaker than the first in its demand for commission. It arises from a source that is probable with respect to its authenticity. The demand, however, has been expressed in binding terms.
3. *Mandub:* (Recommended) The difference between recommendation and the two kinds of obligation above, it should be recalled, is based on the binding nature of the command. The source is probable here, but the demand is expressed in non-binding terms.
4. *Makruh Karahat al-tanzih:* (Disapproved) It is an act, whose omission is demanded by the Lawgiver through a probable evidence *expressed in non-binding terms.*
5. *Makruh Karahat al-tahrim:* (Reprehensible) This category arises from a probable evidence *expressed in binding terms.* It is close to prohibition.
6. *Haram:* (Prohibited or duty not to commit an act) This arises from a definitive evidence.
7. *Mubah:* (Permissible) No duty is created and the subject is given a choice to perform the act or not to perform it. We may also say here that the subject is sometimes given the power to create obligations and duties with respect to other individuals. This may occur, for example, in the case of a person appointing another his agent or concluding a contract with him.

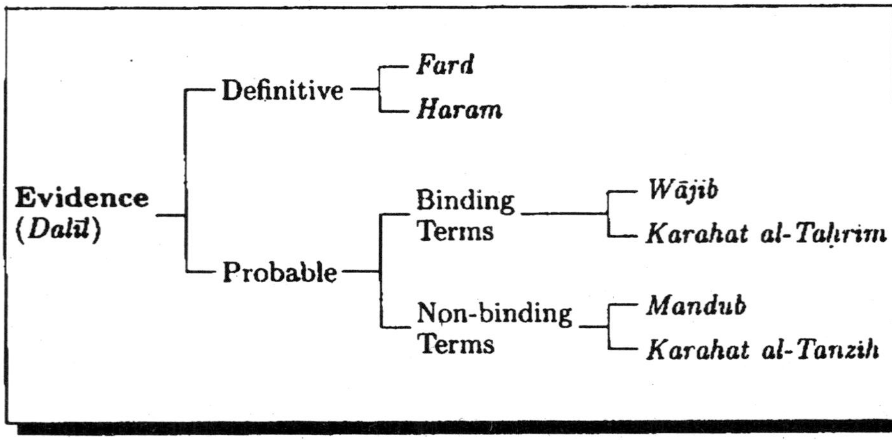

Some modern writers try to ignore this division by saying that the addition of two categories by the Hanafis has no practical significance. This seems questionable for there are some practical consequences though they relate mostly to ritual and in one case to apostasy. Let us now examine the classification of the declaratory rules that flows from the definition provided by Muslim jurists.

The Hukm Wadi— Declaratory Rules : The definition of the *hukm shari* provided above stated that the communication from Allah may be related to the acts of the subject in a manner that is declaratory. This is stated in order to accommodate rules that cannot be classified under the obligation creating rules. The following classifications are made:

1. Classification of secondary rules into *sabab, shart* and *mani.* The *usuli* is concerned more with this classification.
2. Classification into *sihah, butlan,* and *fasad* (validity, nullity and vitiation). This classification is more important for the *faqih,* because it pertains to the performance of acts.
3. Classification into *azimah* and *rukhsah* (general rules and exemptions). This classification helps the jurists to identify the general principles of the law or initial rules and the exceptions to these general principles. It is used as a tool for achieving analytical consistency.

The Distinction between the Hukm Taklifi and the Hukm Wadi

1. The aim of the *hukm taklifi* is to create an obligation for the commission or omission of an act or to grant a choice between the commission or omission of the act. The *hukm wadi* has no such aim. Its purpose is to either inform the subject that a certain thing is a cause of, condition for or obstacle to a *hukm* or it is to explain the relationship that exist between two rules or to provide the criterion for judging whether an act performed is valid or void.
2. The act or event that is affected by the *hukm taklifi* is within the ability of the subject with respect to its commission or omission. The act affected by the *hukm wadi* may or may not be within the ability of the subject with respect to commission or omission. In other words, it is always possible for the subject to commit or omit an act affected by the *hukm taklifi,* but it, may not be possible for him to commit or omit all acts that fall within the domain of the *hukm wadi.* Thus, theft is an act the omission of which is required and it is possible for the subject to avoid it, but the setting of the sun is the legal cause for the evening prayer, and it is not possible for the subject to bring it about. *Rushd* (discretion) is a necessary condition for contracts, but it is a condition that is beyond the power of the subject to create. Insanity is a defence against criminal liability, that is, it is an obstacle *(mani)* for the *hukm* to take effect, but it is beyond the power of the subject (he can only feign it for some time).

It is not to be assumed that the *hukm taklifi* and the *hukm wadi* are always stated in separate texts. It is possible for them to exist in the same text. For example, the verse about theft states: "The thief, male and female, cut off their hands." Here the *hukm* is the obligation to cut off the hand, the cause for it is *sariqah* (thief), thus, both occur in the same text.

STRATIFICATION OF LAW

The main categories of rules emerging from the definition of the *hukm shari* have been identified earlier, both in terms of obligations and in terms of duties. The details of these categories will be taken up in this chapter. The discussion of *wajib, mandub, mubah, makruh* and *haram* will be taken up first. This will be followed by the discussion of the types of *hukm wadi.*

The Meaning of Wajib (Obligatory Act) and its Different Types : The term *wajib* means an act the performance of which is obligatory for the subject. In its technical sense, it is an act whose commission is demanded by the Lawgiver in certain and binding terms. The binding and certain nature of the demand may be inferred from the syntax of the statement in which the demand is expressed. It may also be inferred from an evidence external to the syntax, for example, the existence of a consequential punishment for omission. Examples of these are: the performance of *salat,* the payment of *Zakat,* pilgrimage to the Kaaba, the fulfilling of promises and many other acts that, are required by the Lawgiver from His subjects. The Lawgiver has determined penalties for the omission of such acts.

Hukm or Rule for the Wajib : The rule for the *wajib* is that it must be brought about by the subject and for doing so there is reward *(thawab)* for him, while omitting it, without a legal excuse, entails a penalty. The rule further says that a person who denies the legality of a *wajib* when it is based upon a definitive *(qati)* evidence is to be imputed with *kufr* (infidelity). This is the rule according to the Sunni (sect) majority. The rules according to the Hanafis for the *fard* and for the *wajib* are as follows:

- The *wajib,* according to the Hanafis, is what has been made binding for the subject by the Lawgiver, but which has been established through a probable *(zanni)* evidence, whose strength is not that of a definitive evidence. The examples are: *sadaqat ul-fitr, witr* prayers, prayers of the two *Ids* and reciting *surat ul-Fatiha* in prayers. These cases have been established, according to the Hanafis, through a *khabar wahid,* which is a probable evidence.
- The *fard,* on the other hand, has been made binding for the subject and is established through a definitive *(qati)* evidence. The evidence may be a verse of the Quran or a *mutawatir* or *mashhur* tradition. Examples of

the *fard* are: the five daily prayers, *Zakat, Hajj,* recitation of the Quran in prayer and so on.

- The rules for *fard* and *wajib* are different in their view. The rule for *fard* is the obligation of performance and liability for punishment on omission as well as imputation of *kufr* for denying its legal validity. The rule for the *wajib* is the obligation of performance and liability for punishment for omission, but of a lesser gravity as compared to the *fard.* They also do not impute with *kufr* the person who denies the *wajib.*
- This distinction, drawn by the Hanafis, has an effect on the opinions derived in *fiqh.* For example, they say, if one forgets to recite the Quran in prayer, the prayer is a nullity *(Batul),* because this is non-compliance with a definitive evidence in the Quran requiring such recitation: "Then recite what is easy from the Quran." On the other hand, if one forgets to recite *Surah-Fatiha*[6], but does recite something else, it does not invalidate the prayer, although this is non-compliance with a tradition that says: "There is no prayer for one who does not recite the *Fatiha* of the Book." This, however, is a *khabar wahid.*

The Classifications of the Wajib (Obligatory Act) : There are several classifications for the *wajib* (obligatory act) based upon different criteria. These are described below.

Classification based on the time Available for Performance: Mutlaq and Muqayyad: On the basis of the time of its performance, the *wajib* is divided into *wajib mutlaq,* which is absolute or unrestricted by time, and into *wajib muqayyad* or *wajib* with a time limitation.

Wajib Mutlaq (Obligatory Act Independent of Time) : *Wajib mutlaq* is an act whose performance has been demanded by the Lawgiver, but He has not fixed a definite time for its performance. An example is the payment of expiation *(kaffarah)* and the *nadhr* for fasting sometime in the future.

The rule for *wajib mutlaq* is that the subject may perform the act whenever he likes. For example, if he took an oath to do something and then broke his oath, he may pay the *kaffarah,* for which he is liable, anytime he wishes to do so.

Wajib Muqayyad also Called Wajib Muwaqqat (Obligatory Act Limited by Time): It is an obligatory act demanded by the Lawgiver from the subject for which a time period is also determined having a beginning and an end. Examples are: the five daily prayers, fasting during month of the *Ramadan*, and *Hajj.*

The *wajib muqayyad* or *muwaqqat* gives rise to two further subdivisions depending on the performance of the act within time and depending on the time available for the performance of the act, that is, whether the time is just enough for the act or exceeds the time required. Let us look at both divisions.

First Subdivision of the Wajib Muwaqqat: Early, Timely and Delayed Performance or Tajil, Ada and Qada : The three types are as follows:

1. *Tajil* or early performance of an obligatory act, if permitted by the Lawgiver, amounts to performance in time, like the early payment of the *sadaqat al-fitr.*
2. *Ada* is the timely performance of the act, that is, the time that, the Lawgiver has fixed for it, without there being any shortfall in such performance. In case, the act has not been properly performed and is repeated within time and is performed properly, it is called *iadah* (repetition), like a person praying with *tayammum* finds water, performs ablution and prays again within time. There are some fine distinctions about the term *iadah* among the majority and the Hanafis, that is, when a repetition is called *iadah* and when *ada.*
3. *Qada* is the performance of an obligatory act after the time fixed for it by the Lawgiver, like offering the morning prayer after the sun has risen or like offering *zuhr* in the time of *asr.* The jurists agree that one who misses the determined time is obliged to offer the act as *qada'* and if the delay was without a valid excuse, he is liable for blame. The Zahiri jurists confine the excuse to one who forgot or one who missed the act while he was asleep, thus, it is obligatory only for these two cases in their view and not for one who misses it intentionally.

Second Subdivision of the Wajib Muwaqqat: Wide, Narrow and Dual Duration for the Performance of the Act or Muwassa, Mudayyaq and dhu Shibhayn : The three types are as follows:

1. *Wajib muwassa* (Obligatory act with extra time) is an act for which the time given by the Lawgiver is enough for this act and others like it. The time for the act is called *zarf* according to the Hanafis. An example is the time for the *zuhr* prayer. The subject is permitted to perform the required act in any part of this time period. After agreeing on this, the jurists disagreed as to which part is the *wujub* (obligation) connected to: the beginning or the end of the period. Suppose a woman starts menstruating in the middle of the period for the *zuhr* prayer, when she has not offered the prayer. Is she liable for *qada?* This problem is actually related to the issue in *usul* whether a command necessitates immediate or delayed compliance. It is somewhat complex and lengthy to discuss here.

2. *Wajib mudayyaq* (Obligatory act with time sufficient for a single performance) is an act for which the time granted by the Lawgiver is just enough for its performance and for no other, like the fasts in the month of *Ramadan* or like the evening prayer. The time granted itself becomes the standard *(miyar)* for the validity of this act.
3. *Wajib dhu shibhayn* (Obligatory act with extra time from one aspect and sufficient time from another) or the act that can be performed once in a time period, yet it permits other acts. An example is *Hajj.* It can be performed once in a year in known month, but it permits the subject to perform acts like *tawaf* a number of times during this period.

A major reason for this distinction is that the *wajib muwassa* is not valid if the subject does not form a *niyyah* required for it, because the time available may include other acts and the act has to be identified. As compared to this the *wajib mudayyaq* is valid with a general *niyyah* or even a *niyyah* for another act of the same kind. The *niyyah* will be redirected, so to say, toward the act for which the time is just sufficient.

Classification Based on the Extent of the Required Act : The *wajib* is classified according to the extent or amount of the act required into *wajib muhaddad* and *wajib ghayr muhaddad. Wajib muhaddad* (determinate obligatory act)

It is an act whose amount or extent has been determined by the Lawgiver, like the five daily prayers and the amount of *Zakat.* The rule for this type of *wajib* is that it becomes due as a liability as soon as its cause is found. A demand for its performance or payment is valid without waiting for a judicial verdict or on the willingness of the subject to perform the act. The subject is not absolved from the liability to perform or pay unless he does so in the way determined by the Lawgiver and in the amount fixed by Him.

Wajib Ghayr Muhaddad (Indeterminate Obligatory Act) : It is an act whose amount or extent has not been fixed by the Lawgiver, like spending in the way of Allah, feeding the needy or hospitality for guests. These things depend upon the need and capacity of the individual and thus vary. The rule for this kind of *wajib* is that it does not become a liability, unless it is imposed by a judicial decision or through willingness and acceptance.

The jurists have differed as to which act is to be attached to which type of *wajib.* For example, maintenance of wife and children, or support for the next of kin: are these to be linked to *wajib muhaddad* or *wajib ghayr muhaddad?* According to some Hanafi scholars, these are to be linked to the *ghayr muhaddad,* because there is no fixed amount for them. A court decision would, therefore, be required or it will become obligatory through an agreement between the parties.

The majority link these to the *muhaddad* and no court decision is required in their view for a claim.

Classification Based on the Subjects Who are Required to Perform : Depending on who is required to perform the act, the *wajib* is divided into the universal obligation and the communal obligation or the *wajib ayni* and the *wajib kifaya.*

Wajib Ayni (the Universal Obligatory Act) : *Wajib ayni* or the universal obligation is a demand by the Lawgiver from each subject, or each subject with legal capacity for the act, to perform the act, like prayers, fasting, *Hajj* and *Zakat.* The rule for this type of obligation is that it is to be performed by each person from whom it is demanded. The individual is not absolved of the liability even if some other persons have performed the act.

Wajib Kifaya (the Communal Obligatory Act) : The *wajib kifaya* is an act whose performance is required from the whole community and not from each individual, like *Jihad,* answering the *salam,* and rendering testimony. The rule for the *wajib kifaya* is that if it is performed by some individuals in the community, the rest are no longer liable for it, as the required act stands performed. The communal obligation may turn into a universal obligation, however, in certain cases. For example, if there is only one doctor in the community, it will be his personal obligation to look after a patient.

Classification Based on the Identification of the Object of the Required Act : The obligatory act is divided into two types on the basis of the determination of the object of the act. The types are *wajib muayyan* and *wajib mukhayyar.*

Wajib Muayyan (the Specified Obligatory Act) : The *wajib muayyan* is an act that is required by the Lawgiver specifically; there is no choice in it with respect to the act to be performed. The examples are prayer, fasting, payment of due wages and so on. The rule is that the subject is not free of the liability without specific performance.

Wajib Mukhayyar (the Unspecified Obligatory Act or Obligatory Act with an Option as to its Performance) : This type of act is required by the Lawgiver not as a specific act, but as one out of several determined acts, like the *kaffarah* (expiation) for breaking the oath: feeding ten needy persons, or clothing them, or the freeing of a slave. If the subject is not able to perform one act, he may perform the other. Each of these three acts, however, are required by way of a choice. When one is performed, the subject is absolved of liability.

The Meaning of Mandub (Recommended Act) and its Different Types : *Mandub* or the *mandub ilayh* is defined as "a demand by the Lawgiver for the commission of an act without making it binding and without assigning any blame for its omission." The non-binding nature of the demand can be inferred from the syntax. Sometimes the syntax may indicate that the demand is binding, but there may be related evidence showing that the demand is non-binding. The related evidence may be a text or a general principle of the *Shariah* or some other indication, like the absence of a penalty for non-performance. For example, in the verse,

O you who believe, when you enter into a transaction involving a *dayn* (debt), write it down. [Quran 2 : 282] the demand for the recording of the debt is a recommendation and is non-binding, because of an associated evidence that indicates this. The evidence is found in the following verse:

> And if one of you deposits a thing on trust with another, let the trustee faithfully discharge his trust. [Quran 2 : 283]
>
> This indicates to the creditor that he may trust the debtor without the writing down of the debt. Likewise in the verse And if any of your slaves ask for a deed in writing (to enable them to earn their freedom for a certain sum) give them such a deed, if ye know any good in them. [Quran 24 : 33]

The command requires the agreement of *mukatabah* with the slave (in which the slave pays for his freedom in instalments). It is, however, not binding on the owner. This is inferred from the established principle of the *Shariah* that an owner of property is free to dispose of it as he likes. It is not permitted to coerce him into a specific transaction, unless there is a legal necessity for doing so.

Types of Mandub : The recommended act *(mandub)* sometimes has some additional legal emphasis behind it for persistent or continued performance. On this criterion, it has been divided into two broad types:

Sunnah Muakkadah (the Emphatic Recommended Act) : *Sunnah muakkadah* is a recommended act that was persistently performed by the Prophet (peace be on him). He did not give up its persistent performance, except on some occasions. This again is of two types:

- *Sunnah muakkadah* that complements and completes a *wajib,* like *Adaan* and congregational prayers. The rule for this category is that the person who gives up such acts is liable to some blame, though this does not reach the level of punishment. The person who performs them is entitled to reward in the hereafter. If an individual gives up such acts totally, he is liable to lose his *adalah* (moral probity), which may in turn result in the rejection of his testimony. If a township collectively decides to give up these recommended acts, it exposes itself to legal and military action.

The reason is that these acts are part of the fundamental practice *(shaair)* of Islam. (An act essential for completing an obligatory act becomes an obligation in itself).

Sunnah muakkadah that does not complement or complete a *wajib,* though it is generally supportive of it, like praying two *rakas* before the *fajr* prayer, or after *zuhr, maghrib* and *isha.* There is reward for the performance of such an act and blame for giving it up, however, the person giving it up totally does not lose his *adalah.* If a township gives them up, it does not become liable for civil or military action, because these acts are not considered part of the *shaair* of Islam.

Sunnah Ghayr Muakkadah (Non-emphatic Recommended Act)—Nafil, Mustahab : The recommended act that is not emphatic is called *sunnah ghayr muakkadah* or *nafil* or *mustahab.* It is an act that was not performed persistently by the Prophet (PBUH), that is, he performed it several times and did not do so at other times. Examples of this type are the four *rakahs* before *asr* and *isha'* and giving *sadaqah*[7] to the poor. The rule for this type of act is that one who performs it is entitled to *thawab,* but one who does not, is not subject to blame.

Sunnat Zawaid : This term is used by some jurists for the acts of the Prophet (PBUH) pertaining to ordinary daily tasks as a human being, like his dress, food and drink, as well as his dealings with his family members. The rule for such acts is that one who adopts them seeking to follow the Prophet's (PBUH) example, out of love for him, is to be rewarded. The person who does not adopt them is not blameworthy in any way.

The Meaning of Haram (Prohibited Act) and its Different Types : The prohibited act *(haram)* is one whose omission is required by the Lawgiver in binding and certain terms. According to the majority of the jurists *(jumhur),* it does not matter whether the evidence informing us of this omission is definitive or probable. According to the Hanafis, however, the act that is *haram* is based upon a definitive evidence. The prohibited act that is based on a probable evidence expressed in binding terms, falls within the category of the abominable act that is closer to prohibition *(makruh karahat al-tahrim).* The rule for the prohibited act in their view is the imputation of *kufr* for the person who denies its legal validity. The rule according to the majority is also the same, that is, the imputation of *kufr* is applicable when the prohibition arises from a definitive evidence.

The binding and certain terms in which the demand is expressed are understood either from the syntax of the text alone or from other supporting evidence. Some examples of the prohibited act *(haram)* are: 1. Eating of carrion; 2. infanticide; 3. marriage with mothers or step mothers; 4. false evidence; 5. the misappropriation of another's wealth; 6. murder; and 7. unlawful sexual intercourse. The texts on which these are based are:

> Forbidden to you (for food) is dead meat. [Quran 5 : 3]
>
> Do not kill your children on plea of want. [Quran 6 : 151]
>
> Prohibited to you (for marriage) are your mothers. [Quran 4 : 23]
>
> And marry not women whom your fathers married. [Quran 4 : 22]
>
> And shun the word that is false (perjury). [Quran 22 : 30]
>
> And do not eat up your property among yourselves for vanities. [Quran 2 : 188]
>
> If a man kills a believer intentionally, his recompense is Hell, to abide therein (forever). [Quran 4 : 93]
>
> Nor come nigh to unlawful sexual intercourse, for it is a shameful deed. [Quran 17 : 32]

The communication in all the above texts is expressed in binding terms, and this is obvious either from the word prohibition or from the negation of permissibility or from the demand for the avoidance of the act.

Types of Haram : The prohibited act is divided into two types: prohibited for itself and prohibited due to an external factor.

Haram fi-dhatihi (Prohibited for itself) : The act that is prohibited for itself is one that was declared prohibited for itself ab *initio* and right from the start, and not for an external category. Examples of this type are: unlawful sexual intercourse, theft, and selling of carrion.

The rule for this category is that it is not permissible *ab initio* and if the subject commits such an act, there will be no beneficial legal effects or the gains desired. Thus, unlawful sexual intercourse; cannot lead to the establishing of paternity or claims of inheritance, while theft cannot be a reason for the claim of ownership, nor can the selling of carrion lead to ownership.

Haram fi-ghayrihi (Prohibited for an External Factor) : The act that is prohibited due to an external factor was not prohibited initially, and was legal in itself, but an external factor intervened and led to its prohibition, like fasting on *Id* day. Fasting is legal otherwise, but the Lawgiver prohibited it on the day of *Id,* because the subjects that day are the guests of Allah, and fasting becomes a hurdle for this hospitality. Another example is the sale that involves *riba.* Sale is legal in itself, but a condition stipulated in it that requires the charging and giving of interest leads to its prohibition.

The rule for this type is that as the act is valid in itself, if it is possible to remove the obstructing factor the act may be declared valid. Thus, according to the Hanafis, if the condition of *riba* is removed from the *riba* based sale, the sale may be declared valid. It is for this reason that they place this type of contract in the category of *fasid* (vitiated; unenforceable and not *Batul* (void).

DISTINGUISHING KINDS

There are two basic distinctions between acts that are prohibited for themselves and those that are prohibited due to an external factor:

1. When an act prohibited for itself becomes the subject-matter of a contract, the contract is void, that is, it will have no legal effects. As compared to this, when the act prohibited for an external factor becomes the subject of a contract, it is not void, but is valid or is vitiated with partial or suspended legal effects, according to the varying opinions of jurists on this. Thus, if the sale pertains to carrion or to wine, the contract is void having no legal effects. Likewise, a contract of marriage within the prohibited degree is void and has no legal effects. As for the contract of *riba* mentioned above, it is vitiated.

   The reader will come across many examples that are said to fall in the category prohibited for an external factor. However, in most examples one finds that they fall in this category according to the majority of the jurists; the Hanafis would place them in the category of *makruh* that is closer to prohibition. Thus, some care is to be exercised in studying the examples.

2. The act prohibited for itself cannot be permitted, except in the case of duress *(idtirar)*. For example, wine is prohibited for itself and cannot be permitted, unless the person affected is dying of thirst and there is nothing else available. The reason is that preservation of life is a vital interest secured by the *Shariah*. As compared to this, an act prohibited for an external factor may be permitted in case of dire need to the extent of the need. Thus, the covering of private body parts is prohibited not for itself, but for what it leads to. It is, therefore, permitted to uncover these parts in case of need, as when it is necessary for medical treatment.

The Meaning of Makruh (Disapproved Act) and its Different Types : The *makruh* (disapproved act) is a single category according to the majority of the jurists, but is divided by the Hanafis into two types: *makruh tahrimi* and *makruh tanzihan*. The first is what has been called reprehensible as it is closer to the category of *haram*. This type of act is the opposite of *wajib*, according to the

Hanafis. It is an act whose omission has been demanded by the Lawgiver in certain terms through a probable evidence, like making a proposal for marriage where the proposal of another is awaiting response or even making an offer for sale where the offer of another is pending. Each of these has been established through a *khabar wahid.* The *hukm* or rule for this type of *makruh* is punishment for the person denying it, though he is not imputed with *kufr.*

The simple *makruh* (disapproved) act is one whose omission is demanded by the Lawgiver in non-binding terms whatever the type of evidence from which it arises. It is one for which omission is better than commission. For example, a verse of the Quran proscribes sale at the time of the Friday congregational prayer, and asks the believers to avoid it at that time. This, however, may be interpreted as *makruh* rather than prohibited; and even if it is interpreted as prohibited due to an external factor, the result is the same.

The above division of *makruh* into two types is based on the Hanafi opinion. The majority of the jurists place *makruh tahrimi* into the category of *haram* insofar as it is a demand for omission expressed in binding terms.

Al-Shatibi[8], the *Maliki* jurist, explains that something that is considered disapproved in an individual case may be deemed prohibited as a whole. This means that a person should not make a habit of indulging in disapproved acts.

The Meaning of Mubah (Permitted Act) and its Different Types : The *mubah* or permissible act is one in which the Lawgiver has granted a choice of commission or omission, without blame or praise for omission or commission. It is also called *halal.*

The *mubah* that is mentioned in the texts is usually expressed in words like "There is no harm for you...," or "It is no sin for you" and so on. The *mubah* is also understood through the principle of *Istishab,* which states that anything that is not expressly prohibited or considered abominable by the *Shariah* is permissible.

According to the above rule, all contracts and transactions are permissible, unless there is an evidence indicating that they are not. This principle emphasises the fact that underlying rule for all things is permissibility. It will be explained, however, in detail in the sources for the *mujtahid.*

There is an interesting discussion in *usul ul-fiqh* about the *hukm* of *mubah.* It is generally maintained by the jurists that once an act is established as *mubah,* the Lawgiver cannot be assumed to have an intention of omission or commission related to it, and the performance or non-performance cannot be deemed an act of worship or required obedience.

On the other hand, there are certain groups, like a section of the Sufis, who are attributed with the statement that the omission of *mubah* is a required act. They rely for this on certain verses and texts of the traditions in which the temporal world and its pleasures have been looked down upon by the Lawgiver. They also argue that indulging in the permitted pleasures of this world leads to the commission of the disapproved and the forbidden. The jurists, however, reject such opinions and maintain that omission of the *mubah* is not a required act.

There have been other jurists who insist that as the commission of a *mubah* act amounts to the non-performance of a prohibited act, the commission of *mubah* becomes *wajib*. *Al-Shatibi*, thinking in different terms, has explained in great detail how the *mubah* may be permitted for individual cases, but taken as a whole may be considered obligatory or permitted. For example, eating and drinking is permitted and the subject has a choice in eating or not eating, but overeating may destroy his health and not eating at all may kill him too; a balance, therefore, has to be maintained. He calls such an act *wajib bul-kulli* and *mubah bi al-juzi.* This means that at the level of a specific evidence it is permitted, but when it attacks a purpose of the law it becomes obligatory or prohibited, as the case may be.

We may raise the question here as to whether the *mubah* is permitted by itself or whether it becomes permitted with the approval of the *Shariah?* For example, whether eating and drinking was permitted anyway or only when the texts said "eat and drink". This question is directly concerned with the principle of *Istishab.* The answer will, therefore, be provided there.

Hukm Wadi or the Declaratory Rule : The declaratory rule or the *hukm wadi does* not create an obligation; it is a rule that facilitates the operation of the obligation-creating rule or it explains the relationship between different obligation-creating rules. The major classifications are:

1. *sabab, shart* and *mani;*
2. *sihhah, fasad* and *butlan;* and
3. *azimah* and *rukhsah.*

Sabab, Shart and Mani : The secondary or declaratory rules primarily include the causes of, conditions for, and obstacles to the *hukm.* These may be described very briefly.

Sabab (Cause) : *Sabab* is the cause on the basis of which a primary rule or *hukm taklifi* is invoked or is established. The literal meaning of *sabab* is the means to a thing. In its technical meaning it is what the Lawgiver has determined to be the identifier of a legal rule so that its existence means the presence of the rule, while its absence means the absence of the rule. Thus, it is each entity or incident whose existence the Lawgiver has determined to be the prerequisite for the existence of the *hukm,* and its absence an indication of the absence of the *hukm.* Unlawful sexual intercourse, for example, is a cause for the obligation of implementing *hadd,* while *safah* and insanity are the causes for interdiction, but when these causes are missing there is no obligation to impose *hadd* or interdiction.

The cause *(sabab)* is divided with respect to the act of the subject into two types. The first is not dependent on the act of the subject, nor is it within his power to bring it about. Yet, when such a cause is found the *hukm* exists, like the setting of the sun as a cause for the obligation of the evening prayer, and the beginning of the month of Ramadan as a cause for the obligation of fasting, and like *safah* for the obligation of interdiction.

The second type is an act of the subject and is within his power to bring about, like journey for the permissibility of not fasting, or murder *(qatl-e-amd)* for the obligation of *qisas,* or the formation of contracts as a cause for enforcing their performance. Such an act may itself be the subject of a *taklifi* rule, that is, it would be required or prohibited or recommended, and it may fall under the category of declaratory rules. Thus, marriage is a cause for the permissibility of marital relations, but it becomes obligatory when there is fear of falling prey to unlawful sexual intercourse.

The distinction between a *sabab,* that is, a *sabab* alone and a *sabab* that amounts to an *illah* for a *hukm* is important and must be understood. The simplest way to understand this distinction is to say that when a cause can be rationally perceived to be the reason for the existence of the *hukm* it is an *illah,* but when the cause is obscure for human reason and it is not possible to understand why the cause has been associated with a *hukm,* the cause is simply a cause and not an *illah.* For example, human reason can comprehend why journey has been determined to be the cause for the permissibility of not fasting, but it may not understand why the month of Ramadan has been fixed for fasting. Another way of looking at it would be to say that the *illah* is a *sabab* that can be rationalised.

Shart (Condition) : The Lawgiver may declare that a set of facts must exist or an act must take place before the cause can take effect and invoke the related *hukm.* The existence of such a set of facts is called a *shart* or condition for the *hukm.* A *shart* or condition then is a sign or an indication on which the existence of another thing depends, but the existence of this sign does not necessarily mean the existence of that thing however, its absence does mean the non-existence of the other thing. By existence and non-existence of the *hukm* here is meant something of which the *Shariah* will take cognisance and to which it will also assign legal effects. In its technical sense, however, it implies a necessary condition for a *hukmi.* Ablution is a condition for prayer and the presence of witnesses a condition for the marriage contract. The existence of witnesses, however, does not necessarily mean that a marriage has taken place, yet without witnesses a marriage would not be valid.

The meaning of *shart* is understood clearly by distinguishing its meaning from those of other attributes. There are similarities and differences between a *shart* and a *ruku.* The similarity is that the legal existence of a thing depends on both; if either is missing the act is not valid or the *hukm* does not exist. The difference between the two is that a *ruku* (element) is always part of the act, while a *shart* is external to it. For example, bowing is a *ruku* or prayer and is a part of it, while ablution is a condition and is external to prayer.

There are similar distinctions between *sabab* and *shart.* The similarity is that both are external to the act and on both depends the existence of the *hukm.* The difference is that the existence of the cause necessarily leads to the existence of the *hukm,* but the existence of a *shart* does not necessarily mean the existence of the *hukm,* as in the case of witnesses to a marriage contract. A *shart* is divided into two types by the jurists: *shart shari* and *shart jali.* These are conditions imposed by the Lawgiver and conditions imposed by the subjects, as in contracts that accept them.

Mani (Obstacle) : A condition or set of facts may exist that prevent the *hukm* from being applied even if the cause is found and the condition is met. The obstacle or *mani* is a factor whose existence indicates the negation of a *hukm* or its *sabab.* This implies that an obstacle is of two types. The first type negates the *hukm* or prevents it from coming into operation, like the negation of the *hukm* of retaliation when the accused is the father of the victim.

The other type is the obstacle that affects the cause and prevents it from coming into being. The majority of the obstacles are of this type. Those who will study Islamic criminal law should understand that the first kind of *mani'* constitutes the doctrines of criminal law also called general defences.

The principle is the same as in Western criminal law where the definition of the crime is not constituted unless the doctrines are read in with them, that is, the general defences are implied in the definition. We shall be discussing some of these general defences under the heading of legal capacity of the *mukallaf* (subject).

Issues of Genuineness and Defects

An act that is obligatory, recommended, or permissible may be required to be performed in a certain manner by the Lawgiver. When the act is performed properly it is deemed as valid *(sahih)* otherwise it is null and void *(Batul)*. Here too the Hanafites add another category called irregular or vitiated *(fasid)*. Such an act can become valid if the cause of the irregularity is removed, otherwise it stays suspended. It may, however, have some legal effects. An example is a contract involving *riba*.

Under Hanafi law such a contract is considered vitiated *(fasid)*. This means that it can become a valid contract if the offending condition is removed. Such a contract is to be distinguished from the voidable contract under law. A voidable contract is dependent upon the option of the parties, while in a *fasid* contract the offending condition must be removed; the parties have no option in this.

Suggestive Measures

The Lawgiver may indicate that one *hukm* is to be considered as an obligation imposed initially as a general rule *(azimah)*. This may be followed by another rule that is an exemption *(rukhsah)* from the general rule. Drinking of wine is prohibited as a general rule. In cases of duress *(idtirar)*, however, one is allowed to consume it, if it saves one from dying of thirst. This is a *rukhsah*. According to some jurists, the entire law may be classified into general rules and related exemptions. This division has important methodological consequences and helps the jurist achieve analytical consistency.

One important significance is that analogy *(qiyas)* cannot proceed from an exemption, it must be based on a general rule. Thus, if the contract of *salam* is an exemption from the rules of *riba*, it cannot be used as a basis for constructing further analogies to obtain exemptions. This provision, considered with other strict conditions, further narrows down the operation of *qiyas*.

Purpose of Classification

The primary purpose for Muslim jurists in classifying the *hukm shari* into obligation-creating rules and into declaratory or rules was to show that by the term law we mean not merely the command of the Lawgiver, but also categories like *mubah* and the declaratory communications that include secondary rules. This gives us a meaning that is much wider than the simple literal meaning of the word "command."

John Austin, in his imperative theory of law, had defined law as a "command" for which he has been taken to task by legal philosophers like H.L.A. Hart, because it cannot explain the power-conferring rules that are not really commands. Such rules under the Islamic legal system fall within the category of *mubah*. It is also for this reason that the *hukm shari* cannot be translated as a "command."

In addition to this, the classification helps us to understand how the *taklifi* and *wadi* rules interact to create obligations and determine the operation of law. The declaratory rules facilitate, so to say, the application of the obligation-creating or *taklifi* rules.

References

1. *A religious and theological decree.*
2. *A prominent Islamic scholar turned sufi.*
3. *Alms-giving.*
4. *A book on, Science of deriving Islamic laws.*
5. *The followers of Hanafi school of thought.*
6. *The opening chapter of the Holy Quran; a prayer.*
7. *Charity.*
8. *A great Philosopher of Islamic law; Maliki school.*

2

THE BACKDROP

PHILOSOPHY OF SUNNIS

Let's begin with a brief account of the customs and usages that prevailed among the Arabs at the time of the promulgation of Islam, for such customs and usages form an integral part of the history of the Islamic legal system. The Islamic legal system, as in well known, had its origin in Arabia, and has been developed by Arab jurists, and we should, therefore, naturally expect to find on it the impress of Arabia's social history and of the Arab mind and character. Moreover, it would not be correct to suppose that Islam professed to repeal the entire customary law of Arabia, and to replace it with a code of altogether new laws. The fact is, the groundwork of the Islamic legal system, like that of other legal systems, is to be found in the customs and usages of the people among whom it grew and developed.

The author of the '*Hedaya*'[1] in establishing the legality of partnership says: 'Partnership is lawful because the Prophet (PBUH) found people practising it and confirmed them therein.' In commenting on this passage, *Ibn Hammam* remarks: 'There is a clearer authority in favour of legality of partnership than certain traditions, namely, continuous practice among men from the time of the Prophet; and thus there is no need for relying on any particular dicta.' The general principle is thus expressed: 'We hold permissibility to be the original principle, and prohibition to be equivalent to abrogating, with reference to the interval of time between Jesus Christ and the Prophet (PBUH), when lawfulness was the original attribute of human action; then the Prophet (PBUH) came and declared some acts to be unlawful, so that the rest remained lawful and permissible' The Muhammadan Code, in fact, includes many rules of pre-Islamic customary law which have been embodied in it by express or implied recognition.

Administration of Arabs

The constitution of Arab society, when the laws of Islam came into force, was that of a people which had not yet, generally speaking, completely lost its nomadic habits and characteristics. The Arabs were divided into tribes and sub-tribes, and these latter again into families. They were often at hostilities with each other, and on such occasions there was no 'recognised usage or general public opinion restraining the actions of the members of one tribe towards those of the other. But for sometime a number of tribes had united together by compact for the purposes of offence and defence, and this had the effect of ensuring peace for a sufficient length of time to allow for the growth of law. Such was specially the case in large cities like *Mecca* and *Medina*. *Mecca*, which was the place of pilgrimage, contained a large and powerful population, composed of several tribes bound together by ties of kinship and interest.

These two cities and some seaport towns were centres of busy trade, and the merchandise of, at least, some parts of Asia passed through them to Europe. We also find that marts used to be held at different places almost the entire year round. Besides the town populations there were the Arabs of the desert known as the Bedouins. They led a roving life, removing their tents as time and opportunity offered from place to place. Each of these tribes had no doubt its own peculiar usages. Our account is mostly concerned with customs that prevailed among the inhabitants of the principal cities; but the general characteristics of the customary law of the populations of the towns and of the desert did not differ in essentials. Only the one tended to a more settled form than the other. The bulk of the Arab population were idolaters, but there were some among them who had adopted Christianity, and some were Magians in religion. A large and influential community of Jews had for a long time settled in Medina with their own laws and usages. They were also found in Southern Arabia.

Role of the Chief

The *Arabs* of Arabia at the time of the Prophet (PBUH) had no certain constitution and nothing like a settled form of government, whatever might have been the condition of things previously. Each tribe elected its own chief. He was generally a man who, by his nobility of birth, age and reputation for wisdom, won the confidence and respect of his fellow tribesmen. His most important function was to represent his tribe in its relations with the other tribes. Sometimes he was assisted in the discharge of his duties by a council of elders. Within the limits of his tribe his orders and decisions were enforced not by any fixed machinery at his disposal, for properly speaking there was no constituted State, but by the force of tribal opinion. Sometimes it happened that the culprit belonged to a powerful family, and his kinsmen would refuse to surrender him to the chief of the tribe for punishment.

That family would then break away and join another tribe and become their Ahlaf (sworn allies). If the culprit escaped alive and took refuge with a rival tribe, he would be called *Dakhil* (*lit.* one who has entered.)

Things were Tending towards Settled Government at Mecca : In *Mecca*, however, things were tending towards the formation of a government. The tribes that composed the non-migratory population of that city had in their custody the *Kaaba*, which was a place not only of public worship, but of many social and political ceremonials. The public offices were divided among the twelve principal tribes or families. Of these the office of deciding disputes was delegated to one tribe and used to be exercised by its chief.

The duty incidental to another important office was for the chief who held it to pay from his own pocket fines and compensations for wrong doings committed by any of his tribesmen towards a member of another tribe. *Abu Bakr*[2], who afterwards became the first Caliph in Islam, held this office for some time.

What Happened in the Case of an Offence Committed by a Member of one Tribe Against a Member of Another Tribe : If a member of one tribe killed a member of another tribe, no distinction being made whether it was wilful or otherwise, the heirs or chief of the tribe of the deceased were entitled to demand that the offender should be given up to them to suffer death. But the matter might be compounded by payment of a fine or compensation amounting to a hundred camels. If the two tribes happened to be, at amity with each other, and the person accused denied the charge, then, on a number of men belonging to his tribe pledging their oaths to his innocence, the matter would be dropped. A case is reported in *Al-Bukhari*[3] which is important as illustrating the custom of the Arabs in this connection. A man of the family of *Banu Hashim* was hired by a man called *Khadis*, belonging to another branch of the tribe of *Quraish*, to go with him to *Syria* in charge of his camels. On the way, because the hired man had given away a tether rope to a passer-by without his master's knowledge, the latter in rage threw a stick at him which, happening to strike the man in a vital part, caused his death. But before he died, a man of *Yaman* happening to pass that way, he requested him when he arrived in *Mecca* to tell *Abu Talib*[4], the chief of his family, how he had been killed by his employer for the sake of a tether rope.

When the employer afterwards returned to *Mecca*, *Abu Talib* inquired of him what had happened to his man, and he said that he had sickened on the way and died. Subsequently, however, the man of *Yaman* who had been charged with the message by the deceased, came to *Mecca* and communicated the same to *Abu Talib*. The man who had engaged the deceased was then making the circumambulation of the *Kaaba*. A member of the family of *Banu Hashim* went up to him and struck him saying: 'You have killed one or our men', but *Khadis* denied the charge. *Abu Talib* next went up to the man and said: 'Choose at our hands one of three things: if you wish, give a hundred camels for the murder of our kinsman, or, if you wish, get fifty of your tribesmen to swear that you have not killed him. If you refuse either of these we will kill you in his place'. But, according to *Zubair-ibn Bakr*, both the parties referred the case to *Walid Ibnul Mughira* who decided that fifty men of Banu Amir— the family of the man charged—should swear before the *Kaaba* that *Khadis* had not killed the man.

Khadis spoke to his kinsmen, and they said that they would swear that he had not killed him. Then a woman of *Banu Hashim*, who was married to a man of *Banu Amir* and had borne him a son, came to *Abu Talib* and requested him to accept her son, as one of the fifty and forgo his oath. *Abu Talib* acceded to her request. Next a man of the family of the accused person came to *Abu Talib* and said: 'You want fifty men to swear in lieu of payment of a hundred camels, so it comes to two camels for every man's oath. Take from me two camels and do not insist on my taking the oath at the place where oaths are taken'. *Abu Talib* accepted the two camels, and forty-eight men came and took the oath.

Way of Working

The procedure that used to be adopted when a dispute or claim had to be decided was to call upon the plaintiff to adduce proof in support of his claim. If he had no witnesses, the defendant, in case he denied the charge, would be given the oath, and if he took it he would be absolved thereby from all liabilities. Sometimes the parties would go to a diviner and abide by his decision. If a suspected person was a slave, torture was sometimes resorted to in order to extort a confession.

The Oaths

Oaths formed an important part of the procedure in settling a dispute. An oath was held in great reverence, not merely as an inducement to speak the truth, but was regarded in the nature of an ordeal finally settling the dispute. Much solemnity was attached to the ceremony of administering it and a place called *Hatim* (lit. one that destroys, referring to the belief that a man taking a false oath would be destroyed by the deities) was set apart just outside the *Kaaba* for this purpose. The exact form of the oath is not known, but it appears that the pre-Islamic Arabs used to swear by *Hubal* their chief deity, or by their ancestors, and at the end of the ceremony would throw down a whip or sandals or a bow as a token that they had taken a binding oath.

Revenge : a Fine

The principle of punishment for all crimes against the person was retaliation commutable to a payment of blood-money or compensation for the injury. If the injury resulted in death, the loss caused was regarded as a loss to the tribe or family of the deceased, and it was their right to demand satisfaction from the tribe or the family of the offender. This would often assume the form of Vendetta. We also find that the doctrine of retaliation underwent modification according to the relative positions of the families of the parties. If a member of an inferior tribe killed a member of a nobler tribe, the latter would exact the blood of two men in lieu of one, of a male in lieu of a female, of a freeman in the place of a slave.

Kinds of Fine

Among other forms of punishment that prevailed among the Arabs, it appears that they used to cut off the right hand of the thief. Among the Jews of *Medina* an adulterer used to be stoned to death if he was poor, but latterly they punished the adulterer, rich or poor, by blackening his face and flogging him.

Customs Regulating Relations between the Sexes; Temporary or Muta Marriage : The customs regulating the relations of the sexes and the status of the children, issue of such relations, were at the time of the establishment of Islam uncertain and in a state of transition. Side by side, with a regular form of marriage, which fixed the relative rights and obligations of the parties and determined the status of the children, there flourished types of sexual connection under the name of marriage, which are instructive as relics of the different stages through which the Arabian society must have passed. It is narrated that there were four kinds of marriage in vogue at the time when the Islamic laws came into force:

(1) A form of marriage which has been sanctioned by Islam, namely, a man asks another for the hand of the latter's ward or daughter, and then marries her by giving her a dower (mahr).

(2) A custom according to which a man would say to his wife: "Send for so and so (naming a famous man) and have intercourse with him." The husband would then keep away from her society until she had conceived by the man indicated, but after her pregnancy became apparent, he would return to her. This originated from a desire to secure noble seed.

(3) A number of men, less than ten, used to go to a woman and have sexual connection with her. If she conceived and was delivered of a child, she would send for them, and they would be all bound to come. When they came and assembled, the woman would address them saying: "You know what has happened. I have now brought forth a child. O so and so? (naming whomsoever of them she chose), this is your son." The child would then be ascribed to him, and he was not allowed to disclaim its paternity.

(4) A number of men used to visit a woman who would not refuse any visitors. These women were prostitutes and used to fix at the doors of their tents a flag as a sign of their calling. If a woman of this class conceived or brought forth a child, the men that frequented her house would be assembled, and physiognomists used to decide to whom the child belonged.' Of the above, the first form of marriage must have been of the latest growth, and apparently it is a mere contradiction in terms to call the rest examples of forms of marriage. It admits of no doubt that the Arabs used also to contract what has been called a temporary marriage under the name of *muta*. It is stated in the '*Fathul-Qadir*'[5] : When a man came to a village and he had no acquaintance there (to take care of his house), he would marry a woman for as long as he thought he would stay, so that she would be his partner in bed and take care of his house'.

The Dower : In the regular form of marriage the fixing of *mahr* or dower for the benefit of the wife was in vogue among the pro-Islamic Arabs. It formed a part of the marriage contract, but in some cases the guardian of the girl used to take the dower himself. Whether such an appropriation was a mere violation of the ordinary usage, or whether it showed that dower was originally the price paid for the bride to her parents, and that the payment to her was but a later development, can only be a mere matter of conjecture.

At all events, at the time of the Prophet (PBUH), dower was regarded as a principle term of the marriage contract and the right of the wife. Its payment, in the event of divorce or death of the husband, was enforced by the voice of public opinion, or by the power of the woman's relatives, unless it had been paid at the time of the marriage.

A device used at times to be resorted to under the name of *shighar* marriage in order to deprive the wife of her dower. A man would give his daughter or sister in marriage to another in consideration of the latter giving his daughter or sister in marriage to the former. In such a form of marriage neither of the wives would get a dower. Unchastity on the part of the wife made her liable to the forfeiture of her dower and frequently a false charge used to be brought against the wife by the husband, so that he might get rid of her without paying the dower. And many a time a divorced wife or a widow would be coerced to give up her claim to dower or to restore it, if it had been already paid.

Woman not a Free Agent in Marriage : Before Islam a woman was not a free agent in contracting marriage. It was the right of her father, brother, cousin or any other male guardian to give her in marriage, whether she was old or young, widow or virgin to whomsoever he chose. Her consent was of no moment.

There was even a practice prevalent of marrying women by force. This often happened on the death of a man leaving widows. His son or other heir would immediately cast a sheet of cloth on each of the widows (excepting his natural mother), and this was a symbol that he had annexed them to himself. If a widow escaped to her relatives before the sheet was thrown over her, the heirs of the deceased would refuse to pay the dower. This custom is described as the inheriting a deceased man's widows by his heirs, who, in such cases, would divide them among themselves like goods.

No Restriction on the Number of Wives : There was no restriction as to the number of wives an Arab could take. The only limit was that imposed by his means, opportunity and inclinations. Unrestricted polygamy which was sanctioned by usage was universally prevalent. This was exclusive of the number of salve-girls which a man might possess.

Ways Disliked

The limits of relationship within which marriage was prohibited were narrow and defined only by close degrees of consanguinity. There can be no doubt that an Arab could not marry his mother, grandmother, sister, daughter or granddaughter, and perhaps he was not allowed to marry his aunt, and niece. But those among them that followed the Magian religion could marry their own daughters and sisters. An Arab was permitted to take as his wife his stepmother, cousin, wife's sisters, and could combine in marriage two sisters or a woman and her niece. It is doubtful whether he could marry his mother-in-law or step-daughter.

The Separation

Unrestrained as an Arab was in the number of his wives, he was likewise absolutely free to release himself from the marital tie. His power in this connection was absolute, and he was not required or expected to assign any reason for its exercise, nor was he under the necessity of observing any particular procedure. The word commonly used for this purpose was *talaq*. It depended upon his discretion whether he would dissolve the marriage absolutely and thus set the woman free to marry again or not. He might, if he so chose, revoke the divorce and resume marital connection. Sometimes an Arab would pronounce *talaq* ten times and take his wife back and again divorce her and then take her back and so on.

The wife in such a predicament was entirely at the mercy of the husband and would not know when she was free. Sometimes the husband would renounce his wife by means of what was called a suspensory divorce. This procedure did not dissolve the marriage, but it only enabled the husband to refuse to live with his wife, while the latter was not at liberty to marry again.

Another form of divorce in use among the Arabs was *ila* the husband swearing that he would have nothing to do with his wile. According to some, such an oath had the effect of causing an instant separation, but others say that it was regarded as a suspensory divorce. Sometimes when an Arab wanted to divorce his wife, he would say that she was like the back of his mother. This would have the effect of an irrevocable divorce and was known as *zihar* (from *zahr Zihar* back).

Khula : The wife among the Arabs had no corresponding right to release herself from the bond of marriage. But her parents by a friendly arrangement with the husband could obtain a separation by returning the dower if it had been paid or by agreeing to forgo it if not paid. Such an arrangement was called *khula lit*, stripping, and by it the marriage tie would be absolutely dissolved.

Influence of Divorce

A woman if absolutely separated by *talaq, zihar, ila*' or *khul* might remarry, but she could not do so until sometime, called the period of *iddat* had elapsed. This precaution was evidently observed in the interest of the child that might be in the womb. But an Arab before Islam would sometimes, divorce his pregnant wife, and she would under an agreement with him be taken over in marriage by another. On the death of the husband the period of *iddat* was one year.

Law at Work

The status of a child was determined not merely by marriage, but also as may be gathered from what has preceded by other forms of sexual relations. Regarding the issue of a regular form of marriage no doubt was entertained as to the establishment of the descent of the child from the husband of its mother. In the other cases, as we have seen, it was the right of the mother of the child to affiliate it to anyone with whom she had sexual connection.

Foster Child

Adoption among the Arabs was also in vogue as a legitimate mode of affiliation. Whether any form of ceremony was observed at the time of adoption is not known, but it seems that it was generally effected by a contract with the parents of the boy. The right to adopt was not based on any fiction, and it was not restricted by any condition as to the age of the adopted child, or the absence of a natural born son to the adoptive father. The adopted son passed into the family of his adopter and assumed his name, and his rights and disabilities were the same as those of a natural born son.

Eves' Killing

In proportion to his eagerness to have a son, an Arab father regarded the birth of a daughter as a calamity, partly at least because of the degraded status of women. Even in the time of the Prophet (PBUH) female infanticide was prevalent, and many fathers used to bury their daughters alive as soon as born.

Estate Proprietorship

The property of an Arab generally speaking was of a simple description. Camels, cattle, tents, clothes and a few utensils usually composed the bulk of his possessions. The use of money had been known to him for some time, and slaves were a common and valuable form of property. In towns there were properly built houses and shops, and land had value. Proprietorship was individual, and the principle of a joint family, with reference to the holding of property, was unknown. No distinction was made between ancestral and self-acquired movable and immovable property. Except the places of worship there was hardly any public property.

With the exception of a slave who himself was the property of his master, the Arab customary law recognised the right of every one to hold property. Though a woman, as we shall see, was debarred from inheriting, she was under no disability in the matter of owning property. Anything that she might receive from her husband as dower or by gift from him or her parents and relatives was absolutely hers. Sometimes women acquired riches by trade and commerce and some of them were owners of land and houses. But neither the person nor possessions of a woman were safe unless she was under the protection of her parents or some male relatives or her husband. If her protector proved rapacious or dishonest, she hardly had any remedy. The position of an infant or a *non compas mentis* was still worse, and the customary law of the Arabs provided no protection to him from the dishonesty of his guardian.

Power of Alienation; Different Forms of Sale : An Arab owner had absolute power of disposal over his property. He could, by an act *inter vivos,* alienate his entire interest by a sale or gift or only a partial or limited interest by lending, pledging or leasing. Under the name of sale he enjoyed a perfect freedom of contract. Some of these transactions were purely speculative and even of a gambling nature.

The following list of the different kinds of sale in vogue among the pre-Islamic Arabs will furnish a clue to many of the principles of transfer of property established by the Islamic Jurisprudence:

1. Sale of goods for goods (*Muqayada*), being an exchange or barter.
2. Sale of goods for money (*Bai*), a form of sale commonly in use.
3. Sale of money for money (*Sarf*), or money-changing.
4. Sale in which the price was paid in advance, the article to be delivered on a future date: this sale was called Salam.
5. Sale with an option to revoke.
6. An absolute or irrevocable sale.
7. Sale of goods, the price to be paid in future.
8. *Murabaha* a transaction in which the vendor sells the article for the cost price and certain stated profits.
9. At-*Tauwaliya* sale at the cost price.
10. *Wadi* sale at less than cost price.
11. *Musawama* sale by bargaining.
12. Sale by throwing a stone several pieces of cloth, for instance, being exposed for sale, the buyer throws a stone and whichever piece it falls upon becomes the property of the buyer, neither party having the option of revoking the sale.
13. *Mulamasa* in this form of sale the bargain was concluded by the buyer touching the goods which at once became his property whether the vendor agreed to the price or not.
14. *Munabadha* a sale in which the shopkeeper would throw an article towards the intending buyer, this having the effect of completing the sale.
15. *Muzabana* sale of dates on a tree in consideration for plucked dates.
16. *Muhaqala* sale of wheat in the ears or of a foetus in the womb.
17. *Muamila* or *Baiul-wafa*; in this form of sale the vendor of the article says to the buyer, I sell you for the debt which I owe you on condition that

when I repay the debt you will give back the article to me'. The buyer, however, could not make use of the article without the vendor's permission.

18. A form of sale called 'two-bargains-in-one' in which the conditions was that the buyer should sell the article back to the vendor within a stated period.
19. Urbun in this sale the purchaser pays a portion of the price to the vendor stipulating that, if he approved of the article, he would pay the balance, otherwise he would return it and the amount paid by him would be forfeited.
20. A sale in which the subject-matter was not in possession of the vendor at the time of the contract, but which he was to secure afterwards in order to fulfil the contract.

The Agreements

A lease of land used to be granted generally for the term of a year, but sometimes though rarely for two or three years. There is no record of a lease for a long term. The rent was paid either in money or part of the produce or wheat. Sometimes it used to be a condition of the lease that the lessor should supply the seed for cultivation, and sometimes that it should be supplied by the lessee. Of the former the tenure was called *mukhabara* and of the latter *muzaraa*. Sometimes the stipulation used to be that the lessee should cultivate the land with seed found by himself, and the lessor would have for his share the crops that would grow on the portion adjoining the stream or on some other specified plot. The Arabs also used to farm out the fruit trees.

Custom of Mortgages

The Arabs used to lend out money on interest, and at least among the Jews of *Medina* usury was rampant under the name of riba. Loans of articles by way of accommodation were designated ariya the borrower in this, form of contract enjoying the use and income without consuming or disposing of the substance.

Testamentary Dispositions of Property : An Arab's capacity to dispose of his property by will was as full as his power to deal with it by acts *inter vivos.* He was not limited in making testamentary dispositions to any proportion of his possessions, nor to any particular description of property. He could make the bequest in favour of anyone he chose, and there was nothing to prevent him from giving away his entire property to some rich stranger, leaving his own children, parents and kindred in want. Or if he chose he might give preference to one heir to the exclusion of the other.

The Heredity

On the death of an Arab his possessions, such as had not been disposed of, devolved on his male heirs capable of bearing arms, all females and minors being excluded. The heirship was determined by consanguinity, adoption or compact. The first class consisted of sons, grandsons, father, grandfather, brothers, cousins, uncles and nephews. The sons by adoption stood on the same footing as natural-born sons.

The 'third class of heirs arose out of the custom by which two Arabs used to enter into a contract that, on the death of one of them, the surviving party to the contract would be an heir to the deceased or receive a certain fixed amount out of the estate. The shares of the different heirs in the heritable estate were not fixed, and it is not easy to ascertain what was the order of succession among them, if any. It appears that the chief of a tribe used to divide the estate of a deceased person among the recognised heirs, and possibly the shares allotted varied according to the circumstances. If there were grown-up sons they probably excluded daughters; wives, sisters and mother did not inherit at all, but the estate was considered liable for the payment of the widow's dower, and among some tribes at least for her maintenance.

Such briefly was the state of Arabia's social life when Muhammad (PBUH), himself an Arab belonging to a prominent family of the tribe of *Quraish*[6], began to promulgate the principles of Islam. We now pass from the stage of unconscious evolution of laws by the customs and usages of a people to that of conscious law-making, always a most important step in the progress of communities. But Muhammad (PBUH) preached Islam not merely for the municipal government of the Arabs, but for the guidance of men's lives generally. In other words he propounded the principles of municipal law as an integral part of a comprehensive scheme of universal religion.

***The History of Islamic Law and Jurisprudence Broadly Divisible into Four Periods*:** The history of Islamic law subsequently to the promulgation of Islam and of the Muhammadan legal science is divisible into four distinct periods. The first period commenced with the *Hijrat* or retirement of the Prophet (PBUH) of Medina (A.D. 622) and ended with his death (A.D. 632). This has been rightly called the 'legislative period' of Islam when laws were enacted by the divine legislator and promulgated in the words of the Quran, or by the precepts of Muhammad (PBUH). These are the texts upon which as their foundation the superstructure of the four Sunni schools has been constructed.

The second period extends from the date of the Prophet's death to the foundation of different schools of jurisprudence, and would cover, roughly speaking, the time of the Companions of the Prophet (*Ashab*) and their successors (*Tabiun*)[7]. It was an age as has been observed mainly of collection and of interpretation and extension of laws by collective deliberations.

The third period was marked by a theoretical and scientific study of the law and religion, and it was then that the four *Sunni* schools of jurisprudence were established. It commenced about the beginning of the second century of the *Hijra* and practically ended with the third century.

Since then there has been no independent exposition of Islamic law, and jurists have been engaged within the limits of each school to develop the work of its founders. This may be called the fourth period in the history of Islamic law and cannot properly be said to have yet come to an end. An elaborate classification has been made of the jurists of this period and their work, but it will be more appropriate to deal with that question in any detail in connection with the doctrine of *taqlid*.

Starting Period

Quran is the name of the collection of those revelations which were made to Muhammad (PBUH) when he was vested with the office of the Prophet (PBUH) and Messenger of God. The revelations were made in God's own words as containing his wishes and commands. Its text which existed from eternity was communicated from time to time in pieces called ayat or verses. Many of the verses laying down rules of law were revealed with reference to cases which actually arose. Sometimes God in His wisdom repealed some previous injunctions, and laid down others in their stead more suitable to the needs of men.

The other sources of the ordinances of God, during the lifetime of the Prophet (PBUH), were his precepts or *Ahadith.* Often questions arose for decision, for the solution of which no direct revelation was forthcoming, or certain points had to be explained and made clear. The pronouncements made by the Prophet (PBUH) on all such occasions are known as *Ahadith* or precepts, and are regarded as of sacred authority. His dicta in all matters of law and religion were inspired and suggested by God, though expressed in his own words, while the Quranic texts were God's, both in language and thought. The Prophet's precepts and usages were likewise guided by God, and, in the same way as the texts of the Quran, furnished an index of what was right and lawful. His approval or disapproval was sometimes implied from his conduct. If, for instance, a certain usage or course of action was followed by the Muslims within his knowledge, and the Prophet (PBUH) expressed no disapproval thereof, its legality was presumed. Similarly, if the Prophet (PBUH) studiously avoided a certain course of conduct, it has to be presumed that he disapproved it.

Later Period

When the Prophet (PBUH) died in June A.D. 632, the eleventh year of the Hijra, the task of the spiritual and worldly government of the Islamic commonwealth devolved on his Companions, and a new era commenced in the history of Islamic Jurisprudence. He being the last of the prophets, there was no longer anyone through whom God could promulgate his wishes and commands for the guidance of the Muslims. The divine Book and the precepts and the precedents of the Prophet (PBUH) were, however, still left for reference and instruction. If a text of the Quran or pronouncement of the Prophet covered a point, or if the Prophet had decided a similar case, there could be no difficulty. But fresh facts and new circumstances often arose for which no provision had been made, specially as the affairs of the community became more complex with the growth of empire. In the absence of authority, the Companions had to guide themselves by the light of their reason, having in regard those usages of the community which had not been condemned by the Prophet (PBUH).

Those who were associated with the Prophet (PBUH) as his companions, and often shared his counsels, must have known, as if by instinct, the policy of Islamic law, and whether a particular rule or decision was in harmony with its principles. It is presumed, therefore, that an agreement among the companions in a particular view vouched for its absolute soundness, and even their isolated opinions are regarded as of high authority.

Election of the Caliph, the Executive Chief of the Community : The first and the most momentous problem that the community had to solve on the Prophet's (PBUH) death was that of finding a successor to him as the head of the Muhammadan Commonwealth. Over this question the Muhammadan world has since then divided itself into two hostile factions, the *Shiahs* who assert that the *Imamat* or Caliphate should have continued in the family of the Prophet (PBUH), and the rest of the Muhammadans who support the right of the community (*Jamat*) to elect the chief. At the time of the Prophet's (PBUH) death, however, the claims of *Ali*[8] according to accepted history were not openly put forward, and *Abu Bakr* was elected the first Caliph. He was the head of the State, and as *Imam* he led the Friday prayers. He was no doubt in his capacity of Caliph the chief executive authority, but he had no sovereign power not any royal prerogative. He was simply the principal magistrate to carry out the injunctions of the Quran, and the ordinances of the Prophet (PBUH). He had no legislative functions, for God alone is the legislator in Islam.

Compilation of Quran

As the Islamic community was to be governed in the main on the principles already laid down for the purpose, the necessity of collecting the verses of the

Quran and the precepts and precedents of the Prophet (PBUH) forced itself upon the attention of the early Muslims. The texts of the Quran during the lifetime of the Prophet (PBUH) had been preserved, either in the memories of his companions, or by being inscribed on bones, date-leaves and tablets of stone. In an expedition against the imposter *Musailima*, a large number of the reciters of the Quran (*Qurra*), were slain, and at the suggestion of *Umar*[9], *Abu Bakr* had the divine book collected. *Zaid*, who used to be constantly with the Prophet (PBUH) and often acted as his amanuensis, was employed at this task which he accomplished between A.H. 11 and 14.

But several different versions and readings of this edition soon crept into use, and *Uthman*[10], the third Caliph, perceiving the need for a correct version again utilised the services of *Zaid* in revising the First edition. On the revision being completed, *Uthman* caused all the remaining editions to be destroyed, and it is due to this fact that at the present day only one authentic and uniform text is in use throughout the Muslim world.

The Traditions were not Collected by Authority of the State : The sayings and decisions of the Prophet (PBUH) were not, however, collected by the authority of the State as was done in the case of the Quran. What the reason was can only be conjectured. Their collection was left to the piety and private enterprise of the Islamics. Men who were most learned in the traditions soon gathered round them an increasing band of students eager to learn and store up every saying of the Prophet (PBUH). It seems that this very zeal gave rise to many a false and inaccurate tradition, for *Umar*, during his Caliphate, discouraged and even stopped for some time the reporting of traditions. But his action had only a temporary effect, and the study of traditions continued with the progress of time to be pursued with all the greater vigour.

Islamic Law and Lawyers

All traditionalists, however, were not necessarily jurists. Among those who, by their learning and aptitude in deducing rules of secular and canon law, acquired eminence among the Companions of the Prophet (PBUH), the names of *Ali*, *Umar*, *Ibn Umar*, *Ibn Masud* and *Ibn Abbas* stand out most prominent, and many important principles of Islamic Jurisprudence are based on their opinion. *Ibn Masud* for a long time gave lectures in *Hadith* and law at *Kufa*, while other jurists and traditionalists carried on the work of teaching at *Medina*.

These two places, especially the latter, continued for a long time to be the seats of sacred learning. Of *Ibn Masud's* pupils the names of *Al-qama* and *Aswad* are best known. *Al-qama* occupied the professional seat, and when the latter died he was succeeded by *Aswad*. On *Aswad*'s death the mantle of the teacher fell on the shoulders of the famous *Ibrahim an-Nakhai*[11], who was known as 'the jurist of Iraq'. *Ibrahim* is reported to have made a collection of the principles of law that had been hitherto established, and *Hammad*[12], under whom *Abu Hanifa*[13] afterwards studied jurisprudence, had a copy of this collection.

The study of the traditions was the especial feature of the Medinite schools, though it is not to be supposed that other jurists in any way overlooked or minimised the importance of this subject which is one of the fundamental sources of law. A jurist must be learned in the traditions, though every traditionalist was not a jurist. The mode of teaching the traditions was like this. The teacher or reciter used to call out from his seat: It was related to me by so and so, to whom it was related by so and so that the Prophet of God said this...' The students would then take down word by word the tradition, as well as the chain of authorities with which it was prefaced. This statement of authorities was called asnad and as time receded from the age of the Prophet (PBUH), the chain of narrators necessarily lengthened.

Justice and Islam

For some time after the death of the Prophet (PBUH), no *Qadi* was appointed, and *Abu Bakr* himself administered justice as the Prophet (PBUH) had done before him. But when the political affairs of the community increased and pressed upon his time, he delegated his judicial functions to *Umar*. *Abu Bakr* was the first to establish a prison-house for the malefactors. His successor *Umar* appointed the first *Qadi*, and he enforced the principle that the majesty of law was supreme, and that the administration of justice must be above the suspicion of subservience to executive authority. He had once a lawsuit against a Jew, and both of them went to the *Qadi* who, on seeing the Caliph, rose in his seat out of deference. *Umar* considered this to be such an unpardonable weakness on his part that he dismissed him from office.

It does not, however, appear that during *Umar*'s time the power and jurisdiction of the *Qadi* were properly defined, or that any distinct machinery was provided for the execution of decrees and sentences. But by the time of *Ali*, who like *Umar* was noted as a jurist, the jurisdiction of the *Qadi* and the legal procedure appear to have acquired a greater fixity and certainty. He was assassinated in A.H. 40, and, this brought to a close the age of 'the rightly-guided Caliphs.

This period, from the point of view of jurisprudence, was characterised by a close adherence to the spirit of the ordinances of Islam. Law as administered either by the head of the State and the Church, or under his direct supervision. The boundaries of Islam expanded with growing rapidity, and it came into contact with the laws and customs of the different subject nations. The first four Caliphs were men of action and experience of the world, and law in their hands, while it was not separated from religion, became imbued with principles of practical application.

The Study of Law and Traditions During the Umayyad Caliphate; Commencement of the Study of Law as a Science : The first act of the *Umayyad* dynasty, their successors, was to remove the seat of the Caliphate to *Damascus*, outside the limits of Arabia proper. Though they were at the head of the State as Caliphs, they were not generally speaking noted for their knowledge of the sacred laws A bright exception must, however, be made in favour of *Umar ibn Abdil-Aziz*, who was remarkable not only for his rigid piety, but also for his extensive knowledge of the law and the traditions. There are many traditions which rest upon his authority.

The *Qadi* still administered justice, but law during the reign of the *Umayyads* grew and developed only in the lecture rooms of the professors, who did not come into contact with the practical concerns of the administration of justice. The zeal, however, for the study of law did not abate, and during the latter days of the *Umayyads* it was largely influenced, at least in *Iraq* and *Mesopotamia*, by the recently introduced sciences of divinity and scholastic logic. It is in this newly awakened scientific spirit that we must seek the beginning of the science of Islamic Jurisprudence. The distinction of first classifying the laws under different subjects, of introducing the use of technical phraseology, and of arranging the different sources of law is ascribed by some of *Wasil-ibn-Ata*[14] the founder of the *Mutazila* sect.

CONTRIBUTION OF ABBASIDS

With the fall of the house of the *Umayyads* and the accession of the *Abbasides* to power, in A.H. 132, a new impetus was given to the study of jurisprudence. The *Abbaside* Caliphs loved to patronize learning and extended special encouragement to the jurists, partly it may be from political motives. Baghdad their capital became the centre of culture and attracted jurists and traditions from *Hijaz, Syria, Mesopotamia* and other parts of the empire. The Abbaside Caliphs appointed as *Qadis* men noted for their learning and legal acumen, and gave them handsome salaries and a high place of dignity in the State.

Was Islamic Jurisprudence Influenced by the Roman Jurisprudence? : During this period, though for a short while, Islamic law once more, as in the age of the Companions, came into contact, with the practical concerns of life, and the study of the Greek and perhaps Roman literatures and sciences also came into considerable vogue about this time. To the students of comparative jurisprudence it must be interesting to note the points of resemblance between the rules of the

Islamic and the Roman laws and the theories of their respective jurisprudence, but since the Islamic jurists themselves make no allusion to the Roman system, and their theories exclude its recognition as a factor in moulding the Islamic system, it is difficult to determine with any degree of certainty the extent of the obligations, if any, of the Islamic jurists to the Roman jurists.

The Third Period; Foundation of the Sunni Schools of Law : It was during the reign of the *Abbasides* that the four *Sunni* schools of law, with whose jurisprudence we are now concerned, were founded. The principals of these four Schools are substantially the same, and they differ from each other merely in matters of detail. They are classed together in contradistinction to the only other important existing school of law among the Islamics, namely, the Shia school, though the differences even between the Shias and the Sunnis centre more round questions relating to political events of the past, rather than to any general principles of law of jurisprudence. We are not, however, called upon to deal with the legal system of the Shia school.

Abu Hanifa; Abu Hanifa known as the Upholder of Private Judgement; Upholders of Traditions : *Abu Hanifa* an-Numan ibn Thabit, commonly known as Imam *Abu Hanifa*, the founder of the most important of the Sunni schools, was born in the year A.H. 80, during the time of the *Umayyad* Caliph, *Abdul-Malik*, and died at an advanced age, eighteen years after the *Abbasides* came to power. He first studied scholastic divinity, but soon abandoned it in favour of jurisprudence. He attended the lectures of *Jafar-as-Sadiq*[15] and of *Hammad*, the first of whom, a descendant of the Prophet (PBUH), was noted for his great learning and piety, and is regarded as an *Imam* of the Shia School.

The latter, as already stated, was a disciple of *Ibrahim-un-Nakhai* and enjoyed high reputation as a jurist. The traditionalists from whom he heard traditions were *Ash-Sahbi, Qatada, Al-Amas*, and other men of eminence in that branch of learning. *Abu Hanifa* was endowed with talents of an exceptional nature and had the true lawyer's gift of detecting nice distinctions. He possessed remarkable powers of reasoning and deduction, which, combined with the resources of a retentive memory and a clear understanding, brought him into rapid prominence as a master of jurisprudence. Men flocked to his lectures, and among his pupils the names of *Abu Yusuf, Muhammad* and *Zafar* are intimately connected with the science of Islamic Law.

The teachings of *Abu Hanifa* acquired for him the title of 'upholder of private judgement' and his school of Law was distinguished by that epithet. There can be no doubt that he was considered by his contemporaries to rely less upon the traditions in arriving at legal conclusions and more upon deductions than the other jurists. In fact in his time, it must be noted, the jurists were broadly divided in two classes: those of *Hijaz* or *Arabia* Proper who were called 'the upholders of the traditions and those of Iraq who were known as 'upholders of private opinion'. It would not however be correct to suppose that *Abu Hanifa* lacked a sufficient knowledge of the traditions, or that he did not regard them as a legitimate source of laws. *Ibn Khaldun* observes: 'Some prejudiced men say that some of the *Imams* had a scanty knowledge of the traditions, and that is the reason why they have reported so few of them.

This cannot be true regarding the great Imams, because the law is based on the Quran and the *Sunna* (*i.e.*, Traditions), and it is a duty incumbent on them to seek put the traditions. But some among them accept only a small number of traditions, because of the severity of the tests they apply.' In sifting the traditions *Abu Hanifa* was undoubtedly more strict than the others, and the tests that he applied to them resulted in excluding many traditions which the people generally accepted as genuine. Further, the principles that he laid down confined within a narrow compass the traditions from which a rule of law might be legitimately deduced. It is said that he felt justified in acting upon eighteen traditions only out of the great mass that was then in vogue.

Qiyas or Analogical Deduction; Istihsan or Juristic Equity; Ijma or Consensus of Opinion; Urf or Usage : But his chief work lay in formulating the theories and principles of jurisprudence, and he was in fact the founder of the Islamic science of law as we find it. He was the first to give prominence to the doctrine of *Qiyas* or analogical deduction, though, as a principle of law, it was undoubtedly in practiced operation before his time. He, however, assigned a distinctive name and prominent position to the principle by which, in Islamic jurisprudence, the theory of law is modified in its application to actual facts, calling it (*istihsan lit.* preference), which bears in many points remarkable resemblance to the doctrines of equity.

An example will best illustrate the respective operation of the doctrine of *Qiyas* and of *istihsan*. A contract of the nature of sale according to the Islamic law in order to be valid requires that the subject-matter must be in existence at the time of the contract. Arguing analogically a contract with a manufacturer or artisan that he is to supply goods of a particular description for a specified price would be invalid. The principle of *istihsan*, however, intervenes and establishes the legality of such a transaction on the ground of necessity based on the universal practice of mankind. *Abu Hanifa* also extended the doctrine of *Ijma*' (consensus of opinion) beyond what many of the contemporaries were willing to concede. Some were of opinion that the validity of Ijma as a source of laws should be confined to the companions of the Prophet (PBUH) and others would extend it to their successors, but no further.

Abu Hanifa affirmed its validity in every age. He also recognised the authority of local customs and usages as guiding the application of law. It is laid down in *Al-Ashba* wan-*Nadhair*: 'Many decisions of law are based on usage or custom, so much so that it has been taken as a principle of law'. The Quran and the precepts of the Prophet were with him as with all other jurists, the primary sources, *Ijma*' coming next to them, and analogy, juristic preference and local customs being regarded merely as secondary sources.

Codification of the Laws by Abu Hanifa and his Disciples, and their Works : In the work which *Abu Hanifa* did in the domain of jurisprudence, he was assisted by many able disciples, some of whom have already been mentioned. He also instituted, it is said, a committee consisting of forty men from among his principal disciples for the codification of the laws. Of this committee *Yahya-ibn-Abi-Zaid*[16], *Hafs-ibn-Ghiyath*[17], *Abu Yusuf*[18], *Daud-at-Tai*[19], *Habban*[20] and *Mandal*[21] were men of great reputation as traditions. *Zafar* was noted for his power of deducing rules of law and *Qasim ibn Nuim* and *Muhammad* were great Arabic scholars. The committee used to discuss any practical and theoretical question that arose or suggested itself, and the conclusions which they agreed upon after a full and free debate were duly recorded. It took thirty years for the code to be completed, but each part as it was finished was circulated broadcast.

The entire code, however, has now been lost, an irreparable loss no doubt to the cause of Islamic Jurisprudence. With the exception of his contributions to this code, it is doubtful whether *Abu Hanifa* wrote any other book for '*Fiqhi-Akbar*'[22] commonly attributed to him is not considered by some well-informed authorities to be his production. We have, however, a small collection of traditions based on his authority and called '*Musnadul-Imam Abu Hanifa* and a letter which he wrote for the instruction and guidance of his disciple *Abu Yusuf* in his office of *Qadi* is still in existence.

Abu Yusuf, who for a long time acted as the chief *Qadi* of *Baghdad*, enjoyed the confidence of his teacher and was held by him in great esteem for his talents, learning and knowledge of the world, and many a principle of practical application in *Hanafi* law may be traced to his influence. Muhammad, the other well-known disciple of *Abu Hanifa*, was a copy writer, but only some of his books are available. *Abu Hanifa* was offered the office of *Qadi*, and because he refused to accept it on conscientious grounds, *Ibn Hubaira*, the Governor of *Kufa*, had him flogged. *Al-Mansur* at last cast him into prison, ostensibly for the same reason, and there the great jurist expired, having been, as believed, poisoned at the instance of the

Caliph. He was held in such esteem that his funeral prayers, it is reported, were said for ten days, and on each day about fifty thousand people attended. The Muhammadans of India, Afghanistan and Turkey are mostly *Hanafis*, and the followers of his school are also largely found in Egypt, Arabia and China.

Malik; He Leaned more upon Traditions and the Usage of Medina : The age of *Abu Hanifa* was the age of jurists. At *Medina*, the city where the Prophet (PBUH) fulfilled his mission and died, a great jurist arose in the person of *Malik ibn Anas*. We have seen that ever since the death of the Prophet (PBUH), that sacred city continued to be regarded as the home of traditionary learning. *Malik* was born in A.H. 95, at *Medina*, and there he studied and taught and did all his work. In his time he was looked up to as the highest authority in *Hadith*, and his fame in this respect has not suffered by the lapse of time. He was not only a traditionist but a jurist, anti founded a school of law which exercised great influence in his life time. The Moors of Spain belonged to his school, which still counts numerous followers in northern Africa. *Muhammad*, the disciple of *Abu Hanifa*, studied traditions under him for three years. His doctrines were not, however, essentially different from those of *Abu Hanifa. Malik* leaned more upon traditions and the usages of the Prophet (PBUH) and the precedents established by his Companions. He upheld the exercise of judgement when the other sources failed him Being in a better position than *Abu Hanifa* to be acquainted with the laws as laid down by the Companions and then successors, he embodied them more largely in his system. He attached a preponderating weight to the usages and customs of *Medina*, relying on the presumption that they must have been transmitted from the time of the Prophet (PBUH). He recognised a principle, corresponding to that of *Abu Hanifa*'s *istihsan*, namely, that of public welfare (*maslihat*) as a basis of deduction.

To the four main sources of law, the Quran, the *Hadith*, *Ijma* and analogical deduction he would add Istadlal as a fifth source. Istadlal is a principle of juristic deduction which according to his School does not come within the scope of analogy. *Malik ibn Anas* died twenty-nine years after *Abu Hanifa*. *Imam Malik*'s *Al-Muwatta*[23], a collection of traditions, is well known and contains about three hundred traditions.

Shafii; He Adopted the Middle Course between Abu Hanifa and Malik in the use of Traditions and Analogy : Among *Malik*'s pupils, *Muhammad ibn Idris Ash-Shafii* attained even greater eminence as a jurist than the master himself. He was born in Palestine, being descended from *Abdul-Muttalib*[24], the grandfather of the Prophet (PBUH). He attended lectures on law and traditions not only of *Malik ibn Anas*, but of other noted doctors in law including *Muhammad*, the disciple of *Abu Hanifa*. At an early age he evinced proofs of great talents, and while still a youth delivered lectures in jurisprudence. His fame soon spread and the doctrines which he enunciated found great vogue. The school of law with which his name is associated takes rank in the number and importance of its followers next only to the *Hanafi* school.

He was noted for his balance of judgement and moderation of views and though reckoned among the upholders of traditions, he examined the traditions more critically and made more use of analogy than *Malik*. He allowed greater scope to *Ijma'* (consensus of opinion) than *Malik*, putting a more liberal and workable interpretation on the well known dictum of the Prophet (PBUH), 'My people will never agree in an error. But he agreed with *Malik* in adopting istadlal as a fifth source and rejected *Abu Hanifa*'s equity of the jurist. He was the first to write a treatise on *Usul* or principles. Egypt is the principal stronghold of his doctrines, but his followers are to be found in other parts of Africa, in Arabia and also some in India, specially in Bombay and Madras.

Ahmad ibn Hanbal; more a Traditionalist than a Jurist : Among the scholars who attended *As-Shafiis* lectures was *Abu Abdullah Ahmad ibn Hanbal*, known as *Imam Hanbal*, who founded the fourth and the latest of the *Sunni* Schools of jurisprudence. He was born at Baghdad (A.H. 164) and studied under different masters including *Shafii*. But from all the accounts that are left of him, he appears to have been more learned in the traditions than in the science of law. As a traditionist and theologian his reputation stood very high, and in the number of traditions that he recollected no one, even in that age, approached him. In law he adhered rigidly to the traditions, a much larger number of which he felt himself at liberty to act upon than any other doctor. His interpretation of them was literal and unbending, and according to some he allowed a very narrow margin to the doctrines of agreement and analogy. He was a man of great piety and uncompromising opinions, and was persecuted by the Caliph *Al-Mamun*, because he adhered to his own views on certain points of divinity, and refused to conform to those that had found favour in court.

This unjust persecution served only to enhance the great reverence in which he was held by the people, and it is said that, when he died in A.H. 241,800,000 men and 60,000 women attended his funeral. His followers, who were regarded as reactionary and troublesome, were persecuted from time to time. Now his School consists only of a few followers and those only in certain parts of Arabia. He himself does not appear to have written any treatise on law, and I have been able to secure only one treatise which expounds his doctrines. One also meets with occasional references to his views in the law-books of other schools. His great work, a collection of 50,000 traditions reported by him and known as '*Musnadul-Imam Hanbal*', has now been printed and forms a valuable addition to the literature on the subject. But, as it is not arranged according to the subjects, its usefulness for purposes of reference is much impaired.

Study of the Science of Traditions during this Period : The age of the four *Imams* produced other teachers who had for sometime a considerable following of their own. Among them *Sufyan-Thuri* and *Daud-uz-Zahiri* (the literalist) attained eminence as jurists. But their systems are now extinct and do not call for any notice here. With *Imam Hanbal*, therefore, the age of independent jurists came to an end, and the work that has been done since then in developing the laws and legal science has been, mainly supplementary.

Study of the Science of Traditions during this Period : But before continuing the narrative of jurists, I ought to make some mention of the great teachers of traditionary learning who succeeded *Imam Hanbal*. These men do not rank as great jurists, but the influence of their labours on the development of laws cannot be overrated. *Imam Hanbal*'s remarkable erudition in traditionary learning combined with the austere piety of his life gave a fresh impetus, if any indeed was needed, to the study of traditions. A new band of scholars, the most prominent of whom are known as the *Imams* of traditions as distinguished from *Imams* of jurisprudence, headed by *Abu Abdullah Muhammad Abu Ismail al-Bukhari* commonly known as *Bukhari*, a pupil of *Hanbal* himself, devoted themselves exclusively to a scientific investigation of this important branch of religious learning. *Zuhri, Malik* and *Ibn Juraij* had already set the example in collecting traditions in the more durable and reliable form of a book, and the jurists generally had demonstrated the need for critically sifting and examining them, laying down, each according to his own light, rules for their interpretation and application as a source of laws. From the latter half of the third until the earlier part of the fourth century (A.H.) the task of collecting and sifting the traditions was undertaken in the same spirit of comprehensive thoroughness which characterised the work of *Abu Hanifa*, *Shafii* and *Malik* in the domain of jurisprudence.

Bukhari was the pioneer in this enterprise and his collections are regarded by the Muhammadans of *Sunni* Schools as the most authoritative. His book contains about 7,000 traditions which he selected as authentic out of 6000.000. He died in A.H. 256 (A.D. 869). Side by side with *Bukhari* and in the same field and with same scientific methods though independently, worked Muslim *ibnul-Hajjaj* or *Nishapur* known as Muslim. He died in A.H. 261 (A.D. 874). Muslim's work, though smaller in bulk, can hardly be said to be of inferior authority to that of *Bukhari*, and the collections of these two are pre-eminently distinguished as the two '*Sahihs*' or the two correct collections out of the six collections which are regarded by the *Sunnis* as authentic.

The remaining four collections are by *Tirmidhi*[25] (died A.H. 279 or A.D. 892), *Abu Daud*[26] (died A.H. 275 or A.D. 888), *Ibn Majah*[27] (died A.H. 273 or A.D. 886) and *Nisai*[28] (died A.H. 303 or A.D. 915). They all worked independently of each other, so that the same tradition is often to be met with in more than one of their books, and the greater the number of collections in which a particular traditions find a place, its authority is held to be proportionately strengthened. *Bukhari* and Muslim and the others did a great service to the Muslim community by the care and assiduity with which they examined the traditions. Still it is not to be supposed, because a tradition is reported in one of these collections even in *Bukhara*'s or Muslim's, that it is always accepted as genuine by the followers of the *Sunni* schools. Indeed nothing has been a more fruitful source of conflicting opinions in matters of law among the Sunni jurists than the question, whether a particular tradition is to be regarded as genuine or not, although it may be one for whose authority one or more of these writers may have vouched.

Role of Islamic Scholars

It may be observed here that the influence which Bukhari and Muslim have exercised on Islamic Jurisprudence, though not, perhaps, apparent at the first sight, has been great. Their work has directly tended, as was to be expected, to strengthen the position of the jurists of *Hijaz*, or 'the upholders of traditions', especially of the *Shafii* and *Maliki* school of thoughts.

Though indirectly and perhaps more or less imperceptibly it has also exercised considerable influence on the 'followers of private judgement;, that is the Iraqi school of thought with which the name of *Abu Hanifa* is especially identified. In fact, it has served to draw both the schools of thought together, so that traditions reported in the six correct collections are constantly, and at every step, referred to in the most authoritative writings of the *Hanafi* jurists in support of their propositions. If we bear in mind that *Abu Hanifa* himself, who lived at a time when the precepts and usages of the Prophet (PBUH) were fresh in the memories of the successors of the Companions, and came into contact with almost all the great traditionalist of the age, is reported to have accepted only seventeen or eighteen of them as genuine, and that the number of traditions, which his followers since his time have acted upon as authentic, may be counted by hundreds, one cannot help inferring that the standpoint of the *Hanafi* school of thought must have undergone great modification under the influence of *Bukhari* and his collaborators.

In fact, though *Bukhari* was strongly opposed to the doctrines of *Abu Hanifa*, and laboured to show from the traditions which he collected that, on many questions, the view which found support of the latter's Schools was wrong, his name and his book stand high in the reverence of the *Hanafis*. At the same time, just as the *Hanafis* have made considerable advance towards the 'upholders of traditions' in making larger use of traditions in matters of law, the jurists of the latter school of thought have also shown an increasing inclination to use those methods of interpretation and deductions of which *Abu Hanifa* was the most eminent exponent. The result has been to hold them all together as 'followers of the middle course'. To what extent the latest phase of the doctrine of *taqlid* will serve to stereotype the differences among the four *Sunni* schools of thought by destroying that spirit of compromise, which has been their most attractive feature, remains yet to be seen.

The Study of the Quran and the Science of its Interpretation : It will not be out of place to mention here that the study of the Quran, the primary source of all laws, also occupy some of the best talents among the Muhammadans and the science of its interpretation (*tafsir*) was naturally regarded as of the highest importance. Of the numerous commentaries that have been written, those by *Tabari* (died in A.H. 310 or A.D. 922), *Zamakhshari* (died in A:H. 538 or A.D. 1143), *Baidawi* (died in A.H. 685 or A.D. 1286), *Ghazzali* (died in A.H. 504 or A.D. 1110), the two *Jalaluddins* (one of whom died in 1459), and *Fakhruddin-ar-Razi* are well known. To this list may be added '*Tafsiri-Ahmadi*'[29], a most useful commentary on those verses of the Quran, from which rules of law have been deduced, written by *Ahmad*, commonly known as *Mulla Jiwan*, who lived in the time of *Aurangzeb*. In this connection it must be borne in mind that commentator of the Quran like traditionalist, however distinguished in their own sphere, do not as such have a recognised place in the rank of jurists.

Philosophy of Law

To resume the narrative of jurists: the work which has been done by the foremost jurists of the third period, especially *Abu Hanifa*, *Shafii* and *Malik*, is of twofold character. Not only are many rules of law traced to their dicta, but they were the first to formulate the principles of the science of *Usul*. *Usul* literally means roots and *ilmul-Usul*, or the science of *Usul*, is the name for the legal science which concerns itself mostly with a discussion of the sources of law, and matters appertaining thereto as contra-distinguished from *ilmul-Furu'* (*Furu* literally means branches), which is the name for the material science of law among the Muhammadans.

The science of *Usul* corresponds to European jurisprudence, though the two sciences cannot, as we shall see, be said to cover quite the same ground. Unlike European jurisprudence, particularly as conceived by Mr. Holland and jurists of his persuasion, *Usul* is not a purely formal science. While it includes within its scope the discussion of the theories and general properties of law, the application of law to men's actions through the media of rights and obligations, and the classification of legal concepts, the main object of this science is to discuss rules relating to the interpretation of texts of the Quran and the *Hadith*, the constitution of Ijma' and analogical extension of the laws established by these three sources to cases not falling within the language of the texts, but coming within their intendment.

The need for such a science in the Islamic system is obvious. The only law-making that there has been among the Muhammadans was during the lifetime of the Prophet (PBUH). The principle of *Ijma'* doubtless admits of what for all practical purposes may be called legislation, but for lack of a definite machinery for the purposes of collective deliberation, development of laws through the agency of *Ijma'* has been slow, uncertain and fitful. The only other means left of expanding the laws has been juristic interpretation and deduction A science of the nature of *Usul* which is described as leading to *Fiqh* or the knowledge of laws, became, therefore, indispensable in the Muhammadan system. The four principal teachers above mentioned agreed in the main theories and principles, of this science, though they differed among themselves in certain details.

After the close of the third century of the *Hijra*, no one has succeeded in obtaining the recognition of the Islamic world as an independent thinker in jurisprudence. A succession of jurists have, on the other hand, applied themselves to the task of completing the work done by the founders of the four schools, especially the *Hanafi*, the *Shafii* and the *Maliki*, both in the domain of material and theoretical science of law. As regards the former they devoted their attention to concrete questions, which had not been dealt with by the founders of different schools and their immediate disciples, and to the collection and arrangement of the opinions of the masters. This work continued among the *Hanafis* until about the age of *Qadi Khan*, who died in the sixth century of the *Hijra*.

The jurists that succeeded took even a narrower view of their functions in this connection. They occupied themselves in determining which of the conflicting versions of the views of the principal jurisconsults, that is, the founder of each school and his disciples, on a given question was correct, and in the event of difference of opinion among them, whose dictum was to be taken as representing the accepted law.

One of the last of these lawyers among the *Hanafis* was *Sadrush -Shariah*, who lived in the eighth century of the Hijra (died A.H. 750 or A.D. 1349). I may observe here that a notion exists that henceforward there has been no further exposition of Islamic law, the ancient doctors having anticipated every question and laid down a rule for its solutions. Such a notion is prima facie untenable, nor is it founded in fact. It would be more accurate to say, as held by jurists of authority, that the principles that have been hitherto established would, if properly applied, furnish an answer in most cases.

At the close of the fourteenth century we arrive at the age of commentators and annotators. Though carrying on their work under a modest title, the contributions of these learned men to the science of law, at least of the more prominent among them, have been most valuable and important. It would be as much a fallacy to suppose that commentators merely explain their texts and add nothing to the law, as a similar assertion with respect to the judgements of judges in the English system. In fact, it is only in writings of these commentators that it is possible to find the doctrines of the different schools expounded in their fullness.

It would be mere pedantry to deny, for instance, that the labours of such jurists as *Ibn Hamman, Ibn Najim* and *Ibn Abidin* among others have largely helped to develop the *Hanafi* law. And, as a matter of fact, no Islamic lawyer of the present day would undertake to answer a question of *Hanafi* law without consulting their writings. The contribution by the Muhammadans of India to the legal literature has not been very considerable, but *'Fatawa Alamgiri'*, complied under the orders of *Aurangzeb* in the eleventh century of the *Hijra*, is as great and achievement of learning, industry and research as perhaps any legal literature can boast of.

As regards the science of law or *Usul*, *Shafii* is reported to have written the first book on the subject, but it was not until the fourth century of the *Hijra* that *Usul* began to be studied as a separate science. Among the writers on this subject a few of the more prominent names may be mentioned here; on *Hanafi* jurisprudence *Abu Bakr Jassasur-Razi* (died A.H. 370), *Fakhrul-Islam Bazdawi* (died A.H. 482), *As-Sarakhsi*, (died A.H. 483), *Al-Kurdri* (died A.H. 562), *Hisamuddin* (died A.H. 710), *Sadrush-Shariat* (died A.H. 747), *Saduddin Taftazani, Ibn Hammam* (died A.H. 861), and among the moderns *Muhibulla* (died A.H. 119) and *Bahrul-Ulum;* on *Shafii* jurisprudence *Abu Bakr Muhammad ibn Abdullah* (died A.H. 330), *An Nawai* (died A.H. 676), *Tajuddinu's-Subki* (died A.H. 771), *Al-Mahalli* (died A.H. 864), and *Ahmad ibn Qasim;* on *Maliki* jurisprudence *Ibn Hajib* (died A.H. 646), and *Qadi Udud* (died A.H. 756); and on *Hanbali* jurisprudence *Qadi Alauddin* and *Abu Bakr ibn Zaidinil-Khariji* (died A.H. 836). Of their writings those that are ordinarily available and in vogue, *Al-Usul* by *Fakhrul-Islam Bazdawi, 'Taudi'* by *Sadrush-Shariat* with its commentary *'Talwi'* by *Taftazani* among the *Hanafis; Jamul-Jawami* by *Tajuddinu's-Subki* with its commentary by *Al-Mahalli* and an annotation by *Ahmad ibn Qasim* called *Al-Ayatul-Baiyinat'* among the *Shafiis;* and *'Mukhtasar'* by *Ibn Hajib,* with its commentary by *Qadi Udud* in *Maliki* jurisprudence, are regarded as the most authoritative.

It may be noted here that, though *Taftazani* was a follower of the *Shafii* School of law, his commentary on *'Taudi'* is held in great esteem by the *Hanafis*. *At-Taqrir Wat-Tahbir'* by *Ibn Hammam,* the author of *'Fathul-Qadir'*, is also a book of high authority on *Hanafi Usul,* and *'Nurul-Anwar'*, a commentary on *Al-Manar'*, by the author of *'Tafsiri-Ahmadi'*, and *'Musallamuth-Thabut'* and its commentary by *Bahrul-Ulum* are also commonly used in India. I have not come across any book on *Usul* by a *Hanbali* jurist, and it is doubtful whether one is available.

Governance of Judiciary

With the establishment of the Anglo-Indian courts, the Islamic law has entered upon a new and interesting phase in India. It is no longer the law of the land and is applicable to the Islamics so far as its administration by the courts is concerned only by the declaration of the Sovereign power.

In the early days of the British Settlement the Islamic Code was enforced in all its departments, but in the course of time Islamic Laws relating to the crimes and punishments, revenues, land tenures, procedure, evidence, and partly transfer of property have been gradually abandoned and replaced by the enactments of the Legislature. Questions relating to family relations and status, namely, marriage, divorce, maintenance and guardianship of minors, succession and inheritance, religious usages and institutions and dispositions of property by *hiba*, will and *waqf* are still governed by the Islamic law so far as the Muhammadans are concerned, and in some parts of India the Islamic law of peremption, is also recognised. And if any sect of Islam has its own rule, that rule, generally speaking, should be followed with respect to litigants of that sect, as laid down by the Privy Council in *Raja Deedar Hussain's* case where the question related to the right of succession to the estate of a Shia Muhammadan.

Law and People at the Helm

The administration of the Islamic, as well as Hindu laws, was for sometime carried on with the help of Indian officers, who acted as expert advisers to the courts, the Islamic law officers being called *Muftis* and *Maulavis* and the Hindu law officers *Pundits*. But for a long time the employment of such experts, being considered undesirable and unnecessary, has been abandoned. In *Hart Das Dabi v. The Secretary of State for India* it was observed by Mr. Justice Louis Jackson: I confess it seems to me to be among the advantages for which the people of this country have in these days to be thankful that their legal controversies, the determination of their rights and their status have passed into the domain of lawyers, instead of *pundits* and casuists; and in my opinion the case before us may very well be decided on the authority of cases without following *Sreenath,*

Achyutan and others through the mazes of their speculations on the origin and theory of gift'.

These remarks were appropriated by Mr. Justice Trevelyan to the consideration of a question regarding the law of *Waqfs* which arose in the Full Bench case of *Bikani Mian v. Sukhla Poddar.* But whatever may have been the demerits of the condemned system, to should, in fairness, be admitted that the fatwas of the *Maulavis* so far as they can be found in the pages of the old law reports, are a faithful exposition of the Islamic law on the points covered by them.

Solidity of the System

Since the services of the law officers were dispensed with, two features, one closely allied with the other, have been noticeable in the Anglo-Indian administration of Islamic law. In the first place, the courts have experienced no small difficulty in ascertaining the Islamic law. In the case of *Khwaja Hussain Ali v. Shahzadi Hazari Begum,* Mark by, J., observed: As I shall have to point out presently, the means of discovering the Islamic law which this court possesses are so extremely limited that I am glad to avail myself of any mode of escaping a decision on any point connected therewith.' And it is to be feared that generally speaking the courts and the profession do not, even at the present day, feel themselves on familiar and certain ground when a question of Islamic law not settled by a course of decision arises for discussion, although several more books on the subject are now available for reference than in the days of Mark by, J., for instance, Mr. Syed Amir Ali's well-known work on Islamic law and Sir Ronald Wilson's Anglo-Islamic Code'.

Some would attribute the phenomenon to the 'complexity, uncertainty and artificiality' of the system itself. This is an important question and requires to be considered.

Alleged Complexity, Uncertainty and Artificiality of Islamic Laws : The alleged complexity of the system, would, I apprehend, be mainly attributed to the fact that the Islamic municipal laws are treated as part of the Islamic religion; its uncertainty is generally imputed to the differences of opinion which undoubtedly exits on many questions among the jurists, and the charge of artificiality is made with reference to the character of many rules of Islamic law and the reasoning by which rules in themselves reasonable are supported.

So far as complexity of the system is concerned, it is one of the chief objects of the science of Islamic Jurisprudence to explain the principle concepts which connect the different parts of the system, and to enable a lawyers by the classification and analysis of different kinds of laws, of actions, rights and obligations to discriminate between purely religious and legal ideas.

As for uncertainty, the description would hold good in the domain of such matters as are not covered by a plain text of the Quran or the *Hadith*, and have not been settled by consensus of opinion, that is, in respect of laws which are based on juristic deduction. And there can be little doubt that a considerable body of legal rules belong to this category. I am not, however, sure that the recognition of a fairly wide area of legal questions on which difference of opinion is admissible, leaving as it does a large margin of discretion in the courts to adopt on such points rules, which are best suited to the exigencies of particular circumstances, and calculated to meet the requirements of substantial justice should not counterbalance the inconvenience arising from uncertainty. At all events, that is how the matter is regarded by the Islamic jurists themselves, who apply in this connection the well known saying of the Prophet (PBUH): 'difference of opinion among the people is the grace of God'.' As for the charge of artificiality the position seems to be this: according to the theory of Islamic jurists not only do the texts of the Quran and authentic traditions contain within them principles which are sufficient for religious guidance, as well as for the purposes of civil administration, and any rules which are not covered by the words of a text are deducible by the application of analogy to some rule expressly laid down by the texts, but the relation between an original rule and the deduction therefrom can always be expressed in the forms of syllogistic logic.

An inevitable consequence of this theory has been that the paucity of express texts, added to the exigencies of dialectical controversy among rival jurists, often led them to hunt out analogy between questions quite unconnected with each other, such as a question relating to ablution and one relating to guardianship of minors.

The form of reasoning in such cases, was bound to be more or less artificial. It must, however, be remembered that whatever the process of ratiocination, the soundness of the conclusion itself has always to be tested by its conformity to some broad principle and purpose of law, such as necessity or the needs of society.

In this connection the further fact is to be borne in mind that the Islamic system has been developed by jurists, many of whom were not directly in touch with the practical needs of administration of justice. It must also be admitted that many of the rules of law enunciated by the jurists, whether based on a formal and literally interpretation of the texts, or on analogy, are narrow and artificial. This is mostly noticeable in the rules of evidence, and in the law relating to contracts and dispositions of property.

It is, in fact, a general feature of Islamic juristic interpretation that questions, which in the modern systems of law are left for decision to the judgement and discretion of the court, are embodied into rigid rules of law leaving the court no discretion in the matter. For instance, on questions relating to assessment of damages arising either in cases of contract or of tort, very little is left to the discretion of the judge; a hard and fast scale of compensation being laid down in particular classes of cases. So also what in English law would be regarded as rebuttable presumptions of law or of fact are treated as conclusive presumptions of law, and thus we find that rules of evidence are largely treated as part of the substantive law.

Similarly, freedom of contract and of disposition of property is much hampered by restrictions and limitations, the most far-reaching of which are traceable to the wide operation which has been accorded to the doctrine of *reba*, the principle of which is to secure a man from loss arising from hazardous and unequal bargains. These results are partly to be attributed to a tendency, which is observable in the earlier history of most legal systems, to attach more importance to the words of a text rather than to its sense, and partly to the age in which the Arab jurists lived, when disposition of property, in most legal systems, was not so free as in the modern times, and the procedure for trial of suits was only beginning to emerge from the test of ordeal, and the idea of ascertaining the truth in cases where the facts are in dispute, by weighing the evidence on both sides, was just finding a faint expression in juristic consciousness.

It seems to me, therefore, that the difficulty in understanding and ascertaining the Islamic law is mostly due to a more or less natural inclination of the mind of a lawyer of the present day to construe it by the light of modern theories and principles with which he is most familiar, more especially as few people have the time or opportunity to study the Islamic laws as part of a comprehensive scientific system.

Difficulty in Translating Islamic Legal Textbooks : There is another stumbling block in the way of a lawyer who has not studied Islamic law in the original Arabic writings; it is not always possible for a person translating the ideas of Arab jurists into English to find words which will convey the exact legal significance of many technical Arabic expressions.

That difficulty is enhanced when an attempt is made to translate a textbook like the *'Hedaya'*, which is written in the most concise language, and in which the author in discussing the various problems proceeds on the assumption that his reader is familiar with the principles of jurisprudence, the Quran and the *Hadith*, and with the exact significance of legal phraseology. It is less difficult, however, to translate a collection of opinions like *'Fatawa Alamgiri'*[30] and that is one main reason why Mr. Hamilton's *'Hedaya'* has often to be critically compared with the original Arabic text, while Mr. Bailie's digest is generally found to be a more reliable guide. But here I must not be understood in any way to depreciate either the high authority of *'Hedaya'*, or to deny that Mr. Hamilton has rendered valuable service to the administration of Islamic law in India by his publication.

As regards the *Hedaya,* it occupies the foremost place among textbooks on *Hanafi* law and, there can be no doubt that the work deserves its high reputation; in fact, one feels at a loss whether to admire most the purity and lucidity of its diction, the scrupulous care and accuracy with which the legal propositions are discussed, the authorities weighed, and the conclusions stated or the profound learning of the author, who is reputed to have devoted forty years of his life to the compilation of the book.

The terseness of its style, however, makes *'Hedaya'* a most difficult book to translate, and that is apparently the reason why Mr. Hamilton did not attempt to translate the bare text, for his work as is well known is a translation of a Persian commentary of the *'Hedaya'* especially prepared for him.

On doubtful points, therefore, it often becomes necessary to refer to the original *'Hedaya'*, and its authoritative commentaries, in order to verify the statements in Mr. Hamilton's books, and I am further afraid that Mr. Hamilton's way of stating the arguments of jurists has at times led to the misapplication of their dicta.

Principles on which Rules of Islamic Juristic Law are Applied **:** The other result of the passing of the Islamic law into the domain of lawyers and judges, trained in the modern English system, is manifest in a reluctance on the part of judges to adhere literally to the reported opinions of Arab jurists, when such rulings from their narrowness and inapplicability to modern conditions of life stand in the way of substantial justice and of the requirements of a progressive society.

In a well-known passage in his judgement in *Malick Abdul Ghafoor v. Mulika,* Garth, C.J., in dealing with the question how far the doctrine of *musha'* is applicable to a gift of rents, *malikana* rights, and the like, observes: In dealing with these points we must not forget that the Islamic law, to which our attention has been directed in works of very ancient authority, was promulgated many centuries ago in Baghdad and other Islamic countries under a very different state of laws and society from that which now prevails in India; and although we do our best here in suits between Muhammadans to follow the rules of Islamic law, it is often difficult to discover what these rules really were, and still more difficult to reconcile the differences, which so constantly arose between the great expounders of the Islamic law ordinarily current in India, namely, *Abu Hanifa* and his two disciples.

We must endeavour as far as we can to ascertain the true principles upon which that law was founded, and to administer it with a due regard to the rules of equity and good conscience, as well as to the laws and state of society and circumstances which now prevail in this country'. The doctrine thus enunciated, as far as it goes, is undoubtedly in accordance with the root ideas of the Islamic system, the opinions of the most authoritative doctors, and the practice which prevailed, at least, as long as the writers on law still thought for themselves, and were not out of touch with the requirements of society.

Necessity and the wants of social life are, as we shall see, the two all important guiding principles recognised by Islamic Jurisprudence in conformity to which laws should be applied to actual cases, subject only to this reservation, that rules, which are covered by a clear text of the Quran or a precept of indisputable authority, or has been settled by agreement among the learned, must be enforced as we find them. It seems to me beyond question that, so long as this condition is borne in minds, the court in administering Islamic laws is entitled to take into account the circumstances of actual life, and the change in the people's habits and modes of living.

Whether this principle, so far as it relates to administration of justice, has been affected by the doctrine of *taqlid* and, if so, to what extent is a question which we shall consider hereafter; but it must be borne in mind here that the Anglo-Indian courts administer Islamic laws by virtue of power derived from the Sovereign and from the enactments of the Legislature, and neither the rules and conditions laid down by the Islamic law relating to the qualifications of *Qadis* and *Muftis*, nor all the limitations on their authority and discretion in ascertaining and administering the Islamic laws can be said consistently with principle to bind the modern judges. At the same time, however, it is obvious that the courts must have regard in determining questions of Islamic laws, to the sources and authorities of those laws, and to such interpretations of them as are regarded as binding by the Islamics themselves.

Administration of Muhammadan Family Laws : This, in substance, is the spirit in which the courts have been administering Islamic laws in India, though it may be that, in some particular instances, there has been a lapse from the principle. If we analyse the rulings, the results may be thus summarised. In the domain of law governing domestic relations and succession, the courts have allowed themselves a much narrower margin of freedom, if any freedom at all, in applying the rules laid down in books written by mediaeval writers to the altered circumstances of modern world than in matters relating to dispositions of property, such as by gift, *waqf* or will.

In the well-known case *Bazloor Raheem v. Shumsoon Nissa Begum* the Judicial Committee, in dealing with a Muhammadan husband's claim for restitution of conjugal rights observe, with reference to the argument that the question should be decided without reference to the Islamic law, that 'they can conceive nothing more likely to give just alarm to the Muhammadan community than to learn by a judicial decision that the law, the application of which has been secured to them, is to be overridden on a question which so materially concerns their domestic relations.

The judges were not dealing with a case in which the Islamic law, was in plain conflict with the general Municipal law or with the requirements of a more advanced and civilized society—as for instance, if a Muhammadan had insisted on the right to slay his wife taken in adultery'. In *Aga Mahomed v. Kulsum Bibi,* where the question related to the right of a Muhammadan widow to maintenance, and reliance was placed on the language of a particular verse of the Quran to show that the widow was entitled to maintenance independently of her share in the estate of the husband, the Judicial Committee remark: 'They do not care to speculate on the mode in which the text quoted from the Quran which is to be found in *Sura II, vv. 241-2* is to be reconciled with the law as laid down in the *"Hedaya"* and by the author of the passage quoted from *Baillie's "Imamia"*.

But it would be wrong for the court on a *point of this kind* to put their own construction on the Quran in opposition to express ruling of commentators of such great antiquity and high authority.'

The significance of the Board's emphasis on a point of this kind' has to be understood not only with reference to what has just been mentioned, but also to what it had laid down previously, with reference to the application of rules relating to certain forms of disposition of property in the Islamic law.

The extreme limit to which deference to the opinions of Muhammadan jurists has been carried in determining the Islamic law governing a question relating to family relations is illustrated in a case reported in 12 W.R., 460, where divorce pronounced upon compulsion from threats was held to be effective, Jackson, J., observing: 'We are not at liberty to substitute for the express rule of Islamic law, as expounded by the best authorities, that which according to our opinion might be a more enlightened and proper rule of law'.

Law Relating to Dispositions of Property : As to the mode in which Islamic law is to be applied in questions relating to alienation of property, there seems to be a gradually increasing tendency on the part of the courts, and notably of the Privy Council, to assert a greater freedom of interpretation. In one of the earlier *cases—Khajoorronissa v. Rowshan Jehan,* Sir Robert Collier, in delivering the judgement of the Board, had observed, with reference to the question whether a *hiba*, or gift *inter vivos,* would be valid without delivery of seizin, (page 196): 'But it also appears that a holder of property may, to a certain extent, defeat the policy of the law by giving in his lifetime the whole or any part of his property to one of his sons, provided he complies with certain forms.

It is incumbent on those who seek to set up a proceeding of this kind to show very clearly that the forms of the Islamic law whereby its policy is defeated have been complied with.' But the extent to which such forms are to be complied with is more clearly enunciated in later rulings.

In *Muhammad Mumtaz Ahmad v. Zubaid Jan, the* Judicial Committee held that the doctrine relating to gifts of *Musa*, or undivided share in property, is wholly unadapted to a progressive state of society, and ought to be confined within the narrowest limits, and in *Ibrahim Gulam Arif v. Saiboo* in dealing with the same question, raised with reference to gifts of shares in joint-stock companies, their Lordships refer to the above observations with approval and add: 'The argument of the appellant was not that the law of *Musa*' did in fact embrace (in the sense of having been applied to) such property, but that if the same aspect of life and things were logically applied it involved the invalidity of gifts undisputed. But this is not the true criterion'.

The principle embodied in this passage is, perhaps, even more clearly stated in *Bakar Ali Khan, v. Anjuman Ara Begam,* where the Judicial Committee make the following observations with reference to the arguments of Mahmood, J., in support of his view that a valid *waqf* cannot be created by will under the *Shia* law: In the judgement of this Committee delivered by Lord Hobhouse, the danger was pointed out of relying upon ancient texts of the Islamic law and even on precepts of the Prophet (PBUH) himself, of taking them literally and deducing form them new rules of law, especially when such proposed rules do not conduce to substantial justice.

That danger is equally great, whether reliance be placed upon fresh texts newly brought to light, or upon fresh logical inferences newly drawn from old and undisputed texts. Their Lordships think it would be extremely dangerous to accept as a general principle that new rules of law are to be introduced, because they seem to lawyers of the present day to follow logically from ancient texts, however, authoritative, when the ancient doctors of law have not themselves drawn those conclusions.'

The judgement of Lord Hobhouse to which allusion is here made was delivered in the well known case of *Abdul Fateh Muhammad Ishaq v. Rosomy Dhur*

Chowdly, where it was held that a *waqf,* created with the object mainly to benefit the donor's family and posterity is not authorised by the Islamic law. It is not necessary in this place to consider how far the law in support of the validity of such *waqfs* could be said to be a new deduction; all that we are concerned with here is to indicate the principle on which Islamic Law is interpreted and applied by the Indian courts.

References

1. *A famous book studied in the curriculum of most Islamic Universities.*
2. *First and most beloved Caliph of Prophet Muhammad (PBUH).*
3. *Most authentic and reverend compiler of Tradition.*
4. *An uncle of the Prophet, Muhammad (PBUH) and chief of the family.*
5. *A famous book of Islamic history.*
6. *The most respected clan of Mecca.*
7. *Companions and disciples of Caliphs.*
8. *The fourth Caliph and husband of Muhammad's daughter, Fatima (RAA).*
9. *The second Caliph; the most courageous of his Time.*
10. *The third Caliph of the Prophet (PBUH).*
11. *A renowned jurist of Iraq.*
12. *Disciple of Abu Hanifa.*
13. *Most prestigious scholar of Islamic Law, called scholar the great.*
14. *Founder of Muttazila sect.*
15. *The most prominent scholar and founder of Shia School.*

16-21. *Great scholars of Islamic Law of the time.*

22. *A book written by Abu Hanifa on Islamic Law.*
23. *A collection of tradition by Imam Malik*
24. *Grand father of the Prophet (PBUH).*

25-28. *Famous books on tradition, collectively called Sihah-e-Sitta.*

29. *A commentary of the Holy Quran, especially of the verses related to Islamic Law, by Ahmadi.*
30. *World-known collection of judicial decrees.*

3

Sources of Law

Origin of Islamic Law

The true source for the *ahkam* of Islamic law, as already stated in the first part, is *Allah* Almighty. The *ahkam* of *Allah*, however, are discovered through evidences leading to the *ahkam.* These evidences are the sources of Islamic law. The meaning of the term source as used in Islamic law does not differ much from its use in positive law, but there are subtle differences that must be appreciated.

The obvious difference between the two systems is that the material sources of Islamic law are divine in origin, while those of positive law are not. As regards the sources that are constructed upon human mental processes like analogy, there may be much that is common. To appreciate some of the differences and similarities we need to examine the meaning of the term *source* as used in Islamic law and, in addition, to examine the different ways in which the sources are classified by Muslim jurists.

The Meaning of "Source" in Islamic Law : In Islamic law, the term used for source is *dalil* (pl. *dalail).* The word *dalil* means guide. The person leading a caravan is called *dalil,* and so is a telephone directory, because it leads to a number. The Quran, in this sense, is a *dalil* for the *ahkam* of *Allah*, because it leads us to the *khitab* of *Allah* that contains the *ahkam* related to the acts of the subjects. Thus, an examination of the contents of the Quran yields the information required about a *hukm.* This is how some jurists describe the technical meaning of *dalil:* "A valid examination of which yields transmitted information [which is the *hukm*].

The term *dalil* in this meaning is also considered equivalent to the terms *usul al-ahkam* (the roots of the *ahkam)* and *al-masadir al-shariyyah li al-ahkam* (legal sources of the *ahkam).* As all these terms are considered synonymous, it would be helpful to understand the classification of the sources from various perspectives.

The Classification of the Sources : The jurists state that the sources of Islamic law are: the Quran, the *Sunnah, Ijma* (consensus of legal opinion), *qiyas* (analogy), *istihsan* (juristic preference), *qawl al-sahabi* (the opinion of a Companion), *maslahah mursalah* (jurisprudential interest), *sadd al-dhariah* (blocking lawful means to an unlawful end), *istishab al-hal* (presumption of continuity of a rule), *urf* (custom), and earlier scriptural laws. These sources are classified from different perspectives to facilitate study.

Agreed upon and Disputed Sources : The jurists classify some of the sources as being agreed upon unanimously. These are the Quran and the *Sunnah.* Some of the other sources are agreed upon by the majority of the schools. These are *Ijma* and *Qiyas.* It is said that the principle of *Ijma* was not accepted by *al-Nazam* from the *Mutazila* and some of the *Khawarij. Qiyas,* on the other hand, was rejected by the *Zahiri* school and the *Jafari school*[1]. There is another category of sources that are not accepted by all jurists. These are *istihsan* (juristic preference), *qawl al-sahabi* (the opinion of a Companion), *maslahah mursalah* (jurisprudential interest), *Istishab al-hal* (presumption of continuity), *sadd al-dhariah* (plugging the lawful means to an unlawful end), *urf* (custom), and earlier scriptural laws.

The reader should note that many of the differences, though not all, between the opinions and methodologies of the schools are based upon the acceptance and rejection of the disputed sources.

Transmitted and Rational Sources : The sources of Islamic law are divided into those that are transmitted and those that are rational, that is, those that relate to legal reasoning. The transmitted sources are the Quran, the *Sunnah,* and *Ijma.* To these are also linked the opinion of a Companion, and the laws of the earlier scriptures. These are the transmitted sources, for the legal validity of which reason has little role to play, though it does affect the legal reasoning that proceeds from them. The other kind are analogy *(Qiyas), maslahah, istihsan,* and *istishab.* These sources pertain to the mental processes of human beings and are not transmitted, though their acceptance as legally valid and persuasive proofs does rely upon the transmitted evidences.

Thus, *Qiyas* is the assigning of the *hukm* taken from a transmitted evidence to a set of facts about which there is no express provision in the transmitted evidences. This is a mental process. The acceptance of *Qiyas* as a valid method of reasoning is derived from the transmitted evidences, the Quran as well as the *Sunnah.* In short, the transmitted sources themselves identify the modes of legal reasoning that may be accepted as valid and persuasive proofs.

The transmitted sources, therefore, become sources from three aspects:

- First, by indicating the detailed rules of law, like those of prayer, *Zakat,* and inheritance.
- Second, by providing legal justification for the use of methods of reasoning like analogy and *maslahah.* In fact, all the transmitted evidences themselves find support for their acceptance in the Quran. As an example we may state that the following verses provide the evidence for the *Sunnah* as a valid source:

> O you who believe! Obey *Allah* and obey the Apostle, and those charged with authority among you. [Quran 4 : 59]

> So take what the Apostle assigns to you, and deny yourselves that which he withholds from you. [Quran 59 : 7]

> Then let those beware who withstand the Apostle's order lest some trial befall them, or a grievous penalty be inflicted upon them. [Quran 24 : 63]

In addition to this, the function of the *Sunnah* is also indicated; namely, that it works as an elaboration and commentary on the Quran:

> And we have sent down unto thee (also) the Message; that thou mayest explain clearly to men what is sent for them, and that they may give thought. [Quran 16 : 44]

> O Apostle! proclaim the (Message) which hath been sent to thee from they Lord. [Quran 5 : 67]

- A third characteristic of the transmitted sources is that they provide a basis for the extension of the law through the rational sources. Thus, a rule in the texts may be extended through analogy, but the basis or *asl* is provided by the texts or the transmitted sources.

Definitive and Probable Sources : The sources of Islamic law are also classified, by the majority of the jurists, as definitive (*qati)* and probable *(zanni).* When we use the word definitive, we mean something about which we cannot have two opinions, while probable means something that does not reach this level of strength. From another perspective, the attribute of a source being definitive or probable refers to the strength of transmission of the source, that is, the way it has been transmitted by the first three generations. The classical jurists usually use the terms definitive and probable in the sense of transmission.

Thus, when the *Hanafis* say that the category of *fard* is proved by a definitive evidence, they are referring to an evidence that is definitive by way of transmission. Modern scholars, in their attempt to simplify things, have come up with an instructional device and have generalised the meaning of a text as definitive or probable in meaning. Thus, they refer to a source as *qati al-thubut* (definitive by way of transmission) and *qati al-dalalah* (definitive in meaning). A closer examination shows that there is no such general category called *qati al-dalalah* (definitive in meaning) in the systems followed by the classical jurists. When these jurists wanted to refer to such meanings, they listed separate individual categories: *muhkam, nass, khafi, zahir* and so on. All these categories were based upon the different strengths of meaning emerging from a word or a text. Nevertheless, we are retaining the broad category *qati al-dalalah,* because of its instructional value. The reader is warned, however, to be careful about the distinctions. What follows is, therefore, based on the classification followed by modern scholars.

1. With respect to transmission, a source is *qati al-sanad* if it has been reported by a large group of persons from a large group of persons, when in practice a report of such a large group is not subject to suspicion, because they could not have assembled together to fabricate a falsehood. This type of transmission is called *tawatur.* Of this definitive category is the Quran, because it has been transmitted to us, both in memorised and written forms, by way of *tawatur.* The same is the case with the *Sunnah* and *Ijma* when they have been transmitted to us by way of *tawatur.* In the probable category fall individual narrations of the *Sunnah* and *Ijma* when these have not been transmitted in a form that reaches the level of *tawatur.*

2. A source is definitive with respect to the understood meaning when the text of the transmitted evidence indicates something about which there can be only one opinion. Thus, if the text of the Quran says that you have "half" of what your deceased spouses left or when it says that for the fornicator are a "hundred" stripes, the words "half" and "hundred" cannot have dual meanings, because a "hundred" is a "hundred" any way we may read it or understand it. Probable means something that can have more than one meaning, and the examples are many.

There are some texts of the Quran and the *Sunnah* that convey definitive meanings and there are others that convey a probable meaning. As for *Ijma,* it always indicates a definitive meaning, because having more than one meaning negates the very concept of *Ijma.* The rest of the sources, like analogy and *istihsan* all convey probable meanings.

This Division into Definitive and Probable Gives us Four Combinations of the Transmitted Sources

1. Sources that are definitive with respect to *sanad* (transmission) and definitive with respect to meaning. These would be the texts of the Quran and the *Sunnah Mutawatira* that convey single meanings.
2. Sources that are definitive with respect to *sanad,* but are probable with respect to meaning. These would be the texts of the Quran and the *Sunnah Mutawatira* that convey more than one meaning, that is, they are subject to interpretation. When the Quran says: "Rub your heads *(mash)* with water," [Quran 5 : 6] it is probable that the meaning is the entire head or part of it, and both meanings have been upheld by jurists. The same is the case with the *Sunnah.*
3. Sources that are probable with respect to transmission and definitive with respect to the implied meaning. These would include traditions that were transmitted by one or two individuals in the first three generations. Examples would include those traditions that contain definitive words.
4. Sources that are probable with respect to *sanad* and probable with respect to meaning. An example is the tradition that says that "there is nothing out of the inheritance for the killer." The question is whether the killing here means *qatl-e-amd* (murder), *shibh al-amd* (culpable homicide not amounting to murder or voluntary manslaughter), *qatl khata* (manslaughter), or even homicide caused directly or indirectly. The opinions of the jurists, therefore, vary.

As for the sources that are not transmitted, they are not relevant to the discussion of the above four categories; in general they are considered as probable. It is only the opinion of a Companion that may be linked to the above four transmitted categories by some jurists.

Primary and Secondary Means

The classification of the sources of Islamic law into primary and secondary is nothing more than a collection, and the combined effect, of all the characteristics that have preceded in the previous classifications. Thus, when we view the previous characteristics, we distinguish the primary and secondary sources as follows:

1. Primary sources are those that are unanimously agreed upon by the four Sunni schools of thoughts. This would include analogy. When the range

of schools is widened, analogy is excluded and so is *Ijma.* Secondary sources are those that are not unanimously accepted.

2. Primary sources are transmitted sources, while secondary sources are mostly rational sources. This distinction would include the opinion of a Companion among the primary sources, but the previous criterion excludes it.
3. Primary sources are definitive sources, while secondary sources are probable. The *khabar wahid,* we have said is probable, but here we are concerned with the *Sunnah* as a source of law on the whole. Likewise, this classification may be said to include only those types of *Ijma* that are considered definitive, but again we are concerned with consensus as a source of law on the whole. Analogy and other types of rational sources would be classified as secondary sources.
4. Laws discovered through the primary sources may be extended through the rational sources or the secondary sources, while laws discovered through secondary sources cannot be further extended. This, perhaps, is the most important distinction between the primary and secondary sources.

Primary sources, then, are at once agreed upon, transmitted, definitive on the whole, and those upon which further extension can be based. This would mean that the Quran, the *Sunnah,* and *Ijma* are the primary sources, while the rest are secondary sources. To describe the characteristics of secondary sources, just reverse the characteristics listed above. For example, secondary sources are mostly rational sources, or they are mostly disputed sources, or that they depend on the primary sources for their content.

Qualities of Means

It is customary with writers to discuss the grades of the sources under a general and preliminary discussion such as this. By grades is meant the priority assigned to a source in the jurists search for the *ahkam.* This topic pertains to *ijtihad* and the *tarjih.* It is, therefore, discussed briefly here.

Many writers maintain that the first source to be approached is the Quran, the second is the *Sunnah,* the third is *Ijma* (consensus of legal opinion) and the fourth is analogy. These writers also maintain, on the basis of this natural order, that it is not proper to move to another source unless the search in the prior source has been exhausted. Thus, the first search for a *hukm* is to be in the Quran. The jurist should not move to the next source, the *Sunnah,* unless the search in the Quran has been completed. Likewise, the jurist should not move to the consensus of jurists, unless the search in the *Sunnah* is exhausted. Analogy is to be resorted to only when the search in all three prior sources is completed. These scholars rely upon a number of evidences to strengthen this view.

For example, they rely upon the verse: "O you who believe! Obey Allah, and obey the Apostle, and those charged with authority among you. If ye differ in anything among yourselves, refer it to *Allah* and His Apostle, if you do believe in *Allah* and the Last Day." [Quran 4 : 59] In this verse, they maintain, obedience to *Allah* means having recourse to the Book of *Allah*, obedience to the Prophet (peace be on him) means having recourse to his *Sunnah* and obeying those in authority means having recourse to *Ijma.* The order is, thus, prescribed in this verse.

Another Source they Rely upon is the Well-known Tradition of Muad ibn Jabal: When the Apostle of *Allah* intended to send *Muad ibn Jabal* to the Yemen, he asked: How will you judge when the occasion of deciding a case arises? He replied: I shall judge in accordance with *Allah's* Book. He asked: (What will you do?) if you do not find guidance in *Allah's* Book? He replied: (I will act) in accordance with the *Sunnah* of the Messenger of Allah. He asked: (What will you do?) if you do not find guidance in the *Sunnah* of the Apostle of *Allah* and in *Allah's* Book? He replied: I shall do my best to form an opinion and spare no pains. The Apostle of *Allah* then patted him on the breast and said: Praise be to *Allah* Who helped the messenger of the Apostle of *Allah* to find a thing which pleases the Apostle of *Allah.*

This tradition determines the order in which the sources are to be approached. It also indicates that analogy is to be resorted to when the search in the texts has been exhausted.

In addition to these two sources, these scholars mention the letter of *Umar ibn al-Khattab*, may *Allah* be pleased with him, written to the famous *Qadi* Shurayh: "When you are faced with an issue, decide through what is laid down in the Book of Allah. If the issue you face relates to what is not in the Book of *Allah*, then decide by what is in the *Sunnah* of the Messenger of *Allah* (peace be on him)." In another version of this *athar* the words are: "If you find something in the Book of *Allah*, decide through it and do not have recourse to anything else besides it." A third narration explains this meaning: "Examine what is evident for you in the Book of *Allah* and do not ask anyone about it. If nothing is evident for you in the Book of *Allah*, follow the *Sunnah* of the Messenger of *Allah* (peace be on him)."

All these evidences show, it is maintained, that there is a determined order for approaching the sources and that the jurist should not move to the next source, unless the first source has been searched thoroughly for a solution.

A closer examination of the issue reveals that the statement about the order in which the sources are to be examined needs to be qualified somewhat. This is obvious from the following points:

1. *Approaching the Quran and the Sunnah Together:* The first point to notice is that it is not possible for the jurist to understand the meaning of the text of the Quran for the derivation of the *ahkam,* unless he has recourse to the explanation and commentary of the Quran. This explanation and commentary is the *Sunnah* itself. Thus, a jurist may not decide upon the basis of a general or absolute text in the Quran, unless he has ascertained that the *Sunnah* has not restricted the general meaning or has not qualified the absolute text.

   Take the case of the provisions for the thief *(shariq)* in the Quran. It provides that the hands of each thief are to be cut. The *Sunnah* restricts this general rule to the thief who steals wealth equivalent to the *nisab* (prescribed scale). It also restricts it to a person who steals something in protective custody *(hirz).* Likewise, the Quran provides for the payment of *Zakat* in broad terms, that is, for all kinds of wealth, but the *Sunnah* excludes several categories of wealth from this wide provision.

   The *Sunnah* is, therefore, interlinked with the Quran insofar as it restricts its general meaning or qualifies absolute texts or explains its difficult and unelaborated words. It would, thus, be inappropriate, if not incorrect, for the jurist to take the *hukm* directly from the Quran without consulting the *Sunnah.* The statement, then, that the Quran is to be consulted first and the *Sunnah* is to be consulted only if nothing is found in the Quran, is to be qualified to mean that consulting the Quran implies the consulting of the *Sunnah* along with it. In other words, there is a special bond between the *Quran* and the *Sunnah* and this bond must never be severed.

2. In one classification above it is stated that a greater weight is attached to a definitive *(qati)* meaning arising from a *mutawatir Sunnah* as compared to a text in the Quran that can be interpreted in more than one way. In technical terms, it means that such a *Sunnah* is definitive with respect to its transmission as well as its meaning, while a *zanni* text of the Quran is definitive with respect to its transmission, but probable as regards the meaning. In such a case too, it would be inappropriate for the jurist to look at the text of the Quran alone and not at the *Sunnah.*

3. *Ijma and the Texts: Hukm* is sometimes established through consensus of opinion *(Ijma). Ijma* is considered definitive by the jurists and the jurist is bound to follow its directives. According to the principles of *tarjih* (precedence of evidences) it is required of a jurist that he first investigate

whether the case he is examining has been settled by *Ijma.* If it has been, he is to follow the settled rule and give up his own *ijtihad.* This process may be compared with the precedents laid down by higher courts. If the higher court has laid down a precedent and has interpreted a statute in a certain way, the lower court is bound to follow the precedent and construe the statute accordingly. It is obvious that consensus of legal opinion has assigned definitive meanings to texts in which the meanings were not very clear, therefore, *Ijma* will have precedence over the unelaborated or multiple meanings in the texts.

4. *General Principles Derived from the Texts:* According to the methodology of some jurists, especially the *Hanafis* and *Malikis*, broad general principles that have been derived from the entire law through a process of juristic reasoning are to be preferred over the *khabar wahid* in certain cases. This is the view of the *Hanafis* and *Malikis*.

The above discussion shows that the sources cannot be consulted in a simple order of priority advocated by some writers. The matter is much more complex, and it is one task of the subject of *usul al-fiqh* to unravel these complexities for the student of Islamic law.

Starting Means

The primary sources are the Quran and the *Sunnah,* because these sources contain the law for many cases and also serve as the basis for the extension of the law. Consensus of legal opinion (*Ijma)* also contains the law, and its provisions can be used for extending the law further, though some would prefer to have recourse to the basis or the *sanad* of *Ijma* for the new case. For this basis, we have to turn to the Quran and the *Sunnah* again, therefore, some jurists maintain that the primary sources are the Quran and the *Sunnah* alone, and *Ijma* is a kind of secondary source. It is, however, associated with the primary sources for the purposes of this book on the basis of the reasons discussed earlier.

In this chapter the Quran and the *Sunnah* will be studied as the two primary sources. This will be followed by a description of the close relationship between these two sources. Finally, the details of *Ijma* as a source of law will be examined.

Quran as the Primary Source of Law : The words al-Quran and *al-Kitab* are used in the same meaning. The jurists who specialise in *usul al-fiqh* (called *usulis)* are hesitant about providing a definition of the Quran insofar as a definition means enclosing the defined thing within bounds. Yet, many of them, in an attempt to grasp all its noble attributes and characteristics have provided definitions. They maintain that the purpose of the definition is not to enclose the nature of the Quran in a definition, but to identify the book in response to the question: Which book do you mean? One such definition recorded here is from *al-Bazdawi*.

This may be Rendered into English as Follows: The Quran is the Book revealed to the Messenger of *Allah*, Muhammad (peace be on him) as written in the *masahif* and transmitted to us from him through an authentic continuous narration *(tawatur)* without doubt.

Some jurists add the words "revealed in Arabic" to emphasise that it cannot be translated, while others say that "the Quran is the revealed and miraculous speech of *Allah* ...," to emphasise the *ijaz* (inimitable or miraculous nature) of the Book. Still others, like the *Hanafis*, add that it is transmitted in its seven readings all of which are *mutawatir.*

The Attempt in most of these Definitions is to Emphasise the Following Attributes:

1. *The Quran is the Speech of Allah Revealed to Muhammad (Peace be on him) :* This attribute excludes other revealed books from the definition, that is, books that were not revealed to Muhammad (peace be on him). These are like the *Torah* and the *Evangel*. Some jurists maintain that the word Quran applies to the eternal speech of the Almighty as well as to the written text that is recited. To refine their definition some insist that it is the recited text that is meant here, while others maintain that both meanings are included in the definition.

2. *The Arabic Words of the Quran as well as their Meanings are both Revealed :* This attribute excludes the Sunnah from the definition, because the words of the *Sunnah* are not those of *Allah* though its content is inspired and is considered to be revelation in meaning from *Allah*.

   The attribute also excludes the tafsir of the Quran and the translation of the Quran from this definition. It is said that *Abu Hanifah* used to permit recitation in *Farsi* during prayers for those who did not know Arabic, however, authentic reports in the *Hanafi* school confine such permission to converts to Islam for a period in which they are able to learn the Arabic text. Thus, the exemption was for necessity and need and was, therefore, limited. There has been an intense debate on the issue in Islamic legal literature.

   Translation of the Quran is, therefore, not possible and what are termed translations are in fact translations of the *tafsir* (interpretation) of the Quran.

3. *The Quran is Transmitted to us by Way of Tawatur :* This means that the Quran was transmitted to us both in its written and memorised form

by such a large number of people in each generation starting with the first that any doubt about its not being the original text cannot be conceived rationally. This attribute is intended to exclude a few variant readings of the Quran that were not revealed by way of *tawatur.*

4. *Ijaz of the Quran : Ijaz* means the inability of human beings individually or collectively to imitate or bring about something similar to the Quran. This inability was acknowledged by the Arabs during the period of the Prophet (PBUH). The inability also confirms that the Quran is the revealed word of *Allah*, and is therefore a source of law. In other words, for purposes of the jurist, *ijaz* becomes an additional proof of the authenticity of the Quran and the truth of the mission of the Prophet (peace be on him)

Justification of Quran as a Source : The entire *ummah* agreed that the Quran is the primary source for the *ahkam* of *Allah*. It is, therefore, binding upon the jurist to have recourse to it and to rely upon it for the discovery of the law in each case that he faces. They also agreed that the jurist will find each case provided for in the Quran either expressly or by implication, that is, through derivation *(istinbat).* In approaching the Quran for the derivation of the laws, the jurist is also under an obligation to have recourse to its commentary and explanation, which is the *Sunnah* of the Prophet (PBUH). The statement of *al-Shafii* recorded earlier that "there is no incident that befalls one of those who follow the *din* of *Allah* without there being an evidence in the Book of *Allah* providing guidance for it" emphasises this meaning.

Considering the Quran as *the primary source* means that all the other sources are secondary to it; even their legal validity and justification as sources is derived from the Quran.

Recording and Revelation of Quran : The compilation of the Quran has a detailed and well documented history. These details can be gleaned elsewhere. The reason why it is studied under the title of the Quran as a source of Islamic law is to provide further justification for its having been transmitted by way of *tawatur* and also to explain the reason for its unique arrangement.

> The Quran, as is well known, was not revealed all at once to the Messenger of *Allah* (peace be on him), but in stages and in accordance with incidents faced by the Muslim community. The important aspect of the wisdom behind its revelation in this way is considered to be the ease in its memorisation by the Companions. *Allah*, the Exalted, says: "(It is) a Quran which We have divided (into parts from time to time) in order that thou mightest recite it to men at intervals: We have revealed it by stages," [Quran 17 : 106] and "Those who reject faith

say: 'Why is not the Quran revealed to him all at once?' Thus (it is revealed), that We may strengthen thy heart thereby, and we have rehearsed it to thee in slow, well-arranged stages, gradually."

[Quran 25 : 32]

Another reason for the gradual revelation of the Quran is considered to be the implementation of the law in stages. This has given rise to the abrogating and the abrogated verses. The clearest example of the laying down of the law in phases is the case of the prohibition of *khamr* (wine). The incidents, cases, and questions that often preceded the revelation of the verses help, those who came later, in understanding the meaning and import of the verses. These are called the *asbab al-nuzul* or occasions for the revelation. These reasons have facilitated to a great extent the application of the law in all ages.

The Messenger of *Allah* used to memorise a verse or verses of the Quran after their revelation. He then recited these for his Companions who used to memorise them. There were also scribes with the Prophet who used to record the verses after their revelation and recitation.

These written records were then preserved in the Prophet's house, while some of the scribes would record the verses for themselves and preserve them for their own use. *Jibbrail* used to inform the Prophet (PBUH) of the place and location of each verse within its chapter *(surah)*. During each *Ramadan,* it is said, *Jibbrail* used to recite in its proper arrangement with the Prophet (PBUH) what had been revealed of the Quran, and in the last year of his life Jibbrail[2] recited the whole of it in its proper arrangement and the Prophet recited it twice after him. The Prophet, thus, memorised it and recited it for his Companions, who memorised it in this arrangement.

By the time of *Abu Bakr,* the Quran was to be found in its complete form either memorised or recorded in *suhuf*[3]. *Zaid ibn Thabit*, therefore, did not rely upon the memory of the Companions alone when he prepared the official copy; he relied upon both.

Legal Strength and Indication of Ahkam in the Quran : As the Quran has been transmitted to us by way of *tawatur,* its authenticity is definitive *(qati)*. This is from the aspect of transmission. When we read the Quran, however, some of its words convey a definitive meaning, which is not subject to interpretation, while others convey probable meanings, that is, there can be two or meanings for a word. Taking both these aspects into account we say that the Quran indicates the *ahkam* in two grades of strength, as follows:

1. Indications that are definitive with respect to *sanad* (transmission) and definitive with respect to meaning. The examples of such meanings were

the words "half" or "hundred." This type of text is also known as *nass* (explicit). The rule for such indications are: "There is no *ijtihad* in a *nass* (explicit meaning not subject to interpretation)." Some people mistakenly believe that this rule applies to all the texts of the Quran and that *ijtihad* is not possible where a text exists. Accordingly they call *ijtihad* by names like "independent reasoning" and so on, as if *ijtihad* was something independent of the texts. It is for the same reason, probably, that the idea is advanced that *ijtihad* is a source of law.

2. Indications that are definitive with respect to *sanad,* but are probable with respect to meaning. These would be the texts of the Quran that convey more than one meaning, that is, they are subject to interpretation. When the Quran says: "Rub your heads *(mash)* with water," [Quran 5 : 6] it is probable that the meaning is the entire head or part of it, and both meanings have been upheld by jurists. The rule stated for the first category does not apply here. Thus, the texts of the Quran that indicate such meanings are subject to interpretation, that is, *ijtihad.*

Kinds of Ahkam in Quran : There are approximately six hundred verses in the Quran that indicate the *ahkam* of Islamic law. Over four hundred of these pertain to the *ibadat* and the remaining to crimes, personal law, and other *muamalat.* A few of all these verses belong to the first of the two categories mentioned above, that is, they do not need further elaboration. The remaining verses require interpretation and elaboration. The primary means of such elaboration or the choosing of one meaning out of two or more probable meanings is through the *Sunnah.* This relationship of the *Sunnah* with the Quran will be explained later in this chapter. The texts of the Quran also require analysis through the tools and rules of literal interpretation, even when the *Sunnah* is being employed for elaboration, and these tools have been described in the part on *ijtihad.* The kinds of *ahkam* that are contained in the six hundred or more verses of the Quran cover a very wide range of *ahkam.* These may be divided into the following categories:

1. *Ahkam Pertaining to Aqaid (Tenets of Faith) :* These are like belief in One God, His Angels, Books, Prophets, and the Day of Judgement. The discipline dealing with these is that of *Tauhid.*

2. *Ahkam Pertaining to the Disciplining and Strengthening of the Self :* These rules deal with Quranic ethics. The disciplines that deal with them are ethics and *tasawwuf.* Many of the ethical norms of the Quran are to be found clothed in the legal provisions.

3. *Rules of Conduct (Pertaining to the Words and Acts of the Subject) :* This category covers the entire field of *fiqh.*

They are Divided into two Types:

A. *Rules Related to Worship* : The purpose of these rules is to establish the relationship of the individual with his Creator.

B. *All those Rules that Relate to Conduct Other than Worship* : This area is called *muamalat* by the jurists. It regulates the relationship of individuals among themselves, the relationship of individuals with states, and the relationship of the Islamic state with non-Muslim states.

In short, it covers the entire are of substantive and procedural law or to put it differently, it includes private and public law.

It is to be remembered that though the particular cases mentioned in the Quran are few, there are many broad and general principles that facilitate the derivation of countless *ahkam*.

Role of Tradition

Definition of the Sunnah : The word *Sunnah* has a literal meaning and several technical meanings. An indiscriminate use of the term leads to confusion, therefore, it is necessary that most of the technical meanings be understood.

Exact Definition

In its literal meaning the word *sunnah* stands for the "well-known path," or the "well-trodden path," which is followed again and again. This may be the path on which people tread or it may be a practice. It is in this sense that the following saying of the Prophet (PBUH) is understood: "He who establishes a good *sunnah* has its reward and the reward of whoever acts upon it till the Day of Judgement, and he who establishes a bad *sunnah* bears its burden and the burden of whoever acts upon it till the Day of Judgement." The *sunnah* of an individual is a practice that he considers binding for himself and that he attempts to protect and uphold.

Specific Meaning

In its Technical Sense, the Word Sunnah is Assigned the Following Meanings:

1. Some jurists apply it to mean recommended acts of worship, while others apply it to super derogatory acts *(nawafil).*
2. The word *sunnah* as an antonym of *bidah* (innovation), that is, innovations in matters of religion. In this sense, it is said, "This act is a *sunnah,*" that is, it is legal. The meaning of "legal" is assigned to it irrespective of the legality arising from the Quran or the *Sunnah.* When it is said that

such and such act is a *bidah* it means it is not legal according to the Quran and the *Sunnah.*

3. The term *sunnah* is used to mean the practice of the Companions *(Sahabah)* irrespective of their relying in it on the Book, the *Sunnah,* or their own *ijtihad.* An example is the compilation of the Quran for which there was no authorising text either in the Quran or in the *Sunnah,* but it amounted to an interest *(maslahah)* indicated by all the texts; namely, the preservation of *Din.* The saying of the Prophet, "Hold on to my *sunnah* and the *sunnah* of the rightly guided caliphs after me," is understood in this sense.
4. Finally, it is defined as "what was transmitted from the Messenger of *Allah* (peace be on him) of his words, acts, and (tacit) approvals." It is in this sense that we shall be using the term *sunnah,* that is, as the *Sunnah* of the Prophet (PBUH) and a source of Islamic laws.

Types of Tradition

The question that arises here is whether every saying, act and approval of the Prophet (peace be on him) has the same status for purposes of acting upon it as a source of law. To be able to answer this question it is necessary to look at the types of the *Sunnah.* For this purpose, the *Sunnah* is classified in two ways:

1. The kinds of the *Sunnah* when we look at the channels through which the *ahkam* are established. This is also called the classification of the *Sunnah* according to its nature.
2. The kinds of the *Sunnah* with respect to the channels through which it is transmitted to us. This may be called the classification of the *Sunnah* according to its written record, that is, the classification of *Hadith,* when this term is used not merely for the sayings of the Prophet (peace be on him), but for the entire written record.

Kinds of the Sunnah with Respect to the Channels of the Ahkam : This type of the *Sunnah* is of three types: *sunnah qawliyyah* or the sayings of the Prophet (peace be on him); *sunnah filiyyah* or the acts of the Prophet (peace be on him); and *sunnah taqririya* or the tacit approval given by the Prophet (peace be on him). Some jurists, like *al-Shatibi,* have discussed another subtype called *sunnat al-tark,* which is discussed briefly here along with *sunnah filiyyah.*

Al-Sunnah al-Qawliyyah: It is defined as the sayings of the Prophet (peace be on him) through which he intended the laying down of the law or the explanation of the *ahkam.* Generally, the word *Hadith* is used for this type of *Sunnah* insofar as the word *Hadith* means "saying." In this sense, the word *Hadith* has a meaning narrower than that of *sunnah.* Some of the traditionalists, however, use the term

Hadith to mean all that is reported from the Prophet (peace be on him), that is, words, acts, and approvals. In this sense, the words *sunnah* and *Hadith* are synonyms. It is in this meaning that *al-Bukhari* calls his book *al-Sahih minal-Hadith* when his book contains all three types.

There are a large number of sayings of the Prophet (peace be on him) that are considered as *sunnah qawliyyah.* Some well known examples are: (Entitlement to revenue depends on a corresponding liability for loss); (The nature of acts is dependent upon the underlying intentions); (No injury is to be caused and none is to be borne); and (Intentional murder leads to retaliation).

It is to be noted that not every saying of the Prophet (peace be on him) is a source of law. This is obvious from the definition stated above. To become a source of law, the purpose of the saying should be the laying down of the law or its elaboration.

Al-Sunnah al-Filiyyah : It is defined as the acts of the Prophet (peace be on him) having a legal content, like his prayer, fasts, *Hajj.* These acts or the method of their performance that he adopted are to be followed in the same way as his sayings. The acts that do not have a legal content do not become a source of law. This may be understood distinguishing between the following types of acts:

1. Ordinary physical acts performed by every human being, like eating, drinking, walking and sitting. Such acts are not meant to lay down laws, though some jurists consider them to be *mubah.* This becomes clear when such acts are compared with acts that lay down the law. Jurists maintain that an act of the Prophet (peace be on him) pertaining to law indicates absolute or unqualified permission, which includes *wujub, nadb,* and *ibahah,* till such time that another evidence fixes the meaning for one these. This means that if no other evidence is available, the acts of the Prophet (PBUH) will be interpreted to mean permissibility. As compared to this, the ordinary acts mentioned above, like eating and drinking, indicate *ibahah* or permissibility *ab initio;* they do not indicate recommendation or obligation.

   In addition to this, there may be acts that pertain to his experience as a human being, like the organising of the army, war tactics, trading skills, and so on. These acts too do not become precedents of law, because their basis is skill and experience rather than revelation.

   Some jurists say that accepting evidence for proving facts in a trial or case cannot be considered as binding either. The reason is that they treat this as a skill. On the other hand, they would consider a decision rendered in a case as a binding precedent. He is reported to have said: "I am a human like you. When you come to me as litigants, some of you have better evidence than the others, and I decide according to what I hear. Thus, if I have given to one something that was due to the other, I have given him a piece of hellfire."

2. Acts that are specific to the Prophet (peace be on him) and the rest of the *ummah* is not to follow him in such acts. For example, in the case of the number of his marriages, which is based on a law specific to him.
3. Acts that are intended to be explanations of unelaborated rules in the texts. All such explanations have the status of law. The persuasive force of such explanations is the same as that of the text being elaborated. The explanation of a *mujmal* (unelaborated) word will take the force of the *mujmal* on which it is based. The acts of his prayer, after his saying, "Pray as you see me praying," as well as his acts concerning the rites of *Hajj* based on his saying, "Take (the knowledge of) your rites from me," are examples.
4. Acts that establish new laws obviously have the force of law.

Intentional Omissions (Sunnat al-tark) : Some jurists divide the *Sunnah filiyyah* into acts and intentional omissions, and this leads to a further subtype: *sunnat al-tark.* Omission or abstention from an act by the Prophet (peace be on him) indicates that the act he has given up is not permitted, and this includes disapproval and prohibition, and one of these will be determined by circumstantial or related evidence. The Prophet's (PBUH) omission of the act indicates that giving up the act is better than its performance. An example is the Prophet's refusal to become a witness for a person who had given most of his wealth to one child. He asked the man: "Have you treated each child like this." He said: "No" The Prophet (PBUH) said: "Then get someone else as a witness. I will not be a witness to injustice." The omission here indicates that the act is not legal. It covers both disapproval and prohibition, and the jurists have differed in determining one of these according to the evidences they have relied upon.

It may sometimes become obvious that the omission is not because of disapproval, but due to some other reason, like a natural aversion for a thing. The Prophet (PBUH) refused to eat a *dabb* (a small animal of the rodent family) and then explained that he did not feel like having such food. As it was something personal to him, it means that it is not prohibited to eat such things. Again, the omission may be for fear that the act may be construed as an obligation, when the act itself is required by law. Examples are the avoiding of *tarawih* prayer during *Ramadan* on certain occasions as well as his saying: "If I did not foresee hardship for my *ummah,* I would have ordered them to use the *siwak* (brushing of teeth) before each prayer."

Sunnah Taqririyyah : It is defined as the commission of certain acts, by word or deed, by some Companions and the maintenance of silence by the Prophet (PBUH) without expressing disapproval. His silence in such a case is called *taqrir* or tacit approval and is considered a *Sunnah* that becomes a source for the permissibility of an act or a statement. An example of this type is the statement of *Muad-ibn-Jabal*[4] when he was sent to Yemen and the Prophet (PBUH) asked him how he will decide cases. This approval, however, was a little more emphatic than mere silence.

Kinds of Sunnah with Respect to its Modes of Transmission : *Ahadith* (traditions) are divided, with respect to narration, into two types. First, the *ahadith* whose chain of narration is complete. These are the ones in which the narrators are mentioned from the beginning of the *sanad* upto the Messenger of *Allah,* and no narrator is missing. Second, the *ahadith* from the chains of which one or more narrators are missing. The *hadith* from which a narrator is missing is called *mursal* by the *Hanafis.* The Traditionalist (Muhaddithun) confine the term *mursal* to a tradition from the chain of which the name of the Companion is missing, while they term as *munqat*a tradition from the chain of which the name of a narrator other than a Companion is missing. Both types of *hadith* will be discussed and within these the types of *Sunnah* they give rise to.

Hadith Muttasil

The majority of the jurists divided the *muttasil ahadith* into two types: *mutawatir* and *ahad.* In between these two, the *Hanafi* jurists added a third category called *mashhur.* It is very important to note that for purposes of working out the number of narrators of a tradition, only the first three generations are taken into account. After their periods, the reports were compiled and all the reports became well-known.

Hadith Mutawatir : The *mutawatir hadith* is one that is related by such a large number of people that their agreement to propagate a falsehood cannot be conceived. This applies to the narration from the beginning of its chain to its end, where it reaches the Prophet (PBUH). An example of such a *hadith* is:

> Acts are determined by intentions, and to each person belongs what he intends.

In the same category are the reports about the number of daily prayers and the rates of *Zakat.*

Tawatur is of Two Types : *Tawatur* in words and *tawatur* in meaning. When all the narrators are in agreement about the words as well as meaning, the *hadith* indicates *tawatur* by its very words. An example are the words of the Prophet

(PBUH): "He who intentionally attributes a falsehood to me should prepare his abode in the Fire." This tradition was related by a large number of Companions in these words. The narration was reproduced in great numbers in the following generation when it was finally recorded. This makes it *tawatur lafzi.* The other kind is known as *tawatur manawi,* which is a tradition that conveys the same meaning even if the words are not exactly the same. Most of the *mutawatir* traditions are of the latter category.

The *mutawatir* tradition conveys definitive knowledge *(ilm)* and is also definitive with respect to its authenticity. It is, therefore, said that a *mutawatir* tradition is *qati* with respect to *ilm* as well as *thubut.* In other words, it must be followed under all circumstances. *Qati al-thubut* means that we are certain about its narration from the Prophet (PBUH). It is to be noted, however, that the words of such a tradition may be subject to interpretation, in which case the meaning arising from such a tradition (its *dalalah)* will not be definitive, but will be probable. Such a meaning will be definitive, of course, if only one meaning can be derived. For example, in the case of the tradition, mentioned above, saying that "acts are determined by intentions", some jurists may say that this means "for the purposes of the hereafter," while others may interpret it to mean acts in this world and thus apply it to contracts and other acts.

Hadith Mashhur : It has been stated above that the majority of the jurists classified the tradition with a complete chain into two types, but the *Hanafi* jurists added a third category called *mashhur.*

The *mashhur* tradition is one the number of whose reporters do not reach the level of *tawatur* in the first generation. Thus, if one or two Companions related the tradition from the Prophet (PBUH), but in the next generation, that is, the generation of the Tabiun, a very large number narrated from them and so on till the end of the chain when the traditions were compiled, then, such a tradition is called *mashhur.* The factor that makes such a tradition *mashhur* (well-known) is the number of persons in the second and the third generation narrating it, because after this compilation started and all traditions became well-known. The *mashhur* tradition, according to the *Hanifis*, falls into a category that is lesser in strength than the *mutawatir* tradition, but is stronger than the *khabar wahid.* The majority of the jurists, however, consider such a tradition to be a *khabar wahid.* According to *al-Sarakhsi*, the tradition about the prohibition of marrying the maternal or paternal aunt of an existing wife belongs to this category.

Hadith al-Ahad : The *hadith al-ahad* or the *khabar wahid* is reported by one or two persons from the beginning of its chain upto its end when all traditions were recorded. Thus, the narrators do not reach the level of *tawatur* in either of the first three periods: the period of the Companions, the *Tabiun,* and the *Tab*

Tabiun. After the third period, as stated above, the traditions were compiled and all became well known.

The *khabar wahid* is generally not relied upon by jurists in matters of faith *(aqaid),* but it is accepted in matters of conduct, that is, in matters covered by the *muamalat.* In fact, there is generally an agreement of the Muslims about the acceptance of the *khabar wahid* in matters of *fiqh.*

Justification of Sunnah as a Source of Law : The *Sunnah* is unanimously accepted as a primary source of law and *ahkam* can be derived from it independently of any other source. The jurists provide transmitted as well as rational arguments for its justification as a primary source of law.

1. *From the Book :* There are several ways in which this justification is understood:

   - The Book indicates that what the Prophet (PBUH) lays down as law is based upon revelation. *Allah,* the Exalted, says: "Nor does he say (aught) of (his own) desire. It is no less than inspiration sent down to him." [Quran 53 : 3, 4]

     Thus, the words of the Prophet (PBUH), being based upon revelation, are a valid source of law, except that the *Sunnah* is revelation in meaning alone, not in words.

   - *Allah* granted the Prophet (PBUH) the task of elaborating the meanings of the Quran as well as the explanation of the unelaborated words. His elaboration, therefore, complements arid completes the meanings in the Quran and becomes a valid source or evidence for law. The verse of the Quran supporting this is: "And we have sent down unto thee (also) the Message that thou mayest explain clearly to men what is sent down for them." [Quran 16 : 44]

   - A number of verses in the Quran that indicate definitively that the *Sunnah* is to be followed as a source of law:

     (1) O you who believe! Obey Allah, and obey the Apostle, and those charged with authority among you. If you differ in anything among yourselves, refer it to *Allah* and His Apostle, if ye do believe in *Allah* and the Last Day. [Quran 4 : 59]

     (2) He who obeys the Apostle, obeys *Allah.* [Quran 4 : 80]

     (3) So take what the Apostle assigns to you, and deny yourselves that which he withholds from you. [Quran 59 : 7]

     (4) But no, by thy Lord, they can have no (real) faith, until they make thee judge in all disputes between them, and find in their

souls no resistance against they decisions, but accept them with the fullest conviction. [Quran 4 : 65]

(5) It is not fitting for a believer, man or woman, when a matter has been decided by *Allah* and His Apostle, to have any option about their decision. [Quran 4 : 65]

2. *On the Basis of Ijma (Consensus):* The Muslims all agreed during the period of the Prophet (PBUH) upon the obligation of acting according to the *ahkam* laid down by the *Sunnah* and upon the necessity of having recourse to it for the derivation and discovery of the *ahkam.* There was no one among the Companions who disputed this, because the true source of these *ahkam* was revelation.

3. *Rational Argument:* First, it is a part of a Muslim's faith that Muhammad (PBUH) is the Messenger of *Allah* charged with the mission of conveying the commands of *Allah*. It is, therefore, obligatory to follow the Messenger of *Allah* in all that he lays down by way *ahkam.* Yet, the most powerful rational argument is to be found in the bond between the Quran and the *Sunnah* and this is visible when we examine the relationship between the two. The rational argument for the necessity of the *Sunnah* can thus be seen in section 10.3 below dealing with the Status of the Quran with respect to the *Sunnah.*

Justification of Different Types of Sunnah : The Muslims agreed unanimously that the *Sunnah* is a source of the *Shariah,* as detailed above. It is an evidence to which recourse must be had for the derivation of the laws, if it meets the conditions that each *Imam* has laid down for it with respect to authenticity.

A group deviated from this unanimous agreement and denied the employment of the *khabar wahid* for establishing the *ahkam. Imam al-Shafii* gave detailed arguments in support of the *khabar wahid* with the intention that once this is established there can be no question about the validity of the *(mashhur* and) *mutawatir.* A few of these arguments are provided below:

1. The companions accepted the report of a single person when he informed them that *khamr,* which was hitherto permitted, had now been prohibited. In response to this report they broke the wine containers. This is proof that the report of an individual is valid.

2. The Messenger of *Allah* ordered *Unays* to go to the married woman about whom an allegation of unlawful sexual intercourse had been made. He said to him, "If she confesses, subject her to *rajm.*" Thus, his report alone about her confession would be sufficient for *rajm.*

3. The Messenger of *Allah* used to send his envoys on various missions. These envoys used to be alone.

Conditions for Acting upon the Muttasil Hadith : The traditions *(ahadith)* differ with respect to their narration and reporting. It is for this reason that the *mujtahids* laid down specific conditions for the acceptance of each category. The purpose of these conditions is to verify the strength of the authenticity of the report.

The *mutawatir hadith* is considered certain proof of the *ahkam* insofar as the conditions of *tawatur* are found in it according to all the jurists; so also the *mashhur* tradition according to the *Hanafis,* because it offers certain knowledge coming down from the Messenger of *Allah,* even if the strength of this knowledge is a little less than that of the *mutawatir.*

With respect to the *khabar wahid,* each *mujtahid* has laid down specific conditions, when it is relied upon for the derivation of the law.

Thus, the Hanafis Stipulate three Conditions for the Khabar Wahid

1. That the narrator should not have acted against the implication of the report. If he does act against it, the reliance will be upon his reported act rather than on the report. A narrator does not act against a report from the Prophet (PBUH), unless he knows that the content of the report was abrogated. A deliberate act against the report would raise doubts about the *adalah* of the narrator, and his report would not be acceptable, because the presumption is that the narrator is *adl.*
2. That the report should not pertain to a matter of universal need, that is, something which is performed often and continuously repeated. Such an act requires that it be known to many people due to their need to know it prior to performance. An act that should be known to many people by necessity will push its report to the level of a report that is *mutawatir* or *mashhur,* and it cannot be the subject-matter of a *khabar wahid.* The narration of an individual regarding such a matter provides circumstantial evidence of its not having been said or done by the Prophet (PBUH).
3. That it should not oppose analogy *(qiyas).* By this is meant opposition to general and fundamental principles. If a report opposes a general principle it ceases to be a valid proof for the *ahkam.* The reason is that the principle is usually not derived from a single text, but is based upon a number of texts, which together indicate a definitive meaning. As compared to this, a *khabar wahid* indicates a probable meaning that cannot be preferred over a definitive *(qati)* meaning. The *Hanafis* made an exemption from this rule in the case of traditions reported or upheld

by the Companions who were well known as jurists and *mujtahids,* like the first four caliphs, *Ibn Abbas* and *Ibn Masud.*

Imam Malik stipulates for the *khabar wahid* that it should not oppose the practice of the people of Medina. If it does oppose it, the obligation is to follow the practice of the people of Medina and to forgo the requirement of the *khabar wahid.* The reason is that the practice of the people of Medina amounts to a *mutawatir* report, and the *mutawatir* being definitive is to be preferred over the *khabar wahid,* which is probable. It appears that he would also uphold the rule about analogy above.

Imam-al-Shafii[5] does not stipulate for the *khabar wahid* any other condition except that it have a sound and complete chain of narration. If this condition is met the report is to be accepted.

The condition stipulated by *Ahmad-ibn-Hanbal*[6] is similar to that laid down by *Imam al-Shafii,* however, he sometimes accepts traditions that do not strictly meet this condition. He is reported to have preferred even *mursal* traditions over analogy.

Hadith, not Muttasil

A tradition that is not continuous *(muttasil)* is one that has the names of one or more narrators missing from the chain of narration. This is called a *mursal* report. It is like a reliable narrator from a later generation saying: "The Messenger of *Allah* said that ...." As for the Traditionalist, they apply the term *mursal* to a tradition from the chain of which the name of the Companion is missing. If the name of someone other than a Companion is missing, they term the tradition as *munqati.* The jurists disagreed about the employment of a *mursal* tradition as proof for a *hukm.* Thus, *al-Shafii* does not rely upon it, unless its authenticity is supported by another tradition.

Status of the Sunnah with Respect to the Quran : The jurists maintain that the *Sunnah* is the second source among the sources of Islamic law. If the *mujtahid* does not find a text in the Quran for a case he has to settle, he has recourse to the *Sunnah* for the derivation of the *hukm.* The evidence for this is the well known tradition of *Muad ibn Jabal* who was sent to Yemen by the Prophet (PBUH). In addition to this there is the letter of *Umar ibn al-Khattab* to *Qadi Shurayh* in which he instructs him to follow the Quran first and then the *Sunnah.*

As regards the status of the *Sunnah* being secondary to the Quran for proof of the *ahkam,* the jurists maintain that the Quran is definitive *(qati)* with respect to its narration in its details and as a whole, while the *Sunnah* is definitive as a whole, but not in all its details, because many of the reports are of the status of *khabar wahid.* The *Sunnah* being an elaboration and commentary on the Quran, it is not required to have recourse to it unless a text requires elaboration and commentary. If the text of the Quran is explicit *(nass)* in its meaning it is to be acted upon, but if it is apparent *(zahir)* having more than one meaning it is necessary to have recourse to its commentary, which is the *Sunnah.*

The Manner in which the Sunnah Lays down the Ahkam : As the *Sunnah* is a primary source of law, the jurist has recourse to it for the derivation of the *ahkam;* it is secondary and complementary to the Quran. The authority of the *Sunnah* as a source of law is derived from the Quran. The *ahkam* derived from the *Sunnah* are, therefore, considered an explanation of the meanings in the Quran. Even when the *Sunnah* appears exclusively to be dealing with a *hukm,* a close examination reveals that the *ahkam* so revealed are based upon principles found in the Quran and the *Sunnah* is merely extending the meaning of these principles or is linking up the rule with the principle.

This may be elaborated in the following points:

1. *The Sunnah is a Commentary of the Quran :* The *ahkam* are often found in the Quran in general, undetermined, or unelaborated form. The *Sunnah* restricts, qualifies, or elaborates these *ahkam.*

   Examples of the *Sunnah* elaborating the unelaborated are like (1) the timings of prayer and their number as well as their *rakas;* (2) elaboration of the kinds of wealth in which *Zakat* is to be paid and the amount to be paid in each as well as the time of obligation; (3) the case of *riba.*

   An example of the restriction of a general meaning is to be found in inheritance: "For the male two shares of the female." The *Sunnah* explains that the murderer will not inherit.

   The example of elaboration is in the case of theft where the *Sunnah* elaborates the meaning saying that the property must be removed from the *hirz* and that it is the right hand that is to be cut.

2. *The Sunnah Links a Vacillating Case with a Known Principle:* The *Sunnah* sometimes lays down rules that are not mentioned in the Quran. These rules appear to be additions over the meanings in the Quran and cannot be considered as elaborations or qualifications within the categories explained in the previous section. Some jurists, however, are of the opinion that a closer examination reveals that these rules are an elaboration in the sense of classifying a rule under a principle. Often a case vacillates between two principles and the *Sunnah* links up the case with one of these principles.

For example, the Quran has in a general way permitted all good things and has commanded the avoidance of *khabaith.* The *Sunnah* has linked with the *khabaith* the consumption of animals with molars and birds with claws, just as it has prohibited the consumption of domesticated donkeys.

The Quran has permitted the consumption of seafood and prohibited carrion. The dead fish in the sea vacillated between these two principles. The *Sunnah* linked it with permitted food: "Its water is pure and its *maytah* (carrion) is permissible."

The Quran permitted a slaughtered animal and prohibited carrion. The separated foetus of an animal after slaughter vacillated between the two principles. The *Sunnah* linked it with the slaughtered animal: "The slaughter of the foetus is the slaughter of its mother."

In these examples, we find that Quran laid down two general principles, but there were certain cases that vacillated between them with the possibility of falling under either principle. The *Sunnah* attached the case to one of the general principles. Thus, the principle is mentioned in the Quran and what appears to us as an additional rule laid down by the *Sunnah* is actually a category of the principle. The function of the *Sunnah* here is the analytical development of the law.

3. *The Sunnah Performs Analogy on the Basis of a Rule in the Quran:* The Quran sometimes lays down a principle or a rule without elaborating all the categories falling under that principle or covered by the rule. The *Sunnah* links a resembling case with this rule, and this function appears to be similar to analogy.

   The Quran prohibits marriage of two sisters to one man and then says that what is besides this is permitted. The cases of a woman along with her maternal or paternal aunt are also similar because of a common underlying cause. The *Sunnah,* therefore, prohibits such marriages too.

   The Quran mentions that pure water descends from the sky and is preserved in the earth. The case of sea-water was not settled. The *Sunnah* declared that it is pure and even its carrion is lawful.

4. *The Sunnah Lays Down General Principles:* The *Sunnah* sometimes lays down a general principle the individual categories of which have been mentioned by the Quran. For example, the *Sunnah* lays down the principle: "No injury is to be caused or borne." The Quran mentions a number of cases in which injury to others has been prohibited, like injury to a parents because of their child or injury to wives and so on. The prohibition of injury or harm is a general principle that is formulated by the *Sunnah.*

5. *The Sunnah Elaborates the Meaning of Words in the Quran:* An example of this the distinction of the white thread from the black thread during the month of *Ramadan.* The *Sunnah* explains that this is the light of day and the darkness of the night.

6. *The Sunnah Abrogates the Quran:* The jurists provide several examples of this that we shall have occasion to look at later. *Imam al-Shafii* does not accept this and says that only the Quran can abrogate the Quran and the *Sunnah* can abrogate the *Sunnah.* Some modern scholars deny the theory of abrogation altogether.

Modern Views about the Relationship between the Quran and the Sunnah : In the 20th century, there have been a number of debates about the relationship of the Quran and the *Sunnah.* It is not possible to record the various views expressed in these debates in this book. There is a huge amount of literature that the reader can access. These debates have by no means come to an end.

While there are many types of view on the subject, a broad classification yields three types of trend.

1. The first is that of those people who wish to give greater prominence to the Quran and wish to emphasise its coherence. Their view appears to be that only that *Sunnah* is to be accepted as authentic that is compatible with the Quran. This is an extreme view and if applied would demolish a greater part of the Islamic legal system as it exists today.

2. On the other extreme are those who maintain that the acceptance of a *sunnah* should be based on its chain of transmission. If the chain is sound the content of the tradition should be accepted and absorbed, whatever the consequences for the legal system. In other words, they relegate to the background the importance of examining the content *(matn)* of the traditions.

3. The third group consists of those who give importance to the *isnad* and also to the *matn.* This third group appears to represent a kind of a middle path, however, the situation here is somewhat complex. Within this group may be those who are inclined to check the *matn* against the Quran alone, and this takes them closer to the first group. Then there are those who focus more on the chain of transmission and check the *matn* not against the Quran alone, but also against the *Sunnah,* i.e., other traditions. In case of conflict, however, they accept the content of the conflicting tradition as an exemption from a broad rule, but then, following the *Shafii* rule, they consider the exemption as a broad principle in itself. This takes them closer to the second group.

To understand the problem, a few things have to be kept in mind. First, the *Sunnah,* like the Quran, deals with life and not with the legal system alone. The meaning derived by a *sufi* from a tradition may not be same as that understood by a jurist. Second, a Muslim may be ready to follow any tradition in its literal sense out of his love for the Prophet (PBUH) and his *Sunnah,* but the same person may understand the same tradition in a different way if he is asked to make law for the subjects to follow: his approach may be different.

Here we are concerned with what is binding and generates obligatory law. A sound method, therefore, has to be followed, a method that ensures that the intention of the Lawgiver is implemented and at the same time taking care that it will not upset or unduly disturb the functioning of the rest of the legal system.

Having said this, we notice that there has never been and, perhaps, there never will be a single system even for the law. Elsewhere, we have discussed the methods followed by the jurists on their different approaches to the *Sunnah.* The two methods that emerged were as follows:

1. The method of the literalists, who gave more importance to the *isnad.* Once a sound chain was established, they tried to implement the content of the tradition even at the risk of losing analytical consistency.
2. The second method was followed by schools who preferred the analytical method based upon the general principles of the law, whether these principles had emerged out of the Quran or the *Sunnah.*

In that work, we had suggested that the first method may be more suitable for what we called the fixed part of the law, i.e., matters of *ibadat, hudud, qisas* as well as some other areas of the law that do not accept change and which deal with the relationship between the subject and the Creator (the right of *Allah* is involved). The second method, on the other hand, is more suitable for the rest of the *muamalat* where the relationship is either between individuals or between individuals and the community as a whole, i.e., the state. In the second area, reason has wider role to play and the examination of the *matn* for analytical consistency is essential.

The second method was refined further by *al-Ghazzali* (d. 505 A.H.) in his theory of the general purposes of the law. He suggested that any new principle made for the law must not only be checked against the *tasarrufat* of the *Shariah* (the established general propositions or principles of the law arising from the Quran and the *Sunnah),* but also against the purposes of the law, the *maqasid al-shariah,* which are taken to be the ultimate general principles. This method ensures the sound development of the law along with the implementation of the overall intention of the Lawgiver. The method is equally valid for the reconciliation of traditions. The method also explains why *Abu Hanifah* would sometimes accept a tradition that did not have a sound chain of transmission. The reason was that a broad general principle, compatible with the tradition, was already present within the legal system, and the law would have still been the same even without the tradition. For the jurist, this may be the only method that can be followed.

Law and Contract

The word *Ijma* has literal meanings as well as a technical meaning. Literally, it is used in two senses. The first is determination and resolution. The words of *Allah,* the Exalted: "Determine your plan and among your partners," [Quran 10 : 71] convey this meaning, that is, decide and determine the matter. So also the words of the Prophet (peace be on him), "The person who has not resolved to fast prior to dawn has no fast," convey the meaning of deciding and resolving. The second way in which the word is used is agreement upon a matter. It is said: "the people agreed upon such and such matter." The difference between the two literal meanings is that *Ijma,* in the first meaning, is possible from one person, but in the second sense it requires two or more persons.

Technicality at Work

In the technical sense, *Ijma* is deemed as:

> The consensus of *mujtahids* (independent jurists) from the *ummah* of Muhammad (peace be on him), after his death, in a determined period upon a rule of Islamic law *(hukm shari).*

Conditions for the Validity of Ijma : The definition given above shows that there are seven conditions that must be met before *Ijma* can be said to have taken place. These conditions are imposed by the majority of the jurists. Two more conditions (nos. 8 and 9 below) are imposed by some of the jurists; however, the majority do not follow them.

1. The agreement or consensus must take place among *mujtahids,* that is, those who have attained the status of *ijtihad.* Thus, an agreement among those who have not reached this status or who are not qualified will not constitute *Ijma.* This will exclude all *non-mujtahids,* the general public, the members of a modern legislature, unless all of them are *mujtahids.* As to the number of *mujtahids* agreeing upon a legal issue, there is a disagreement. Some say that this number must reach the level necessary for *tawatur,* while others say that three is enough. One thing is clear, though, that if there is a single *mujtahid* in a certain period, his view or verdict will not amount to *Ijma.*

2. The agreement must be unanimous, that is, among all the *mujtahids.* If the majority of them agree upon a *hukm shari,* it will not amount to *Ijma* according to most jurists, howsoever small the number of the opposing minority. The reason is that there is a possibility that the minority opinion may be correct. There are, however, those jurists who consider a consensus of the majority as valid *Ijma* when they are being opposed by a minority. Some jurists, on the other hand, consider the agreement of the majority as persuasive, but would not call it *Ijma,*

3. All the jurists participating in *Ijma* must be from the *ummah* of Muhammad (peace be on him). Thus, an agreement of the jurist of another *ummah,* one of the earlier nations of the earlier prophets (PBUH), will not be considered *Ijma,*. The reason is that there are textual evidences supporting the fact that it is only the *ummah* of Muhammad (peace be on him) that is protected against error in collective agreements.

4. The agreement or consensus must have taken place after the death of the Prophet (peace be on him). Thus, an agreement during his lifetime is not considered *Ijma.* If the Prophet (peace be on him) agreed with the Companions on an issue, then, he was the source of the rule and not *Ijma.* If he went against their agreement, their agreement was not considered nor did it become a rule of law.

5. The agreement must be among the *mujtahids* of a single determined period, even if some of the jurists of the following or subsequent period opposed them. The reason is that the constitution of *Ijma* depends upon the unanimous agreement of jurists and this is only possible in a determined period, like a generation. If the period were left open and the opinions of all the jurists of all periods were to be taken into account, the occurrence of *Ijma* would become impossible.

6. The agreement must be upon a rule of law, the *hukm shari.* An agreement upon the rules of grammar in Arabic would not be *Ijma,* nor an agreement upon other rational propositions, like the creation of the universe. Thus, the rule must state that a certain thing is prohibited, permitted, valid, or void. All non-legal matters are excluded from the domain of *Ijma.*

7. That the *mujtahids* should have relied upon a *sanad* for deriving their opinion. A *sanad* is an evidence in one of the accepted sources of law. This is dealt with in some detail below. Does this mean that every rule that is agreed upon must have some evidence as its basis in the Quran and the *Sunnah?* If this is the case, the stipulation takes away something from the strength of *Ijma* as an independent principle. While it is obvious

that the jurist agreeing to a rule would be relying upon an evidence from the legal system, it cannot be a condition that the *sanad* must be found in a text. If it is, then, the *sanad* is the basis of the law. Yes, it can be said that the function of *Ijma* is to make definitive an evidence that is probable and subject to interpretation. It should be noted that the strength of *Ijma* lies in the agreement itself. Another reason for insisting on the *sanad* could be that those who stipulate this condition want to ensure that the jurist has undertaken proper *ijtihad* to arrive at his opinion.

8. The death of those jurists who participated in the *Ijma,* either explicitly or by silence, is not a condition for the validity of *Ijma* according to the majority of the jurists. *Ijma,* according to these jurists, becomes valid as soon as agreement is found. There are a few jurists who maintain that it is possible for a jurist to change his view and as long as a jurist is alive, this possibility exists. They quote the example of *Hadrat Ali* in the case of the sale of the *ummahat al-awlad.* They maintain that *Ijma* cannot be treated as final as long as the participating *mujtahids* are alive. The view of the majority in this case appears to be more practical, otherwise one would have to wait for many years to finally benefit from a decision.
9. That the *Ijma* should have been transmitted to the later jurists by way of *tawatur.* The argument is that as *Ijma* is a definitive evidence, its mode of transmission should also be definitive. The majority of the jurists, however, do not accept this condition.

Types of Ijma : *Ijma* is divided into two types on the basis of the way it is made known. These two types are: (1) *Ijma sarih* or *Ijma qawli* and (2) *Ijma sukuti* or tacit *Ijma*

Explicit Ijma or Ijma Qawli : *Sarih* or explicit *Ijma* is one in which the legal opinions of all the jurists of one period converge in relation to a legal issue, and each one of them states his opinion explicitly. This may happen when all of them are gathered in one session and an issue is presented to them and they collectively express a unanimous opinion. It may also take place when an issue is raised in a certain period and all the jurists, in turn, issue similar *fatwas* independently and at separate times.

Tacit Ijma or Ijma Sukuti : This form of *Ijma* takes place when some *mujtahids,* one or more, issue a verdict on a legal issue and the rest of the *mujtahids* come to know of it during the same period, but they keep silent; they neither acknowledge it nor refute it expressly.

Conditions for Tacit Ijma: For the occurrence of tacit Ijma, the following conditions must be met:

1. The silence must be free of all external indications that point to agreement or disagreement. If an indication of some sort is found that conveys agreement, then, *Ijma,* is not tacit, rather it is explicit. If, however, an indication is found that points to disagreement, no *Ijma* can be said to have taken place.
2. The silence of a *mujtahid* should be maintained for a considerable period of time. The duration, however, cannot be fixed, because the issues subject to *ijtihad* and the formulation of an opinion require time, which may vary for each *mujtahid.*
3. The issue must be one in which *ijtihad* is permitted. These are issues in which the available sources are probable *(zanni).* If, however, the issue is one in which *ijtihad* is not permitted, that is, the controlling evidence is definitive *(qati)* having one meaning, then, the silence of some jurists cannot be considered tacit approval, because jurists are not supposed to open up these issues.

The Legal Force of Ijma as a Source : *Ijma,* as we have said, is either explicit or it is tacit. Each has a rule *(hukm)* that differs from the other with respect to binding strength as a source of law. This distinction is presented below:

The Binding Strength of Explicit Ijma : The majority of the jurists agreed upon the rule that explicit *Ijma* is a definitive source and it is obligatory to act upon it; its opposition is prohibited. Thus, if explicit *Ijma* occurs on an issue and is published, then, the *hukm* upon which agreement is found stands established definitively *(qatan)* and it is not permitted to oppose it. Further, the issue that has been settled through such *Ijma* can no longer be opened up again and subjected to *ijtihad.* In other words, the issue is no longer a moot point.

Al-Nazam-al-Basri[7], a leading *Mutazilite,* and some of the *Khawarij* said that *Ijma* is not a binding source. The majority, who upheld *Ijma* as a binding source, as well as those who opposed them on this issue, argued on the basis of the Quran and the *Sunnah.* Their arguments were as follows:

Arguments of the Majority : The majority gave the following arguments:

1. The words of the *Allah:* "If anyone contends with the Messenger even after guidance has been plainly conveyed to him, and follows a path other than that of the believers, we shall leave him in the path he has chosen, and land him in hell. What an evil refuge." [Quran 4 : 115]

   Allah has promised hell and a bad ending to those who follow a way different from that of the believers, and the way of the believers is determined by explicit and unanimous *ijtihad.* Thus, consensus after *ijtihad* is the true path to be followed, and it is not proper to go against it.

This argument may be refuted in the following way. The intended meaning in this verse of the way of the believers is following the Prophet (peace be on him), helping him, and repelling his enemies. It does not mean following what the *mujtahids* have agreed upon with respect to the *ahkam*. This is the apparent meaning of the verse, from its *sabab-al-nuzul*[8], and from the verse that follows, which says that *Allah* will not forgive *shirk* and may forgive what is less than that.

2. The tradition related from the Prophet (peace be on him) about the freedom from error when the *ummah* is unanimous about the matter, like his words: "My *ummah* will not collectively agree upon an error," "What the Muslims consider good is good in the eyes of *Allah*," and "I asked *Allah* that my *ummah* not agree on an error and He granted it (this prayer) to me."

They said that these traditions had been related by trustworthy narrators, and though they are not *mutawatir* in words, they are continuous *(mutawatir)* in the meaning they convey, and which is that my *ummah* is protected against falling into collective error. It was on the basis of these evidences that the majority accepted *Ijma* as a source of law and acted upon it as such.

Arguments of al-Nazam al-Basri Against Ijma : *Al-Nazam* and those who supported him argued on the basis of the following evidences:

1. In the words of the God, "O you who believe, Obey Allah and obey the Prophet (PBUH),..." Muslims have been commanded to refer each dispute to *Allah* and His Prophet (PBUH), and the meaning of referring disputes to *Allah* and His Prophet (PBUH) is reference to the Quran and the *Sunnah*. There is no command in this verse, he said, to refer the disputed matter to the agreement of the jurists.

   The response to this argument is that it is the Book of *Allah* and the *Sunnah* of His Prophet (peace be on him) that give us guidance about *Ijma* as indicated in the arguments of the majority above.

2. When the Messenger of *Allah* (peace be on him) asked *Muad ibn Jabal* about the sources for his decision, he did not mention *Ijma*. Had *Ijma* been a valid source, it would not have been abrogated.

This argument is considered weak because *Ijma* is a source that comes into operation after the death of the Prophet (peace be on him) and *Muad* could not have possibly mentioned it.

The reasoning and arguments of the majority, who accept *Ijma* and act upon it as a source of law, are considered stronger than those of the opponents.

The Binding Strength of Tacit Ijma : As for tacit *Ijma,* some of the jurists who upheld the binding strength of explicit *Ijma,* objected to tacit *Ijma* as a source of law. Some of them even refused to call it by the name of *Ijma.* Among these jurists are *Imam al-Shafii* as well as *Malikites.*

Those who object to it argue that silence on the part of some jurists could possibly mean that they agree with the opinions expressed explicitly. It could mean that they are not willing to express an opinion on the issue due to respect for the person who has done so or out of fear or some other reason. Silence, therefore, cannot be considered as an evidence of agreement.

The majority of the jurists, however, maintained that tacit *Ijma* is a legally binding source, but they differed with respect to its strength. Some said that it is a definitive source, like explicit *Ijma,* and these are the *Hanafi* jurists and *Imam Ahmad ibn Hanbal.* Their argument is that evidences for *Ijma* in the Quran and the *Sunnah* do not differentiate between explicit *Ijma* and tacit *Ijma.* Some of the jurists said tacit *Ijma* is a probable *(zanni)* source. Among these jurists is *al-Karkhi*[9], the well known *Hanafi* jurist and *al-Amidi*[10], a later *Shafii* scholar.

It is well known that the Companions of the Prophet (peace be on him) used to speak out without fear whenever they felt that a decision could be improved. For example, when the mighty *Umar ibn al-Khattab* decided to award the penalty of stripes to a pregnant woman for her offence, *Muad ibn Jabal* pointed out that he would be awarding the punishment to her as well as to what was in her womb. *Umar* said, "Had *Muad* not been here, *Umar* would have perished." There are many such examples. Further, one would expect from a person who has attained the status of a *mujtahid* to speak his mind whenever he feels that the truth is different. He should not remain silent because of fear or some other expediency, for he is no ordinary individual and it would be his duty to speak out if he disagrees. It is, therefore, felt that those who maintain that *Ijma sukuti* is equally binding as *Ijma qawli are* making a sound argument, and it appears better to consider both types of *Ijma* as having equal strength.

The Sanad of Ijma : The *sanad* of *Ijma* is the evidence upon which the jurists rely for arriving upon a consensus. The majority of the jurists agree that each *Ijma* must have a *sanad* on which the jurist should rely, while arriving at the opinion, otherwise the resulting *Ijma* would be based upon *ray* (personal opinion) and this is rejected by the *Shariah.*

Evidences Qualifying as a Sanad : There is no disagreement among the jurists that evidences from the texts of the Quran and the *Sunnah* are to be treated as valid *sanads* for *Ijma.* Thus, for the *Ijma* on marriage being unlawful with grandmothers, the *sanad* is the verse, " (forbidden unto you (for marriage) are your mothers). For the *Ijma* on the prohibition of sale of food prior to possession by the buyer, the *sanad* is the tradition: (Whoever buys food should not sell it until he has taken possession of it).

As regards *Qiyas* (analogy) being a *sanad* for *Ijma,* there is disagreement among the jurists. Those who object to *Qiyas* being a *sanad,* maintain that *Qiyas* is a probable *(zanni)* evidence, while *Ijma* is a definitive evidence, and it is not proper to construct a definitive evidence upon a probable evidence. The majority of the jurists, however, accept *Qiyas* as a valid *sanad* for *Ijma.* They argue that even a *khabar wahid* is a probable evidence, yet it is accepted as a valid *sanad* for *Ijma* by agreement of the jurists. Further, they argue that even an analogy traces its logic back to an *asl* in the texts of the Quran and the *Sunnah,* so accepting *Qiyas* as a *sanad* should not be a problem.

Similar arguments are advanced with respect to *maslahah mursalah* as a *sanad* for *Ijma* and it has been used as a *sanad* in practice. The examples they cite are the collection of the Quran into a *mushaf.* All the Companions agreed on this in the interest *(maslahah)* of the *ummah.* Another example they cite is about the *kharaj* lands of Iraq, which were conquered during the period of *Umar.* These lands were not divided up as *ghanimah,* but were left in the hands of those in possession as *kharaj* lands, again in the interest of the *ummah.* Those who upheld using *maslahah mursalah* as a *sanad* agree that an *Ijma* based on it cannot be permanent, and will last as long as the *maslahah* persists. If the *maslahah* changes, the *Ijma* will also have to be altered.

Likelihood of the Occurrence of Ijma : There is some disagreement about the possibility of consensus and its actual occurrence. The majority of the jurists maintained that such a consensus is possible and actually did take place. *Al-Nazam* and his followers maintained that such a consensus is not possible. They argue that a condition for *Ijma* is the participation of all the *mujtahids* of a particular period and this requires the identification of all *mujtahids* as well as the identification of their opinions. This they argue is not possible, because there is no criterion for distinguishing a *mujtahid* from a *non-mujtahid,* and even if there was such a criterion, the *mujtahids* are spread all over the Muslim lands and it is not possible to gather them in one place nor to ascertain where they are. They argue further that a *mujtahid* has to rely on an evidence in the sources for the formulation of his opinion.

Now, such an evidence is either definitive or probable. A definitive evidence conveys a single meaning and there cannot be two views about it, therefore, there is no function that *Ijma* can perform in this case. If, on the other hand, the evidence is probable, that is, it has more than one interpretation, getting all the *mujtahids* to agree upon a single meaning is an impossibility.

To these arguments, the majority respond by saying that there have been such agreements in Islamic history. The examples they quote pertain to the period of the Companions. For example, the granting of one-sixth share in the inheritance to the grandmother, the prohibition of sale of food before the buyer has taken possession, the prohibition of the marriage of a Muslim woman to a non-Muslim, and the validity of marriage *(nikah)* when a dower has not been mentioned.

The objection to this argument may be that even if this were possible during the period of the Companions, when all the *mujtahids* were well known and easily accessible, it would be impossible today when the Muslim world is composed a large number of states. Some may respond, however, that the world is once again becoming a smaller place with the rapid advancements in technology, and we cannot call the possibility of the occurrence of *Ijma* as impossible.

Cases of Ijma Transmitted in Books of Fiqh : For an agreement to constitute valid *Ijma* it must be among all *mujtahids* in a determined period upon a legal issue. The jurists have argued in support of this concept of *Ijma* on the basis of the texts of the Quran and the *Sunnah.* The question is: Have the rules about *Ijma* laid down in these texts, and formulated by the *fuqaha,* been followed in books of *fiqh?*

Those who study these books notice that instances of *Ijma* mentioned in the books of *fiqh* are either among the majority of the jurists or they are agreements pertaining to the jurists of one school. On a number of occasions, the cases cited are those of tacit rather than explicit *Ijma.* Thus, for example, we may find, in the *Hanafi* books, statements to the effect that such and such jurist upheld such an opinion and no one opposed him, thus it constitutes *Ijma.* It is obvious that such claims of *Ijma* do not meet all the conditions that the *fuqaha* have themselves laid down for valid *Ijma.*

In addition to this, there is no compiled source for cases of *Ijma.* There are a few books, like the one by *Ibn Hazm,* who belonged to the *Zahiri* school, which is now extinct. The name of the book is *Maratib al-Ijma.*

Role of Ijma in the Modern World : In the preceding discussion, it has been stated that there are various objections against the principle of *Ijma.* Some of the objections pertain to the conditions of *Ijma* as stipulated by the jurists, while others relate to the possibility of its occurrence. Some practical difficulties have also been pointed out. *Ijma* is a source that is accepted by all the Sunni schools of thought, just as they accept the two primary sources, yet there is no established system for its transmission. The only transmission of *Ijma* one finds is within the schools; in the books of each school. Further, some of the cases or instances of *Ijma* that are cited do not meet the conditions stipulated for *Ijma* when they are examined outside the schools of *ijtihad* and *fiqh*. Due to these factors and objections, some modern scholars have said that *Ijma* does not appear to be a practical principle and cannot operate as a source of law, at least in the modern times. The view of the present author is that the very fact that *Ijma* has been accepted as a primary source of law for so many centuries by the leading jurists of Islam, it has to have a greater or deeper role than is exhibited by the external conditions imposed by jurists. In other words, the matter needs to be examined a little more deeply, perhaps, in the context of modern law.

An examination of the principle of *Ijma* in a general way reveals that all it saying is that if a rule or principle is upheld collectively by the highest legal forum in the land, then, such a principle or rule must be followed by those subordinate to this forum. This is exactly what the doctrine of *stare decisis* says in the English common law system. The deeper the examination of the principle of *Ijma,* the greater is the conviction it requires that the decision of the higher forum, or the full bench of the highest court (en banc), so to say, must be followed and maintained by the lower courts. In the earlier stages of the growth of Islamic law, the forum was confined to the jurist Companions. Later, when the schools of law emerged, the forum moved to the leading jurists of each school and operated within the schools. Today, when the *ummah* is composed of different jurisdictions in Muslim countries, the forum would automatically be the highest court in each Muslim country. In fact, the principle fits in perfectly with the legal system in those countries that have the English common law as the modern tradition.

Means of Lesser Significance

The term "rational" with respect to secondary sources means that these are not material sources in which the rules are stated. The rational sources are techniques of legal reasoning that the *mujtahid* employs during his *ijtihad.* The material sources used during this legal reasoning are the Quran, *Sunnah* and *Ijma,* and the rational secondary sources provide the means of extension for the law stated in these primary sources. The secondary sources of Islamic law to be discussed in this chapter are: *Qiyas* (analogy); *istihsan* (juristic preference of the stronger principle); *Istishab al-hal* (presumption of continuity); *maslahah mursalah* (extended analogy); and *sadd al-dhariah* (blocking the lawful means to an unlawful end). The first study taken up is that of *Qiyas.*

The Assessment

The discussion of *Qiyas* covers several topics. These are: definition; elements; conditions pertaining to the elements; types of analogy; and justification of *Qiyas* as a source of law. Some topics that are of practical significance, like deriving the underlying cause *(illah),* will be taken up under the second mode of *ijtihad* in the next part, where it will be shown how the *mujtahid* undertakes *ijtihad* based on analogy.

Definition of Qiyas (Analogy) : In its literal meaning, the word *Qiyas* means measuring or estimating one thing in terms of another. Thus, measuring cloth against the metre rod is *Qiyas.* It also applies to making two things equal, that is, comparing. This comparison may be physical or it may be rational.

Thus, mapping a shoe upon a shoe to see their equality is *Qiyas.* The word *Qiyas* is sometimes used in its figurative sense, and not its actual sense, to mean examination *(nazr)* or even *ijtihad,* which is its method, by the application of the term used for the cause to the resulting activity. The distinction between these terms needs to be maintained to avoid confusion.

In the technical sense, as defined by the jurists, it applies to "the assignment of the *hukm* of an existing case found in the texts of the Quran, the *Sunnah,* or *Ijma* to a new case whose *hukm* is not found in these sources on the basis of a common underlying attribute called the *illah* of the *hukm."* Another definition is: "the equality of a case, whose *hukm* is not mentioned explicitly in the texts, with a case whose *hukm* is mentioned, on the basis of the equality between the underlying causes found in the two cases."

If the texts of the Quran or the *Sunnah,* or *Ijma* contain a case whose *illah* is known to the *mujtahid,* that is, the underlying reason because of which the *hukm* has been laid down, and he then sees a new case which has the same *illah* in it, he will assign the *hukm* of the existing case to the new case. By such an assignment, he renders the two cases equal in terms of the *hukm.* This assignment or rendering equal is called *Qiyas* in the terminology of the jurists.

Elements of Qiyas

The definitions of *Qiyas* show that it has four ingredients or elements :

- the case (set of facts) mentioned in the text with its *hukm;*
- the *hukm* of the set of facts mentioned in the text;
- the *illah* or the underlying cause that has led to the *hukm;* and
- the new case or the set of facts for which the *hukm* has not been explicitly mentioned and which needs a *hukm.*

The case mentioned in the text (the first element) is called the *asl,* that is, the root case or even the base. It is also called the *maqis alayh* or the case upon which analogy has been constructed. The *hukm* of this case (the second element) is called the *hukm al-asl* or the rule to be passed on. The underlying cause of the *hukm,* which is determined by the jurist, is called the *illah* or the *hukm.* The new case to which the *hukm* is extended is called the *far* or the offshoot. It is also called the *maqis* or the case for which analogy is constructed. The *hukm* that has been established for the new case is called the *hukm al-far* or the rule established.

Examples of Qiyas

We may now look at some examples to understand the operation of *Qiyas:*

1. *The Prohibition of Khamr (wine from grapes) is Laid Down in the Quran :* The text prohibits *khamr* along with a statement of the disaster it leads to, that is, enmity and hatred among people. Now, *khamr,* according to some jurists (the *Hanafis*), is the name of an intoxicating liquor made from grape juice, called wine in English. The Arabic term *khamr* in their view does not include other intoxicating liquors like whiskey and beer that are made from other substances. The other intoxicants, according to the *Hanafis*, are prohibited separately by the texts of the *Sunnah.* The *Hanafis*, therefore, see no need to use analogy in this case. The majority, however, say that even if the word *khamr,* in its literal meaning, does not cover the other types of intoxicating liquors, the *hukm* of *khamr* can be extended to them through *Qiyas* (analogy). Their reasoning takes the following form:

   The jurists first decide that the *illah,* or the underlying cause for which *khamr* has been prohibited is intoxication. On examining the other intoxicating liquors, they find that the property of being intoxicants is found in them. When it is verified that this property is found, they extend the *hukm* of *khamr,* which is prohibition, to the other intoxicating liquors as well.

   Thus, *khamr* in this case is the *asl,* or the *maqis alayh,* each one of the intoxicants, other than *khamr,* is the *far* or the *maqis,* and the property of being an intoxicant is the *illah.* The prohibition of *khamr* is the *hukm ul-asl,* while the prohibition of whiskey, say, is the *hukm al-far,* which has been established through *Qiyas.*

2. *There is a Tradition from the Prophet (peace be on him) that Says:* "The murderer will not inherit." This tradition prohibits the granting of inheritance to an heir who kills his predecessor from whom he is to inherit. The punishment for such an offender, in addition to the punishment for his crime, is deprivation from inheritance.

What about a bequest *(wasiyyah)?* The tradition mentions inheritance alone and not bequest. Supposing a legatee murders the testator, who has bequeathed his property to the legatee in his will. The offending legatee will be prevented from taking the bequeathed property on the basis of *Qiyas,* because the *illah* in the two cases is similar, which is "hastening the benefit prior to its appointed time through a criminal act or unjustified enrichment."

Murdering the predecessor in the case of inheritance mentioned in the tradition is the *asl* or the *maqis alayh,* while murdering the testator is the *far* or the *maqis.* Hastening death prior to its appointed time through a criminal act is the *illah,* because of which the *hukm* has been assigned. The *hukm al-asl* is prevention from inheritance, while deprivation from the bequest or legacy is the *hukm al-far* established through *Qiyas.*

3. *A Tradition from the Prophet (peace be on him) Says :* "A believer is a brother to his believer, therefore, it is not permitted for a believer to make a proposal (for marriage) where the proposal of his brother is still pending, or to make an offer of sale where his brother's offer is pending." This tradition proscribes proposals or offers to the same party till such time that similar offers made to this party by another person are pending and have not been refused or accepted. The underlying cause or *Illat* is causing harm to anothers interest. This tradition does not mention the hiring of services or property. The proscription can be extended to hire through analogy.
4. *Indulging in Sale when the Call for the Friday Prayer is made is Prohibited by the text of the Quran :* The underlying cause is reducing the incentive to offer the Friday prayer. This *hukm* can be extended to other contracts like pledging or marriage that may have been planned at such a time.

Conditions Pertaining to the Elements : As stated above, analogy has four elements: *asl; hukm al-asl; illat;* and *far.* The conditions pertaining to the remaining three elements are stated below:

Conditions of the Asl or the Case in the Texts : A single condition is stipulated by the jurists for the *asl.* The condition is that the base case, on which analogy is being constructed, should not be an extension *(far)* of another case mentioned in the texts. The reason is that if it is so, the analogy will be constructed upon the original case and not upon the extension.

Conditions Pertaining to the Hukm of the Asl

The *Hukm* has several conditions :

1. It should be a *hukm* that has been established directly from the Quran, *Sunnah* or *Ijma*. This means that it should not be the *hukm al-far* or a *hukm* extended to a new case through analogy or some other method of legal reasoning.

   There is some disagreement among jurists whether a *hukm* established through consensus *(Ijma)* can become a basis for extension through analogy. Those who oppose this say that it is difficult to determine the underlying cause for a *hukm* established through *Ijma*. In addition to this, each consensus has relied upon some evidence (which is called its *sanad)* in the texts. It is, therefore, better to rely upon the *hukm* in the *sanad* rather than upon *Ijma*. Those who favour extension of the *hukm* from *Ijma* maintain that there are several modes of discovering the *illah,* and this can facilitate the extension of the *hukm* in *Ijma*. They maintain that this is possible even when the *sanad* is not evident.

2. That a determined *illah* (cause) should be found for the *hukm* of the text. The jurist should be able to determine an *illah* for the *hukm,* and *illah* that can be rationally under stood to be the cause of the *hukm*. It should not be *hukm* that has no understandable *illah* and is *taabbudi* (requiring ritual obedience). Thus, the setting of the sun is the cause for the evening prayer, but we cannot understand or are not required to understand why it has been determined as the cause. As compared to this "intoxication" as a cause for prohibition of wine is a cause that can be rationalised. Analogy is permitted where the *illah* can be rationalised; in other cases there is no *illah* and analogy fails.

3. That the *hukm* should not have been abrogated. Analogy cannot be constructed on the basis of a *hukm* that stands abrogated. This depends upon the acceptance of the theory of abrogation. All four schools accept this theory.

4. That the *hukm* should not be restricted to a specific case by another text. If a *hukm* is specific for someone or some occasion it cannot be extended to other persons. Thus, the permission for the Prophet (peace be on him) of marrying more than four wives or the prohibition of marrying his wives after his death cannot be extended through analogy; these *ahkam* were specific to him.

5. That the *hukm* should not pertain to an exemption. The majority of the jurists maintain that analogy should not be constructed upon exemptions.

The contract of *salam* (advance payment), for example, is an exemption from the rules of *riba;* further analogy cannot be constructed upon it.

Some of the *Shafiis* maintain that once the exemption is granted through a text, it becomes a principle in its own right and may be used for further analogy. The pursuit of analytical consistency in the law and reasoning from principles would resist such a view. For how can you maintain two contradictory principles and still be able to extend them through legal reasoning; the results will be contradictory. It can be done, however, if one is using a literal system of interpretation that has no room for reasoning for broad general principles.

6. That the *hukm* should not pertain to the criminal law. This condition is imposed by the *Hanafis* and pertains to the disagreement among the jurist about the meaning of *dalalat al-nass.* It may be mentioned here that this rule is observed in Western law as well. If the criminal law and crimes are permitted to be extended through analogy it will violate the principle of legality, which states that there can be no crime and no penalty without prior legislation.

Conditions Pertaining to the Far or New Case Needing a Hukm

The jurists lay down three conditions for the far :

1. That the texts should be silent about its *hukm.* This means that it should not be expressly mentioned in the texts or in *Ijma.* There is no *Qiyas* for a case that is expressly mentioned in the text, because it has already been settled.
2. The *illah* of the *asl* should be found in the *far.* The jurist should be able to find the same *illah* in the new case that he has found for the case mentioned in the texts.

When this condition is not met fully and there is a difference between the *illah* established for the *asl* and that for the *far,* the analogy undertaken is called *Qiyas ma al-fariq* or analogy with a distinctive attribute. An example is the division of the property through preemption between co-owners of the property from which the right emanated. Should the property be divided equally among them, or should it be divided in proportion to their shares? The *Hanafis* maintain that they should be given equal shares irrespective of the proportion of their shares in the original property that gave them the right of preemption. The other jurists maintain that this right is similar to a partnership and they should be assigned the right of preemption in proportion to their property.

The *Hanafis* object that this is *Qiyas ma al-fariq,* and the distinction is that in a partnership the revenue grows out of the property owned, while the right of preemption is not the result of a growth in property and cannot be compared with revenue.

Conditions Pertaining to the Illah and Meaning of Illah : The discussion of the *illah* is, perhaps, the most important topic within the subject of rational sources. The limits and the conditions of the *illah* not only determine the nature of analogy, but also determine the scope of other rational sources or techniques of legal reasoning like *istihsan* and *maslahah mursalah.*

The larger doctrine of *maslahah* partly discussed earlier has also grown out of these discussions. This section is devoted to the conditions of the *illah.* The modes of discovering the *illah* called the *masalik al-illah* will be discussed in the next part under the second mode of *ijtihad.*

Before the conditions pertaining to the *illah* are discussed it is important to note certain distinctions. The first distinction is between *illah* and *sabab.* The second distinction is between *illah* (underlying cause) and *hikmah* (wisdom). These distinctions become obvious when the *illah* is defined and its conditions are stated.

The Meaning of Illah (the Underlying Cause) : The underlying cause of a *hukm* or its *illah* is perhaps the most difficult concept in Islamic jurisprudence. Accordingly, many of the earlier jurists have avoided a definition. Instead, they try to focus on what it can be or what it cannot be. For example, *al-Ghazzali* begins the discussion of the *illah* by saying:

> "It is permitted that the *illah* be a *hukm* itself, like our saying that the sale of wine is void, because its utilisation has been prohibited..." He then goes on to mention a large number of shapes that the *illah* may acquire.

Modern jurists have tried to give definitions, but such definitions can be shown to be defective in the light of what the earlier jurists have said. In some of these definitions importance has been given to the securing of *maslahah,* while in others the importance has been given to the relationship between the cause and the *hukm.* We will extract the text of *al-Tanqih* that is woven into the text of *al-Tawdih* to show how *Sadral-shariah* describes it.

We have given this text above to acknowledge the skill of this learned man, however, we will focus on the overlined part:

> An apparent and stable attribute that is either coterminous with the underlying rationale or the rationale is usually present when the attribute exists.

In this definition we will focus on the words "apparent" and "stable," because they explain some important features of the underlying cause.

Conditions for the Validity of the Illah : The Analysis of this Definition Yields the Following Conditions for the *illah:*

1. That the *illah* must be an apparent cause. An apparent cause is one that can easily be perceived by the senses. It is an outward attribute and not something internal and concealed. This apparent attribute can be identified with ease both in the *asl* and in the *far.* As compared to the *illah,* the *hikmah* (wisdom) of the law is something internal and concealed and cannot be verified with ease. An internal or concealed reason does not qualify for becoming an *illah.* The *hikmah,* according to *al-Razi,* is the *illah* of the *illah.* He maintains that the *hukm* can be based upon the *hikmah* as well.

   In contracts, for example, the objective theory is favoured, because inner intention is something difficult to verify. It is difficult to verify what the contracting party really intends. The cause that makes a contract valid is, therefore, the outward expression of offer and acceptance *(ijab* and *qabul).* Accordingly, the jurists maintain that the validity of contracts does not depend upon intention, but on the outward expression. In this case, verification of the intention is the *hikmah,* while offer and acceptance are the *illah.* The *hukm* of validity is tied to the cause, offer and acceptance, in a way that the existence of the cause means the existence of the *hukm* and the non-existence of the cause its non-existence.

   In the case of curtailment of prayer on a journey, the *hikmah* is the hardship that a person will face. This is something internal and it cannot be verified whether the traveller is actually facing hardship. The *hukm* is, therefore, tied to the *illah,* which is "journey" in this case.

2. *That the illah Should be a Constant and Stable at. Tribute:* A constant and stable attribute is one that does not change with a change in circumstances and does not vary from person to person. In the example of curtailment of prayer on a journey, the *illah* was "journey" itself. This attribute does not vary from person to person, that is, it does not matter whether the person going on a journey is young or old, strong or weak, healthy or ill. As compared to this, "hardship" is something that may vary from person to person: a strong person is not likely to face the same hardship as a weak person.

   The *illah* does change due to a change in circumstances either. In the same example, when "journey" is the cause of the *hukm,* it will not matter whether the subject is going on foot or on horseback, on a train or by car. The cause remains the same. If the wisdom, that is, "hardship" is deemed to be the cause, it will alter with the means adopted for travelling. A person going by car will suffer a lesser amount of hardship as compared to one going on foot.

3. *That the Illah Should be Extendible and not Confined to the Asl:* If the attribute determined by the *mujtahid* cannot be extended to other cases, the determination of such an *illah* is futile and will not constitute a valid analogy. In the case of *riba,* trading in gold and silver with an excess or with a delay is restricted. The *illah* determined by *Shafii's* here is "currency-value" *(thamaniyyah).* The *Hanafis* maintain that this is an *illah* that is *qasirah* (confined to these two metals and coins made from them). It cannot be extended to other things, therefore, it is not a valid *illah.* It is for this reason that the *Hanafis* determine "weight and measure" to be the *illah* along with "genus."
4. That the *illah* should be an attribute that is compatible with the purposes of the law *(munasib).* The reason is that the purposes of Islamic law, in reality, provide the underlying rationale of all the rules. That is why the *hikmah* has been emphasised.

Most of the attributes that have been determined as causes for the *ahkam* are compatible with the purposes of Islamic law. The reason is that the purposes of the law have emerged from a collective consideration of the various *ilal.* An *illah* derived by a jurist must, therefore, meet this condition. "Intoxication" as an *illah* for the prohibition of *khamr* is compatible with the "preservation of the intellect." As compared to this, the colour of wine or its smell have no compatibility with this purpose and are not suitable causes. There are different levels of compatibility and the concept of suitability *(munasabah)* is not confined to *Qiyas* alone. The concept covers other forms of legal reasoning, like *maslahah mursalah,* where it is not always the *illah* that is relevant; the *hikmah* (wisdom) may also be used for determining the law. The concept of *munasabah* will be discussed within the second and third modes of *ijtihad* in the next part.

Types of Analogy (Qiyas) : The majority of the jurists classify *Qiyas* into two broad types. The first type is determined by looking at the strength of the similarity of the two *illahs* in the *asl* and in the *far.* The second type is based on the manner in which the *hukm* is established in the new case. In addition to this, the *Hanafis* classify analogy into *Qiyas jali* (manifest analogy) and *Qiyas khafi* (concealed analogy). The classification according to the majority of the jurists is discussed first.

The First Type: Probable and Definitive or Qati and Zanni : *Qiyas* is definitive when two conditions are met:

- That the *mujtahid* is fully convinced about the *illah* he has discovered in the *asl.*
- That exactly the same *illah* is found in the *far,* that is, there are no distinctive attributes.

The example of *qati* analogy is the proscription of saying "fie" to parents. The *illah* discovered here by the *mujtahid* is "torment." In other words, saying "fie" to parents is something that causes grief or pain to them. This satisfies the first condition, because there is no doubt that the underlying cause is torment. When the *mujtahid* face cases like abuse of parents or beating of parents, he is also sure that this underlying cause of torment is definitely found in such acts. This satisfies the second condition with certainty.

The underlying certainty in the discovery of the *illah* and its application to the new case makes the analogy definitive or *qati.*

The`same conditions, when reversed, need to be fulfilled in the case of *zanni Qiyas* or analogy with a probable strength. If the *mujtahid* is not certain about the *illah* in either or both cases, the *Qiyas* is said to be probable. An example of *zanni Qiyas* is the assignment of the *hukm* of *riba* from food items mentioned in a tradition to the water-melon on the basis of "food-value" as the *illah.* The *illah* of "food in general" is not a very convincing underlying cause; the *Hanafis* and *Malikis,* therefore, reject it. Identifying it as a cause violates the first condition. The reason is that all the items mentioned in the tradition are basic foods with the significant attribute of being stored over long periods. This attribute is missing in the water-melon and, therefore, violates the second condition pertaining to the *far.*

It may be noted here that even if the number of traditions in the case of *riba* has reached a level that makes it *mutawatir manawi,* which makes the *hukm* definitive, the *Qiyas* in the above example is still *zanni* due to a weakness in the *illah* both for the *asl* and the *far.*

The Second Type: Classification According to the Strength of the Hukm Established in the Far : This classification is based on the nature of the *hukm* in the *asl.* It is a classification of analogy when the *hukm* in the *asl* is *zanni.*

When the *hukm* in the *asl* is probable *(zanni),* the *Qiyas* constructed upon it may be of three types. This is based upon the strength of the *hukm* established in the *far.* Is the strength of the *hukm* of a higher order than that in the *far ?* Is the established *hukm* of the same order or strength? Is it of a lesser strength or order?

1. *Qiyas that is of a Higher Order is Called Qiyas Awla :* The example again is of constructing analogy for beating parents upon saying *"uff"* or *"fie"* to them. The *illah* is torment and the torment inflicted in beating them is more than that in saying *"uff."* In another example, the consumption of the wealth of the minor, or even transferring it to one's own name, is proscribed by the Quran. Consumption leads to the destruction of this wealth. By analogy it is said that destruction of any other type with respect to such wealth is also proscribed on the basis of the *illah* of destruction *(itlaf)*. Destruction by arson, for instance, is of a higher-order, because there is no chance of retrieval or recovery of the same wealth.

   This type of analogy is called *Qiyas al-mana* by *Imam al-Shafii* and is considered by him to be the strongest type of *Qiyas.* According to the *Hanafis,* this is not *Qiyas* at all, but a literal mode for establishing the *hukm* called *dalalat un-nass.*

2. *The Second Type of Qiyas is where the Hukm Established is of an Equivalent order or of the Same Strength:* There is a tradition about the male slave jointly owned by two persons to the effect that if one of the co-owners sets him free, to the extent of his own share, he becomes liable to pay the value of the other co-owner's share to him. The case of the female slave is held to be identical on the basis of the *illah* that is considered to be the "gifting of freedom by the *Shariah"* or freedom by operation of the law. The *hukm* for the male and female slave is deemed equal for this purpose.

   Another example given by some jurists is that of reducing the penalty of a married male slave, for extra-marital sexual intercourse, to half of 100 stripes on the analogy of the female slave whose case has been mentioned in the Quran.

   Most of the cases of analogy will be covered by this type. It is called *Qiyas al-illah* and also *Qiyas jali* or manifest analogy.

3. *The Third Type is that of Qiyas Adwan or Analogy of a Lower Order :* The example is that of extending the prohibition of *riba* to all types of food on the basis of "food in general" as the *illah.* This *illah,* as stated earlier, is upheld by *Imam al-Shafii. Imam Malik* disagrees with him by saying that the *illah* in the food items mentioned in the tradition is food, but food that can be stored and preserved not all types of food. This attribute is missing from the water-melon, which lacks such attributes. Analogy if undertaken will be of a lower order due to a lesser number of attributes in the *far.*

Qiyas Jali and Qiyas Khafi or Manifest and Concealed Analogy : The term *Qiyas jali* (manifest analogy) has been used in various senses by the jurists, depending upon the school to which they belong. In the previous section, the term was used for the second type of analogy where the *hukm* established is of the same strength. Some have used it for the first type as well. Under this heading we are concerned with the way the *Hanafi* jurists have used it.

The *Hanafis* use the term *Qiyas jali* to mean analogy for which the underlying cause is more or less apparent or can be discovered with relative ease. The jurist does not have to ponder too much over the attributes of the *illah.* Almost all types of analogy are classified under this meaning. As compared to this, the real *illah* may be less apparent and the jurist has to expend considerable effort to discover it; the *illah* is concealed so to say. This type of analogy is considered *Qiyas khafi* or concealed analogy. In reality this is not analogy at all. In Islamic jurisprudence, according to the *Hanafis,* concealed analogy is called *istihsan.* The next section deals with this form of analogy: *istihsan.*

Justification of Qiyas as a Source of Islamic Law : The majority of Muslim jurists consider *Qiyas* to be a valid evidence for proving the *ahkam.* The *Zahiris,* some of the *Mutazila* and the *Jafari* school of though (Shias) rejected it as a source and a form of legal reasoning. Both sides, those who accept it and those who reject it, give arguments in support of their view. Some of these arguments are recorded below:

Arguments of those who Uphold Qiyas : The arguments are provided from the Quran, the *Sunnah,* from the practice of Companions and as rational propositions.

1. (Consider, then, O you with eyes (to see) [Quran 59 : 2]). This verse asks those with eyes (intellect) to consider things, compare them, and ponder over them. The word *itibar* implies moving from one thing or place to another. In the present context it means moving one's thoughts between things in an effort to compare them. As *Qiyas* is a method of legal reasoning that requires comparison between two things and moving the *hukm* from on to the other, it falls within the implications of this verse.
2. The famous tradition about *Muad ibn Jabal* when he was sent as a *Qadi* to Yemen. He stated before the Prophet (peace be on him) that if he was not able to find a direct evidence in the Quran and the *Sunnah,* he would use his considered opinion. This was approved by the Prophet (peace be on him). As considered opinion in the context of law is nothing more than proper legal reasoning, and *Qiyas* is the soundest method of legal reasoning, this amounts to an approval of *Qiyas.*

3. There are many cases in which the Prophet (peace be on him) in response to the queries of the Companions tried to give answers in a form that was supposed to train them in legal thinking, and in many such cases the method is quite similar to analogy. For example, a person came to the Prophet (peace be on him) and said that his mother had resolved during her lifetime to perform *Hajj,* but she died before she could fulfil this promise, and could he now perform it on her behalf? The Prophet (peace be on him) replied: "If she were under debt would you pay it back on her behalf?" The man said: "Yes." *The Prophet* replied: "Then pay the debts of Allah for these, have the highest priority."
4. The Companions used to settle cases by performing analogy on already settled cases, that is, they followed precedents and performed analogy. In addition to such cases, there are instructions from the Companions to this effect. For example, the well known letter written by *Umar,* may *Allah* be pleased with him, to *Abu Musa al-Ashari.* In this letter he advised him: "Compare cases with settled precedents, and then select what you think will please *Allah* and is closer to the truth."
5. The cases in the texts of the Quran and the *Sunnah*[11] are limited and the cases that are faced by human beings are unlimited, therefore, there has to be some way of extending the law in these sources to cover new cases as well so that the new cases are settled according to Islamic legal norms. *Qiyas* is a very strict and tested method of extending the law, and in reality is nothing more than legal reasoning.

Arguments of those who Reject Qiyas

1. A verse of the Quran says: "O you who believe! Put not yourselves forward before God and His Apostle, but fear God: for God is He Who hears and knows all things." [Quran 49 : 1] The person who upholds analogy acts against the implication of this verse, because analogy means "putting yourself forward" before *Allah* and His Messenger when the Quran and the *Sunnah* have not settled a case.
2. Another verse says: "And pursue not that of which thou hast no knowledge." [Quran 17 : 36] Analogy is something that is probable *(zanni)* and doubtful, and acting upon it would amount to acting according to something of which we have no knowledge. This is particularly so when the Quran says: "And We have sent down to thee the Book explaining all things, a guide and a mercy and glad tidings to Muslims." [Quran 16 : 89] As everything is to be elaborated by the Quran, there is no need for analogy.

3. There are many sayings of the Companions in which they have condemned the use of *ray* (personal opinion), and analogy is personal opinion.
4. Analogy leads to discord among the Muslims, because it does not lead to exactly the same opinion when different jurists are exercising it. The reason is that they may be trying to use a different precedent for solving the same problem. Something that leads to differences should be shunned.
5. It cannot be said that the *ahkam* of the *Shariah* are based upon similarity and equality. For example, the thief who steals is to be given the penalty of cutting of the hand, while the embezzler is not punished in the same way, although there is no difference between them. Water and clean soil have both been considered means of ritual cleanliness when they are opposites.

The weaknesses in the arguments of those who reject analogy can be seen with ease. The main point here is that the judge has to give relief to the litigants who come to him. It is not possible for him to say to them that "I cannot find anything in the Quran and the *Sunnah* to settle this case, therefore, I cannot help you." The presumption is that a solution exists in the *Shariah* and the judge has to adopt some method of legal reasoning to extend the law from the limited number of texts that he can employ. As long as he is required to do so, analogy is a good and strict method of legal reasoning that maximises the chances of the discovery of the intention of the Lawgiver. The assertion that analogy is based on probable *(zanni)* knowledge is also without foundation, because there are many verses that are *zanni al-dalalah,* that is, there can be more than one way of interpreting them and understanding their meaning.

Speciality at Work

The Meaning of Istihsan : In its literal sense the word *istihsan* means "to consider something good." It is also applied to mean something towards which one is inclined or which one prefers, even if it is not approved by others.

Technically, it has been defined in several ways. *Al-Bazdawi* defines it as "moving away from the implications of analogy to an analogy that is stronger than it, or it is the restriction of analogy by an evidence that is stronger than it." *Al-Halwani* defines it as "the giving up of analogy for a stronger evidence from the Book, the *Sunnah,* or *Ijma."* The *Maliki* jurist, *Ibn al-Arabi* defines it as "sacrificing some of the implications of an evidence by way of exception insofar as the exception opposes some of these implications."

From all these definitions it is obvious that istihsan means the preference of a stronger evidence over analogy. In other words, it means:

- The preference of *Qiyas khafi* over *Qiyas jali,* as explained in the previous section.
- It also means following the requirements of a stronger general principle that requires something different from strict analogy.
- It may also mean the creation of an exception to a general principle due to a stronger evidence when the general principle is based upon analogy.

Al-Sarakhsi points out that some jurists have criticised *istihsan* on the grounds that analogy is being given up for the personal opinion of the jurists. He responds that this is totally misfounded for how can a jurist give up a *hujjah* (legally admissible authority) for something that has no authority. In modern times, the words "juristic preference" may have implied something similar. The reader should note that analogy is given up by the jurist only when he has a stronger evidence to rely on and this stronger evidence is one that is valid according to the *Shariah. Istihsan,* he says, is merely the comparison of two valid evidences (sources) and the preference of the stronger over the relatively weaker. It may also mean the restriction of one with the other. He concludes that "giving up of *Qiyas* is sometimes due to the text, and at other times due to *Ijma* or due to the principle of necessity."

Istihsan is a Method for Looking at the Consequences of a Decision : *Al-Sarakhsi* explains that *istihsan* is a way of looking at the consequences of the application of two legal rules and the selection of one that creates ease and facility. He says that analogy is of two types. The first one is *jati* or manifest where the strict rules of logic require a certain thing, but the consequences of implementing it are injurious. On the other hand, the second type of legal reasoning called *Qiyas khafi* may not appeal very much to the rules of logic, but its consequences are good and beneficial. He gives a number of examples to explain this, and some of these are given below.

Examples of Istihsan (Juristic Preference)

1. *Abu Hanifah* on deciding the issue of the person who eats during a fast out of forgetfulness, is reported to have said: "Had it not been for the report by the people, I would have said that he should repeat his fast." What he meant by this was that strict application of the rules of fasting requires that anyone eating food has broken the fast. A report from the Prophet (peace be on him) says that "liability for three things has been lifted from my *Ummah:* forgetfulness; mistake; and duress." This is a case of *istihsan* where a text has been preferred over analogy, and by means of which an exception has been created.
2. *Qiyas* prohibits the contract of *salam,* because it involves delay in the exchange of food items listed in the tradition of *riba.* There is, however,

the tradition from the Prophet (peace be on him) that says that "he made an exemption in the case of *salam.*"

3. Similar to *salam* is the case of the contract of *istisna* or the manufacturing contract with advance payment. Analogy prohibits it on the basis of the same rules as in the case of *salam.* It is, however, permitted on the basis of *Ijma* according to the *Hanafis.*
4. Analogy requires that ritually pure water should be used for ablution. In the case of wells in which dirt or carcasses of animals have fallen, following strict analogy would mean the non-use of these wells, and this would cause hardship to the people. The principle of necessity requires that use of these wells be permitted. This is done after observing formal cleaning methods.
5. The general principle of sale requires that a thing that does not exist cannot be sold. In the contract of hire, *(ijarah),* the benefits or services that are being paid for do not exist at the time of the contract. The contract has been permitted on the basis of necessity, seeking support from the contract made by the Prophet *Yaqub*[12] *(Jacob)* as mentioned in the Quran.

In all these cases, the consequences of the application of strict analogy have figured significantly in the decision and the decision preferred was one that had more healthy consequences for the people.

Types of Istihsan : We may now list the various methods through which *istihsan* is employed in legal reasoning.

1. *Istihsan Through the Text (Nass) :* A general principle emerging from the texts may not permit something, yet another text may provide an exception to this broad principle. An example of this is the contract of *salam* explained above; it has been permitted on the basis of a tradition when strict analogy would not permit it. Another example is that of *khiyar al-shart* (stipulated option). The general principle requires that all contracts become binding on their conclusion. A tradition permits the stipulation of an option for three days as an exception to this principle.
2. *Istihsan on the Basis of Ijma :* The example is again the contract of *istisna* mentioned above. The general principle for bids transactions in things that do not exist at the time of contract. An exemption was made on the basis of consensus for the manufacturing contract seeking strength from the exemption made for the contract of *salam.*
3. *Istihsan on the Basis of what is Good (Maruf) :* Some writers have used the word *urf* (custom) to indicate that this one method of employing

istihsan. Care has to be exercised in using such concepts. *Al-Sarakhsi* explains that one meaning of *istihsan* is where the *Shariah* is asking us to follow what is good and has left the determination of this *maruf* to our opinion. For example, the words of the Quran: (A gift of a reasonable amount is due from those who wish to do the right thing [Quran 2:236]). So also the words: (But he (to whom the child is attributed) shall bear the cost of their food and clothing [Quran 2:233]). In such cases, the principle is that we follow what the *Shariah* would consider to be good, that is, we determine it in accordance with the general principles of the *Shariah.* It does not mean following each and every custom in accordance with what the people have been practising. Even if it is an age old custom and is generally considered good, the ruling of *Shariah* must be given before it can be accepted. The point is explained under the discussion of custom as a source of law.

4. *Istihsan on the Basis of Necessity (Darurah) :* The example of wells has already been given above. So also *Imam Malik* permitted slight uncertainty that will not lead to a dispute where the general principle requires the avoidance of uncertainty *(gharar)* that will lead to a dispute.

5. *Istihsan on the Basis of Maslahah :* This is attributed to *Imam Malik.* The example, however, is from the time of the Companions and pertains to the liability of artisans. The general principle required that artisans were not to be held liable for things handed to them, unless it could be proved that they were guilty of negligence. In other words, the burden of proof of negligence was placed on the customer. *Ali,* may *Allah* be pleased with him, changed the rule, because the artisans were misusing the facility. He placed the burden of proof on the artisans who were required to show that there had been no negligence. The *Hanafis* call this *istihsan* on the basis of necessity of the preservation of wealth, which again is similar to *maslahah.*

6. *Istihsan on the Basis of Qiyas Khafi :* The general rule required that if beasts of prey had drunk from water it was no longer pure. Strict analogy required that the rule be applied to domestic animals as well. Pondering over the issue the jurist finds that beasts of prey have soiled saliva, whereas domestic animals do not. The rule was not applied to such animals.

Distinction between the Various Types : *Al-Sarakhsi* says that if *istihsan* is based upon the text or upon *Ijma,* the derived rule can serve as a further basis for analogy. In the other cases, like *istihsan* based upon necessity or concealed analogy, it is not possible to extend the new rule further.

Justification of Istihsan : Some jurists, especially the *Shafii's*, have objected to the use of *istihsan. Imam al-Shafii* said that *istihsan* is the following of one's personal whim and amounts to unjustified legislation. The dispute, however, appears to be around the literal meaning of the word *istihsan* rather than its technical meaning. The above examples show that many of the opinions stated above, especially those based on the texts, are held by the *Shafii's* as well. *Istihsan* is an efficient method of legal reasoning that ensures analytical consistency in the system and helps the jurist identify general principles and exceptions besides giving importance to the consequences of the decision.

Istishab (Presumption of Continuity) : The word *istishab* means the continuance of companionship. Technically it means the presumption of continuance of an earlier rule or its continued absence. In this sense it means the maintenance of a status quo with respect to the rule. The previous rule is accepted, unless a new rule is found that goes against it. As an easy reference one may refer to *istishab al-hal* as the "accompanying rule." In reality, *istishab al-hal* is not a source of law nor is it a source for establishing new rules; it is merely a set of presumptions. This will be obvious from the discussion below.

Principles that form the basis of Istishab

The following general principles form the basis of *istishab :*

1. The original rule for all things is permissibility, that is, the presumption is that all things are permitted, unless prohibited by the *Shariah.* This rule applies to beneficial things alone, like food, drink and benefiting from all good things. It is known that spilling blood without justification is prohibited. The taking of wealth without a legal right is prohibited. Indulging in sex without lawful permission is prohibited. In general, the commission of any act that is injurious to another is prohibited, like defamation and all kinds of falsehood. This narrows down the scope of this principle. It is for this reason that some of the *Hanafis* are considered to maintain the opposite principle: (the presumption is that all things are prohibited, unless the *Shariah* permits them). If we assume that most beneficial things are originally permitted, it means that they have been permitted by the Lawgiver. Can the state today prohibit some of these things? It is obvious that the evidence to do this must come directly from the sources of Islamic law. This shows that the principle may have some problems.
2. *Also Called Baraah Asliyyah:* This principle means that there is no presumption of liability against any one, and all liability has to be proved.

This principle is more of a procedural nature and places the burden of proof on the person making a claim.

3. *Certainty does not give Way to Doubt :* This means that once a thing is established beyond doubt, it can only be set aside through an equally certain evidence. If a person is sure that he has performed ablution and later doubts this he is presumed to be ritually pure till he is certain that he is not. The above principles highlight the different ideas associated with the principle of *Istishab.*

Types of Istishab and their Legal Validity : The principle of *Istishab* in certain forms was accepted by *al-Shafii* and in some of its forms by the *Hanafis* as well. The following discussion by *al-Sarakhsi* is expected to throw light on the issue. *Al-Sarakhsi* first discusses a broad principle in legal reasoning where there is no *dalil.*

The issue is whether "no *dalil*" can be a form of legal proof. He says that some jurists lay down the following principle: *"No-dalil* is an evidence for purposes of defence, but not for asserting a claim." He maintains that an analysis of issues settled by the *Shafii* school shows that "it is a defensive presumption for the continuance of an existing rule, but not for establishing what was not there from the start." He then says that an analysis of cases in the *Hanafi* school shows that what *al-Shafii* states is valid only to the extent where the right of *Allah* is involved, but where the right of the individual is concerned it is not an evidence for either of the litigants, neither for purposes of defence and denial nor for purposes of establishing claims.

After dealing with this general approach, *al-Sarakhsi* states that "among the forms of reasoning without any *dalil* is one called *Istishab al-hal."* This type of reasoning he states is *Batil.* He then analyses the various types of *Istishab* to show what is acceptable and what is not. He divides *istishab* into four types:

1. *Where the Absence of Dalil is Known with a Certainty:* This type of certainty can come only from the texts themselves and should be similar to the words: (Say: "I find not in the message received by me any (meat) forbidden" [Quran 6:145]). When it is known with a certainty that there is no evidence that will change the existing rule, and the *dalil* of the existing rule is known, the continuance of the *hukm* is valid. This rule requires a thorough examination of a new issue in the light of the general principles of the *Shariah.*

2. *Where after Pondering over the General Evidences it is Obvious to the Jurist that there is an Evidence that will Change the Existing Hukm.* This means a negative *istishab* where a jurist wishes to allege a change in an

existing *hukm* established through valid evidences. In such a case, it can only be used as a defence and not for establishing a claim, because the opponent will say that in his opinion there is a contrary evidence.

3. *Where the Continuance of a Hukm is Alleged with out Making an Effort for Seeking an Evidence that will Change the Rule:* According to *al-Sarakhsi* this is ignorance. The reason is that before searching for such an evidence the jurist cannot know whether the *hukm* has changed or an evidence is available for settling the case. This ignorance can in no way become an argument against others.

4. *Istishab for Establishing a Rule ab Initio:* To use *istishab* to establish a new rule is a grave mistake according to *al-Sarakhsi. Istishab al-hal,* he says, is the name for the continued following of a *hukm* that had been established through a valid evidence. Where there is no such *hukm,* the principle of *istishab* does not apply.

Istishab al-hal cannot Establish a New Rule : The above discussion shows that *Istishab* is a procedural rule that creates a presumption for denying something, but not for establishing a claim. As a source of law, the principle has little value as it cannot be used to establish a new rule.

Istishab al-hal and the Islamisation of Laws : The law obtaining in Pakistan is based on the English law. It is the practice of some institutions to say that where a direct evidence is not found to show that the law is against the Quran and the *Sunnah* it will be accepted as valid.

According to this reasoning some people can be heard saying that only 5% of the laws need to be changed, because they clash with the texts and the rest should be accepted as Islamised. In the same spirit, perhaps, the Council of Islamic Ideology says that they have reviewed a large number of laws.

The principle of *Istishab* asserts that the continuance of a rule is conditional upon the fact that it was originally established by an evidence from the *Shariah.* Does the acceptance of existing Western laws, on the grounds that they are not repugnant to the Quran and the *Sunnah,* enough to justify their validity? Will it not be better if each and every law on the statute book is justified *ab initio* on the basis of the sources of Islamic law?

Will this not help in the application of these laws by the judiciary who deal in general principles as well as rules? It is, therefore, suggested that the CII should publish its legal reasoning underlying its recommendations and so should the Islamic Fiqh Academy of the OIC.

Detailed Analogy

Maslahah is defined in its literal sense as "the acquisition of *manfaah* (benefit) or the repulsion of *madarrah* (injury, harm)." In the technical sense it means "the preservation of the purposes of Islamic law in the settlement of legal issues." The purposes of the law are interests recognised by the *Shariah. Maslahah mursalah* is also referred to as *istidlal mursal.*

The jurists classify *maslahah,* in accordance with the acceptance and rejection by the *Shariah,* into four types:

1. The first type is *maslahah* acknowledged by the Lawgiver at the level of the lowest category *(naw).* This is called *Qiyas* (analogy).
2. The second type is *maslahah* that is acknowledged by the Law giver at the level of the genus *(jins).* This is called *maslahah mursalah.*
3. The third type of *maslahah* is one that is not acknowledged by the *Shariah.* This is called an interest that is rejected or *mulgha.*
4. The fourth type is a *maslahah* that is neither acknowledged by the *Shariah* nor is it rejected. This type of *maslahah* is called strange *(gharib).*

In the present section the meaning of the second and the fourth types will be examined, that is, *maslahah mursalah* and *maslahah* that is strange or *gharib.* The examination of the *gharib* is expected to sharpen the understanding of *maslahah mursalah.*

The Meaning of Maslahah Mursalah and the Conditions for its Validity : *Maslahah mursalah,* sometimes referred to in the plural as *masalih mursalah,* is a highly flexible and advanced type of analogy. It is employed when the jurist cannot find a rule for the case at hand through literal interpretation nor can he extend the meaning through strict analogy *(Qiyas),* because there is no specific base *(asl)* from which he can extend the rule by analogy. In other words, individual or specific evidences do not control the law any more. The word *irsal* means to "let go." We can say here that the individual or specific texts have "let go" of the issue or they have released their hold. The case now has to be settled by "looking at all the texts collectively." This is achieved by referring to the purposes of Islamic law or the *maqasid al-shariah.* The first thing that a jurist employing *maslahah mursalah* has to do is to "formulate a new principle that will control the problem being faced by him." The new principle he has formulated must meet the following three conditions identified by *al-Ghazzali:*

1. He has to make sure that the new principle he has formulated does not clash with a text *(nass)* or attempt to alter the implication of a text.

2. He has to make sure that the principle does not clash with the existing principles and propositions of Islamic law. *Al-Ghazzali* calls these principles and propositions the *tasarrufat* (established practices) of the *Shariah.*

3. The jurist must ensure that the principle he has formulated is not *gharib* (strange) for the *Shariah.* This is in reality means that the norm it promotes must be among the purposes of Islamic law recognised by the *Shariah.*

Illustrations of Maslahah Mursalah : The jurists provide a number of examples to elaborate the meaning of *Maslahah Mursalah.* Some of these are listed below:

1. The compilation of the Quran after the death of the Prophet (peace be on him). Although the Prophet (PBUH) had indicated the order of the *surahs,* he had not given the orders for its compilation in the form of a book between two covers. The Companions were, therefore, not sure whether this should be done, because it was something that the Prophet (PBUH) had not done himself. They decided that it was essential to gather it and compile it in the "interest of the preservation of *din.*" History has shown that this was a very wise decision.

2. The rule for murder *(qatl amd)* provided in the texts was that one life could be taken for one life by way of retaliation. It was not clear whether a number of persons could be subjected to *qisas* when they participated in killing a single person. *Umar* decided that all of them should be put to death. This rule it is said was based on the "preservation of life," which is a purpose of Islamic law. This is strengthened by the words of the Quran: "In retaliation there is life for you." *Umar* is reported to have said (in this decision) that if all the people of *Sana* had conspired to kill a single person he would put all of them to death.

3. The rule for artisans accepting goods from people for doing work on such things was that they were not required to show negligence if the thing was destroyed. The burden of proving negligence was on the customer. The artisans started misusing this facility. The Companions, therefore, decided to change the rule. After this decision, if a thing was destroyed in the hands of the artisans, the artisan would be required to show that there was no negligence on his part. The decision is based upon the need to "preserve the wealth of the community." This decision was given by *Ali.*

4. *Al-Ghazzali* has stated that on the basis of *maslahah mursalah* it is permitted to the ruler to impose taxes if the coffers are empty and he

needs money for *Jihad* or for preserving the security of the Muslim *Ummah.*

5. There is no penalty in the Quran for drinking of wine. In the *Sunnah* the traditions vary, with some providing 80 lashes and others 40. Ali fixed the penalty at 80 on the analogy of *qadhf.* This is the most elaborate and instructive of the examples and is explained below.

These examples may appear simple in the identification of the rule, but the mental process required for employing it is somewhat complex. The process is quite similar to what is referred to in Western law as "reasoning from legal principles." This process is highlighted in the examples below. The first case is that of fixing of 80 lashes as a penalty for drinking wine. This is followed by two examples, one of *gharib* and the other of *mulgha.* These two examples are hypothetical and have been constructed by *al-Ghazzali* to show the operation of the conditions.

The Process of Using Maslahah Mursalah : In this example it is shown that the jurist usually has a principle that is valid. He also has another principle about the validity of which he is not sure. The jurist makes a third broader principle that accommodates the two existing principles within it. In law this is considered to be a broad form of analogy and is called reasoning from legal principles.

The purpose of this example is also to show how the three conditions identified by *al-Ghazzali* above are satisfied. These conditions are that the new principle should not be *gharib,* it should not conflict with a text, and it should not attempt to alter the implications of the text, that is, of other established principles, and that it should conform with the *maqasid.*

The case, as is well known, was decided by *Ali.* The drinking of wine is prohibited by the texts, however, no fixed penalty is prescribed. The penalties that appear in the traditions vary and are not fixed. He is reported to have said:

He who drinks is intoxicated; he who is intoxicated raves; he who raves slanders; I (therefore) uphold the penalty of the slanderer for him.

This, according to *al-Ghazzali,* is based on *maslahah mursalah.* The principle quoted in the above statement is not mentioned in the texts, nor can it be derived from a specific rule. The first principle that the jurist possesses here and under which the penalty of slander *qadhf* is covered is that the "person who slanders is to be awarded the penalty of *qadhf* (slander)." This is explicitly mentioned in the Quran, and the penalty is eighty stripes:

Al-Ghazzali says that this principle is *munasib* (suitable), that is, it conforms with the purposes of the law. However, if we attempt to apply it to the case of the person who drinks, it does not appear to be *mulaim* (compatible) with the general practices and principles *(tasarrufat)* of the law. The reason is that it would amount to giving him a penalty for an offence that he did not commit; namely, *qadhf. Al-Ghazzali* maintains that when probed deeply we find it to be *mulaim* (compatible). This is based on the following legal reasoning.

The law, he says, often assigns the outward indication *(mazinnah)* of a thing the *hukm* of the underlying intended act or happening. Thus:

- penetration is considered to stand in place of actual ejaculation for purposes of bathing to achieve ritual purification;
- *bulugh* (the age of puberty), which is the outward indication of discretion and maturity, is assigned the *hukm* of actual discretion to determine majority;
- sleep is assigned the *hukm* of ritual impurity, because one who sleeps is liable to becomes ritually impure.

Examining the Last Case : He who sleeps becomes ritually impure; he who becomes ritually impure performs ablution; therefore, he who sleeps is to perform ablution (for the next prayer).

This is the Same as Saying: He who drinks is intoxicated; he who is intoxicated raves; he who raves slanders; therefore, he who drinks is to be awarded the penalty for slander. This reasoning leads to the conclusion that drinking of *khamr* is the outward indication of the loss of one's senses that leads to slander and finally to enmity and hatred. As a punishment for slander has been provided by the texts, it should be awarded for drinking wine, which is its outward indication. A new, and much wider, principle has now been formulated. The larger principle now includes both cases of *qadhf* (slander) and *shurb* (drinking).

Further, we notice that this case meets all three conditions prescribed by *al-Ghazzali,* that is, it is not *gharib,* it does not conflict with an explicit text, and it does not alter the implications of the general propositions of law. The case, then, falls within the principle of *maslahah mursalah* proper. It may be mentioned here that this illustration is not intended to show that a new rule was laid down. The penalties are provided in the texts of the *Sunnah,* and this legal reasoning was used as an aid to interpret the texts for choosing the appropriate penalty. Establishing a new rule for the criminal law through analogy or other forms of legal reasoning is not approved by all the jurists as it is against the principle of *nulla poena sine lege,* which is approved by Islamic law.

Identifying Maslahah that is Gharib : The second example is being stated here to show the operation of the three conditions stipulated by *al-Ghazzali,* as well as further conditions on the basis of which a case that appears to be based on the *mursal* principle, but which is actually *gharib,* may be accepted. The case is purely hypothetical.

Al-Ghazzali gives the example of Muslims besieged in a fort by the enemy. The enemy is attacking this fort and is using Muslim captives as shields in the hope that the Muslims in the fort will not fire at them. The question is should the Muslims fire at the enemy, even if the Muslims being used as human shields are killed?

This case violates all three conditions that al-Ghazzali has stipulated for maslahah mursalah.

- First, it conflicts with the texts that clearly lay down that no one is to be killed intentionally.
- Second, it violates the general propositions of the law, which prescribe that only those persons can be killed who have committed an offence. It is, therefore, not *mulaim* (compatible) with the general principles, which means it is *gharib* or unacknowledged by the law.
- Third, by permitting the killing of Muslims under certain circumstances due to necessity, it attempts to alter the meaning of the implications of the texts, which is the third condition stipulated by *al-Ghazzali.*

Al-Ghazzali appears to be saying, although he does not say it explicitly, that even such a case may be drawn into the fold of the *istidlal mursal,* which is *mulaim,* but with additional conditions. These conditions are:

- that the case should lie in the area of the *darurat* (necessities), that is, it should be one of the five top purposes of the Islamic law;
- that it should be definitive *(qati),* that is, we should be certain about the resulting consequences;
- and it should be general *(kulli),* that is, it should affect the entire Muslim *ummah* and be a public interest.

This hypothetical case can be approved only if it assumes that the entire Muslim community is being attacked at once. If the entire community is destroyed or eliminated, Islam as a religion will disappear. If the entire Muslim *ummah* is threatened, this case would lie in the area of the *darurat,* as it affects the first primary purpose of the law, that is, the preservation and protection of *ummah.* The second assumption is that we are certain that if we shoot at the disbelievers, who are using the Muslim captives as shields, they will be driven away and the Muslims, at least some of them, will be saved. This certainty about survival makes the case definitive *(qati).* The third assumption is the same as the first that the entire Muslim community is being attacked. Thus, there is the interest of a few Muslims pitted against the community as a whole, and the latter is to be preferred.

With these three conditions, then, this *mursal gharib* may be accepted, however, it can be seen that the three conditions are impossible to meet in this case, even though they are hypothetically possible.

Identifying Maslahah that is Rejected (Mulgha) : As compared to the above hypothetical case, *al-Ghazzali* presents another hypothetical case. The case is that of a number of people in a boat who are cast out at sea and are about to die from hunger. They cast lots to choose one of their companions who will be killed and his flesh will be eaten so that the others are saved. For legality, this requires a *gharib* rule that is rejected by the *Shariah,* because it does not meet the three additional conditions imposed by *al-Ghazzali.*

- First, though it is obligatory on the people in the boat to save their lives even if they have to consume *haram,* they cannot kill someone else to do so. The reason is that killing another person is prohibited without legal justification. Saving themselves by killing one whose life the *Shariah* protects is not a purpose defended by the *Shariah.* In other words, it is not *daruri.*
- Second, the people in the boat are not sure that they will be saved even if they consume the flesh of the person they kill. It is possible that they will stay at sea and will not be saved. The issue is, therefore, not *qati.*
- Third, and this most important, the issue concerns only a few individuals in the boat and not the entire Muslim *Ummah.* It is, therefore, not *kulli* and, thus, cannot be a public interest.
- Killing of one individual here cannot be permitted by the *Shariah* as the issue fails to meet the additional conditions identified by *al-Ghazzali.* The interest of these individuals is thus rejected.

Justification of Maslahah Mursalah : The main objection against the use of *maslahah mursalah* in particular and the concept of *maslahah* in general is that it is based upon the *hikmah* (wisdom) of the rule rather than on the *illah.* The jurists have been very cautious in the use of *hikam* for the determination of laws. This argument is based on the use of strict analogy *(Qiyas)* as the sole rational secondary source for the derivation of rules. The principle of *maslahah* is more flexible than strict analogy and is based on an interplay of general principles and the purposes of Islamic law. The general principles and the *maqasid* are based on the *hikmah* underlying the various rules.

Another argument that is sometimes advanced is that it will be misused by ignorant people. The response to this is that the legal system must ensure that its professionals observe the proper methodology that meets the conditions imposed above. Further, the principle is to be used mostly by the judges of the Higher Courts of the country and by the lawyers who assist these Courts. It is not upto every person to employ legal reasoning.

Sadd al-Dhariah (Blocking the Lawful Means to an Unlawful End) : The word *dharai* is the plural of *dhariah* (means to an end). It is the means to an end irrespective of the end being lawful or unlawful, beneficial or harmful. The term *sadd al-dhariah,* however, means "blocking the lawful means to an unlawful end." As compared to this, the term *fath al-dhariah* is also used, which means "permitting the unlawful means to a lawful end."

The principle of *sadd al-dhariah* is attributed to *Imam Malik.* Some modern writers insist that its use can be seen in the rulings of most schools, however, the classical jurists have not acknowledged or even discussed it. It has been given attention by al-Shatibi.

The principle is not concerned with unlawful acts, because those are prohibited anyway. It is concerned with lawful acts that may be prohibited as they lead to unlawful results. For example, the cultivation of poppy has been banned in many countries, because it is leading in most cases to the production of opium and heroin, which is a deadly drug that is being misused. Here an act that was basically lawful has been declared unlawful. This prohibition in the terminology of the jurists would be called *sadd al-dhariah* or the "blocking of lawful means to an unlawful end." The question in each individual case would be: Is the end unlawful according to the *Shariah?*

Law at Work

For purposes of this principle, the jurists divide acts into three kinds :

1. *Those that Rarely Lead to Harmful Results:* The interest *(maslahah)* to be secured in such acts is greater than the injury *(mafsadah)* to be sustained. Examples are: looking at a woman to be proposed to and maintaining vineyards for grapes. The injuries that may arise from these acts are less than the benefits. Thus, the first usually leads to marriage and lawful relations, though it may sometimes lead to illicit relations as well. Grapes are used for a large number of purposes though they may also be used for making wine. The benefits in both are more than the harm.
2. *Those that Usually Lead to Harmful Results:* The injury in such acts is much more than the benefits to be derived. Examples are: the sale of arms during waves of terrorism and rebellion; renting out property to one who

will use it for unlawful purposes, like maintaining a brothel; like the selling of grapes to a winery; like the sowing of poppy from which heroin will be made.

3. *Those in which there is an Equal Probability of Harm and Benefit:* This is a difficult area. Examples are: Marrying a woman with the intention of divorce so as to enable her to remarry her previous husband; prohibiting multiple transactions that may lead to *riba* when combined, like *bay al-inah.*

Disagreement of Jurists about the Legality of the Principle : Out of the three types of lawful acts discussed above, there is no dispute that the first type do not fall within the purview of the principle of *sadd al-dhariah.* The jurists disagree about the remaining two categories, that is, the second and the third. The *Malikis* and *Hanbalis* say that acts in these two categories may be prohibited if they are leading to unlawful means. The *Shafii's* and the *Zahiris* say that these are lawful acts and they cannot be prohibited.

Those who prohibit them argue that *sadd al-dhariah* is an acknowledged principle of *Shariah* and as long as these acts lead to unlawful results, they should be prohibited. For the last category of acts, the *Maliki* jurists would say that "repelling of injury is to be accorded greater weight than the securing of benefit."

The root of the problem is based upon two theories in the law of contracts, because most of the acts mentioned above are contracts and are mostly lawful transactions (except for looking at a woman for purposes of marriage). These are the objective theory of contracts and the subjective theory of contracts. According to the objective theory, the law goes by the obvious meaning of the words used for offer an acceptance. It does not attempt to investigate the inner intention of the contracting parties. If the parties are entering into a contract that is lawful on the face of it, this theory will permit it.

As compared to this, the subjective theory tries to investigate the inner intention of the parties as well. If it can be shown that the ultimate purpose is unlawful, the subjective theory will declare the contract unlawful. Take the case of *bay al-inah* or the buy-back agreement, for instance. It consists of two separate transactions. If A sells a book to B for $100 in cash paid on the spot, and then after a few minutes B sells the book back to A for credit of one year for a sum of $120, the two separate transactions when combined are a transaction for lending on interest at 20%. *Imam al-Shafii* following the objective theory looks at them as two separate transactions having their own offer and acceptance; he does not bother about their real inner intention (which here appears to be the conclusion of an interest bearing transaction).

The principle of *sadd al-dhariah,* then, revolves around these theories. The *Malikis* and *Hanbalis* favour the subjective theory and declare the principle of *sadd al-dhariah* to be lawful. The rest of the schools favour the objective theory and, therefore, find it difficult to accept this principle. As the bulk of the rulings in Islamic law are based upon the objective theory, it would be better to side with those who favour this theory.

The two sides provide detailed arguments for the acceptance or rejection of the principle. It is, however, suggested that the principle should not be rejected outright or even accepted outright. The principle should be linked with empirical evidence. If all the scientific and other evidence is pointing to the fact that an act is certainly leading to greater harm than benefit, the state should consider prohibiting the act in the greater public interest.

Although the jurists have deemed *sadd al-dhariah* to be an independent principle, there is no reason why it cannot be considered part of *maslahah mursalah.*

This brings to an end the study of the rational secondary sources in Islamic law. Some modern writers have also tried to include the use of legal fictions *(hiyal)* in such sources. Legal fictions, however, are procedural devices and part of the law of conveyancing. As such they cannot be considered a source of Islamic law.

Means of Differing Nature

We have already discussed the study of the rational sources or the rational secondary sources. There are a few other secondary sources that depend upon transmission *(naql)* and not on methods of reasoning. These will be considered in this chapter. The sources are the opinion of a Companion, earlier scriptures and custom.

Theory of Comrade

A Companion, according to most jurists, is someone who saw the Prophet (peace be on him), believed in him, supported him and was in association with him for some time so that he could understand something of the ways of the *Shariah* from him. After the death of the Prophet (peace be on him), it was the Companions who interpreted the law and developed it where needed. They undertook *ijtihad,* issued rulings, settled cases and became a source of guidance for later generations.

Views of those who Accept it as a Source : The main issue faced by the jurists under this source is whether *the opinion of* a *Companion is to be preferred over analogy (Qiyas) undertaken by a later jurist?* In general, the *Hanafis* maintain that if there is a clash between the opinion of a Companion and analogy, the analogy is to be given up and the opinion of the Companion is to be followed. The *Shafii's* uphold that it is not binding on the jurist to give up analogy, he may or may not do so at his discretion. *Al-Sarakhsi,* the *Hanafi* jurist, has the following to say:

> In the opinion of a Companion there is a chance that it is based on a narration of the revelation. It appears from their practice that if one of them possessed a text, he would either narrate it or he would base his opinion on it. There is no doubt that the opinion in which there is a chance of transmission from the Prophet (peace be on him) (the possessor of the revelation) is to be preferred over mere opinion. It is in this context that the preference of the opinion of the Companion over opinion is analogous to the preference of a *khabar wahid* over analogy. And even if their view was based upon analogy, their view is stronger than all who are not Companions.

The reason is that they were witness to the practice of the Prophet (peace be on him) in the elaboration of the *ahkam* and they saw the events that were the cause of revelation. It is on this basis that their view is to be preferred over the view of those who did not witness any of these things.

The second area in which the *Hanafis* maintain that it is binding to follow the opinion of a Companion is where the Companion is talking about quantities, numbers and periods. The reason is that analogy has no role to play in this area, and most jurists are agreed that the opinion of a Companion is to be followed. *Al-Sarakhsi* points out that it is for this reason that we have followed the opinions of Companions in the following cases (examples):

- The rates of *Zakat.*
- The determination of the amount of dower.
- The determination of the minimum and maximum for the period of menstruation.
- The determination of the post-natal period.
- The determination of the maximum gestation period.

Views of those who do not Consider it Binding : Those who do not consider the opinion of a Companion to be binding maintain that they are under an obligation to follow the Quran and the *Sunnah,* as well as those sources that are indicated by these two primary sources. These primary sources have not asked us to follow the opinion of a Companion as a source of law.

Opinions of the Followers of the Companions (Tabiun) **:** *Al-Sarakhsi* maintains that there is no dispute that the opinions of the *Tabiun* are not binding in the sense that analogy should be given up in their preference. If one of them holds an opinion contrary to the consensus of the Companions, his opinion is not given weight in opposition to theirs.

Shar Man Qablana (Earlier Scriptures) **:** The meaning of *shar man qablana* is the body of rules ordained by *Allah* for the nations before the Muslim *ummah* through revelation to their Prophets (PBUH) and Apostles. Muslim jurists have differed somewhat about the relationship of such laws with the *Shariah,* as well as about their binding force for the Muslims. Some maintained that it was abrogated by our *Shariah,* while others said that those parts that were not abrogated are binding on us.

Law and its Types

1. Rules that have been repeated in the Quran or the *Sunnah* and made obligatory. These texts themselves provide the evidence about the binding nature of the laws and we do not have to refer to the earlier scriptures. These laws are binding on us just as they were binding on the earlier nations. Example: Fasting during *Ramadan.* [Quran 2 : 183].
2. Rules that have been described in the Quran or in the *Sunnah,* but are considered abrogated. Rules about carrion, blood, flesh of swine and the like.
3. Rules that are not mentioned in the Quran and the *Sunnah,* but are found in the earlier Scriptures. There is no dispute that these are not binding on us.
4. Rules that are mentioned in the Quran and the *Sunnah,* but there is no evidence whether or not they are to be followed. The example given by some jurists under this heading is that of *qisas* (retaliation). There is, however, ample evidence in the texts that it is binding on us.

This shows that the real source for all such rules are the Quran and the *Sunnah,* and they become binding on the Muslims when these primary sources grant the authority.

Reason why the Earlier Laws are not Binding

To Elaborate the Basis for not Accepting the Rules in the Earlier Scriptures, Al-Sarakhsi Makes the Following Statement: The most authentic statement in our view is that what is confirmed as an earlier law through the Book of *Allah,* or the elaboration by the Prophet (peace be on him), becomes a law for us, unless it is abrogated. As for what is transmitted by the People of the Book or is understood by the Muslims from their Scriptures is not binding on us, *because of the established evidence that they altered their Books.* Their transmission is, therefore, not accepted on the assumption that what is transmitted is entirely changed.

The Practices

The earlier jurists make only a passing reference to custom, and they have never considered it as a source of law. In modern times, under the influence of Western jurisprudence, some writers have given more importance to custom as a source of law. Custom has been a source of law, but in a limited sense. This will be obvious from the discussion below.

The word *urf* is usually associated with the word *maruf* (good) in the texts. In this sense, it is what the *Shariah* considers to be good, and not what human reason or the prevalent practices consider to be good. If some of these practices are approved by the *Shariah,* then, they are acceptable to the law. The process of approval, prior to acceptance, is necessary.

Types of Urf : There are different ways of classifying *urf,* and each classification is intended to bring out its nature.

Division into Usage and Practice : *Urf* is divided first into *urf qawli* (usage) and *urf fili* (practice).

Urf Qawli : The first type, or usage, may be analysed into the following types:

1. *The Meaning of Terms During the Period of the Prophet (Peace be on him):* This is the usage that was prevalent during the time of the Prophet (PBUH). The meaning assigned to words at that period is used to understand the true intention of the Lawgiver.
2. *Technical Terms of the Law or urf Shari:* The jurists usually employ the term *urf shari* to denote the technical sense that a term may have acquired in Islamic law. This technical meaning is usually different from the literal meaning in which the term is used. Thus, the word *salat* means any type of prayer or supplication, but in the technical sense it means the entire form of the prayer that has been transmitted from the Prophet (peace be on him). The word *riba* literally means excess and in general usage it means "interest" in the sense of *sud* in *Urdu,* but in the technical sense it has a much wider and comprehensive meaning assigned to it by the Quran and the *Sunnah.* For legal purposes, it is the *urf shari* that has to be followed.

3. *Usage in a Local Area for Purpose of Transactions:* It is obvious that people using languages other than Arabic, undertake their transactions in their own language. Islamic law will recognise the meaning in such usage, but only if it conforms with the forms prescribed by the law, that is, if such use of words achieves the same purpose as the one prescribed. If it does not, the law will declare it *fasid.* In other words, such usage has to be measured against the permitted rules before it can become permissible. It will not be recognised automatically.

It is obvious that none of these can be called a source of law in the sense that we understand custom to be a source in Western law.

Urf Hili (Practice) : This is of two types:

1. *The Practices Prevalent During the Period of the Prophet (Peace be on him):* These practices were either approved by the Prophet (peace be on him), either expressly or tacitly, or they were rejected. As such they became part of the *Sunnah.* The source of the law here was not custom, but the *Sunnah,* even though customs and practices did provide the raw material. Each practice was subjected to the norms of the *Shariah* by the Prophet (PBUH) himself, and was either accepted or rejected.
2. *Practices During the Later Periods:* These practices were faced by the jurists like new instances or cases and each one of them was subjected to scrutiny by the jurists. The jurists either justified these practices in the light of the principles of Islamic law or rejected them in the light of the same principles. No practice could automatically be approved just because it was a long standing custom.

We see from the above that though custom may provide the raw material to be considered by the jurist, no practice or custom can automatically be accepted as law. It has to be analysed and Islamised before it may be accepted. It may be noted that even in Western law, customs become law only when they are recognised by courts as such, and recognition means weighing them against the rest of the law for compatibility.

Can the Western Laws Obtaining in Pakistan be Treated as Custom? : It has been suggested by some that all the laws prevalent in Pakistan may be treated as *urf* (custom) and thus declared valid. The idea behind this suggestion is that customs attain automatic validity just by being called customs. The idea is used by those who maintain that only five percent of the law needs to be changed for purposes of Islamisation and the rest should be left untouched. This is not correct. Each prevalent law must be treated as a new case and be analysed in the light of the principles of Islamic law. It is not sufficient to say that there is nothing in the Quran and the *Sunnah* that clashes with a certain law, that is, the law has passed the repugnancy test. This way the law will not develop further on Islamic lines. Each law must be shown to be valid according to a principle of Islamic law. The Courts will then be able to develop the law and the principles further.

Means of Law

We have identified the *faqih* as the jurist, who performs the judicial function, and follows the methodology called *takhrij*. It should not be assumed that the function of the *faqih* is in any way less than that of the *mujtahid*. The *mujtahid* built the legal system by going directly to the primary sources of Islamic law and identifying its basic general principles, besides laying down the law itself. The *mujtahid* helped to bring the legal system to maturity; it is the task of the *faqih* to implement the general principles and to ensure that the system runs smoothly and in an analytically consistent manner. The task of the *faqih* is, therefore, more critical and important in many ways.

It should also not be assumed that the *faqih* cannot approach the sources that we have described in part two and called the sources for the *mujtahid*. He certainly can, but the system erected by the *fuqaha* appears to be saying that there is no need to reinvent the wheel. The entire law, after analytical systematisation, has been organised around a large body of principles, precedents and rules. This body of principles, precedents and rules provides enough flexibility for expansion and change. So why go through the whole process once again, a process over which centuries of labour has been expended by the *mujtahid?* Why not build on the work that has been done already; why lose the heritage?

In the same way, the *mujtahid* responsible for the legislative function can access this body of principles for the derivation of the law. In fact, most of the principles that we find in the books of Islamic law are traced back to the work of the *mujtahids*. Finally, it is to be noted that the role of the *faqih* as well as his methodology have been neglected by researchers. This field of study needs penetrating research before something final can be said about this methodology. At the same time this area provides a rich field waiting for the modern researcher. Those who may be unsure of the methodology we are talking about need to focus on the statements like the following that are often made by *al-Sarakhsi:*

The Explanation of the Extension of the Law (Takhrij) to Issues from this Principle is as Follows: After making such statements, he goes on to derive rule after rule from general principles. We would, therefore, suggest that researchers should focus on this area of the law, an area that offers the most fertile ground. Nevertheless, we have to say a few things on the issue. This is based on our understanding and research, yet there is a need to form a collective opinion.

The Task of the Faqih : We may now identify the task of the *faqih* in more specific terms, as it will help us identify the sources that he uses. The *faqih* has the following main tasks:

1. *To Settle Disputes in the Light of the Existing Case Law:* This means maintaining the decisions already settled by the *mujtahid.* It is an activity that is similar to the doctrine of stare *decisis* in the law. It makes the following of precedents necessary for the *faqih.* It is in this sense that we can say that the *ijtihad* of the *mujtahid* is a source of law for the *faqih.*
2. *To Extend the Law, if Necessary, From the Existing General Principles of Islamic Law:* These principles are basically of two types: those that have been stated explicitly in the texts of the Quran and the *Sunnah* and those that have been derived by the jurist through the existing law settled by the *mujtahid.*
3. If the new case faced by the *faqih* cannot be settled on the basis of the two previous methods, to formulate a new principle provided that this new principle meets the conditions laid down by the jurists. Briefly, these conditions are that the new principle should not attempt to overturn the meaning or implication of a text of the Quran or the *Sunnah;* it should not alter the meaning of an established principle of the law (as mentioned in the previous paragraph); and it should be in conformity with the purposes of Islamic law *(maqasid al-shariah).*

We may now Proceed to List the Sources

The Output/Result of Ijtihad is a Source for the Faqih : Some writers have erroneously stated that *ijtihad* is a source of Islamic law. For the *mujtahid,* it is a process, the effort that he expends, for the derivation of the law. For the *faqih,* it is the result of the *ijtihad* that is a source, not the *ijtihad* itself. The output or the result of *ijtihad* is the record of the decisions given by the *mujtahid.* It provides the precedents required by the *faqih.*

In the *Hanafi* school of thought, the first such source are the books called the *Zahir al-Riwayah* written and compiled by *Imam Muhammad al-Shaybani.* These are followed by others as shown below:

1. *Masail al-Usul or the Zahir al-Riwdyah:* These are books that record not only the opinions of the leading jurists of the *Hanafi* school, but also those of other leading jurists like *Ibn Abi Layla* and *al-Awzai.* The first book is called *Kitab al-Asl* or *al-Mabsut.* This is the first book on Islamic law, and most of the opinions recorded there are to be found today, either in the *Hanafi* school of thought or even in other Sunni schools of thought.

The other books under this heading are: *al-Ziyadat* (also a huge book), *al-Jami al-Saghir, al-Jami al-Kabir, al-Siyar al-Saghir,* and *al-Siyar al-Kabir.* All these books have been called *Zahir al-Riwayah* as they represent the most authentic formulation of the school. What we mean by this is that the methodology used in these books is definitely that of the first jurists of the school.

2. *Masail al-Nawadir:* These are cases narrated in books other than the *Zahir al-Riwayah.*
3. *The Fatawa and al-waqiat:* These are opinions of later jurists, or the *faqihs* on cases not contained in the books listed at (1) and (2) above.

The rule for the above texts is that the issues in the first category are to be preferred over those in the second and third category, in case there is a contradiction.

The *Zahir al-Riwayah* were summarised under the title of *al-Kafi.* It is on this summary that several important books by later jurists were constructed. For example, *al-Sarakhsi* wrote his famous 30 volume book *al-Mabsut* as a commentary on this summary. *Abu Bakr al-Kasani* also relies on it for his *al-Badai al-Sanai.* Later books like *al-Hidayah* by *al-Marghinani* rely on the original as well as on later commentaries. Books in the *Maliki* and *Shafii* school of thought that can be compared to the *zahir al-riwayah,* though written sixty to seventy years later, are *al-Mudawwanah al-Kubra* by *Sahnun* for the *Maliki* school of thought, and the *Kitab al-Umm* written by *al-Shafii* himself. The *Zahir al-Riwayah,* however, are much more extensive.

Ibn Abidin has Given a Few Words of Warning when it Comes to Consulting Later Books. His text is Reproduced below: As you have known the obligation to follow the preferred opinion out of the various opinions... know then that most of the verdicts handed out today by merely referring to the books of the later jurists are not trustworthy, especially the unverified verdicts in books like *Shark al-Niqayah* by *al-Quhistani, al-Durr al-Mukhtar,* and *al-Ashba wa al-Nazair...* for they contain in many cases the preference of a rejected opinion and the preference of that which is the opinion of another school, not preferred by anyone in this school. The transmission of an opinion may occur in about 20 books of the later jurists and still the opinion may be incorrect as the first jurist has erred and those coming after him have transmitted the opinion from him.

Ibn Abidin is trying to tell us that a case should first be traced in the earliest books, and then in the later. When a case is found it needs to be subjected to verification. This verification means determining the underlying principle. Without tracing the principle employed, the *faqih* can never be sure how the new case is to be settled. The tracing of the principle is a process that is identical to tracing the *ratio decidendi* in modern law and separating it from the *obiter dicta.* This process is the essence of the methodology of *takhrij.* The principle once extracted is used to settle the new case.

The Established Principles of Islamic Law are a Source for the Faqih : The first type of established principles are those that are either stated explicitly in the texts of the Quran and the *Sunnah* or are discoverable by the implication of these texts. The second type of principles are those that have been derived from a large number of cases by the jurists. The derived principle may or may not have the approval of *Ijma;* what makes it an established principle is the recognition that it receives from the jurists of a school. We will first state a few of the textual principles and then list a number of those derived by the jurists.

Principles Stated Explicitly or Impliedly in the Texts : The texts clearly lay down a number of principles that in one way or another govern Islamic law and jurisprudence. Such principles are found for almost every part of the law. The principles stated below, as an example, are those that govern the commercial law.

1. *The Prohibition of Riba:* One of the major principles of Islamic law is the principle of prohibition of *riba.* It is well known that the broad general principle is stated in the Quran and its sub-principles are to be found in the *Sunnah.* The principle is stated in the words of the *Allah,* "And *Allah* has permitted exchange and prohibited *riba.*" [Quran 2 : 275]

   This means that all types of bilateral contracts are permitted except those bearing *riba.*

   It would not be an exaggeration to say that the jurists have checked almost each and every transaction to see whether it violates the principle of the prohibition of *riba* in some way. Even the payments made or amounts returned in case of marriage and divorce may not be spared. This shows that the prohibition of *riba* determines the nature of the law of contract in Islam. The principle has been reaffirmed for the Pakistani legal system by the recent judgement of the *Shariat* Appellate Bench of the Supreme Court of Pakistan. It is yet to be seen, however, as to how it will be implemented.

2. *The Prohibition of Gharar (Uncertainty or Uncalled for Risk):* Islamic law is concerned with uncertainty in dealings that may lead to disputes. It, therefore, requires the parties to the contract to be as specific as possible so that their agreements may not give rise to future disputes. This principle has a role to play in the law of contracts, although it may not prove fatal for some contracts. In cases of minor risk, the jurists have permitted some contracts.

It is to be noted here that Muslim economists have tried to derive a rule against speculation in transactions from this principle, especially from the prohibition of sale of food before possession. This appears to be an exaggeration as it attempts to grant a role to this principle that the law does not recognise. Even is such transactions the law is concerned with uncertainty that may lead to disputes. The law does not attempt to curtail profits or to fix prices, and there are clear traditions on this issue. The economists, therefore, need to rethink the issue of speculation.

Further, it is not clear how far the principle of uncertainty leading to disputes should be emphasised. It is true that there are texts that may be interpreted to mean this, yet the same texts may be interpreted another way to indicate something else. For example, the economists have interpreted them to mean speculation (which is an interpretation with which we do not agree). The principle of uncertainty or concern for uncertainty is a sign of a legal system that is not fully developed. Concern for it was valid during the days of the earlier jurists, but today the law is much more sophisticated and has built in mechanisms to deal with it. Roscoe Pound, for example, while studying a few pages from the *Hedaya* was struck by this feature and said that it is the sign of primitive law to be concerned too much with certainty.

3. *Principle of Liability for Loss and Entitlement to Profit:* This principle is stated in a tradition of the Prophet (PBUH): *al-kharaj bi al-daman.* It means, first, that profit from something or revenue belongs to the person who is bearing the liability for loss of the thing. In the opposite inference, it means that any person who is benefitting from a property will be liable for its loss. In the former sense, the principle is crucial for contracts of partnership and *muddarabah,* while in the latter meaning it tells the jurist about the liability of bearing the loss if a property is destroyed or converted during a sale. The principle covers the rule of *res perit domino—the loss falls on the owner* of Western law, but has a much wider application.
4. *Principle of Unjustified Enrichment:* This principle is called *akl al-mal bi al-Batul.* It is based upon a verse of the Quran: "Do not consume your wealth among yourselves through unlawful means." In Western law, the principle states that "no one will be allowed to enrich himself (unlawfully) at the expense of another." It plays a role in contracts as well as torts. The principle has a wide and general application in Islamic law.

The combined operation of these principles determines the nature of the Islamic law of contract. Today, if the state were to redraft the law of contract in accordance with the provisions of the *Shariah* it would have, at a minimum, to keep in view these fundamental principles. This is not to say that these are the only principles that are operative in Islamic law of contract. There are other principles too, but these principles have a very wide application and cover the entire range of contracts, whatever their nature. In fact, many other principles may be said to be corollaries of these major principles.

Principles Derived by the Jurist from a Number of Existing Cases in the Law : Principles derived by the jurists are called *qawaid fiqhiyya.* Today, the most popular and well known source of such principles are books entitled *al-Ashba wa al-nazair.* A few paragraphs above, while describing the output of *ijtihad,* we have seen that *Ibn Abidin* cautions us against such books. The reason is that the principles should be checked first from their authentic sources and so should the cases listed under them.

The first jurists who derived such principles were the *Hanafis.* The leading works in this area are those of *al-Karkhi* and *al-Dabusi.* There are stories about how the *Hanafi* jurists tried to keep these principles secret and the *Shafii's* tried to obtain them through ingenious means. Even if such stories are not true, they indicate that the development of the discipline of the *qawaid* in the other schools was an afterthought. *Al-Subki* states that it was the great *Shafii* jurist, the *Imam al-Haramayn,* who asked his students to gather the principles, and he described a principle as "something that is remembered when the detail is forgotten." In any case, *Shafii* jurists like *al-Subki* and *al-Suyuti* compiled excellent books called *al-Ashba wa al-Nazair* that contain a number of principles. Surprisingly, it was the *Hanafi* jurist, *Ibn Nujaym* from Egypt, who compiled a book with the same title borrowing the method used by the *Shafii* jurists. The *Majallat al-Ahkam Al-Adliyya* mentions one hundred such principles in the first chapter.

The principles listed here are from *al-Dabusi.* It should be noted, however, that those who are interested in learning how these principles have been employed throughout the law should study *al-Sarakhsi's* famous book *al-Mabsut. Al-Sarakhsi* mentions the *asl* and then shows how it is used. The sources as a whole for tracing the general principles of Islamic law are as follows:

- Principles listed by *al-Karkhi* and *al-Dabusi.* This is the earliest collection of principles in Islamic law, and is presented in the books called *Tasis al-Nazar* and *Usul al-Karkhi.*
  (*Hanafi* works—fourth and early fifth century of the Hijrah).
- *Al-Sarkhsi's* works—*al-Mabsut* and commentary on *al-Siyar*—are an excellent source not only for the principles, but for their use and application.
  (*Hanafi*—5th century *Hijrah*).

- The monumental work of the *Maliki* jurist *al-Qarafi* called *al-Furuq*. It deals with the principles and the art of distinguishing cases. (7th century Hijrah).
- Books called *al-Ashba wa al-Nazair* by *al-Subki* and *al-Suyuti* (both *Shafii*) and by *Ibn Nujaym*. *(Hanafi)*
- The works of the *Maliki* jurist *al-Wanshirisi*.
- The book called *al-Qawaid* by *Ibn Rajab (Hanbali)*.
- The *Majalla* lists about a 100 principles. An explanation of these principles is available in a book by *Mustafa Zarqa*.
- The Islamic Fiqh Academy (OIC) has commissioned an encyclopaedia of general principles. In response, a Saudi scholar has published an encyclopaedia on his own. Unfortunately, he has mixed up rules of literal construction as well as principles of *usul al-fiqh* with the principles of law *(fiqh)*, but it appears that this is how he found them in some works.

Examples of Principles from Al-Dabusi : Abu Zaid, Ubayd Allahibn, Umar ibn, Isa al-Dabusi was a *Qadi* and jurist. His understanding of the principles is unmatched in Islamic law. He states a principle upheld by a jurist of the Hanafi school and then states the opposing principle held by a jurist of the same school or of another school. The principle is then elaborated through cases.

1. The principle according to *Abu Hanifah* is that if a substantial and agreed upon irregularity *(fasad)* enters a contract it spreads throughout the contract. Thus, if a person buys two slaves in a single bargain and it turns out that one of them was a freeman, the contract becomes *fasid* due to this reason. The two disciples maintain that the contract is valid with respect to the slave.
2. The principle according to *Abu Hanifah* is that the *dhimmis* are to be left alone to practice what they believe and to practice their faith. The two disciples maintain that they are not to be left alone to do so.
3. The principle according to *Abu Hanifah* is that if the cause of *itlaf* (damage; destruction; injury) precedes ownership of the owner, it does not obligate *daman* (compensation; damages) on the offender (tortfeasor) in favour of the latest owner. Thus, if a person cuts off the hand of a slave and the owner sells him off and thereafter the inflammation spreads causing loss of life due to the injury, while in the possession of the buyer, then, the offender is not liable for compensation either to the seller or to the buyer. The two disciples disagree.

4. The principle according to *Abu Hanifah* is that if absolute permission (general attorney) is exercised without any imputation or claim of breach of trust, the act (of the attorney) is not to be determined on the basis of prevalent practice (*urf*). The two disciples maintain that it is to be so determined.
5. The principle according to *Abu Yusuf* and *Muhammad* is that what is performed in accordance with the directive of the *shar* (law) is to be deemed to have been performed with the permission of the person having authority *(wilayah)*. According to *Abu Hanifah* this is to be accepted with the condition of proper performance. Thus, if a person shoots at a hunted animal, but misses and hits a human, he is to be held liable.
6. The principle according to *Abu Hanifah* is that the ownership of an apostate *(murtadd)* is lost by the very act of apostasy, a loss of ownership that is suspended (till further legal action). The two disciples as well as *al-Shafii* maintain that ownership is not lost, unless the *Qadi* passes an order about his having crossed over to the *dar al-harb.*
7. The principle according to *Abu Yusuf* is that the conditions pertaining to a contract after its conclusion are considered to exist at the time of the contract. According to *Abu Hanifah* and *Muhammad* they are not to be considered to exist at the time of the contract.
8. The principle according to *Abu Yusuf* is that it is permitted that a thing be considered secondary to another thing even if there is an independent *hukm* for it. According to *Muhammad* if a thing has a *hukm* of its own it does not become secondary to another. *Abu Hanifah* sides with *Abu Yusuf* in most cases under this principle.
9. The principle according to *Abu Yusuf* is that the affirmation of the right of Allah in a thing erodes the title of ownership of the owner. According to Muhammad it does not erode it.
10. The principle according to our three jurists is that it is possible that a thing remain suspended in contracts and other things due to an attribute that is to arise or is to develop in it, but according to Zufar when a thing is declared valid or vitiated it cannot be converted to another form due to an attribute that is to take place or arise in it, except by re-conclusion or renewal.
11. The principle according to our three jurists is that an obstacle to a contract toward the end has a *hukm* different from the state of the contract at the beginning. According to Zufar it has the same *hukm* as the state at the beginning.

12. The principle according to *Ibn Abi Layla* with respect to *muamalat* is that a contract rescinded in part is rescinded as a whole.
13. The principle according to *Ibn Abi Layla* is that rights of Allah are taken into account through rights of individuals.
14. The principle according to our jurists is that a matter that is not litigated before a *Qadi* is not affected by a minor uncertainty *(jahala)* nor by an excess of it with respect to vitiation. According to *Ibn Abi Layla* a small amount of uncertainty does not vitiate a contract, but when it is excessive it does vitiate the contract (concept of voidable).
15. The principle according to *Ibn Abi Layla* is that a single right cannot be established in two independent subject-matters, because its operation in one subject-matter eliminates it from the first subject-matter.
16. The principle according to our jurists is that the opinion of a Companion is to be preferred over analogy if it is not opposed by any of the Companions, because it is not proper to say that he said it by way of analogy as analogy contradicts it and it is also not proper to say that he said it by guesswork—the presumption is that he said it after hearing it from the Prophet (PBUH). According to *Imam al-Shafii* analogy is preferred because he does not follow precedents from the Companions *(taqlid)* nor does he adopt their opinions.
17. The principle in our view is that things compensated are owned through prior liability and ownership is extended in them till the time of compensation when the property in question is one that is capable of being owned through consent. According to *Imam Shafii* things compensated are not owned through *daman* (liability).
18. The principle according to our jurists is that the world is divided into two *dars: dar al-Islam* and *dar al-harb.* According to *Imam al-Shafii* the entire world is a single *dar.*
19. The principle in our view is that each member of a woman's *asabah* who is in charge of his own affairs is her guardian, and it is permitted to him to give her away in marriage if she is a minor, and with her consent if she is a major, like the father and grandfather.
20. The principle in our view is that anyone who is guilty of a transgression (tort) against another person by way of taking away his property is not liable for the cutting of the hand if the property is destroyed (lost) while in his possession, as in the case of *ghasb.*
21. The principle in our view is that the permissibility of sale follows *daman* (liability for loss), thus, anything that is to be compensated due to

destruction may be sold, but a thing that is not compensated in case of destruction cannot be sold. According to *Imam al-Shafii* the permissibility of sale follows ritual purity, thus, anything that is ritually pure may be sold, but a thing that is not pure may not be sold.

Al-Dabusi on the Methodology of the Faqih : The question is what are these distinctive principles that are different from those prevailing in other systems? When the state steps in to enforce the law, a new element is visible. There is a need to deal in rules covering not one but many situations. Further, the area under the jurisdiction of the state is much wider and it makes laws for situations that cannot be determined through the explicit evidences in the Quran. The state has to rely on broad general principles.

The jurists did not assume such a wide authority for themselves and they confined themselves to those norms that they found directly stated in the texts. The reason is that they were dealing with that part of the law that would remain stable and complete irrespective of the backing of the state.

In other words, it would be possible for a Muslim to practise this law even in a non-Muslim state. Today, the state may use general rules based on the principles of Islamic law to cover the entire area of contracts. In fact, the jurists were fully aware of the possibility of the extension of the law and use of general principles. The situation is summed up by *al-Karkhi* in a comprehensive principle:

The principle is that if for a new case, the seeker does not find an answer or a precedent in the books of our school, then, it is necessary for him to derive the answer from other sources, either from the Book or from the *Sunnah* or from other evidences, moving from the strongest to the stronger, however, the *hukm* will not lie outside of these principles.

Al-Nasafi (the commentator) said: The settled issues have been derived from these principles, and new cases and incidents can be derived from them as well. This principle is designed to lay down a methodology. It indicates that there are principles derived by the jurists that will usually help settle a case, but these principles are derived from, and operate around, another set of principles that are laid down in the Quran, the *Sunnah* and other evidences like *ijma.* The jurists must be aware of their operation during his study and application of the law. In other words, the principles are to be "read in" by the jurist when he is trying to discover or interpret a law.

The methodology of extending the law from these general principles to new cases has been implemented in the works of *Hanafi* jurists, especially in the monumental works of *al-Sarakhsi.* It is the duty of researchers to highlight this methodology and to show how the law may be extended to new cases. In fact, such research is already under way.

The Faqih may Formulate a New Principle if it Meets the Prescribed Conditions : As shown in the discussion of *maslahah mursalah,* the jurist may formulate a new principle and then check it for compatibility with the purposes of Islamic law and the primary general principles. If the principle is compatible he can construct his reasoning on the basis of this new principle. This is the only way that the law will be extended. In fact, this type of legal reasoning is the essence of the methodology of *takhrij.* It yields a legal structure in which the automatic generation of new principles takes place.

Conclusion : Islamic law has a chance of rapid development if the methodology of the *faqih,* based on reasoning from principles, is developed and linked to that of modern judges and lawyers of higher courts. God knows best.

References

---

1. *Islamic Theory propounded by Imam Jafar As-Sadiq (Shiite Sect).*
2. *Jibbrail : the archangel who would bring revelation to the prophet (PBUH).*
3. *Suhuf : Divine books, like, the Torah, the Injeel, the Zaboor.*
4. *A Caliph of the Prophet (PBUH).*
5. *A great scholar of Islamic law; founder of Shafa'z' School.*
6. *A great scholar of Islamic law; founder of Hanbali School.*
7. *Prominent scholar of Muttazilait sect.*
8. *Reason or purpose or the context in which a revelation was made.*

9-10. *Famous Scholars of Islamic law from the school of Hanafiits.*

11. *Tradition of the Holy Prophet (PBUH).*
12. *Father of Prophet Yusuf (PBUH).*

4

Holy Quran, the First Source

The Covenant

What is the consequence of abstracting the text and treating it symbolically? Our impression is that such an interpretative approach either becomes trivialising or fascist. The trivialising aspect comes about because truths are abstracted from their context and end up being recorded as bland statements, like 'Islam is peace', or 'Islam teaches us to be just', or '*Jihad* means to struggle for peace'. In such a context, how important could careful adherence to the *ahkam* (legal properties) be? The fascist part comes about because the key interpreter gets to play games with symbols that are manipulated exclusively by him and his cohorts. In that context, external or outward or literal Islam, with its laws and regulations, is so much drivel for people not sufficiently elevated. (One could call the first approach *ibahiyyah* and the second *batiniyyah).*

Holy Quran First : In contrast, the consequence of closer readings of the revelation, of more grammatically aware and precise readings, of increased attention to the tiniest details of the revelation in its original language is, ironically, a discovery of a polysemantic and multifaceted text. The broadest, most varied and dynamic, vibrant and living understanding of the revelation comes from the closest, most careful, detailed, linguistic, and literally based reading. It happens too that the closest fidelity to the *ahkam* (such as those related to placing one's hands while standing during the *salah,* for example) opens up a range of authentic and true positions. Instead of denigrating the truth of following normative practices by trivialising them, this interpretation invests great significance and relevance to multiple true positions; instead of in-group fascism, this interpretation affirms other true positions, without denying any one of them.

In one passage we saw *Ibn al-Arabi* incorporating the peculiar linguistic fact that in the Arab language the word *khafiya is* its own antonym, such that, for those of the perception, the Hidden is the Manifest, the exposed is the concealed. When I mentioned this to a colleague of mine, she said that the secrets of the Quran are safely hidden away—in the outside, literal text! As with Poe's purloined letter, the best place to hide something is in the most exposed place. The *haqqiqah* is the *Shariah.*

Let us examine the depths, details, and particularities of one portion of a verse to show what kind of polysemanticism comes about with a close; literal reading of the revelation. This portion of a verse in the chapter *al-Maidah* sets down the description of *wudu.* The portion reads, *O you who believe. When you go to the salah, wash your faces and your hands to the elbows and wipe your heads and your feet to the ankles [5:6].* The two operative imperatives are wash *(ghusl)* and wipe (m.s.h.). The question is which imperative governs the phrase 'your feet'.

Wiping is where wet hands brush over the bodily part in question, whether head or foot. Wiping the feet entails a brisk movement similar to the wiping over the shoes, and *Sunni* scholars have generally believed this movement of wiping over the bare feet to be negated by the *Hadith* evidence in which the Prophet Muhammad (PBUH) admonished a group of Muslims to pay attention to their heels in *wudu,* saying, 'Woe to the heels in hell-fire'.'

This particular line of argument unfolds as follows. The obvious and literal meaning of the verse in the Quranic Arabic indicates the feet, much as in English 'wipe your heads, and your feet', means 'wipe your heads, and wipe your feet'. But the *Hadith* seems to indicate 'washing' the feet, so as to make sure the heels are covered in *wudu*[6]. How should these two different indications be reconciled? We examine some of the major arguments which seek to do just that below, and then we examine *Ibn al-Arabi's* treatment of this issue.

Let us look first at three areas essential to this *fiqh* debate. First, the recitations involved for the verse; that is, the authentic, correct *(sahih)* recitations of the word 'your feet'. Second, the list of authorities and what method of *wudu* of the feet they practised, and why. Third, the arguments proffered by scholars over the ages to address this issue. The raw citations and data are to give the reader a glimpse of the intricacies and fine points of the classical scholarly discourse, where the direction one moves toward truth is not outwards abstraction and generalisation, but inwards detail and specificity. As with fractal geometries, Escher's drawings, Borges and Eco's writings, the 'truth' of things lies in the patterns one perceives as one peers closely and with a narrower field of view. The weight of this massive debate should demonstrate the futility of the desire for conclusion and answers, and should begin to show us instead the value of searching for polysemanticism in randomness, complexities, and ambiguities.

Melodious Reading

There are three recitations of 'your feet', namely *arjulakum* (with *nasb),* *arjulikum* (with *khafd),* and *arjulukum* (with *raft*) :

1. The first recitation is recited by *Nafi-ibn-Abu-Nuaym*[2] (169/785), *Asim-ibn-Abu-al-Nujud*[3] (127/744), and *Ali-ibn-Hamzah-al-Kasai*[4] (189/801).
2. The second recitation of *arjulikum* with *khafd* is that of *Abd-Allah-Ibn-Kathir*[5] (120/737), *Abu-Amr-ibn-al-Ala*[6] (1455/771), and *Hamzah-ibn-Habib*[7] (156/772).
3. For the third recitation, *Nafi* is reported, by *Walid ibn Muslim,* to have also recited *arjulukum* with *raft*, and it is the recitation of *Hassan*[8] and *al-Amash Sulayman?*

Generally, but not necessarily, as we shall see, the recitation of *arjulakum* supports a reading that implies that the operative imperative here is 'wash'; the recitation of *arjulikum* supports a reading that implies that the operative imperative is the proximate verb 'wipe'; and the rare recitation *arjulukum* supports a reading that implies that either of the two imperatives are operative—wipe *and wash* your feet.

Effective Authorities : The following are authoritative positions of early Muslims.

Arjulakum : Washing

Urwah ibn Zubayr (nasb): recorded in *Ibn Mundhir.*

Mujahid ibn Jabr (nasb): in *Ibn Mundhir.*

Nafi ibn Abd al-Rahman (nasb): reported from *Abu Ubayd,* in *Ibn Mundhir.*

Qusai (nasb): in *Ibn Mundhir.*

Abu Ubayd al-Qasim ibn Salam (nasb): in *Ibn Mundhir.*

Al-Shafii (nasb): in *Ibn Mundhir.*

Ali (nasb): al-Qurtubi records, *'Asim ibn Kalib* reported from *Abd al-Rahman* that he said, *Hassan* and *Hussain,* Allah's mercy on them, recited *wa arjulakum,* and Ali heard that, and was adjudicating between the people, and said *arjulakum.'* *Ibn Mundhir* confirms that *Ali* recited with *nasb.*

Arjulakum : Wiping

Ibn Masud : *(nasb :* wiping);

Ibn Abbas (nasb : wiping): *al-Qurtubi* records, 'It was reported from *Ibn Abbas* that he said *wudu* is two washings [arms and face] and two wipings [head and feet]'. *Ibn Qudamah* records, 'It is related from *Ibn Abbas* that he said, I do not find in the Book of Allah anything but two washings and two wipings."

Ibn Kathir records that *Ibn Abbas*[9] wiped the feet. He says, *'Ibn Abu Hatim* said, *haddathana* my father *haddathana Abu Mamar al-Mungari haddathana Abd al-Wahhab Haddathana Ali ibn Zaid* from *Yusuf ibn Mohrin* from *Ibn Abbas* about this verse that it is a wiping. '

Ibn Majah records in his *Sunan, 'haddathana Abu Bakr ibn Abi Shaybah haddathana Ibn Ulayyah,* from *Ruhi ibn al-Qasim from Abd-Allah ibn Muhammad ibn Aqil from Rubayya,* who said, *Ibn Abbas* came to me and he asked me about this *Hadith,* that is, the *Hadith* in which it was mentioned that the messenger of Allah *(sallallahu alayhi wa sallam)* did *wudu* and washed his feet. *Ibn Abbas* said, "The people insist on nothing but washing, but I do not find in the Book of Allah anything but wiping"."

Arjulikum : Wiping

Al-Hassan al-Basri : in *Ibn Mundhir.*

Sulayman ibn Mohrin al-Amash : in *Ibn Mundhir.*

Abu Jafar : al-Razi records, 'The people disagree about wiping the feet and washing them', and *Ibn Abbas, Anas ibn Malik, Ikrimah, Shubi,* and *Abu Jafar Muhammad ibn Ali* obligate wiping, and it is the position of the *Imamiyyah* among the Shia.'

Ikrimah ibn Abd-Allah: al-Qurtubi records, *'Ikrimah* used to wipe his feet. He said there is no washing for the feet: The Quran was sent down with wiping them.' He also records that *Ibn Jarar* said, *'haddathana* Yaqub *haddathana* Ibn Uliyah *haddathana* Ayub who said, "I saw *Ikrimah* wiping his feet, and he argued for it".'

Abu Dharr: Ibn Hajar (852) in *Fath al-Bari* records that to the *Hadith* 'woe to the heels in hell-fire', *Abu Dharr* added, 'And he did not wipe his feet."

Al-Qatadah : al-Qurtubi records that *al-Qatadah ibn Daamah* (117/ 735) said, 'Allah made required two washings and two wipings.'

Arjulikum : Washing

Amr ibn Sharhbil al-Shubah : in *Ibn Mundhir.* He is recorded as saying, 'The Quran came down with wiping but the Sunna is for washing.'

Al-Thalab : Ibn Manzur in *Lisan al-Arab* cites *Abu al-Abbas al-Thalab* (291/903) as saying, 'The Quran came down revealing wiping but the Sunna is for washing."

Anas : al-Qurtubi records that *Al-Hajjaj ibn Yusuf al-Thaqafi* (95/ 714), governor of the eastern provinces, 'gave a *Khutba* in Ahwaz and mentioned *wudu.* He said, "Wash your faces and hands and wipe your heads and feet because there is nothing of the sons of *Adam* closer to filth than his feet, so wash them, their bottoms and their tops, and their tendons." *Anas ibn Malik* heard that and said, "Allah spoke the truth and *Hajjaj* spoke a lie, because Allah said, Wipe your heads *wa arjulikum.* When he wiped his feet, he (simply) moistened them".' *Al-Qurtubi* also records, 'It is also reported from *Anas* that he said the Quran was sent down with wiping but the Sunna is with washing.' *Ibn Mundhir* records the above from *Ibn Umar* and also records, *'haddathana* Ismail *haddathana Abu Bakr haddathana Muhammad ibn Abi Adwi* from his father that Anas used to wash his hands and feet until they dripped.'

Ibn Kathir records the same story about *Hajjaj: 'Ibn Jarar* said *haddathani Yaqub ibn Ibrahim haddathana* Ibn Uliyah *haddathana* Hamid who said *Musa ibn Anas* said to *Anas,* when we were with him, O *Abu Hamzah, Hajjaj* gave us a *Khutba*[10] in *Ahwaz,* while we were with him and he mentioned purification. He said, "Wash your faces and wipe your heads and feet because there is nothing of the sons of *Adam* closer to filth than his feet, so wash them, their bottoms and their tops, and their tendons." Anas heard that and said, *Hajjaj* spoke a lie: Allah said, *Wipe your heads wa arjulikum.* When Anas wiped the feet, he moistened them. The chain is authentic.' *Ibn Kathir* also confirms: *'Ibn Jarar* said *haddathana* Ali ibn Sahl *haddathana* Mumal *haddathana* Hammad *haddathana Asim* about the case of Anas, and he said. The Quran came down with wiping but the Sunna is for washing. This too has an authentic chain.'

The Cleanliness

Hassan (combine): *al-Zamakhshari* records that *Hassan* said, 'It is a combining of two matters.' He also records, *'Hassan* recited *arjulukum* with *raf,* with the meaning *wa arjulukum,* washed or wiped to the ankles'.

Daud (combine): *al-Razi* records that *Daud al-Isfahani al-Zahiri* obligates combining the two; it is also the position of *al-Nasir* of the *Zaidis.*

Al-Nuhhas (combine): *al-Qurtubi*[11] records, '*al-Nahhas* said one of the best things said about the issue is that wiping and the washing are both obligatory together, so the wiping is obligatory because of the recitation of one who recites *nasb,* and the two recitations have the status of two verses.'

Arjulikum or Arjulakum : Wash or Wipe

Al-Tabari (choice): *al-Qurtubi* records that '*Ibn Jarar al-Tabari* (310/ 922) judged that required for the feet is to choose between the washing and the wiping.' *Al-Razi* adds that this was *Hassan al-Basri's* position too, recording, 'The position of *Hassan-al-Basri*[12] and *Muhammad-ibn-Jarar-al-Tabari*[13] is that the one responsible [for *wudu]* chooses between wiping and washing.' *"Ibn al-Arabi al-Maliki* records that *Muhammad ibn Jarar al-Tabari,* reasoned that the recitation *is arjulikum* with *khafd* in conjunction with the head, so the head and feet are wiped, and the recitation with *nasb is* in conjunction with the face and arms, so they are washed; so in that way it functions in accordance with both recitations." *Al-Nawawi* adds, "*Jubbai,* the head of the *Mutazilahs,* chose between wiping and washing'."

IMPORTANT DISCUSSION

Arguments from Sunna : The conclusive argument for the classical *Sunni* scholars for washing is based on *Sunna.* A terse argument for washing is that given by *Ibn al-Arabi al-Maliki,* who says, 'Our proof is the continuous practice *[amal al-muttasil,* that is, from the time of the Prophet (Pbuh) to today, of washing the feet] and the multiple unbroken chains of transmitted text *[naql al-mutawatir]'.* Related to this argument for washing is the consensus of the scholars, described by *Al-Qurtubi* as his last proof, namely.

Consensus *[ujma].* They agree that the one who washed his feet has in fact fulfilled his obligation, but they disagree about one who has wiped his feet. Certainty is with what they have agreed about and not with what they have disagreed about. The transmitted tradition of all the vast majority *[jamhur]* is from their Prophet (Pbuh) that he washed his feet in his *wudu,* once, twice, and thrice, until he had cleaned them.

But while the *Sunna* is to wash, this was not always the case. *Ibn Qudamah* reports, 'Said *haddathana* Hashim that *akhbarana* [it was told us in the form of a report] *Ibn Ata* from his father that he said *akhbarani* [it was told me in a report] *Aus ibn Aus Abi al-Thaqafi* that he saw the Prophet (PBUH) come to a *kizamah* of the people of Taif, and he did *wudu* and wiped his feet. *Hashim* said this was in the initial period of Islam.' Interestingly, the *Sunna* of washing is so established that when *Ibn Manzur* cites this *Hadith* in order to explain *kizamah* in his dictionary, he says this:

> 'The *kizamah* is a pipe under the ground and water flows through it. It is mentioned in the *Hadith* that the Prophet came to a *kizamah* of the people and did *wudu* with its water and wiped over his *shoes'*. But besides the argument from *Sunna,* the classical *Sunni* scholars also provide numerous arguments for washing based on the Quran. Most of these arguments are linguistic, but some fall into other categories. Let us look at the other categories first.

Symbolic Arguments : *Al-Zamakhshari* (d.538) in his commentary *Kashshaf* records *wa arjulikum* and says, 'The majority recite *arjulakum* with *nasb,* thereby indicating that the feet are to be washed. If someone asked me why did you [O *Zamakhshari*] make it recite with *jarr* [that is, *khalf arjulikum]* and make the admission of a property of wiping [when you actually argue for washing the feet], I would say that the feet are among the three bodily parts washed with a pouring of water on them, so they are places of anticipated wastefulness—that is blameworthy, and actual wastefulness is forbidden—so the feet are placed in conjunction with the third part, which is wiped (i.e., the head), not so as to wipe them, but in order to remind one of the obligation of frugality in pouring water over them.'

So avoiding waste is a consideration which explains away the linguistic inclination toward wiping. This argument relies neither on the *Sunna* of *wudu* nor on other linguistic possibilities. This is *al-Zamakhshari's* major argument, and it is repeated by many of the great classical scholars.

Another argument which does not rely on the *Sunna* nor on linguistic evidence appeals to a sense of symmetry in *taharah.* The argument is recorded by *Al-Qurtubi* in this way:

> *Amr al-Shabi* said *Jibbrail* sent down wiping: Do you not see that *tayammum* has wiping for what was washed [in *wudu*—hands and face] and eliminates what was wiped [in *wudu*—head and feet]?

Ibn Kathir uses this argument too, recording that

Ibn Jarar said *haddathana Abu al-Sayb haddathana* Ibn Idris from *Daud ibn Abu Hind* from *Shaabi* that he said, Jibbrail came down with wiping, then *Shaabi* said, Do you not see that *tayammum* is wiping what was washed and it eliminates what was wiped?

Ibn Qudamah uses this argument as well.

Linguistic Arguments : Now let us turn to the linguistic arguments. I have collated six different linguistic arguments. These include attempts to show that it is possible in the Arab language (meaning the Arabs have used such a linguistic configuration in the period before and during the descent of the Quran) to have 'your feet' be governed by the initial verb 'wash'.

The first linguistic argument we consider is lexigraphic. *Al-Qurtubi* records, *Abu Zaid al-Ansari* [215 A. H./830 C. E.] said, wiping in the Arab language is washing and wiping. An example is that the Arab says about someone after *wudu* who has washed the limbs that *tamassaha* [he has wiped].' This argument accepts that 'your feet' is governed by the proximate verb 'wipe', but goes on to posit that `wipe' in effect means a light washing.

Al-Qurtubi also argues that the word 'wipe' may also apply to 'wash'. However, wipe is usually seen as a subset of wash. The argument of *al-Qurtubi* is that *Abd al-Haqq ibn Atiyah* (546 A. H./1151 C. E.) said, "There are people among those who recite with a *qisrah [khalf]* who judged that the wiping of the two feet is a washing. It is correct that the word wiping shares multiple meanings, applying to wiping and to washing".'

A second argument takes the instances of imperative verb plus a delineated or non-delineated object, as they occur in the verse for wudu and for *tayammum.* We have for *wudu* a clear 'wash the hands to the elbows'. When it comes to *tayammum,* we have a clear 'wipe your face and hands'. Based on these instances, the arguments goes, we see that objects governed by the imperative 'wipe' are not given delineations, and the object that is definitely governed by the imperative 'wash' is given delineation, that is, up to something. Therefore, when we come to 'your feet', and we note that they are delineated with 'up to the ankles', we can conclude that the governing verb must be 'wash'. *Al-Qurtubi* says, 'Allah bounded the area and said *to the ankles* as He said about the arms *to the elbows.* This proves the obligation of washing the feet, but Allah knows best.'

Ibn Hisham in his *Mughni al-Labib* and *al-Zamakhshari* in his commentary on 5:6 say, 'It was said *to the ankles,* so He mentioned the end-point, and that dismisses the supposition that the feet are wiped, because wiping is not given an end-point in the *Shariah.*'

A third argument is based on the idea that the sequence of bodily parts purified in wudu-face, hands, head, feet-is given precedence over syntactical considerations. To illustrate this argument, suppose that the imperatives were given precedence. We would then have, 'Wash your face, hands, and feet, and wipe your head'. But because the head should be washed before the feet, we have, 'Wash face, hands, (but wipe) head, and feet', meaning 'and wash too your feet'.

Al-Qurtubi with this argument, juxtaposes the strong case for wiping based on the Quran and the strong case for washing based on the Surma. Given this tension he argues that there must be an overriding concern which motivates the inclination of the Quranic phrase towards wiping. That concern, he says, is the sequence.

Al-Qurtubi says :

> And it is said, Allah has *wiped* what you have when He has *washed* and purified you from your sins. *So* if it *is* from Arab tradition that the wiping may mean washing, then the statement which preponderates is this statement: *if* the consequences of the recitation with *khalf is* washing. . . and the many *Hadiths* fix washing, and there is the warning not to neglect the washing *of* the feet in the numerous reports published by the Imams, then the wiping for the head *is* rather inserted between the things which are washed [arms and feet] for the sake of sequence, that the head should be wiped before the feet are washed, according to this syntax: so wash your faces and your arms to the elbows, and your feet to the ankles, and wipe your heads. But as the head is done before the feet, it precedes them in the recitation—Allah knows best—not because they share with the head in being wiped, but because the head precedes the feet in the process of purification.

Abu Thawr (d. 240) also explains that there must be some overriding concern which interrupts the list of bodily parts and their imperative verbs. He says that the reason your 'feet is placed' after 'your head' is not because it should take the imperative 'wipe', but because the verse is rather establishing the sequence of *wudu.* He says, 'The munificent verse mentioned something wiped [the head] among the things washed.

The custom of the Arab when he mentioned like things and unlike things [e.g., wiped and washed bodily parts] is to gather the like things and then to put the other thing in conjunction to them [last], and that custom is not opposed except for a bounty, and the bounty, here, is the [teaching of the] sequence [of *wudu]."* *Ramli* [d. 1004] uses this argument too in his commentary to the *Minhaj* called *Nahayat al-Muhtaj.*

A fourth argument is that in the Arab language before the descent of the Quran, there is a kind of poetic sentence which puts two objects into conjunction, but where the second object is not governed by the same verb as the first object. This would explain how the Quranic phrase puts 'your heads' into conjunction with 'your feet'., while the first object is governed by 'wipe' and the second is governed by something else, in this case 'wash'.

Ibn Manzur argues this way in *Lisan al-Arab.* He says, 'So one who recites it *arjulakum* does so for two reasons. First, in this there are things anterior and things posterior, as if He said, 'Then wash your faces and arms to the elbows, and your feet to the ankles, and wipe your heads', thereby putting things first and putting things last so that *wudu* would be a succession of things one after another. Then, it is as if He meant, 'Wash your feet to the ankles' because His statement *to the ankles* has already proven that is just as we described it [that is, the argument of delineation], so 'your feet' is arranged with washing, as the poet said:

If only your husband had come tomorrow!

Armed with sword, and lance

meaning 'armed with sword, and carrying a lance', where the verb 'carrying' is supplied, as 'armed' is an inappropriate verb for 'lance'. *Ibn al-Arabi al-Maliki* uses the same verse to show that the noun of 'feet' may be in conjunction with the word 'head' but not in conjunction with its meaning (that is, 'wipe'), like the poet's verse:

I saw your husband, clamoring

Armed with sword, and lance.

Al-Qurtubi multiplies the examples of this use of language. He says, 'The Arab puts something in conjunction with something with an act which applies to only one of them. The Arab says, "I ate bread, and milk", meaning, "I ate bread and I drank milk".' Another example is the statement of the poet:

I fed them straw, and cold water.

Another example is [from *Labid ibn Rabiah*]:

The two used the leaves of the cabbage plant, Giving birth

On the banks to her gazelle, and her brood.

Another example is:

I drank milk, and dates and cheese.

'The *taqdir* [the meaning of sentences with ambiguous syntactical elements] is as follows: I fed them straw, and gave them water to drink; the one giving birth on the banks to her gazelle; and the other brooding her ostrich (the ostrich does not 'give birth to' but rather 'broods' the egg); and finally, I'drank the milk, and I ate the dates.

So, His phrase *Wipe your heads, and your feet* could be in conjunction with washing in spite of the conjunction with wiping, carrying the meaning and purport of washing. But Allah knows best.'

Al-Jurjani (d. *816), al-Zamakhshari's* commentator, also uses the poet's verses:

Armed with sword, and lance

And feeding the animal straw, and cold water.

A fifth argument is based on the different instances of *jarr,* which means the vowel 'i' *(khafd)* given to a word because of proximity. *Al-Qurtubi* finds this in the Quran, where we have, *Sent down to you will be a flame of fire, and smoke (55:35),* where 'and smoke' *is muhasin* (in some recitations), which *is khafd* because of *jarr,* because 'the smoke' means 'fumes', so the meaning is 'sent down to you will be *smoke,* and a *flame* of fire', where *smoke* and *flame* are the direct objects of the sentence, even though *smoke* is in *khafd.*

Also, *al-Qurtubi* adds, 'He said, *No, it is a glorious Quran, in a tablet preserved' (85:21-2).* Here *preserved is mahfuz-in,* which *is khafd* because of *jarr.* In this sentence, *Quran-un, majid-un,* and preserved are all nominatives (raft so that one would say, 'It is a Quran, it is glorious, and it is preserved, in a tablet', but instead of *mahfuz-un,* we have *mahfuz-in,* which is explained as being from proximity to *fi lawh-in* (in a tablet).'

Al-Qurtubi also cites *Imru al-Qays,* who said: *kabir-u unas-in* fi *bijad-in muzammal-i* meaning, 'He is great among the people, in his striped garment, wrapped up.' *Al-Qurtubi* remarks, *'muzammal-i is* made *khafd* by proximity, because "wrapped up" refers to the man, not to the striped garment, so that its inflected termination would otherwise be *raf".'*

He also says, 'It is like the Arabs say, *hadha juhr-u dabb-in kharib-in* [this hole of a lizard, deserted]. The word *kharib-in* [deserted] is made *jarr* even though it would be *raf.'* That is, the sentence reads, 'this deserted hole of a lizard.' He says, 'This is the position of *Akhfash* and *Abu Abidah,* but *al-Nahhas* rejected it and said this statement is a great error, because it cannot be that the proximate be brought into relationship with something in such a sentence, but it is really an error, like changing the vowel to achieve a rhyme.'

Ibn Kathir remarks that the recitation with *khafd is* 'produced because of proximity and the relationship [to wipe your heads] in the sentence, as in the Arab's sentence *juhr-u dabb-in kharib-in,* and as in His statement, *They will have on them clothes of silk, green, and brocade [76:21].* This is common in the language of the Arab.'

The grammarian *Ibn Hiṣham* says, 'A word gives governance to another word when it is in proximity to it, like the statement of some of them: *hadha juhr-u dabb-in kharib-in* with *jarr* but most of them make it *raf.*' That *is, kharib-un;* this is a hole *(juhr-u)*, deserted *(kharib-un)*, of a lizard *(dabb-in)*. He also cites *Imru al-Qays's* verse:

ka-anna abanan fi *afanini wadqihi*

kabir-u unas-in fi *bijad-in muzammali.*

Ibn Hisham al-Ansari also argues from a passage in 56:11-22, which reads in part, 'These will be nearest to Allah, in gardens of bliss .... Circling them will be ever fresh youth, with goblets, glasses, and cups ... and fruits ... and flesh of fowl ... and black/white eye'." One question in this passage is what governs the phrases. *Ibn Hisham*[14] notes that some take 'black/white eye' as *jarr*, that *is*, *hur-in*, so that 'black/white eye' is governed by 'ever fresh youth'. The meaning is then 'ever fresh youth ... with black/white eye'. But the conjunction could go all the way back to 'gardens of bliss'. Then, we would have 'gardens of bliss', with 'many fruits', and 'flesh of fowl', and *hur-in ayn-in*, which is then read as a synecdoche, as in 'companions with *hur-in ayn-in*'. *'Cups'* would be in conjunction with 'ever fresh youth', so that it would be 'ever fresh youth, circling them with cups'. But *Ibn Hisham* ends his discussion with the comment, 'Actually, the *khafd* of proximity is rare.'

Ibn Qudamah quotes *Imru al-Qays's* verse which we saw and also:

fa-zalla tuhatu al-lahm min bayni mundij-in

safifa shiwa-in aw qidir-in mu ajjabi

The meat cooks erred between a well-cooked

grilled row and quick boil

where *qidir-an* (cooked in a pot) is made *jarr—qidir—in—by* being in conjunction with what is proximate, but referring back to *al-lahm* (the meat).

Ibn Qudamah also cites the Quran, where we have *inni akhafu alaykum adhaba yawm-in alim-in (I* fear for you the punishment of a grievous day) (11:26), saying that *alim-in is jarr* because of the proximity of 'day', while it is a description of the punishment, which is *nasb* (the direct object), because of its proximity to the proximate *yawm-in.*

But *Ibn Manzur* questions the occurrence of the *khafd* of proximity as proving 'washing' in this verse by citing *Abu Ishaq,* the grammarian, who said, 'Making a noun *khafd* because of proximity is not permitted in the Book of Allah, while it is permissible for poetical imagery.'

Al-Razi too, is doubtful about this argument. He says that the *jarr* of proximity means that the 'feet' are the conjunction with 'wipe your heads', and are governed by 'wipe'. He cites the arguments that this *jarr* is not conclusive, saying 'If it is said no, it is not possible to say that this vowel "i" is there just because of proximity [while "feet" is still in conjunction with "wash your faces"], as it is in the statement:

juhr-u dabb-in kharib-in

and the poet's verse:

kabir anas fi *bijad-in mazmal-i*

we say that is false.' Al-Razi says the above examples may be explained by poetical exigency.

Second, in the above examples, there is no question of ambiguity. In the statement *juhr-u dabb-in kharib-in* the word, 'deserted' cannot be describing the lizard but must be describing the hole. So, he concludes, 'in this verse certainty in the face of ambiguity is not produced.' For al-Razi, the linguistic argument of *jarr* is ultimately inconclusive.

Al-Shawqani cites the possibilities of an argument of *jarr,* but then acknowledges its weakness and sustains an argument from *Sunna.* He says,

The ones who argue that washing the feet is not obligatory, argue from a recitation of *jarr* in His statement *arjulikum* being in conjunction with His statement *your heads.* They say *arjulikum is* one of the [three of the] seven recitations which are authentic. There is an argument for the conjunction being with washing the faces, even though it is recited with the *jarr* of the proximate; this has been related by the majority of the Arab 21 Imams, like *Sibawayh* and *Akhfash,* but it certainly *is* very rare; it differs from the obvious meaning and it cannot sustain the contested position. We argue instead that obligatory is carrying the argument with *his (sallallahu alayhi wa sallam)* consistent practice of washing the feet.

Finally, there is an argument that there is an ambiguity in washing or wiping the feet precisely so that the verse can bear two contexts: wash the feet in one context, and wipe the feet when they are shod.

Al-Qurtubi says, 'It has been said that if the *khafd* of the feet rather mentions restrictively wiping them, it could be for when the feet have shoes on. We learn this restriction from the messenger of Allah, as it is not correct about him that he wiped his feet, except when they were shod. So thereby the messenger of Allah explained with his action the context for washing the feet and the context for wiping them. This is a fine argument.'

Ibn al-Arabi al-Maliki also gives this argument, saying 'Or, the meaning of "wiping" could be for the context of wearing shoes, so the two recitations could be for both contexts [bare feet and shod feet], once *nasb* for the bared feet and once *khafd* for the covered feet.'

Ibn al-Arabi's Position : Ibn al-Arabi alludes to this argument when he discusses the *fiqh* disagreement about what to do when wiping over the shoe when there is a tear in the shoe. He says, 'We argue for wiping what emerges, because we were commanded in the Book of Allah to wipe the feet, so when something of the foot emerges, we wipe it. Thus, there should be no obstacle in wiping the torn shoe where some of the foot sticks out, because the verse's imperative of 'wipe' fits both cases of shod/bare foot.

Ibn al-Arabi reviews the various positions of the *Ulema,* saying, 'The *Ulema* concurred that the feet belong to the bodily parts of *wudu*, but they disagreed about a format of their *taharah,* whether that is through washing, wiping, or choosing between the two.' As we saw, the position of washing is the position of the majority of the classical *Sunni* scholars; the position of wiping is the position of many companions and successors, including *Ibn Abbas, Anas,* and *Ikrimah;* the position of choosing between the two is that of *al-Tabari, Hassan al-Basri, Jubbai, Nasir,* and *Daud.* It is appropriate here to emphasize that *Ibn al-Arabi* is neither part of the *Zahiri* school of jurisprudence associated with *Daud* and *Ibn Hazm,* nor is he a part of the *Shiite* school of thought.

Ibn al-Arabi says, 'Our position is choice' and goes on to say 'the combination is best'. This last phrase probably refers to *al-Nahhas* own position which is characterised by *al-Nahhas* as `one of the best things said about the issue'. We saw above that *al-Qurtubi* recorded, `*al-Nahhas* said one of the best things said about the issue is that the wiping and the washing are both obligatory together, so the wiping is obligatory because of the recitation of one who recites with *khafd* and the washing is obligatory because of the recitation of one who recites with *nasb,* and the two recitations have the status of two verses.'

There is an argument of *Ibn Hisham* found in his classical grammar *Mughni* which holds that the *wa* (and) could have the meaning of *aw (or).* In this case there is a linguistic argument for choice. The argument goes as follows.

The meaning of the *wa* here could be 'choice'. One of (the poets) said,

They said, Go far away, choosing for her

patience 'wa' crying

She said, Crying is healthier if I want revenge.

The meaning then is patience *or* crying if patience is not joined to crying (that is, patience *and* crying).

Ibn al-Arabi's position embraces two themes, ease and relief of difficulty, based on the verse *We did not make for you in the religion any constriction (22:78),* a verse which begins with *jahidu fi Allahi* (exert for Allah) and suggests the *Ijtihad* of effortful exertion to understand the determined properties *(ahkam)* and the many consequences of a polysemantic text.

Wiping and washing are related as two forms of purification, the one being subsumed' in the other. *Ibn al-Arabi* says, 'Know that washing contains wiping from one perspective, so the one who washed has already subsumed wiping in it, just as star light is subsumed in the sun's light.' He acknowledges too that it is possible to see wiping simply as a synonym for washing, as we saw above, saying, 'The one who has wiped did not wash, except in a position of the one who believes, and quotes the Arabs, that "wiping" is a word for "washing", so they are synonymous.'

In *Ibn al-Arabi's fiqh,* each command which is operative in the outwardness is also operative in the inwardness. The command of this verse, therefore, has an inward dimension. He says,

The correct meaning of the *hukm* for the inwardness is that wiping is used for whatever specific practices are necessitated and washing for whatever general practices are necessitated.

Because of this, we propounded choice commensurate with the moment, because perhaps you run to a philanthropist for a designated need, on behalf of an individual himself, then that is in a way station of wiping. And perhaps you run to the king for a need diffused over the entire population, or needs, so that individual would be included in this general public, so this is in a way station of washing in which is subsumed wiping.

Now *Ibn al-Arabi* investigates the linguistic evidence of the verse. He notes, 'As for the reciting of His statement [Wash *your faces,* and *your hands to the elbows, wipe your head] wa arjulukum* [your feet] [5:6], with either *arjula,* or *arjuli*—on account of the letter *wa*—according to whether the *wa* is in conjunction with "wipe", through *khafd,* or in conjunction with "wash", with the vocalisation *arjula.* Our position is that even the recitation *arjula* does not actually contraindicate wiping, because this wa may be the 'and of simultaneity', and the 'and of simultaneity' makes the word *arjula.*'

Even though the recitation of *arjulakum* which we noted above, was generally associated with the argument for taking the initial verb 'wash' as the operative imperative, the argument for wiping is still linguistically strong. *Ibn al-Arabi* then gives examples of the 'and of simultaneity'. He says:

> You say, *qama Zaid wa Umar-an*; and *wa stiwa-al-mau* was *l-khashabatan*; and *wa ma anta wa qasat-an min tharid;* and *wa marrartu bi-Zaid wa Umar-an*. You mean, (I passed *Zaid*) with *Umar*. And likewise for the one who recites [with *nasb*] *Wipe your heads and your arjula, with a.*

So,

The argumentation of the one who argues for wiping, in this verse, is stronger, because his argumentation shares with the proponent for washing in giving expression to the recitation arjula. But one who argues for washing does not share with the proponent for wiping in giving expression to the recitation *arjuli*.

From the verse 'wiping' is stronger, and the proponent for 'wiping' can point to either vocalisation for proof. Among 'our colleagues', *Ibn al-Arabi* says, there are those who 'preponderate the specific over the general, and among them there are those who would preponderate the general over the specific: all of that absolutely.' Using the metaphor developed above, some of our colleagues always go to a specific philanthropist, and others always go to the king. They are not sensitive to the context, but instead go fixedly and rigidly to one place.

Ibn al-Arabi then says,

> But our position is other than that. We walk with the Real according to a determined property *[hukm]* of the circumstance, so we generalize where He generalised, and we make specific where He makes specific.
>
> We do not initiate a property, because one who initiated a property has already initiated in his self Lordship, and the one who has initiated in himself Lordship has already diminished his servanthood, to the extent of this issue. And if he has diminished his servanthood, to that extent, he shall diminish the divine self-disclosure of the Real in him. And if he has diminished the divine self-disclosure of the Real in him, he has diminished his knowledge through his Lord. And if he has diminished his knowledge through his Lord, he is ignorant about Him to the context he diminished it, because if there should appear to that one, the one who diminished it, a property in the world [the macrocosm] or in his world [the microcosm], he would not recognize it. Because of this, our position is that we do not initiate a property in one fell swoop.

Ibn al-Arabi is completely familiar with the range of arguments produced by the legal scholars of his time. Their arguments generally seek closure and finality—although without exception, the final theme among all the classical scholars is 'But Allah knows best.' That is, even though they desire closure and finality, the classical scholars leave the door open to continuing divine guidance. The desire to achieve a single and monolithic understanding of Islam is a perennial problem. Every *Qadi* who ever insisted on having the right to use *ijtihad* to settle cases, using any of the schools of jurisprudence which best applied for that particular case, was also fighting against the desire of the sultan and state to codify and impose a Procrustean vision of Islam.

So the sum consequence of the polysemantic text of washing/wiping the feet is 'that or perhaps that', or 'this and that'. The more one knows about this verse, the more one is aware of not knowing. For *Ibn al-Arabi,* the response to 'not knowing' is not *qiyas* or *ray* but *taqwa,* becoming protected by Allah through doing acts which will protect oneself from His punishment (which is its Arabic definition).

Interestingly enough, the conclusion or last word of *Ibn al-Arabi* for every issue, then, *is taqwa,* and this is a conclusion which is valid for every level of knowledge. *Ibn al-Arabi's* treatment of this particular issue is to multiply its polysemantic nature, to increase the possibilities, to deconstruct false closures and *taqayyid,* and the smugness of 'knowing'. He seeks to convince his audience that for this and every issue we must void ourselves of Lordship and exaltedness, becoming instead humbly receptive and alert to divine command.

In the matter of purity *(taharah)* in the same verse we have been considering (5:6), Allah says that He does not wish for us any constriction *ma yuridu Allahu li-ajala alaykum min haraj,* but instead, *He wishes to make you pure.* Then, following this verse He tells us to remember our covenant with Him, when we said, 'We hear and obey'. One might gloss here we listen, we hear, and we obey. For *Ibn al-Arabi,* assumption of lordship on our part, whether openly or not, precludes our listening, hearing, and ultimately, obeying. And right after that, Allah says, *And have taqwa [fear] before Allah; Allah is aware of the bottom of the hearts! (5:8).*

Divine Teaching

There is a great thirst for the direct word of Allah. Knowledge in the Quran is linked with water; rain comes down from the heavens, the parched earth drinks it, and vegetation is produced. Muhammad received the rain, which comes 'freshly from its Lord'. Rain is the direct knowledge which Allah gives to make us whole. River water is indirect knowledge—knowledge from our intellects—which gets mixed up with impurities and is subject to pollution. I used to joke that now we have acid rain: but, now I think that is our situation indeed. We no longer have the direct, clean, pure rainwater which Allah provides because the medium above us is itself polluted.

Clearing the Air : We have tried here to clear the air of the irritants and obstacles which come in the way of hearing the word directly. What *Ibn al-Arabi* does, above all, is to prepare his audience for the encounter and then to become transparent before the encounter. His intellect, his genius, and his skill pale in comparison with this gift: a way to hear in clear and clarifying language, the divine word. And as therefore neither conclusions nor resolutions are appropriate, we take up three passages from Ibn al-Arabi's *fiqh.*

Quotes from Al-Arabi

The First Passage : In the first passage, we hear *Ibn al-Arabi's* discussion on *awrah.* This word is not translatable, but it is describable. Classically, *awrah* meant the part of the body, men's and women's, which had to be covered. The classical *fiqh* books spent most of their time discussing the man's *awrah* and the man's clothing. Today of course, *awrah* means the shameful part of women, including their voices, smell, and very presence. In fact, in *Urdu,* woman herself is called shameful—*aurat.* In order to recover the direct knowledge of the Quran, let us take up Ibn al-Arabi's discussion here; I have first translated Ibn *Manzur's* descriptions of key words needed for this passage from Ibn al-Arabi's *Futuhat al-Makkivvah.*

Awrah ('w.r.): *Ibn Manzur* says, 'The *awrah* of the man and the woman is their private parts.' And 'the *awrah* is everything that causes embarrassment if it is exposed.' Also, 'The *awar* ['w.r.] has only one eye'. He also says, 'Covering the *awrah* during the *salah* and other than the *salah* is obligatory; about covering it when secluded there is a disagreement'. And 'in the Quran we have, Our *houses* are *awrah* (33:13), that is, they are open to the thief because the houses have been cleared of the men, but Allah caught them in their lie, saying, *But they* were *not awrah, they only, wanted to desert* [33:13]. It is said its meaning is. Our houses are *awrah,* that is, our houses are near the enemy and we were stolen from them. But Allah knew that their intent was deserting the battle.' *Ibn al-Arabi* says, 'The *Ulema* agree that covering the awrah is obligatory, with no disagreement, and absolutely, that is, during the salah I shall mention its boundary of the man and the woman.'

Mayl (m.y.l.): *Ibn Manzur* says, '*Mayl* is inclining toward something.'

Ibn al-Arabi says, 'The crossover for that in the inwardness. It is obligatory on every intelligent person to cover the divine secret which, if it were disclosed, would lead someone, who was neither knowledgeable nor intelligent, to a lack of a sense of taboo toward the Side of the divine, Exalted, Forbidden, because the reality of *awrah* is *mayl*. Because of this that person said *Our houses are awrah*

[33:13], that is, inclined, bent on destruction, when they sought to desert; then Allah caught them in their lie, before His Prophet (PBUH), with His word, *But they were not awrah; they* only *meant* to desert [33:13], that is, to desert what you [Muhammad] called them to. There is also the *awar* [one-eyed man], because his view inclines [m.y.l.] to a single perspective.

'Like that it is appropriate that the knowledgeable one cover from the ignorant one the secrets of the Real; secrets like His word, *There* are *no whisperings of three except He is the fourth [58:7];* His word, *We are closer to one than the jugular vein [50:16];* and His word, *I become his ear, and his eye, and his tongue,* because when the ignorant one hears that, it leads him to forbidden conceptualisations like divine incarnation or bounded divinity. Therefore, it is appropriate that with which the Real turns and inclines to the hearts of the knowledgeable ones—Exalted is He and Holy—with His address, be covered up with whatever His Majesty necessitates of Independence absolutely from the worlds; in addition to His word on the tongue of His messenger, *I was hungry and you fed me not, I was sick and you visited me not, I was thirsty and you did not give me to drink.*

'So he covers up the knowledge of this secret from the ignorant one and he does not add to what He said as a commentary to it [that is, I *was hungry]* at all. He covers up as the Real does with His word, *So and so was sick, and if you had visited him, you would have found Me with him.* This is more ambiguous than the first statement, but He gives in this commentary to the ones who know Allah, another knowledge about Him which they did not have. That is that in the first He made Himself the very same sick and hungry one but in His commentary He made Himself the Helper of the sick one, as He is *with him,* because whoever helps the sick one is with him. How far away is this from the One who made Himself the sick one himself! Each statement in that way is real, and to every real *[Haqq]* is a Reality *[Haqqiqah].'*

Ammi (' m.m.): (This is one of the most loaded classical words, usually full of the absolute class distinctions of the elite and the mass. *Ibn al-Arabi's* use of the word is, however, quite different and is tied into one of the descriptions used by *Ibn Manzur*). *Ibn Manzur* says, 'A *ummayy ['m.m.]* man and a *qusriyy [q.s.r.,* utmost] man. The *ummayy* is the *amm* and the *qusriyy* is the *khass.* In the *Hadith:* When he used to go home, he gave upon entrance three *juz*': a *juz* to Allah, a *juz* for his family, and a *juz* for himself. Then he apportioned *juz* for him and the people and he correlated that portion to the *ammah* through the *khassah,* meaning that the *ammah* were not with him at that moment, so the *khassah* communicated to the *ammah* what they heard from him; it is as if the benefits were transferred to the *ammah* from the *khassah.'*

According to *Ibn al-Arabi*, 'As for the covering up of that before the *ammi,* it is that one say to him about His statement, You *would have found Me with him* that the condition of the sick one is certainly that of dependency and need of the one in whose hand is the cure—and that is no one but Allah, so mostly what we need is to remember *[dhikr]* Allah with each instant to repel what befell him, which is different from the healthy one: He said, I *Myself am seated with the one who remembers [dhikr] Me.* This is the healthy condition. The *ammi* is satisfied with it and the knowledgeable one stays with what He taught him about that upon his knowledge; this is the cover up of the divine *mayl* from the gaze of the *ammi.*

'The Ulama then disagree about whether covering the *awrah* during the *salah* is a precondition for the validity of the *salah* or not. There is one who says that covering the *awrah* is one of the Sunnas [voluntary but customary practices] of the *salah,* and there is one who says that it is one of the obligations of the *salah.*

> 'As for the crossover for that spiritually, we have already taught you the concept of *awrah* above. About this issue, as it is established [by an authentic *Hadith]* that the one praying is in intimate conversation with his Lord and that the *salah* has been divided in two between Allah and His worshipper, so the one who sees predominate [in this issue] that the Real is the One praying through the acts of His worshipper, that is, the outward practices of the worshipper in the *salah,* as it is established that *Verily Allah said on the tongue of His worshipper during the salah, Allah hears the one who praises Him [sami Allahu li-man hamidah],* when one rises after *ruku,* and the worshipper is the speaker, certainly; and He said, *Give him [asylum] so that he may hear the Word of Allah [9:6],* while it is the messenger (Pbuh) of Allah, who is reciting, certainly; [that one who takes this position says] the covering of the *awrah* is one of the obligations of the *salah,* that is, the likes of this should not be made manifest before the *ammi,* meaning its supra-sensory meaning and its secret, which is known by the knowledgeable one; rather, the *ammi* should believe in it [without understanding it], as is mentioned, *Only the knowledgeable ones will understand it.* *[29:43]*
>
> 'And the one who sees that there is no gradation in this issue between the knowledgeable one and the *ammi,* and that there is nothing but what the text relates, and if it causes to lead, before the hearer, towards what it leads to—if he does not go outside of what the language requires for that—even though their degrees are granted preference [one over another], then the covering of the *awrah* in his view is one of the Sunnas of the *salah,* not one of its obligations. *Allah says what is real, and He is the guide of the way.* *[33:4]*

'About the boundary of the *awrah,* there is one who says that the *awrah,* for the man, is the two private parts and there is one who says that it is, for the man, from the navel to the knee. It is, according to us, only the private parts. 'The crossover for that spiritually: whatever is blameworthy, hated, and filthy of humankind is the *awrah* according to Reality. The two private parts are a place for what we mentioned. It is at the location of the unlawful; and in addition to the private parts is what encroaches on the private parts, the navel on the upper and the knee on the lower; the encroaching area is at the location of the Doubtful, and it is appropriate that one protect oneself [w.q.y., cf. *taqwa]* [from the Doubtful], because *The herder going around the enclosed precinct may almost get into it* [and so should stay well away from the boundary of the Unlawful].

'About the boundary of the *awrah* for the woman, there is one who says that all of her *is awrah* except the face and palms and there is one who argues for that and adds that her feet are not *awrah.* And there is one who says that all of her is *awrah.* As for our position, there is nothing *awrah* of the woman, in fact, except the private parts, just as He said, (*their sawah (two private parts) became visible to them, and they [Adam and Eve] started weaving for themselves the leaves of the Garden [7:22],* so He treated Adam and Eve the same in the covering of the private parts; they are the two *awrahs.* Even though the woman is commanded [in the last *Shariah*, of Muhammad] to cover [more], and that is our position, yet this is not because of it being *awrah.* That [covering of the leaves of the private parts] is a legal property set down by Shariah mentioning covering; but it is not necessary that anything else be covered as *awrah.'*

The Second Passage : To understand this second passage, we need to understand *Ibn al-Arabi*'s Arabic conception of *sawm.* It will become immediately clear why this word can not be translated, either by 'fasting' or by any conventional *Arabic* phrase. Ibn al-Arabi begins his large chapter on the *sawm* with its definition. He says, 'You should know—may Allah strengthen you!—that the *sawm is imsak* [abstention] and *rifah* [elevation].' As usual, we turn to the description of the word in *Lisan al-Arrab* and find the same: *Ibn Manzur* says, 'The word *sawm* in the language is *imsak* [abstention] from something and *tark* [leaving] it.' This is the first description. For the second, *Ibn Manzur* says, 'There is *sama* [from the same three letter root s.w.m. from which the word *sawm* is derived] the day when it draws up and rises to the zenith of mid-way. *Imru al-Qays* (one of the pre-Islamic poets whose Arabic usage is authoritative) said, *idha sama an-nahar wa hajjara* (the day rose up and became mid-way).'

To demonstrate the second description, *Ibn al-Arabi* says, 'One says, *sama an-nahar* when the day elevates. *Imru al-Qays* said, *idha sama annahar wa hajjra,* that is, became elevated. Because the *sawm* has been elevated above the rest of the worships [the pillars of Islam, such as *salah* and *zakah]* by a degree, it is called *sawm.* He—Exalted beyond—elevated the *sawm by* refusing any similarity with it to the worships, as we shall explain. He takes the *sawm* away from His worshippers even though they are doing it as a worship and attaches it to *Himself-subhana-hu* [He is exalted beyond]-and gives with His hand the reward to the one with the attribute of *sawm* who does it. He links the *sawm* to Himself by refusing any similarity [of it to the other worships].'

Ibn al-Arabi will explain below why the *sawm* is elevated above the other worships using the same evidence which *Ibn Manzur* uses. *Ibn Manzur* says, 'There is a *Hadith* where the Prophet (Pbuh) said, Allah said, *Every act of the offspring of Adam is theirs, except the sawm, because it is for Me. Abu Ubayd* said, Allah has made the *sawm* special with it being His and as being something which He rewards.'

In fact, the conception of elevation *(rifah)* and abstention *(tark)* both point to the particular description of *sawm. Ibn al-Arabi* says, 'The *sawm* is in reality a *tark,* not a practice, and the refusing of similarity is a negative attribute which intensifies the relationship of the *sawm* to Allah. He said about Himself, *Laysa ka mithlihi shayun* [There is nothing like Me] [42:11], so He refused that there should be to Him a *mithl* [similar], because *He—subhana-hu—has* no *mithl,* according to intellectual and *Shariah* proofs.

And *al-Nasai* [one of the authoritative collectors of *Hadith]* published from *Abu Umamah* that he said, "I came to the messenger of Allah and I asked him, Command me with a command which I can take from you. He said, On you is the *sawm,* because it has no *mithl* [there is nothing like it]." Thus, he refused that any of the worships which are made *Shariah* for the worshippers be made similar to it.' In order to pursue this particular conception, *Ibn al-Arabi* continues with the usual evidence for this worship. He says:

> 'And Muslim published in his authentic collection from *Abu Hurrayrah*[15] that he said, The messenger of Allah said, *Every act of this offspring of Adam is theirs, except the sawm; I reward it.* And *siyam (sawm) is* a shield; when there is a *sawm* day for one of you, do, not be loud and noisy on that day. If someone insults you or fights you, say, I am one with the matter of *sawm [saim], I am a saim* [one fasting]. And by the one in whose Hand the soul of Muhammad is, the breath of the one with *sawm is* better, according to Allah, on the day of judgement, than the scent of musk. And the one with *sawm* has two joys which he enjoys: when he breaks [fast] with his *iftar* there is a joy and when he meets his Lord there is a joy in his *sawm.'*

The last phrase is awkward and not an expected turn of phrase. This should be a signal to us that something quite particular is happening. Indeed, taking the conception of *sawm* which *Ibn al-Arabi* has developed gives an explanation why we have this strange turn of phrase. He says,

> 'Know that as he refused any similarity with the *sawm,* as was established in what preceded with the *Hadith* of *al-Nasai* and the reality that *Laysa ka mithlihi shayun* [there is nothing like Him, 42:11], the *saim* meets with his Lord by the attribute of *Laysa ka mithlihi shayun* and sees Him by it, so He is the Seer who is Seen. Because of this, he said, There is a joy in his *sawm,* and he did not say, There is a joy in meeting his Lord, because the joy is not a joy enjoyed by himself but is a joy enjoyed in *it.* And the one about whom the Real is his eyes with which he sees and witnesses, he himself does not see except by His seeing.'

This last phrase is the thematic *Hadith qudsi* which is as follows: 'My *abd* draws near to Me by means of nothing dearer to Me than that which I have established as a duty for him. And My *abd* continues drawing nearer to Me through supererogatory acts until I love him; and when I love him, I become his ear with which he hears, his eye with which he sees, his hand with which he grasps, and his foot with which he walks.'

Concluding, he says, 'So the joy of the *saim* is his meeting at the degree of refusal of similarity. His joy in the *iftar* [breaking of the fast] is in the world, in respect to giving due to the physical self which needs nourishment for itself.

As the *abd* is described in this *Hadith* as having *sawm,* and deserving the name *saim* because of this description, so after the affirmation of his *sawm* the Real negates it and attaches it to Himself, saying, [Every act of the offspring of Adam is theirs] except the *sawm;* it is Mine [or, it is for Me], that is, an attribute of *samadani* [cf. *Allah ussamad*] [112:2], which is being beyond needing nourishment. "It is Mine only; even though I may describe you with *sawm, I* so describe you by some delimiting metaphor of *tanzih* [being beyond an attribute], not by the absolute *tanzih* which is appropriate to My Majesty.

So I say, And I reward it." So the Real rewards the *sawm* for the *saim* when he turns to his Lord and he is cast to his Lord by the attribute of "He has no *mithl"*— which is the *sawm,* as the one to Whom "There is nothing like unto" cannot see anything but one whom "There is nothing like unto." Abu Talib al-Makki-he was one of the masters of the folk of tasting determined the text *jaza-u-hu man wujida fi rahl-ihi fa-huwa jaza-u-hu* [12:75]—for what this verse requires for this circumstance.'

Now we can turn to the passage in question. 'The most surplusing and balanced *sawm is* "fasting" one day for yourself and fasting one day for your Lord and between them a day breaking fast .... But when some of them saw that the right-claim of Allah is more right, they did not see treating equally the right of Allah and the right of the worshipper, so they fasted for two days and broke fast for one day.

This was the fasting of Mary, because she saw that *men have a degree over women* [2:228], so she said, Perhaps I shall make this second day of fasting one to counter this degree. And that was how it was, because the Prophet (PBUH) *testified* that *she* was complete [perfect], just as he testified to the completion of the Men.' And when she saw that the testimony of two women was balanced with the testimony of one man, she said, "Two days fasting for me is at the level of one day fasting of the Man." Thus, she got the station of the Man for that, and she equalled David in surplus in the fast. So because of this, the one who overcomes in himself his *nafs* has overcome in himself his [tendency to] divinisation; then it is appropriate that he treats his *nafs* as Mary treated her *nafs* in this context, lest her *nafs* overtake her *aql*; this is a fine allusion for the one who understands it.'

Dahr: Ibn Manzur says, *'dahr is* an extremely long time'. And 'there is the *Hadith,* Do not revile *the dahr because Allah is dahr.'*

Qayyum (q.w.m.): Ibn Manzur says, 'The *Qayyum,* one of Allah's names; Allah is Standing up by Himself absolutely, not by [the help of] anyone.' *Ibn al-Arabi* continues, 'When completion became hers, she caught up to the Men, and the most completion was hers in her catching up to her Lord. It was like Jesus son of Mary, her son, because he used to fast *dahr* and not break the fast, and he used to stay up (q.w.m.) at night and not sleep. Outwardly, in the world he was with the name *dahr* in the day and with the name *Qayyum*—the one whom *sleep does* not *seize,* nor *slumber* (2:225) at night. So divinity was claimed for him, and it was said, Allah is the Christ, son of Mary (5:72), and that was not said about any prophet before him, because the most that was said about *Uzayr* was that he was the son *of Allah* (9:30). It was not said, He is Allah.'

Kufr: Ibn Manzur says the word *kufr* is derived from *satr* (veil, cover). *Kanaf: Ibn Manzur* says, In the *Hadith* of *Ibn Umar*, we have about salvation, The believer draws closer to his Lord on the day of judgement until He places over him His *kanaf. Ibn Mubarak* said, He meant, He covers (s.t.r.) him.

> 'So look at what effect this [divine] attribute had,' Ibn al-Arabi says, 'from behind the veil of the unseen, on the hearts of the veiled ones of the folk of disclosure such that they said, *Allah is the Christ, son of Mary* [5:72]; *kufr* is related to them for that, set up as an excuse

for them, because they did not commit *shirk;* rather they said, He is Allah, and the one who commits *shirk* is the one who makes with Allah another god. So this is one doing *kufr,* not *shirk.* Therefore, He said, They have done *kufr* who say, Allah is the *Christ, son of Mary*, thereby attributing to them a *sitr* [a cover, that is, *kufr*]*;* they took the humanity of Jesus to be a locus of divine manifestation [*majalla*]. Jesus warned him [self] about this station, in what Allah reported, as a confirmation for them concerning what they said. Christ said, O *Bani Israil, worship Allah, my Lord and Your Lord.* They said, That is what we are doing! So they worshipped Allah through him. Then He said to them, *The one who commits shirk with Allah, Allah has made forbidden to him the Garden [5:72],* that is, Allah has made forbidden His *kanaf* with which He covers [s.t.r.] him; but Allah already described them with being covered [s.t.r.] in that He described them with *kufr.* This is a verse whose literal meaning gives exactly that which the matter itself gives of that. The *tawil* [allegorical interpretation] of the verse is caught up in blameworthiness; if you comprehend what we have mentioned about it, you will fall into the great ocean and you will not be saved from drowning in it at all, because it is the endless ocean. There is no deeper' word of Allah for the one who sees it and has eyes to see it and is from Allah concerning it *upon insight'.* *[12:108]*

The Third Passage : Iḅn al-Arabi says, '*Abu Ahmad* mentioned in a *Hadith* of *Abd-Allah ibn Rabi ibn Waraqa al-Makki* from *Amr ibn Dinar* from *Ibn Umar* from *Umar* that he vowed to sit ('k.f.) in the sacred mosque, and the messenger of Allah (Pbuh) said to him, Sit in *itikaf* and do *sawm.'*

Awliya: *Ibn Manzur* says, 'The *waliy [* singular of *awliya]* of the right hand is the one who is in charge of one's command and executes his tasks.' 'Its connecting crossover: *Rasululah*, the messenger of Allah commanded the one desiring to stand [q.w.m.] with Allah that they should stand with him by the attribute which is Allah's, and that attribute is the *sawm,* so that one should be with Allah, by Allah, for Allah, so nothing of them would be seen except Allah. This is the circumstance of the folk of Allah. It was asked of the *Rasululah*, Who are the *awliya* of Allah? He said, *Those who, when they are seen, Allah is remembered [dh.k.r,* cf. *dhikr],* that is, in order to be made real by Allah they disappear in him from them and from the eyes of creation, so when the people see them, they see nothing but Allah, so their remembering of Allah is their seeing the *awliya.* It is like the above-mentioned verses.

This is the station which the *Rasululah* asked for in his prayer, *And make me nur [n.w.r.],* and Allah answered his prayer, as we were told that he was sent to people *as one of good tidings, warning, calling to Allah by His leave, and an illumined lamp [siraj munir, n.w.r.]* 33-45-6; so He made him *nur* as he asked.

'His word to his Lord, *And make me nur,* was, So that I would be in my essence the very divine name itself *al-nur,* and the one whom the Real is *his ear, his eye, his tongue, his hand, and his foot;* and one who *would not speak from caprice [53:3].* So he is not he, and nothing remains for the one who sees him, who sees him, except Allah, that being known by the one who sees or not; this is the way the folk of knowledge of Allah witness him.

'Among the believers there are the *khulafa [kh.l.f.,* ones representing someone behind them, singular *Khalifa]* who manifest in the world and among the masses with the attributes of the one who is behind [kh.l.f.] them. *Bilqis* [the queen of *Sheba*] said about her throne, *ka'anna-hu huwa,"* but it was nothing but *huwa [it/Him]!* But her veil was the extreme distance [between her palace and Solomon's] and the force of convention [which says thrones do not transport themselves across large distances instantly], and she was unaware of Solomon's power with his Lord, so this veiled her from saying, *huwa huwa* [it is It; he is He; etc.].

So she said, *ka'anna-hu huwa.* And what distance could be greater than one to whom *there is no mithl* [like] compared to one whose *mithl is* things? The complete one [Muhammad] said, *Indeed I myself am a human being who is your mithl* [like yourselves]-this based on a command of Allah. It was said to him, *Say,* and he said, *Say: indeed I myself am a human being who is your mithl [41:7],* and by this we know that it is based on a command of Allah, because he conveyed the command to us just as he conveyed what was commanded.

'This statement is a remedy for the sickness which arose in the one who worshipped Jesus in his commentary; they said, *Indeed Allah is the Christ, son of Mary [5:72],* missing a great knowledge in that they said *son of Mary* and they did not realize. Because of this, Allah said in raising proof against the one with this description [the *mushrik*], *Say: Name them* [that is, name the partners of Allah, 13:33], but they could not name him [e.g., *Allah, the Christ, son of Mary*] except by one of the names they knew him by, in order that he understand from them what they meant, because when they gave them [the partners] names, it became clear, in the name itself *[Allah, the Christ, son of Mary],* that he was not one of the messengers who were sent demanded that they worship.

'But we rather said, *huwa huwa* [He is He] based on what sound disclosure gives the *khass* and what clear faith gives the *amm,* just as the prophetic report from the divine relates, that Allah, when He loves His worshipper, He becomes his ear, his eye; and He mentions his faculties and limbs. And humankind is nothing but these faculties and limbs which the Real makes his highness itself.' So if you are a believer, do you know what you believe in? And even if you are one with a sound vision, do you know what you saw? Most of this prophetic explanation about Allah is concerned with the human faculty so that the believer would be one with a state of seeing, so that one would know by that the One who is the entity itself of the things and the entities.'

References

1. Ablution' cleanliness before offering Salat.
2-8. Early recitors of Holy Quran, famous for their melodious voice.
9. A companion of the Holy Prophet (Pbuh).
10. A Sermon or Speech.
11. A famous commentator of the Holy Quran.
12-13. Renowned scholars of Islamic law.
14. Prominent writer and a contemporary of companions of Prophet, also the most reliable biographer of the Prophet (Pbuh).
15. Oft-referred to companion of the Prophet (Pbuh), who quoted most of the traditions.

5

TRADITION, THE SECOND SOURCE

GENESIS OF LAW

Notwithstanding the fact of *Shatibi*'s juristic views unfortunately remained external to the mainstream of Islamic legal thought, the principle of *Masla* was suggested to be the essential point for the convergence of all enquiries about the nature and purpose of legal obligation, social and legal change and the method of legal reasoning. It was also thought to provide the culmination for the search of desirable unity underlying the diversity of rules in Islamic Law. The theological objections against the principle were satisfied with the argument that Divine will at the legislative level, in contrast with its manifestation at the level of the creation, allows man's will for freedom to act and holds him responsible for his acts. The translation of human freedom and responsibility in modern terminology will reflect the concept of legal obligation, with the logical derivation of Divine commands to remain within man's capability for compliance, and their necessary intelligibility which cannot be without the inclusion of rational considerations. A collective assessment of all these factors would emphasize the requirement for the explicit or implicit occasioning reasons (*ila*) for the commands in order for their understanding, generalisation and extension to like situations.

The law is recognised to reflect the "soul" of the society to be a social reality, and without coming upto the aspirations of a society and its demands for new adjustments, law can only remain less than a living force. For these reasons law cannot be studied for its own sake as an "introspective science." The decline in the legal development of Islamic Law after the establishment of legal schools, in particular, due to its characterisation as "scholastic law," is explainable against this perspective. This realisation is underscored by the understanding that the primary sources of Islamic Law are a code of life, however, any claim to their being a final code of law is unsustainable. The conceptual adequacy of law as reflected in the harmony of legal principles is a recognised criterion of evolved law. In this setting, it is a common presumption that the legal principles are mutually interrelated and the outweighing of one principle in relation to others is violative of this criterion. A survey of the legal development of Islamic Law is demonstrative of the fact that no such requirements were particularly maintained.

The incompletion and insufficiency of law remain a known issue and the primary sources of Islamic Law do not lend any presumption of substantive corpus juris, and its judicial provisions are inadequate as a statement of Muslim personal relations and some of the basic institutions of Islam are not even mentioned in it. This argument, however, is to favour the idea of the Quran being a set of super-eminent principles which should have formed the basis for the deduction of rules and development of law. Some of the more prominent legal inadequacies in Islamic Law are the law of civil obligations, wide arbitrary powers vested in political sovereign under the Shariah doctrine of deterrence or "*tazir*" as a part of less than developed constitutional law in particular, and public law in general, and law pertaining to the status of women in society as a result of unsatisfactory interpretations.

A survey of the Islamic Law is demonstrative of the lack of imaginative harnessing of full potentials of the Quran as a source of law, because the ground for the law resided in its explicit provisions. In the making of law, reliance was placed upon rules rather than on standards, and ideals were not utilised in the law. This observation is also substantiated by the outlining of some of the more prominent legal inadequacies in the previous section. According to Hart, the question of law concerns the society and the constitutional law is positive morality merely, thus the primary source of Islamic Law could have yielded a prodigious material for law-making. For the same purposes, the far-reaching and wide connotations of Islamic legal "norms" whose value in the modern legal literature is acknowledged beyond doubt," were not beneficially used.

The Muslim legal thought has typically come to be identified with the Islamic laws of inheritance and succession. Similarly, the rights of inheritance in Islam have come to be the facsimile reflection of the social values. The considerations of customary laws prevalent in the Arabian society on the advent of Islam, especially the patrilineal nature of social set-up, the revealed law furnishing vital directions divergent from the customary practices, the critical issue of the revealed standards not accorded any preponderant role in the law-making in relation to the revealed canons, are credible indications of essential Islamic legal thought remaining dormant. In this respect, the issue whether the pre-Islamic customary law underwent replacement or merely modifications following the Quranic legislation is of proximate relevance.

The concurrence with Coulson's view is but unavoidable, for the promulgant or customary law was neither entirely supplanted nor superseded by the revealed tenets, as the latter were merely instrumental in that law's reformation in certain particulars. As an illustrative instance, in the patriarchal social configuration of the tribal pattern of society, male agnate laid claim to the succession as well as the patrimony. The apportioning of legal share in the financial inheritance for the female was the Quranic modification of the customary law whose substitution could only have been the consequence of the legal development in Islam. However, in addition to the factors already stated, this legal transformation remained unattained due to the essential nature of "Jurists' law" in Islam, for the academic law lacked the apprehension of factual situation and human circumstances, and this observation can find assertion due to the available benefit of retrospection. Similarly, the attitude of vehement religious trust in the invocation of Divine name during the course of legal matters and morbid fear of sin are the factors traceable in the lack of development of the law. The reliance upon the force of religious belief, such as was not in legal consonance with the practical circumstances of law and legal proceedings, is reflective of the exercise of religious idealism in a basically academic approach towards law of evidence. The realisation is of fundamental significance that the ascribed idealism cannot be held without deficiency in fulfilling the criteria of objectiveness in religion, as is exemplified by the inadmissibility of circumstantial evidence in legal process, notwithstanding of the fact that the occurrence of deliberate hiding of the silver pale in the ration of grain, as a later pretext of involvement and incrimination, cited in the chapter of *Joseph*[1] in the Islamic Scripture, would have served as an adequate instance to introduce the validity of circumstantial evidence.

The zeal to benefit the great belief-system, by subscribing to the notion that the unflinching obligation of the society is to maintain judicially unprocessed primary ethico-legal "rules" in the provided form, is misconceived, for the ordinary religio-ethical outlook is incapable to encompass the intricacies of law and its making. Fundamental problem facing Islamic Jurisprudence in the contemporary era bears essential resemblance with the one that existed in the past-the need to define the legal standards available in the religion and their interrelationships with the vital social factors which influence society. As a matter of critical differentiation, while law in the modern knowledge is viewed to reflect the soul of a society in order to be a "living force," however, in Islam, the law due to its religious origin is the "animating force" for the soul of society. This aspect is of such fundamental significance in Islam that without designating the pivotal social system as Nomocracy—where "*nomo*" is Greek for law—the claim to essential Islamic character of society cannot be made convincingly. If the same crucial aspect is considered from another viewpoint, wherein the religion is upheld as the basis of comprehension and implementation of the Divine purposes for the Islamic society, then, necessarily the Islamic Law is to be assigned the role of the medium for the attainment of those objectives. Now the emphasis is laid upon the use of reason in the Islamic Scripture, and the intricate yet subtle prerequisite for the possession of understanding is indicated therein for its intended subjects. Thus, in the deliberately patterned texture of the Islamic Law, the warp and woof of the Divine revelation and human reason are to be inseparably interwoven. The observation, that rational justification should have been adopted as the essential religious injunction in respect of law, has sound basis.

Accessible to the Muslim legists were the records of antedating Roman and Greek Civilizations, with the respective legal systems prevalent during their politically ascendant periods as models for comparative study, and so was available the precedent of Canon Law. Evidence to the contrary is available in the instances of Islamic constitutional and other categories of public law, which do not reflect the benefits of such a comparative study. Now recourse to comparison of laws is an indispensable part of legal scholarship and unavoidable in the determination of superior form of political constitution and, therefore, a paradigm of political community. Aristotle studied a large number of constitutions concerned with Greek and other cities in his treatise, Politics. In drafting the Athenian Laws, Solon (640-558 B.C.) proceeded on similar course. Further, the drawing up of the law of the Twelve Tables for Rome was preceded by the enquiries in relation to comparative law concerning the legal systems in the Greek cities. In later periods, the comparative studies of Canon and Roman Laws were conducted and their respective advantages compared. Montesquieu (1689-1755 A.D.) attempted through comparison to penetrate the spirit of laws and, thereby, to establish common principles of sound government.

Due to the essential differentiation that exists between the doctrines of "Kalam" and the principles of "*Usul*," its mitigation during the interpretation of the rules is undesirable. The leading original Muslim legists possessed a theological inclination which permitted an excessive devotion to the letter of law, making it an end *per se,* independent of its underlying purpose. In accordance with the modern legal terminology, such an interpretation earns the designation of "grammatical." As a result, the inter-relationship of rules, vital for the development and efficiency of law, is not satisfactorily maintainable. Besides, such interpretative outcome may cast some aspersions upon the legal system and, upon the translation of this observation into Islamic terms, the implementation of such a rule may result in the besmirching of Islam in the final analysis, an occurrence of which should not allow such a rule to remain any more cherishable. Additionally, the result of this particular interpretative method is not likely to cause the reinforcement of necessary link between the law and society. And, above all else, the underlying principles, functional throughout the law, comprising its spirit as derived from Islam, that perform an important role in the fostering of fundamental values in the society, are unable to leave their desired impact. Now, in order to give full effect to law, its intention must also be interpreted in the light of certain fundamental legal doctrines. The real meanings of the legislative texts cannot be provided elucidation without taking into account the whole of the system and principles by which the legislative policy is unquestionably guided. This particular interpretative approach is designated as "logical." Approximately related issue to this interpretative approach is the spirit of the laws, derived from Islam and enshrined in its Supreme Fundamental Principles, which is indispensable to the concept of the "soul of society."

Law and its Working

Appropriateness of a legal system in meeting the challenge of social change is basically dependent upon its philosophical and methodological adequacy and, in the instance of Fiqh, Shatibi had emphasised these aspects. This approach was a precedence of the Fuero, or Spanish Christian, system of law wherein reliance was placed upon the exposition of the shortcomings of the system and the effecting of the renaissance of the Roman Law, in bringing about its reformation. In this process of the systematisation of Roman Law, the ascertainment of reasons for the rules marked the advent of the philosophy of law in modern legal systems.

The proponents of dynamism in Islamic Law considered "*Masla*" as a principle of adaptability, in contrast with the immutability of the law upheld by the theological and idealistic proponents, and it conveyed a distinct implication of modification in adjustment to emerging social conditions, with the added significance of the expansion of law. The immediate concern of adaptability with social change is not related to the latter resulting from the transformation of society, but due to its happening as an outcome of social needs. The distinction in regard to praiseworthy and condemnable "*bida*," or innovation in Islamic Law consequent to the adoption of *Masla*, was maintained. These measures were deemed necessary, for the methodological issues concerning Shariah as to the application and extension of law to new situations, the interpretation of law in accordance with the principles of jurisprudence developed in the past several centuries, and the eradication of difficulties existing in the then prevalent law had remained undefined. Any satisfactory outcome of those issues was hampered due to adherence to the theological viewpoint concerning the denial of cause in legal reasoning, which was a notion in contrast with that subscribed by the proponents, including Shatibi, of command or edict not to be without some motivating cause. The fact in this respect is of more than passing historical interest that *Suarez* initiated similar improvements in the philosophy of law in the 16th century A.D., which were to influence the fundamental legal developments in Europe. As a tribute to Shatib's legal genius, the ironical instance of *Rashid Rida* is mentionable, who succeeded in blunting the popularity of his views in the 19th century A.D., with the undeserving epithets of conservative, crusader against innovation and traditionalist, which is as noticeworthy as it is instructive.

The search for the principles, such as are the essential point at which all enquiries about the nature and purpose of legal obligation, social and legal change and the method of legal reasoning converge, besides providing the basis for the unity that underlies the diversity of rules in Islamic Law, is indicative that the complete identification of those principles remained unattained in Islamic Law. The justification for this view is available in the modern concept of legal system to constitute a unity, and *Kelsen* proposed basic norms pertaining to each system. The definition of the relationship between these principles, mandated by the religio-legal system of Islam, and the dynamic forces which activate society, is an unfulfilled requirement of the Islamic jurisprudence. The lack of complex congruent practice of a legal system is its recognised malfunctioning. Kelsen presented a related view in the idea of the law as a "hierarchical structure" which rendered it perpetual self-creativeness. On the other hand, Fuller presented a theory, maintaining the implicitness of certain principles in the concept of law and to the extent these principles are violated, the law is lacking, hence, a consideration to be viewed as a matter of degrees. A survey of Islamic Law is suggestive of the non-contribution of these latter-day concepts in the development of the legal system.

Religious idealism characterised the early Islamic jurists, and the concurrence is due Coulson in the observation of the Islamic jurisprudence that began as the formulation of a scheme of law, rather than the formation of an envisioned society. The theological approach to law is considered to "denaturalize" the legal science, for the object of the law, which is intended to be obtained, may be lost in the literal interpretation of the text. The Quran was unquestionably the primary source of law, however, the juridical provisions provided therein were not an all-embracing law, and the possibilities of interpreting the source of law in Islam gradually diminished due to the theological influence and a want of the evolvement of a comprehensive methodology for the development of Law.

The other non-legal influence upon Islamic jurisprudence, in its formative period, was the prevalent social traditions, and the legal interpretation in the area of the status of women, in particular, bears its evidence. It is a reflection of the inadequacy in legal methodology, and not of the want in the content of law specifically, which underscores the necessity for the formulation of a methodology for the fruitful adaptation of Islamic Law to an ascendant social order.

The period between the middle of 7th to the abolition of *Khilafat* in the initial quarter of the last century in the Islamic calendar is identifiable with the juristic phenomenon of "*Taqlid*," which is another way of suggesting the recession of "*Ijtihad*," whereby sapping of the intellectual vitality and inducing the immobility of the legal system are noticeable. In *Shariah* the meaning of the term "Taqlid" is to follow the decisions of a jurist without the demand for the arguments. The jurists of the period followed the views of the founders of the respective schools of law. The development and systematisation of the legal work of the founders of schools constituted main juristic activity, with the exception of dealing such cases as were not evaluated by the founders. The adoption of this legal doctrine of blind orthodoxy was to become the precursor for the "closing of the door of Ijtihad" in the 10th century A.D., and it generally assigned the responsibility of the curtailment of creative force immanent in the Muslim jurisprudence. Similarly, it is not difficult to trace its non-creative influence upon the legal method of analogical reasoning which, translated in present-day terms, resembled with the "distinctions" drawn during juristic decisions, but with the striking difference that the created rules failed to find further application. Now, adherence to the legal orthodoxy is violative of the fundamental truism applicable to the world: Its complete characterisation according to a definite, preset number of features is not feasible. Hence, the legal provisions cannot be made available in advance for every imaginable likelihood, for no expression will then be provided to creative elements in the legal concepts. In sum and substance, the result will be the mechanical application of law which invariably proves inimical to legal development.

The shortcoming of a literal interpretation is the theoretical possibility of the binding application of a rule with pernicious tendency and, on the basis of empirical criterion available in the legal systems, such a rule is treated as void. The Islamic concept of "*riba*" has been extrapolated to exclude any form of interest on a capital loan or investment. Basically a prohibition of usury, the legal concept of *riba* was coupled with the rules concerning the general prohibition on gambling transactions, with the connotation of chance or unpredictable earnings, in accordance with the meanings of their literal interpretation. Including in its legal ambit all speculative transactions, the law has thus excluded from its validity such contracts and business transactions as may ensure the prosperity of commercial and economic system.

No different is the issue of the husband's basic rights of polygamy and repudiation of spouse, an illustrative instance of a literal interpretative technique without consideration for the empirical tendency of the related law. A sound method placing reliance upon recognised legal criteria is likely to demonstrate those rights as an outcome of misinterpretation. Now, irrespective of the actual incidence of the exercise of the mentioned rights on the part of husbands, even if due to social censure and economic impracticability, the recognised existence of those rights in Islamic Law constitutes an adequate basis for the socio-psychological hindrance, from a practical stand-point, to the advancement of Muslim society. As a consequence, for an unaccountably long duration, the basic and prominent Islamic religio-legal principle of the interaction of reciprocal duties, a foundation of social interdependence leading to social solidarity, has been held in abeyance.

Transformation of Law

Failure to Make Law : The impasse faced by the Islamic jurisprudence in the 14th century A.D. was furnished a resolution and *Shatibi* is credited with it, however, the legal ingenuity of an outstanding intellect remained unavailed in the final analysis. Interestingly enough, this situation arose after the four Islamic schools of law were fully established and independent exposition of law gradually dwindled. The result, obviously, was the immobility of law, which is a testimonial, albeit negative, to the absent framework for legal development. An ongoing process, in the form of juristic inquisition, for future development of law, should have been mandatorily available and, additionally, it was required to embody the vital principle of rapid development. These developmental deficiencies in the legal system, however, were to deprive it of the "open" character with a potential for the constant discovery of new rules. On the contrary, the kind of automatism utilised in the application of established law was to paralyse its evolution.

The view, that Islamic Law is essentially rigid and immutable, takes its roots in the two equally unjustifiable misconceptions: its incapacity to accommodate legal change, and the misunderstanding about the comprehensiveness of Divine legislation in the sense of not embodying coverage in all its variety and detail. Recognition is to be granted in this regard to the early Islamic jurists' self-imposed terms of reference.

And the tendency of the mechanical observances of the incidents of a legal rule, rather than designed purposes of the rule, is also a factor. Noticeworthy is the fact, a legal method which incorporates the remedial steps even for these shortcomings, can allay the stationary character of the Law of Islam.

Law of Schools : In addition to the reasons for the decline in the development of Islamic Law-literal interpretation, "*taqlid*" and the exercise of "*Ijtihad*" becoming defunct-a communalism in law on the basis of established schools of law further compounded this hindrance. Juristic disciples from respective schools, in extolling the virtues and authority of the particular master genius almost to the extent of canonisation, became devotedly adherent to its legal expositions. Its one logical consequence was the ratification of the *Shariah* doctrine within each school of law, and the other eventually culminated in the invaluable legal notion of independent juristic enquiry or *Ijtihad* coming to stagnate. In consequence, the creative potential of Islamic jurisprudence was to undergo curtailment. In time, this led to the functional assumption that the material sources of revealed legislation were fully utilised in law-making, and their contents finally determined, which bred legal complacency-the anathema to the science of law.

Religious vs. Legal Outlook : Coulson draws distinctions in the essential nature of legislations on the basis of comparison between the attitudes of religious prophet and political legislator. The concern with the consequences of an act or omission is common to both, however, if the one views such consequences in terms of the attainment of merit or fault in the sight of God, then, the other considers those as practical sanctions enforceable by human agencies. The social problems are viewed by the political legislator in terms of the effects of an individual's behaviour upon his neighbour or upon the community as a whole. In contrast, religious law considers the effect that actions may have upon the conscience and eternal soul of the one performing the acts. In brief, the primary purpose of one is to regulate relationship of man with his fellow beings, and of the other is their regulation with the Creator. The author further observed that the legal verses, or the regulations which are more specifically of a legal tone, cover a great variety of subjects and "often have the appearance of *ad hoc* solutions for particular problems rather than attempts to deal with any general topic comprehensively." Now, the appropriateness of the observations is unexceptionable as to the practical distinction between religion and statutory law is concerned. However, Islam is to be viewed as a composite of these two general categories, and the *ad hoc* nature of revealed rules of legal value remains no more than an appearance once these rules are viewed as juridical guidelines, for the revealed legal injunctions, in purport, cannot be considered as a compendium of law. Nonetheless, in relation to the Islamic religious laws, the issue of *ad hoc* nature of legislation carries significance, for then alone the relevance of the intent of legislation, history of legislation and the law or customs prevailing in the society immediately antecedent to revelation, appear of legal utility. But, more importantly, the necessity for the consideration of the particular modalities of interpretation of the revealed laws and legal application of the vital conception of Supreme Fundamental Islamic Principles, in distinction from the regulatory rules, only then arises.

Realisation is due to the fact that any hiatus or deficiency of juristic merit, in the legal methods, introduces difficulty in maintaining legal relationships in the formulation of legal situations, and hampers legal development, as exemplified by the dormancy of the principle of Ijtihad and the subscription to the approach of "*taqlid*" in traditional Islamic jurisprudence, respectively. Nowhere else, perhaps, than in the sphere of religious law the relevance of the observation made by *Mill* is evident that the political institutions, in every stage of their existence, are the result of human voluntary agency. With the apprehension of this political truism, and within the concept of self-binding force of legislation, whereby, making of law presupposes the existence of certain rules which govern the process, the necessity, on the one hand, for the application of the Supreme Fundamental Islamic Principles of legal value and, on the other, for the predominant activity of lawmaking in Islam, becomes obvious. A legal method entailing the application of the fundamental principles is described in the subsequent discourse. The failure to make law is epitomised by the lack of identification of these principles in view of the fact that direct access to revealed law has ceased as a result of the finality of Prophethood in Islam, and the available source of law must have provided the universal principles against legal status and immobility.

Other Causes : In the enumeration of the causes for failure of law-making, Fuller describes inability to provide effective remedies for non-compliance of law, and to maintain minimal literacy conditions in society required for legal compliance. In the survey of Islamic Law, the maintenance of these causes is conspicuous and, particularly, the Muslim family laws and the laws of inheritance do not impose any other than social censure as the legal requirements for the compliance of various provisions. The observation is justifiable that a certain level of general and legal literacy is a requisite for the Muslim law as a part of "nomocracy", where "nomo" is law in Greek-in Islam. Additional cause for failure to make law is the deficiency in the requirements of "natural justice," such as the judicial impartiality and a right to a hearing, so that, disrespect for law becomes common. In this perspective, restoration of the reverence for law is an inviting issue that resides at the core of a successful legal system, with its foundations in the revealed source of law. It is the social effect that acquires relevance in this context. And excessive use of law in the controlling of human beliefs and passions is another noticeworthy cause from the viewpoint of the subject under review, which brings to apt attention the ramifications ensuing from an exercise of overzeal in law-making.

Rights and Duty : The rights prescribed in a body of law are the partial constituents of its "spirit," and the formalism of law remains devoid of reality without the proper inclusion of rights. In Islamic Law, remedy for any shortcoming in this sphere resides in the investigation of the real nature of its legal theory and the requisite rectifications.

In the adjacent half millennium, *Shatibi* appears outstanding amidst those whose juristic pursuits were dedicated to such an undertaking. As a matter of legal history, guaranteeing of the various types of rights in the law-making of Islam would have been of the fundamental significance, as it would have obviated the subsequent authoritarian tendency in the statecraft. This inadvertent exclusion on the part of Islamic Law was the misdirection in orientation of the law concerning the origin of all interests and concerns. The want of juristic, social and political equality not consonant even with the implication of Islam, was its undesirable outcome.

Apart from moral and ethical considerations of the results of this legal slant in Islamic humanism, an equitable society has become a political pre-condition for religious ascendancy and national independence, without which the vision of national security, social development and political stability may remain an illusion. As an illustrative instance of legal methodology through which the legal development in Islam remained deficient in those desirable objectives, on evaluation in retrospect, the analogy of the Habeas Corpus Acts can be cited. These Acts declare no principle and define no rights but, from a practical standpoint, represent the constitutional guarantee for individual liberty, that is, to provide means for giving legal security to the rights declared by the constitution. The primary sources of law in Islam are replete with such means *par excellence* and, simultaneously, ensure the full-functioning of those rights even in the theoretical instance of the suspension of the relevant constitutional provisions.

In a developed legal system the concepts of rights and duties form a pivotal part in the legal structure, and are proximately allied to the performance of its social functions. The legal connotations of justification and entitlement are conveyed by the concept of right within the framework of a legal system, and it is facilitative of the adherence to a legal order. The legal notions of obligation and right are an essential component of a system of law and, more important, are logically interconnected in the efficiency and development of the system. Pertinent is the fact that the set of rights and the legal framework for their satisfactory fulfilment, in contrast with the gamut and nature of legal obligations, constitute the legal distinction and political identification of a society.

Traditional Muslim Law is assessed to centre upon the legal obligations rather than on lawful rights, and to place reliance upon the religious principles that become inoperative in the instance of non-Muslims.' However, a conscientious and meticulous evaluation of the Islamic Law will demonstrate its subtle legal distinction from the original source of law, due to the self-imposed terms of reference that have found applicability in the former instance. The inference is available that the rights are to be emphasised in the Islamic Law in conformity with the requirements of the original source of law. The methodology of legal change, incorporates the invaluable suggestion for the satisfactory inclusion of the legal rights and the adaptability of the Islamic Law in the event of its application upon the non-Muslims in symmetrical conformity with the requirements of Islamic religio-legal principles.

The delineation of the causative factor for shortcomings in law, in relation to the crucial legal issue of the actual scope of rights, entailing distinction between original limitations of law in granting and the default of society in securing the rights, is an aspect of extraordinary legal and ideological significance. As a prototypical example, the rights of Muslim women, within the jurisdiction of traditional Muslim laws, are not uncommonly deemed to have been abridged especially relative to their Muslim counterparts. The characteristic construction of the relevant provisions in the primary source of law notwithstanding, the customary status of women in society in conjunction with their general inability to clearly understand the valid scope of their legal rights, and the perpetuation of nearly patriarchal pattern of society, are substantive contributory factors in an historic lack of implementation of the legal rights of women within the proper jurisdiction as provided in the primary source of law. This discrepancy in the availing of rights, pertaining to Muslim women, is explainable as the responsibility of society due to custom and socio-political constraints. With this in perspective, a legal methodology, founded upon the fundamental principles available from the primary source of law, which would demonstrate such rights of women as are consonant with the religious purposes and legal meanings of Islam and, hence, restore the legal balance due in favour of the rights, will establish a credible proof of its usefulness.

From among the three verses in the Quran whose misinterpretations have caused misconceptions with an historic consequences, ".... obey those in authority" is one such verse. An out of context interpretation was construed to also refer to jurists of all ages and, hence, was misapplied in support of "taglid, " with lamentable consequences to the Islamic Law. This misconstruction evidently exemplifies an out of context interpretation, notwithstanding of the fact that the legal concept of "*taqlid*" is deviant from the fundamental Islamic precepts whose foundation is the idea of "individual responsibility." The undesirability of *taqlid* according to essential Islamic principles and empirical results of its application are a part of legal history. Another and far more serious drawback emanating from the out of context interpretation of the aforementioned Quranic verse is the distortion in the politico-legal notion of social contract, to adopt the description according to modern terminology, to the extent it contains the idea of the correspondence of rights and obligations between the rulers and the populace. The obligation of allegiance to political authority represents the concurrent demand for the supremacy of Islamic Law to be satisfied by the latter, with the implication of contractual reciprocation and to the exclusion of the "sovereign and subject" politico-legal arrangement. As a matter of history ripe with invaluable lessons, in this correlation of right to the rule of Islamic Law and the obligation of allegiance to political authority, the disruption of the contractual harmony, whereby obligation superseded the right, was the verifiable cause of the consequences to developmental shortfall in the legal and political systems.

The vital scriptural injunction as the epitome of the requirement for the observance of revealed law, and it will be referred repeatedly in this discourse, is quoted here: "O you who believe! obey Allah, and obey the Messenger and those of you who are in authority; and if ye have a dispute concerning any matter, refer it to Allah and the Messenger if ye are (in truth) believer in Allah and the last day. That is better and more seemly in the end." Noticeworthy is the scale of sovereignty and any lack of adherence to the specified sequence is a fundamental breach of the revealed injunction. The evaluation of this Quranic verse in terms of law makes manifest the primary sources of Islamic Law to supersede the political authority as a matter of legal obligation. The dual conceptions of consummate juridical significance and revolutionary political connotation in the tenet are the equalisation of the fundamental religious ideas pertaining to faith with the objective notion of law and the contingency of the allegiance to the political authority upon its compatibility with the sovereignty of Islamic Law.

The importance of these observations is summarily describable as the fact that their complete realisation into definite social institutions has eluded the Islamic Civilization during the course of its history. The conversion of religious obedience into legal obligation is the key factor in the practical realisation of the substantive implications which are conveyed in the revealed precept, and this is inferable from the commentaries by other learned sources. To recognize the obligation towards the observance of Islamic Law constitutes the essential measure in this approach, which has been made manifest in numerous other revealed precepts.

The phraseology of religious commentators, whose representation is provided in the expressions such as "obedient to Allah," "ultimate authority rests in Allah," "cornerstone" of Islam, and "no independent obedience to men in authority," is translatable in modern juristic terms of the sovereignty of law. A meaningful elucidation of this instrumental concept, with its practical significance in view, will be the content of this discourse at appropriate junctures. If Islamic Law is in quest of itself and Islamic Civilization is in search of a definite direction for the realisation of its an historic destiny, then, the implementation of these basic ideas will prove a turning point in the attainment of those objectives.

Constitutional Law-General View : Constitutional law generally includes all the rules which directly or indirectly effect the distribution and the exercise of the sovereign power in the state. As a part of public laws, it is distinguished by the superior importance of the subject therein treated." The constitutional law in Islam remained underdeveloped and the constitutional limits upon the ruler were neither well-defined nor the means and laws for their implementation were made available.

The legal interpretation of the critical Quranic verse, elucidated earlier, was adopted out of context of the verse itself and other legal parameters of the constitutional law in the Scripture. These scriptural parameters included the Quranic requirement of council in managing the affairs, the meritorious attributes for aspiring to the position of public authority, and the Quranic concept of the emancipation of man as a derivative from the precept of the equality of men underwritten by the idea of Oneness of the Creator. In accordance with the expression of the last determining legal standard, no individual was to be subservient to another except through the legal notion of the equality before law. Translated in terms of the constitutional measures, the same legal concept of the rule of law amounted to constitutional limits upon the authority of political ruler and, as a vital legal deduction from the verse (iv : 59); it was to be the evolvement of the constitutional framework for lending security to the society's prerogative to effect change of rule under specific conditions of the infringement or breach of those constitutional limits.

Such a constitutional framework could be constructed through the comparative study of the constitutions ever since the Greek Civilization, and the characteristic vision of the particular society and the state, entertained by the jurists, would have become a political reality. The preceding observations serve as an illuminating instance of the necessity for the development of law from the original sources, which remained unutilised in the area of constitution-making due to the want of methodological approach.

Caliph: Requirements of Law : The historical circumstances of the early part of Islam, bordering upon the "right-guided" Caliphate era, had bequeathed the political tradition of the appointment of the Caliph by consent of the representatives of the community. The Ummayad rule, however, left the legacy of the rule of dynasty and, subsequently, the august office of the Caliph remained unstamped by the valuable procedure of the rule with the political consent, but with rare exceptions. If the constitutional framework for the settlement of the issue of the highest executive office in Islam was not in effect, then, the requirements of the qualifications for the same could not be constitutionally satisfied.

Therefore, the effective promulgation of the Shariah law was at the discretion of the *de facto* ruler." The conditions for the office of the Caliph, as a matter of consensus among all schools of law, comprised of piety of character and ability to ascertain and understand the revealed law. Discretion of political power is a natural result of such a constitutional set-up, and arbitrariness follows unavoidably in its wake. The political view of "sovereign and subject" expresses only one aspect of the relationship between state and individual under these political circumstances, and the political distinguishing mark of such a legal relationship is the unquestioning reception of orders."

This aspect contrasts with the issue of the meticulous observance of law by the political authority, and brings into sharp focus the imperativeness of the accessibility to the constitutional security, provided to the society's prerogative to effect change of rule within the meanings of the Quranic verse of prototypical significance, already alluded. No surprise, therefore, is to be evinced on the reversal of the order of allegiance in that verse and, with the passage of time, the ruler had become the effective object of obedience. To chronicler, a subject of interest, to philosopher, a matter of natural result emanating from the circumvention of law, to a jurist, a legal issue replete with invaluable constitutional instructions for the future, and to a believer, an occasion for lamentation as an historical opportunity was squandered for the political ascendancy over time, the political rulers in era subsequent to the right-guided Caliphs assumed powers which the law did not concede to them and, in their political conduct, abridged or isolated the *Shariah* law's vital principles.

The deterrent punishment or "*tazir*" is discretion made available to the ruler in Islamic Law under the doctrine of "*Siasa Shariah*." The basic premises of the doctrine are the sound order of the state and considerations of public interest; and within the meanings of these broad principles, sufficient discretion for the law-making through ordinances, as an addition to the rules of *Shariah*, is retained.

Siasa Shariah : The public law lacked comprehensive form and, as its component, the law did not comprise of any complete system of constitutional law." Naturally, additional jurisdiction was necessitated in the domain of public law, and the legal doctrine of "*Siasa Shariah*" was evolved to satisfy this legal demand. Under the provisions of this doctrine, generous discretionary powers were available to the ruler for the law-making as a supplement to the *Shariah* law, under the need of the maintenance of state and requirements of public interest. As a reflection of the deficient constitutional law, the doctrine was simultaneously indicative of the non-availability of the law for the ascertainment of the qualifications as an Islamic prerequisite for the rule. For the maintenance of the required order of precedence in the Quranic injunction (iv:59) God, Messenger and ruler-a self-regulatory judicial system was required, and such legal requirements were in obvious conflict with the demands of the *Siasa* doctrine. The discretionary powers available to the ruler were the signal of the *basic drawback* in the legal system. Fundamental problem facing Islamic jurisprudence since is essentially the deficient legal framework for the implementation of Islam, which is a nomocracy, wherein the conscientious judicial system, a demand approximately represented in the latter-day legal notion of the separation of powers, is indispensable.

The settlement of the issues of moral worth and justness of the legal rule should be interrelated with the criteria for its validity. Thomas Hobbes sought to argue that the decrees of the law are synonymous with morality. However, Bentham adjudged the moralness of law according to the dictates of his prominent principle of utility. The essential advantage claimed for this method was the clarity of thinking it imparted in distinguishing between legal and moral obligations. Legal philosophers, however, provided no response to the issue whether the citizen is entitled to disobey a law appearing morally condemnable. In the Islamic conception of the rule of law, in accordance with the requirements of the important verse with substantive connotations on interpretation (iv : 59), the individual is granted the exercise of this choice, once morality is considered in Islamic religious context. This crucial privilege with far-reaching legal implications did not secure due recognition in the Islamic legal system, notwithstanding of the fact that it constituted another of the vital requirements of the Islamic rule of law. This aspect is intimately interlinked with the substantive legal issue of the discretion provided to the ruler without the definite constitutional framework.

Legal Injunctions

Purpose of Law : The subject of the purpose of law is intricately related to the concept of law as an activity, with the emphasis upon its functions, rather than as an entity, with the importance of its nature. Purposive character of law generates principles that regulate the creation and administration of law. These principles amount to an "inner morality" of law because of their implicitness in the concept and nature of law. *Shatibi* defined "*Masla*" as the purpose of Islamic Law, and its assimilation into the Islamic legal theory would have freed its operation from a number of factors of determinism, rigidly arising out of theological and methodological considerations. The pivotal point in the legal philosophy of *Suarez* was the exposition of the end of law which, according to him, was the "common good of the community." Notwithstanding of the fact that an interval of approximately three centuries separated *Shatibi* and *Suarez*, the similarity in their approach towards law and its end is noticeworthy. And, if the latter contributed towards the development of law in Europe, then, the former's juristic expositions did not cross the stage of legal scholarship.

To reiterate, the reformation of the Spanish Christian system of law entailed the measures of the exposition of its shortcomings and the renaissance of the Roman Law. This approach consisted of the systematisation of the Roman Law in accordance with the Aristotelian method in the light of Christian doctrine, which also comprised the ascertainment of the reasons for the motivation of its rules. This trend was to mark the beginning of the philosophy of law in the Western legal system, and it had the far-reaching effects on the evolution of law. *Shatibi* was involved in the investigation of the philosophy of law and this vital pursuit, associated with the shaping of the concept of law, became inconspicuous afterwards. It is of no passing interest then, that the philosophical inadequacy of law has the causative role, in conjunction with the legal methodological insufficiency, for the developmental shortfall in the Islamic Law ("*fiqh*"). This basic concept in legal philosophy was considered an obstacle in the method of legal reasoning, while contrastingly acceptance was given to placing an excessive reliance upon the theological principles in the application of the law.

Irrespective of the evaluation of the laws of inheritance under the Shariah doctrine, as the general functions of law or the relationship between law and morals, which are the concerns of the legal philosophy among other subjects, for those laws to retain their moral nature in Islamic Law, as their infringement did not occasion legal sanction, is one illustrative instance of the inadequate legal development in Islam." The critical differentiation between law viewed as a fixed entity and law considered as an activity was not maintained, and with the general functions taken as the expression of law is also evident.

Particular Concerns : Values resulting from the application of certain laws may lie external to the intended objectives of relevant law, however, their concern is within the purview of the philosophy of law, such as the conceptions of justice and limits of law. The instances of such resultants are not rare, and the values of equality in relation to status, right and opportunity pertaining to the women in a Muslim society, have born such influence as to be the manifest concern of legal philosophy. The consideration for existential interdependence of law and the engendered values raises the issue of the limits of the law. The possibility is entertainable that the beneficial objectives of the law are transferable into their antithesis and, in effect, law ceases to be the original entity. Within the meanings of these estimations, the behaviour of citizens as the outward expression of the internal accompaniments in the form of psychological states, is a consideration not to face omission.

The legislative and judicial justifications, as a concern of the legal philosophy, view the lack of internal consistency of law anathematical to its "inner morality." The requirements of the same justifications are the indications that a legal system which, not unlike an issue or an approach, may be fundamentally misconceived due to the erroneous definition of its objectives. Understanding of the law is also influenced unless its purpose is evident. The failure to separate conceptual issues from those of straightforward facts cannot be deemed out of bounds, within the purview of this concern, of religious laws. Austin's elucidation of legal rule, employing the notions of command and habitual obedience, poses an obstacle in its unquestioning adoption in view of the concept of justice, in addition to the aforeoutlined concern of legal philosophy. And this legal aspect in canonical laws taxes the juristic subtleties to the maximum.

Legal philosophy cannot remain unconcerned about the issues of adaptability of laws, legal concepts, and changing social order. The revealed law itself visualizes a changing social order. And a legal theory falters if the included legal methods are inadequate in encompassing these demands of legal, conceptual and social change.

Judicial justification is instrumental in the jurisprudential reconstruction of the legal system. Definition of the role of jurist in the legal system and the judicious direction for the juristic efforts are its antecedents. As an ensuing step, display of characteristic judicial virtues, with the special appropriateness to legal decisions in this perspective, is an explanation for not designating this judicial activity as "legislative," especially in the Islamic legal context.

The guideline furnished by the Prophet (PBUH) of Islam to a newly appointed judge, in regard to the exercise of personal judiciousness, in legal matters lacking, in effect, appropriate rules and directions from the primary source of law, is citable in support of this assertion. In addition, the juristic principles provided in the original sources of Islamic Law, with the capacity of functioning as a definite legal framework, in conjunction with the adequacy of legal methodology which is an onus of this treatise, are to transform the judicial activity into "finding," rather than "making," of law.

Due to the crucial significance of the subject of appropriate rules and directions in the original sources of law, in particular, the comprehensive ascertainment of those, a formulation to this end is essential.

Importance of Religion

Theological Considerations : Any interest in a religious law is the marked inclination to extend the attitude of worship, or "*tabbad*," to the revealed legal injunctions. The fundamental error introduced into law in this approach is the assignment of value in jurisprudence relative to theological beliefs, rather than to the proven legal principles identifiable with a particular system of law. The reductionist impulse, invariably associated with the theological attitude, imparts its unavoidable influence upon the process of law-making. The characteristic perceptions of reality, whose determinant normally is the current situation, leave their impact upon the shaping of the legal order.

Historically, theological and legal composition in Islam was reflected in the combined office of the "*Qadi*" and "*Mufti*," which could not have been devoid of certain difficulties. The differentiation between two kinds of obligations—absolute and not subject to change, relative and subject to changes-necessitated according to legal criteria, which can resolve some important legal issues, was not maintained. Similarly, a vital legal issue of "mixed obligations," wherein the observance of two related but variant rules is a mutually conflicting obligation, which in a religious law can retain a theological solution, however, a legal solution would prefer a legal framework of reference to establish the preponderance of one of the obligations. For instance, the injunctions pertaining to the equal rights and economic parity between two sexes are a source of mixed obligations, relative to the rules concerning the repudiation of marriage and inheritance of property. The explanation for this variance in legal obligations resides in the divergence between the "spirit" and the "letter" of the law, and this perspective induced *Shatibi* to favour the "meanings" of the law as a predominant measure towards the intelligibility of *Shariah.* To imagine the issuance of divergent obligations as the intention of the lawgiver is without justification and, therefore, the formulation of a legal method for the reconciliation of the seeming legislative duality is a substantive step. Noticeworthy is the fact that these factors can prove impediments in the organisation and evolvement of an enduring legal system.

Deficient Jurisprudential Approach : A crucial discriminating concept of law is the distinction to be drawn between the question essentially pertaining to law, morals or religion. This is necessitated on the basis of cautious evaluation and understanding of the conditions prevalent in legal thinking. The Quranic prohibition of gambling was merged with the revelational demands for usury or "*riba*," to assign the latter an extensive legal scope that included any chanceful and unearned capital gain, not based upon its precise estimation in advance. An outcome of reliance placed upon subjective belief and personal reasoning, rather than the acknowledged principles of Islamic jurisprudence, the law was to perform a critical function in the designing of the Islamic economic system. Similarly, religious law, not unlike natural law, encouraged obedience to established rulers.

However, there was nothing inherent in religious law which compelled allegiance to the existing rulers. And, in resemblance with natural law, the legal notion of certain fundamental rights, possessed by the individual, could not have been absent from the source of religious law. But the demands of religious faith, largely misconceived as imposing duties and prohibitions, were allowed to hold overwhelming precedence over the jurisprudential dictates of individual right to the "rule of law," with the legal implication that makes this obedience conditional upon that right.

In subsequent times, Locke proposed the terms of social contract, whereby the political authority was conceded only on trust, and the infringement of the fundamental rights of the people by the ruler was an evident breach of the same. The distinct change in emphasis from imposition of duties and obligations, previously misconceived as derivatives of natural law, to the source of fundamental democratic rights—or individual political liberty in society—as a restriction upon the absolute political authority of the ruler, was brought according to the suggestions of the social contract. As an instructive happening of legal history, Islamic Law, under the influence of religious belief, in substitution of the legal requirements, adopted a legal course that evolved law in a direction ironically opposite to the valid dictates of revealed law.

The political authority in Islam is a trusteeship of God and, hence, of people, conceded only in accordance as well as in acceptance of the Islamic code of law and its observance, simply translatable in latter-day terminology as the rule of law. Due to the contractual basis of the conceded trust, the Islamic rule of law is a right of people and, as a counterbalance against the tendency of absolute political authority of the ruler, the socio-political system in Islam, therefore, must be designated as "Nomocracy." This legal situation is in contrast with the fundamental democratic rights of the people as a restraint against the assumption of the absolute authority by the political ruler, as envisioned in the original Lockian concept.

The juristic interest notwithstanding, the concept of Islamic "social contract," to adopt a latter-day terminology, with its derivation reposed in the complete corpus of revealed law and epitomised in the Quranic verse aforementioned, establishes a general resemblance with the Lockian social contract, with the difference of rule of law as the fundamental Islamic right in substitution of the fundamental democratic right envisaged in the latter instance. In contrast, Rousseau proceeded from premises different from those of Islam as well as Locke. Natural law, in this case, rather than creating imprescriptible natural rights in favour of individuals, conferred absolute and inalienable authority upon the people as a whole.

Thus, the people *en mass* were regarded to constitute the entity of "general will," which was a legal authority in the state, assignable to a ruler through delegation alone. A matter of intellectually engaging legal distinction, the primary Islamic source of law is the equivalent of "general will" in Rousseau's "social contract," and essentially external to the scope of delegation. Nevertheless, social contract defined by Rousseau, enacted an historic role, because the French Revolution adopted this doctrine for promulgation in the wake of its victory. Islamic legal development sustained a shortfall and, indeed, Islamic Law became virtually stationary due to the deficient jurisprudential approach. This vital aspect is described by *Ibn Khaldun*[2] in an insight imparting way, who deserves to be quoted at some length, given the importance of the subject: "The school doctrine of each authority became, among his adherents, a scholarly discipline in its own right. They were no longer in a position to apply independent judgment and analogy. Therefore, they had to make reference to the established principles from the school doctrine of their authority, in order to be able to analyze problems in their context and disentangle them when they got confused. A firmly rooted habit was required to enable a person to undertake such analysis and disentanglement and to apply the school doctrine of his particular authority to those processes according to the best of his ability. This habit is what is meant at this time by the science of jurisprudence."

Laws of Islam

The word 'Muslim' is the subject noun of the word *Aslama* which means 'he became obedient and submissive' to his (Creator and his Lord). In this sense, the word Islam, applies to the submission of the whole universe to Almighty Allah. The messages and missions of all the Apostles of Allah were also in obedience to the Commands of Allah.

> The Holy Quran says: "Seek they other than the religion of Allah, when unto Him submitteth whosoever is in the heavens and the earth, willingly, or unwillingly, and unto Him they will be returned'. (III: 83)
>
> And again: "Who forsaketh the religion of Ibrahim save him who befooleth himself, Verily we chose him in the world, and lo! in the

Hereafter he is among the righteous. When his Lord said unto him: Surrender: I have surrendered to the Lord of the worlds. The same did Abraham enjoin upon his sons, and also Jacob (Saying): O my sons! Allah hath chosen for you, the (true) religion; therefore thai not save as men who have surrendered (unto Him). Or were you present when death came to Jacob, when he said unto his sons: "What will you worship after me?' They said: "We shall worship thy Allah and the Allah of thy father of Ibrahim, Ismail, and Ishaq the one (true) Allah to Him we bow (in Islam)". (II: 130-133)

Allah mentions the prayer of His Apostle Joseph in these words: "O my Lord: Thou hast given me (something) of sovereignty and hast taught me (something) of the interpretation of events—creator of the heavens and the earth! Thou are my Protecting Friend in the world and the Hereafter. Make me to die submissive (unto Thee), and join me to the righteous". (XII: 101)

It must be borne in mind that the decrees of Allah consist of the following common points:

(1) Allah's worship with sincere devotion.

(2) Humble prostration before Him.

(3) Accepting His commandments cheerfully.

(4) Strict observance of what has been enjoined and abstention from what has been prohibited by Allah.

These points were the integral part of every *Shariah* although the means and the nature of revelations differed. It has been narrated in a Tradition of the Holy Prophet (peace be upon him): "We, the community of Prophets, are like brothers. Our religion is one".

With the Prophethood of Muhammad, Islam has become a symbolic name to denote the *Shariah* of Allah and a title which represents its followers. No man is allowed to transgress the limits imposed by the religion of Islam which was revealed by Allah to the Prophet (PBUH) who conveyed it to the world.

The Surrender : Says the Quran; "Lo! religion with Allah (is) the surrender (to His will and Guidance). Those who (formerly) received the Scripture dittered only after knowledge came unto them, through transgression among themselves. Whoso dis-believeth the revelations of Allah (will find that), lo! Allah is swift at reckoning. And if they argue with thee (O Muhammad), say: I have surrendered my purpose to Allah and (so have) those who follow me. And say unto those who have received the Scripture and those who read not: Have you (too) surrendered? If they surrender, then truly they are rightly guided, and if they turn away, then it is their duty only to convey the message (unto them). Allah is seer of (His) bondmen." (III: 19-20)

"And whose seeketh as religion other than the surrender (to Allah) it will not be accepted from him, and he will be a loser in the Hereafter." (III:85)

"O you who believe! Observe your duty to Allah with right observance, and die not save as those who have surrendered (Unto Him)." (III: 102)

"And whomsoever it is Allah's will to guide, He expandeth his bosom unto the surrender, and whomsoever it is His Will to send astray, He maketh his bosom close and narrow as if he were engaged in sheer ascent. Thus Allah layeth ignominy upon those who believe not". (IV: 126)

In a Tradition regarding *Gabriel* the Prophet (PBUH) has interpreted the word "Islam" as follows:

"Islam is that thou shall bear withness that there is no god but Allah and that Muhammad (PBUH) is the Messenger of Allah and (that) thou keep up prayer and pay the *Zakat* and (keep) fast in *Ramadan* and perform pilgrimage to the House, in case you have means."

In another *Hadith*, the Messenger of Allah said :

"Islam is based on five things: the bearing of witness that there is no god but Allah and Muhammad (PBUH) is the Messenger of Allah and the keeping up of prayer and the payment of *Zakat* and the pilgrimage and fasting in *Ramadan*". At another place the Prophet (PBUH) explained the meanings of *Iman* (faith) in the following words: "Faith is that you believe in Allah and His angels and His books and His messengers, in the Hereafter and in the divine decree to good and evil".

Whenever a mention of Islam and faith is made simultaneously, as has been mentioned in the Tradition regarding Gabriel[3], the word Islam indicated outward actions, whereas faith implies inner beliefs or convictions; and when their mention is made separately, each of these words would mean actions as well as inner beliefs or convictions.

Islam is another name for belief and action, religion and the world, and a code of life. *Sheikh-ul-Islam Muhammad-bin-Abdul Wahab*[4] has defined Islam as follows:

"Islam means bowing before Allah with firm belief in His Oneness, and prostration before Him in complete submission, and abstinence from ascribing partners unto Him". A true Muslim is one who by the grace and favour of Allah embraces Islam, acts upon it and affirms his faith in it by convictions, actions and practice so that he acquires unshakable trust and confidence in it.

The bases of Islamic *Shariah* are the revelations of Allah which He vouchsafed to the Prophet (PBUH). The purpose of these revelations was to bring the people out of darkness into light. These are intact even today in the form of the Holy Quran. There is no question of interpolation or distortion in it from any side. The other source of the *Shariah* is the *Sunnah* of the Prophet (PBUH) which is an interpretation and elucidation of the Quran.

The Book of Allah and the *Sunnah* of the Prophet (PBUH) are co-related with each other just as the bearing of witness to the truth that "there is no god but Allah", and the affirmation of the truth that "Muhammad (PBUH) is the Messenger of Allah", are inseparable from one another.

A further probe would reveal that the foundation of Islamic *Shariah* is based on the following two unique and fundamental principles :

(1) Worship is due to none but Allah who has no partner, may he be an angel or an apostle. Says the Quran: "And the places of worship are only for Allah so pray not unto anyone along with Allah". (LXXII: 18). It has been mentioned at another place: "Say: Lo! my worship and my sacrifice and my living and my dying are for Allah, Lord of the worlds. He hath no partner. This am I commanded, and I am first of those who surrender (unto Him)". (VI: 163-164).

(2) The second fundamental principle is that Allah must be worshipped as has been enjoined in the Quran and according to the *Sunnah* of the Prophet. The Quran says: "And whatsoever the Messenger giveth you, take it. And whatsoever he forbiddeth, abstain from it". (LIX : 7).

At another place it has been said:

> "Say: I am only a mortal like you. My Lord inspireth in me that your God is only One God. And whosoever hopeth for the meeting with his Lord, let him do righteous work, and make none sharer of the worship due unto his Lord". (XVIII : 110)

Hafiz ibn Kathir while interpreting the phrase 'righteous work', writes that it denotes the actions which are in conformity with the decrees of Allah and are performed only to please Allah. There are only two basic conditions, the fulfilment of which make the actions agreeable to Allah. The first condition is that they should be done with the sole intention of pleasing Allah and the second is that these actions should be in accordance with the *Sunnah* of the Prophet (PBUH). It has been reported by *Hadrat Aishah* that the Holy Prophet (PBUH) said: "He who made an innovation in our matter *(Sunnah)* is condemnable".

> Allah has embodied all goodness and virtue in the Islamic *Shariah* so that it has reached its culmination. It has an all-embracing and universal position and has become eternal. So far as the question of its excellence and its being free from all sorts of errors is concerned, the Quran itself affirmed: "This day have I perfected your religion for you and completed My favour unto you, and have chosen for you as religion *Al-Islam*".
> (V : 3)

Explaining this verse, *Hafiz ibn Kathir* states that it is the greatest favour and bounty of Allah on the Muslim *Ummah* that He has perfected the religion for them. Now it stands in need of no other religion or code of life. This is the reason why the Prophet (PBUH) was exalted to the eminent position of the last of the Prophets (PBUH).

What he declared lawful is lawful and what he forbade is unlawful. The only true religion is that which he preached and the only truth is that of which he gave the knowledge. It is free from all errors and blemishes and there is no question of disputing about it. Says the Quran:

> "The words of your Allah are complete as regards Truth and Justice". (VI : 116). That means the events which have been related are based on truth and the verses which enjoin and prohibit certain things and actions are based on justice and equity. With the completion of the religion, the blessings and favours of Allah have reached at the highest. The Muslims should express their delight that the choicest religion of Allah has been sent down for them and this religion has been revealed to the Prophet who handed it down to them through the most exalted divine book, the Holy Quran.

As regards universality, it must be borne in mind that it is incumbent on every Muslim to abide by the all-embracing and universal *Shariah* and none is allowed the slightest deviation from it. So it is essential that every Muslim realise that he is to mould his life according to its behests so that he may earn the blessings and favours of Allah and refrain from incurring His displeasure and wrath.

> Says the Quran: "And it becometh not a believing man or a believing woman, when Allah and His Messenger have decided an affair (for them), that they should (after that) claim any say in their affair;

and whoso is rebellious to Allah and His Messenger, verily he goeth astray in error manifest." (XXXIII: 36).

It is not the only place where such a course has been recommended. I quote below some passages from the Quran where this idea has been emphasised very clearly and unequivocally :

"And whatsoever the Messenger giveth you, take it. And whatsoever he forbiddeth, abstain (from it). And keep your duty to Allah. Lo! Allah is stern in reprisal." (LIX : 7).

"And let those who conspire to evade orders beware lest grief or painful punishment befall them." (XXIV : 63).

"Follow that which is sent down unto you from your Lord, and follow no protecting friends beside Him. Little do you recollect."(VII : 3).

"So tread thou the straight path as thou art commanded and those who turn (unto Allah) with thee, and transgress not. Lo! He is seer of what you do." (XI : 112)

"So hold thou fast to that which is inspired in these. Lo! thou, art on a right path." (XLIII :43)

"And (He commandeth you, saying): This is my straight path, so follow it. Follow not other ways, lest you be parted from His way. This hath He ordained for you, that ye may ward off evil)." (VI : 154)

Say, (O Muhammad, to mankind): It ye love Allah, follow me, Allah will love you and forgive you and your sins. Allah is forgiving, Merciful. Say: Obey Allah and the Messenger. But if they turn away. Lo! Allah loveth not the disbelievers (in His guidance)." (III : 31-32)

Obey Allah.

"The saying of (all true) believers when they appeal unto Allah and His Messenger to judge between them is only that they say: We hear and we obey, and such are the successful. He who obeyeth Allah and his Messenger, and feareth Allah, and keepeth duty (unto Him): such indeed are the victorious." (XXIV: 51-52)

"O you who believe! Obey Allah and obey the Messenger and those of you who are in authority; and if you have a dispute concerning any matter, refer it to Allah and the Messenger if you are (in truth) believers in Allah and the Last Day. That is better and more seemly in the end." (IV : 59)

"But nay, by thy Lord, they will not believe (in truth) until they make thee judged what is in dispute between them and find within themselves no dislike of that which thou decidest, and submit with full submission." (IV : 65)

"Whoso judgeth not by that which Allah hath revealed: such are disbelievers." (V : 44)

"Let the people of the Gospel judge by that which Allah hath revealed therein. Whoso judgeth not by that which Allah hath revealed; such as evil-livers. And unto thee have We revealed the Scripture with the truth, confirming whatever Scripture was before it, and a watcher over it. So judge between them by that which Allah hath revealed, and follow not their desires away from the truth which hath come unto thee. For each We have prescribed divine law and traced out way. Had Allah willed, He could have made you one community. But may try you by that which He hath given you (He hath made you as ye are). So vie one with another in good works. Unto Allah yet will all return, and He will then inform you of that wherein you differ. So judge between them by that which Allah hath revealed and follow not their desires, but beware of them lest they seduce thee from some part of that which Allah hath revealed unto thee. And if they turn away, then know that Allah's Will is to smite them for some sin of theirs. Lo! many of mankind are evil liver. Is it a judgement of the time of (pagan) ignorance that they are seeking? Who is better than Allah for judgement to a people who have certainty (in their belief)?" (V : 47-50)

"Shall I seek other than Allah for judge, when He it is who hath revealed unto you (this Scripture) known that it is revealed from thy Lord in truth. So be not thou (O Muhammad) of the waverers. Perfected is the word of thy Lord in truth and justice. There is naught that can change His words. He is the Hearer, the Knower." (VI : 115-116)

Preach Truth : Success, honour, prestige, victory over the enemies and peace and stability of the Muslims depend on acting upon the *Shariah.* If the condition of the Muslims be reversed to that which has been stated above or, in other words, they become indifferent to the *Shariah,* only loss, ignominy and disgrace would fall to their lot. We must keep this fact in mind that the Almighty Allah has observed, swearing by the age, that all men are in a state of loss save those who affirm belief and do good deeds and preach truth and perseverance. There are many statements in the Divine Book and in the *Ahadith* of the Holy Prophet (peace be upon him) which bear testimony to this fact. Moreover, history also affirms the fact that real honour and respect lie in submission to Allah and he who disobeys

Him nothing but disgrace is in store for him. The Holy Quran affirm this fact at a number of places, such as :

> "He who holdeth fast to Allah, he indeed is guided unto a right path." (III : 101)
>
> "And those who strive hard in Our cause We shall guide them to Our right path. Verily, Allah is with the grateful." (XXIX : 69)
>
> "O you who believe! If ye help Allah, He will help you and will make your foothold firm." (XLVII : 7)
>
> "Verily, Allah helpeth one who helpeth Him. Lo! Allah is strong, Almighty—those who, if We gave them power in the land, establish prayer and pay *Zakat* and enjoin kindness and forbid iniquity and Allah's is the sequel of events." (XVII : 4041)
>
> "O you who believe! Shall I show a commerce that will save you from a painful doom? You should believe in Allah and His Messenger, and should strive for the cause of Allah with your wealth and your lives. That is better for you, if you did but know. He will forgive you, your sins and bring you into Gardens underneath which rivers flow, and pleasant dwellings in Gardens of Eden. That is the supreme triumph." (LXI : 10.12)
>
> "O you who believe: If ye keep your duty to Allah, He will give you discrimination (between right and wrong) and will rid you of your evil thoughts and deeds, and will forgive you. Allah is of infinite Bounty." (VIII : 29)
>
> "Allah hath promised such good deeds that He will surely make them to succeed (the present rulers) in the earth even as He caused those who were before them to succeed (others); and that He will surely establish for them their religion which He hath approved for them and will give them in exchange safety after their fear. They serve Me. They ascribe nothing as partner unto Me. Those who disbelieve henceforth, they are the miscreants. Establish prayer and pay *Zakat* and obey the Messenger, that happily ye may find mercy." (XXIV : 55-56)

Triumph of Logic

The Law in Islam is not comprehensively in revealed form and the need of law is attainable through its ascertainment with reason. Some legal methods have acquired the recognised status of the sources of law, while other methods have remained juristic principles. Deficiencies in the development of the area of legal methods have cast a reflection upon the law. In the view of Mahmasani, foundations of the modern renaissance in Islamic legal thought were laid in the 14th century by the Muslim jurists who wrote on the legal methodology and the end of law. These writings no doubt were the precursors of the modern legal philosophies in the West, however, the Islamic Law *per se* remained substantially unbenefitted, for those legal conceptions stayed without assimilation into Islamic legal thought as a matter of an historic irony. Response of legal theory to social changes, development of law and the completion of the objectives of law were adversely influenced as a result.

Convergence of Opinion (Ijma) : The implications of *Ijma* are the consensus of opinion of Islamic community on a legal issue, the consensus of persons competent for *Ijtihad*, or the unanimous agreement of the jurists of the community in a particular age. Consensus of all Muslims on essentials and of the Muslim scholars on points of detail are the distinguishing features of the "unanimity of opinion." Some eminent jurists also consider the majority of all Muslims to constitute *Ijma* as well. The present-day definition of *Ijma* places reliance upon an agreement of the Muslim jurists in a particular age on an issue of law. The four *Sunni* Schools of Law uphold it as a valid source of law. However, in this perspective, a proper apprehension of the meaning of *Ijma* is lent by considering it as a natural process of the crystallisation of viewpoints into agreement. With wide awareness of the Islamic history, Hurjronge's[5] observation of Ijma as the "foundation of foundations and the moveable element in law" demands attention. In the opinion of Gibb, *Ijma* is described as the third source of revelation, erected with a theory of infallibility. Ascribable advantages to *Ijma* in a sympathetic view would include the resolution of conflicts due to divergent opinions and authentication of the rules of law, formulated by the jurists, and their elevation to a status of law. An aspect of more than academic interest, legal history of *Ijma* takes the juristic curiosity to conclude that its validity should be dependent upon the consonance with the text, general spirit and objectives of *Shariah*. *Ijma* has been an ongoing process, for rules and decisions based upon it may change with the alterations in time and conditions. Nevertheless, as an inductive principle of fundamental import, the construction of Ijma as popular voluntary consensus, obtained in advance of the implementation of the legal measure, and not a sovereign viewpoint which can arrogate to itself the unique authority for overwhelming legal preponderance, remained unutilised in the Islamic constitutional law.

In the opinion of McDonald, the famous Muslim jurist, *Shafii*, is rightly credited with the extension of the principle of agreement and its erection into a formal source of law. According to him, the absolute form of the principle- whatever the community of Islam has agreed upon at any time, is of God-is noticeworthy." The ramifications of this principle upon the political unity of Islam and the critical evolution of Islamic Law is a subject suited to the evaluation for vital legal insight. Now, in conformity with Ijma as a material source of law, the constitutional requirement for the office of the Caliph could have been the consent of the representatives of the ruled, in consonance with the agreed practice of "*baiya*" during the era of the "right-guided" Caliphs. The omission of this constitutional practice from the subsequent political course in Islam, especially, after the enunciation of the principle of consensus, is the expression of the maxim, "what is potent for the good, can also be good for the evil," whose practical manifestations are deceptively rare in life. The principle of agreement must have been of avail in the authentication of the legal tradition of Caliphs assuming political powers which were not sanctioned by Islamic Law. Hence, the substantive issue, whether the common political error can be authenticated by the method of Ijma, is of extraordinary relevance. Obviously, then, the principle of consensus in legal authentication is to be intimately associated with the settled merit of reasons.

The substantive aspects of the utilisation of lawmaking potential of *Ijma* in the present-day constitutional set-ups, the avoidance of the shortcomings such as become apparent from the evaluation of its utility from the Islamic history, and the preservation of the politically unifying role of *Ijma* in Islam will be addressed during the ensuing course of this treatise.

Rational Approach (Ijtihad) : Independent intellectual striving or *Ijtihad* is based upon the premise that on all problems, which confront the Muslims, there is either a binding decision or an indication of the right solution that is to be sought. The implication of reasoning is involved in the exercise of *Ijtihad*, which is based on Islamic criteria, and its Islamic desirability is demonstrated by the emphasis laid repetitively upon the measures of "thinking" and "understanding" in the original source of Islamic Law. As an accepted juristic principle, it is considered to make the legal system of Islam dynamic, and its development and evolution in the changing circumstances possible. In the view of Schacht, the opinion of expert on questions of fact is a parallel of *Ijtihad*, while Coulson describes it as the process of juristic endeavour to ascertain the terms of *Shariah* law. *Shatibi* thought of it as a process of adaptability and, among one of its four functions, deduction of the basis of the rules of *Shariah* law, also called reasoning by analogy, was included. And, most importantly, he considered *Ijtihad* as a necessary duty of Muslims, and suggested that its use should not contradict the objectives of Shariah. The deductions of a jurist, in the course of *Ijtihad*, do not ipso facto attain the status of law, which is consequent to the consensus or *Ijma* of the jurists, and its wide popular acceptance. Now as an inglorious chapter in the Islamic legal history, the "closure of the doors of *Ijtihad*" in the 10th century A.D. curtailed the legal usefulness of analogous reasoning, for it is considered as synonymous with *Ijtihad* by *Shafii* and many other Muslim jurists, and severely eroded the basis of *Ijma*. Thus, the result was destined to reflect as the marked decline in the Islamic legal development. Against this perspective of Islamic legal history, the reintroduction of *Ijtihad* as a process of legal development will depend upon the prerequisite of a functional Islamic legal system, considered strictly according to the accepted denotation of this term, and this treatise is an endeavour in that direction.

Analogical Method (Qiyas) : Analogous reasoning or "*Qiyas*" was adopted by the Muslim Jurist, *Hanifa*, as a source of law-making. A review of relevant literature demonstrates this juristic method as a process, by which the rules of law embodied in the Quran, Traditions and Ijma are extended to cases not covered by their texts. The jurist *Shafii* considered analogous reasoning to be synonymous with *Ijtihad*, and to the extent that the former is a part of the latter, it is a dependable view. The legal authority as a binding precedent in the instance of analogous reasoning is, however, lent by the consensus of jurists in this regard. The crucial issue of the role of human reason ("ray") in relation to revealed law was addressed by *Shafii* to the satisfactory settlement of the controversy, concerning the divine and human elements in law, that surfaced in the 8th century, A.D. This fundamental conflict of principle in Islamic jurisprudence was resolved with the two specified elements, finding accommodation in a complementary relationship, in the process of reasoning by analogy.

This juristic accomplishment was, no doubt, the partial basis for the title of the "father of Muslim Jurisprudence," which was bestowed upon him. Another eminent Muslim legist, who succeeded *Shafii* by several centuries, *Shatibi* viewed analogical reasoning or deduction as a systematic mode of *Ijtihad*, wherein the human reason is assigned the role of discovering the "*ila*" of the text. In turn, this is extended to analogical cases and situations which though are not covered by the language of the text, however, the reason employed therein serves as the coverage. The "*ila*" is definable as the fact, circumstance or consideration underlying the law embodied in the text, as related to the lawgiver. Extension of the law of text is the function of analogical reasoning. In another opinion, the application of the "effective cause of the law" in a text upon new cases and situations is the essence of analogical reasoning.

Theory of Debate

From among other juristic principles, "*Istihsan*" or juristic preference is a legal argument contrary to the apparent analogy. The controversy arose due to the arrogation of legislative privilege, perceived in the application of this principle, and *Shafii* was proponent of such a view. However, *Maliki* jurists defined it in the sense of the attention to public interest and justice. In this perspective, it appears as a juristic and not personal preference, in conformity with its adoption as a doctrine of equity. The same legal attribute is ascribable to another juristic principle of "*Istislah*," and the Muslim Jurist, Malik, favoured it as a legal modality for the deduction of law, based upon the consideration of public interest. The Islamic legal conception of public interest does not carry unlimited or unrestricted connotation, for it is conceived within the scope of *Shariah* law. The recommended conditions for the applicability of the legal notion of public interest excluded matters of religion, and included concerns of transactions.

The precepts of *Shariah* law and its objectives did not come in conflict with the considerations of public interest. And the demands of public interest were of the essential and necessary type, and included the preservation of life, religion, reason, progeny and property, as also the betterment of life. Considered from another viewpoint, "*Istislah*" is a mode of *Ijtihad*, which upholds public interest such as is envisaged by *Shariah* law to be paramount. Although this juristic principle should have developed into the legal concept of adaptability in law, a view ably proposed by *Shatibi* later, but remained unassimilated into Islamic legal theory, however, in actual application, it succumbed to the theological and idealistic limitations. The idealism of literal emphasis in law, without making legal theory in conformity with the principles of jurisprudence, was a causative factor which hampered the development of the principles of 'adaptability in Islamic Law."

The juristic principle of "*Istidlal*" is the deduction of a rule, with the use of reason and logic, on the basis of another rule. The absence of "*ila*," or common cause for the basis of reasoning, is its differentiating feature from the analogous reasoning. This principle relies upon juristic exposition and leads to legal development.

The juristic principle of "*Istishab*" literally means "permanence," and denotes the existence or non-existence of a state which is not proved to have ceased from the past. In the description by Ibn Khaldun it is "the attempt to associate the present legal situation with the past by judging the present in the same way as the past is judged, with the result that the legal situation is left as it had been, for no evidence to change it has been found."

"*Siasa Shariah*" was denoted to administer justice in conformity with the spirit of Islamic Law. According to this legal doctrine, the deficiency in law was no doubt compensated, however, the arrogation of legislative prerogative to the political authority, under the misperceived scriptural precept of sovereignty being

Divine ordained, compromised the development of constitutional law and independence of judiciary. At this juncture, it is suited to the occasion to enunciate the preceding precept as one of the misinterpreted revealed injunctions whose adverse consequences upon the Islamic polity have been no less than substantial.

The principle of "selection" was adopted to choose between variant opinions recognised in jurisprudence as equally authoritative. And the principle of "need or necessity" was viewed as different mode of reasoning, resulted in an exception of rule to accommodate the change in imperative circumstances, and it was not generally considered to be a source of law. In legal writings by Malik, considerable stress was laid upon the maxim that necessity makes prohibited things permissible.

The subject of juristic preference, in the interpretation of law, cannot be completely separated from the interpretative ad hocism, and an opportune selection for a mode of reasoning. A strict conformity with the fundamental principles of Islam, underlying the *Shariah* law, and constituting its spirit, reinforced with the principle of authentication by *Ijma*, is necessitated in the use of the juristic principles and modes of legal reasoning. However, due to the disuse of the principle of *Ijtihad*, these juristic principles would not have been of much usefulness as methods of legal development and change. Therefore, concurrence is affordable to Schacht's observation that these methods were not adopted as principles of change, but were rather employed to interpret and justify the already existing rules of Islamic Law.

References

1. *Prophet Yusuf's name as in the Bible.*
2. *A famous historian who wrote History of Islamic times.*
3. *Gabriel (a Jibbrail), the archangel who used to visit the Prophet (Pbuh) with revelations from Allah.*
4. *The most revered Islamic scholar who founded the Wahhabi movement in the deserts of Arabia.*
5. *A famous historian, outside Arab writing for Arabs.*

6

CONSTITUTIONAL CHARTER

THE DECLARATION

The word, 'constitution' in its legal sense is of recent origin.

A modern writer defines constitution as "codes which aspire to regulate the allocations of functions, powers and duties among the various agencies and offices of the government...."[1] When we apply it, to a document which was signed within a few months of the *Hijrah* of the Prophet (Pbuh), fourteen hundred years ago, we do not get the exact sense and meaning given to it by either the Prophet (Pbuh) himself or those to whom the document was being given. He had called, the Document under study, as:

"A Writing from Muhammad, the Prophet (PBUH) of Allah."

A Document : It could also mean a letter and a document, the last being the most appropriate. This settles one thing. It was neither a 'treaty' nor an agreement, because it was "From Muhammad, the Prophet (PBUH) of Allah," and not an agreement between him and others. They had no objection in receiving it as a Charter laying down the Code of Life for *Yathrib*[1]. They also accepted his position as "The Prophet (PBUH) of Allah," even though some of them desired to retain their attachment to the religion they already professed. They had, as a matter of fact, no option but to accept it or else live in *Yathrib* as aliens.

A few points need to be borne in mind while studying this Document. First, that the Document must be placed chronologically before any of the other objects is studied. This is necessary, because of two reasons. The first reason is that unless its period is determined it will not be possible to determine the object for which it was promulgated.

The document is of a permanent nature. There must, therefore, have been other reasons which are of a lasting nature. The Constitution, if we consider it as such, of the first Islamic State, brought into existence by the Prophet (Pbuh) himself has to remain, in most respects, if not all, a model Constitution for all states established by Muslims. We, therefore, feel that it needs studying from a number of angles.

It is important to bear in mind that the Document was dictated by the Prophet of Allah (Pbuh). He had been receiving Sublime Guidance, for thirteen years, from Allah. A person of his calibre would not issue a document of this nature without an adequate and a set purpose. Furthermore a person of his knowledge, experience and capabilities would not issue a self–contained document piece meal. If a document is issued by instalments it loses consistency and results in being misunderstood. His actions subsequent to the issue of this Document have also great relevancy. They show, if he was in the habit of tackling problems in a consistent or a disjointed manner. It must be kept in mind that he is The Law Giver and laws given by him have stood the test of time. Persons who create and promulgate laws have to consider problems from all angles, otherwise their laws fail to receive such reception as desired. There has to be logic and consistency in the words and actions of men placed in the position he occupied. Written documents become out of date if they are void of consistency. Lastly, it has to be borne in mind that this Document was issued under certain conditions. Therefore, to gauge its proper importance we must bear in mind all the time, the circumstances which necessitated its issue. These have been discussed briefly.

We have referred to the Document as a Constitutional Charter.

"The form and nature of a constitution are dictated by the relationship prevailing among the various sections or classes of people." There was no organised group with whom the Prophet (Pbuh) could have executed a treaty or an agreement. Hence we find that it was neither a treaty nor an agreement. It is important to bear in mind its heading, which also forms the very first Clause.

The heading needs to be given in full.

> "This Document (writing) is from Muhammad The Prophet of Allah (Pbuh) to *Quraish* and *Yathribite* Believers and those who will follow them and fight alongside with them. They will form ONE UMMAH to the exclusion of others."

Primarily the Document has been issued to administer the affairs of *Muhajir* and *Ansar* Believers. Its jurisdiction is then extended to those who live and fight Jihad under the leadership of these *Muhajir* and *Ansar* Believers. Leadership has been given to the entire Muslim community. The Prophet (Pbuh) has not spoken of his leadership. This point has great significance for future generations of Believers.

Promulgation Manner : The manner of promulgation of the Charter may also have a bearing on the circumstances at the time of its issue and the keenness of the recipients to be favoured by inclusion in the *Ummah*. From the wording and placing of concessions to various tribes, it creates the impression that the dictation of the Charter took place in an open Darbar, and as the Arab custom was and still is, those to whom a clause did not apply they spoke up to be included and at once another clause was dictated for inclusion.

The Document was issued within a few months of the Hijrah of the Prophet (Pbuh) which took place in July or August 622 A.C. This is the period when, "a few years earlier, the reign of the grandson of Nousherwan was extended to the *Hellespont* and the *Nile*, the ancient limits of the Persian monarchy; the Christians of East were scandalised by the worship of fire and the impious doctrine of the two principles; the Magi were no less intolerant than the bishops, and the martyrdom of some native Persians, who had deserted the religion of Zoroaster was conceived to be the prelude of a fierce and general persecution. The oppressive laws of Justinian, the adversaries of the Church were made the enemies of the state; the alliance of the Jews, Nestorians and Jacobites, had contributed to the success of Chosroes[2], and his partial favour to the sectaries, provoked the hatred and fears of Catholic clergy."

The Persian monarch was so full of arrogance that, as his predecessors used to carry away the gods of the defeated, back to Persia, he carried away to his capital the Holy Cross from Jerusalem. The situation, however, altered, within a few years as predicted in the Quran. Byzantium, "rallied under Heraclius, who had led his troops in 624 A.C., into the heart of Iran. Chosroes was deposed and executed by his own subjects, and Heraclius recovered the Cross".

It meant a great deal for the prestige of the Emperor. To have brought back Holy Cross, the symbol of true Christianity, to Jerusalem, where the Jews were supposed to have been instrumental in having Jesus Christ crucified, was a great achievement. Syria, at that time was a truly Christian land. "In fact this is the only period in which Syria has been a fully Christian country..... Not only was the country Christian, but the age was an ecclesiastical age".

It was in this age of persecution, religious prejudices, taboos, ethnical differences, and acute hatred resulting in mass killings, when this Document was dictated to an assembly of Believers, *Mushrikeen* and Jews, not far from a totally Christian land, where at about the same time controversies raged, which ended in a, "sentence of excommunication on the tomb of St. Peter; the ink was mingled with the sacramental wine, the blood of Christ; and no ceremony was omitted that could fill the superstitious mind with horror and affright".

It was the same period, when in India, Harsha[3] ruled and according to a Chinese pilgrim, ''The penalty of imprisonment, inflicted after the cruel Tibetan fashion, which left the prisoner to live or die was freely awarded and mutilation was often adjudged".

In spite of it all we are told that in every one of these lands their particular civilization was at its peak and yet man was in bondage and writhed with pain at the feet of other men. Man had forgotten that he and other men were all descended from Adam, and Adam had been created from clay:

"He it is Who hath created you from clay". (6: 2)

How unnatural that men should be regarded as unequal and yet inhabit the same planet. Many prophets had come and tried to teach men and women that they were equal as human beings, but it was left to the Last Prophet (PBUH) of Allah to establish complete equality in those who believed in Allah and him as His Messenger and Servant.

While he was dictating this Document of great consequence he was observing the principle of equality. It would take centuries for mankind to realise the effect and importance of this principle.

The Ultimate Domination : The ultimate destination of mankind, while on this planet is the mastery of elements of nature. He has to achieve vast knowledge of nature of things and elements to an extent that very few can imagine. Acquisition of knowledge at the level of entire humanity demands peace, justice and equality among mankind. This will come about when mankind rises above the level of present ignorance and becomes one *Ummah*. This is the most important lesson taught by the Last Prophet (PBUH) of Allah, while dictating this unique Document. Universal peace will be achieved when the principle of equality of man is universally accepted. The Prophet (Pbuh) when dictating this Document brought the level of all men on an equal pedestal. Jews who, at the time, were looked down upon, except may be in Iran were given equality with Arabs of *Quraish* and *Ansar*[5] origin. Equality of man appears to be one of the main features of his Mission, and, "It is difficult to portray the events of the life of the Prophet (Pbuh) unless we first understand the nature of the Mission entrusted to him"."

This Mission, according to the Quran is complete guidance of mankind in all walks of life. Man has to enter Islam completely.

> "O you who believe! Come, all of you, into submission". (2: 208)

And the Prophet (PBUH) has to bring mankind into Islam-submission to the Will of Allah.

> "(This is) a Scripture which We have Revealed unto thee (Muhammad) that thereby, thou mayest bring forth mankind from darkness unto light, by the permission of their Lord, unto the Path of the Mighty, the Owner of Praise". (14: 1)

The Eternal Message of Allah happens to be placed in a world which, in certain respects, alters with changes in time and geography. And yet this Eternal Message guides men to the straight path. "The glory of Islam is that it distinguishes the universal from the changing particulars".

If we study the Quran and try to locate Eternal Commandments we will find that these happen to be all in respect of those aspects of human life and nature, which remain constant and are not subject to any great changes as a result of time and place. Those aspects of life whether at the level of an individual or at the collective level of society, which are subject to changes due to change in surroundings, have been left to the individual or the society, as the case may be, to find the best solution as long as no other Commandment is violated in the process. This means that no restrictions have been placed on "the changing particulars."

It is the same with the Sunnah of the Prophet (Pbuh). He has set precedents in all walks of life but restrictions are placed only in the field of universals and particulars are left to be decided by the individual and the society, as the case may be. He was the Messenger of the Code of Life Revealed by Allah. He was not sent as a military commander and yet he demonstrated the "why, when and how" of war, because the *Ummah* needed guidance in it. He was not a statesman and yet he demonstrated how justice tempered with mercy was to be administered in a society of equals. He led his army to many a battlefield, keeping in view the principles of war and compulsions of strategy and tactics dictated by geography and other factors and demonstrated all the qualities of a great commander.

His critics fail to keep his Mission in view when commenting on his activities as a soldier or as a statesman because their view of a Way of Life is limited to acts of prayers only. To say that, "Muhammad (Pbuh) himself was not a warrior and had few military gifts. In battle he invariably followed behind the front line, never, if avoidable, himself engaged in hand to hand fighting", amounts to disregarding his role as a guide of commanders. The writer forgets that commanders do not engage, normally, in hand to hand fighting. They have to direct, control and deploy troops as the situation may demand. This vague statement of a British general does not mention those qualities of martial nature which in his opinion were absent in the Prophet (Pbuh).

He would have probably liked to see in him qualities displayed by British generals like Kitchner, who, "sword in hand and Bible in pocket he enjoyed a career of spectacular warfare in Russia, China, India, and Africa...." Kitchner's enjoyment of war amounted to perversity, when he had defeated Mehdi's Army he arranged a victory parade, on 10th of April 1898, in which, he treated the captured enemy commander Amir Mahmud in the most cruel manner. "Dragging chains which were riveted round his ankles, and wearing a halter round his neck the defeated army commander was made to walk, and sometimes run, behind the cavalry. His hands were bound behind his back, and he was driven forward by Sudanese guards who lashed him with whips when he stumbled. Kitchner rode on a white horse in triumph". What a spectacle of British chivalry and martial excellence during the closing years of nineteenth century when European civilization was at its height.

This British general of whom many generations spoke with admiration, gave orders, that the tomb of *Mehdi* be razed to the ground and his bones to be cast into the Nile. *Mehdi's* skull which was unusually large was kept aside to be used as inkstand. One suggestion was to use it as a drinking cup. He had ordered Wingate, another famous British soldier, to "loot like blazes. I want any quantity of marble stairs, marble payings, iron railings, looking glasses and fittings, doors, windows, furniture of all sorts". A victorious general who pardoned his life-long enemies must have appeared to General Glubb, to lack martial qualities common among European generals and conquerors.

The objective of the Prophet (Pbuh) was to establish peace as a precedent for Believers until the end of Time. He had to demonstrate what was an ideal life. This included both war and peace. It included the life of a labourer and also that of a ruler. He demonstrated the life of a man of all walks of life, when he was being persecuted and we find no change in the way he lived, when he was the ruler of entire Arabia and his army had a successful round of exchange of arms with the Byzantines Imperial Army, at the battlefield of Mowtta. As a general his strategy was not only to win the war but to succeed in the days after the war as well, and his war stands alone in the annals of military history, which brought happier days both for the winner and the vanquished although a winner in earlier battles he had accepted armistice on the enemy's terms.

It has been recorded by his biographer "When there was peace and war was abolished and men met in safety and consulted together none talked intelligently about Islam without entering it. In these two years double as many or more than double as many entered Islam as before".

Throughout his life he was keen to use all his resources to bring about peaceful atmosphere in which his Message could be understood and accepted. Today, fourteen centuries after him, the world has accepted the point of view that peace alone can solve mankind's problems. A modern writer has said, "In an age of Total War we will need Total Peace". War, however, has to be catered for." Wars do not break out of themselves, but they may change the course of history and the fate of mankind.... War has, therefore, become the greatest of social problems". For him and for Islam war had become the greatest of not only social but also political problem. He gave to the world, Islam—The Message of Peace-when war had been brought to his doorstep. This Document is of great consequence as it gives an answer to a multi-national *Ummah*, as to how they should face an aggressor and survive. One of the outstanding features of this Document, which cemented the citizens of *Yathrib* was justice with Equality for all. Peace within communities and, at international level, cannot be established without equality and equal status to men and groups of men—the nations. This equality was not acceptable either within Arabia or at the international level at that time. The Arabs of *Mecca*, steeped in the idea of racial superiority, their minds clouded with racial prejudices, and having a class ridden society, were in no mood to accept equality between *Abu Jehl*[5], the high born *Quraishi* chief and *Bilal* the Negro slave.

Principle of Equality : It was the principle of equality of man which evoked the animosity of the two neighbouring mighty empires of Iran and Byzantine, towards Islam and Muslims. The ruling classes of both these empires were securely entrenched as the high born elites, who held the birth right of princely and regal positions. The birth of an Ideology of "Equality before the Eyes of Allah," both in this and the next world, was a revolutionary reality which had to be nipped in the bud. The rest of the world was to array itself on the side of these to Empires, one after the other. The prophesy of *Abbas bin Ubada* was fulfilled soon enough but it was to continue being fulfilled for ever.

It was during the Second *Bayah at al-Aqaba*[6] that *Abbas bin Ubada al-Ansari*, said to the *Ansars* who were swearing allegiance to the Prophet (Pbuh), "O men of *Khazraj*[7], do you realise to what you are committing yourselves in pledging your support to this man? It is to war against all and sundry. If you think that if you lose your property and your nobles are killed you will give him up, then do so now, for it would bring you shame in this world and the next. But if you think that you will be loyal to your undertaking even if you lose your property and your nobles are killed, then take him for by God. It will profit you in this world and the next".

The men from *Khazraj* and many others who followed their footsteps are still being challenged by the enemies of Justice and equality for all. It is, outwardly, that people oppose Islam, while their real opposition is against the principle of equality of man, by those whose vested interest are in danger or being jeopardised. It was a question of life and death in that age. Religion during that age made men of religion oblivious of cruelties perpetuated in the name of religion. Minor differences or even suspicion of minor differences led men to throw others into flames. As has been remarked, "It remained for the Medieval Church, however, to put cruelty and burning and gruesome public executions on the firm popular basis of exalting religious spectacles".

There can be no peace in the world unless the world led by Muslims observes laws relating to Jihad on the Path of Allah and in conducting their foreign affairs as ordained in the Quran. This Document was the first writing, directing towards the principles and the policy according to which human societies should conduct their affairs. It has been universally accepted that in the world of today there is no international law, relating to the conduct of states in matters of conflict or mutual interest, obligations and the making and breaking of treaties. There have been usages in various parts of the world, which have been overlooked more often than not and in all conflicts national interests have prevailed. "International Law, so called, is in reality national law regulating international relations of those states".

Complete Code : Islam has a complete Code of International Law. It, however, operates at the level of the Millah of Islam, on the principle that Believers are an *Ummah* when considered with respect to the rest of humanity. If Muslim States observe in their inter-state relations, the Commandments of the Quran, the super powers will find it difficult to drive humanity in World Wars, as they have done twice during twentieth century. These Quranic Injunctions dictate relations between Muslim states and also between Muslim states and others. Islamic Law is the only Law which forbids states to undertake aggression of any kind; not even for the spread of religion.

This Document, apart from being the Constitutional Charter of the state of *Yathrib* was at the same time the document on the authority of which this state had come into existence. The person proclaiming the coming into being of this new state was Prophet Muhammad (Pbuh), the last of the line of prophets, who had received Revealed Word of Allah. As a result of the contents of this Document, the state of *Yathrib* received all those elements which add up to the formation of a state. "A state exists as soon as the four formal elements (a people, a territory, a government and the characteristics of sovereignty) can be found in it and that recognition by other states merely recognizes the social fact", and non-recognition does not alter its status. The newly created state of *Yathrib* was, however, recognised soon after its establishment. The Prophet (Pbuh), immediately after the promulgation of this Document went out of *Yathrib*, stayed with various tribes, each of which held sovereign status within its tribal territory, and executed friendly treaties with them. Apart from establishing treaty relations with neighbouring tribes, these journeys of the Prophet (Pbuh) fixed approximate limits of the territory of *Yathrib*. The boundaries of an Islamic State, cannot be a permanent feature. Islam cannot have and does not have fixed boundaries. Islam attracts people because of principles of justice and equality. It spreads and with its spreading are extended its boundaries. Islam has not remained static even during its days of political eclipse. The spread of Islam in Africa has been when a greater part of Africa had been occupied by European Colonial powers.

In Malay Archipellago Islam was spread by Muslim merchants at a time, when Spain held sway over the area. "They did not come as conquerors, like the Spanish in the sixteenth century, or used the sword as an instrument of conversion; nor did they arrogate to themselves the privileges of a superior and dominant race so as to degrade and oppress the original inhabitants".

It is said of *Al-Mamun* that when a certain *Yazdanbakht* a leader of the Manichaean sect came on a visit to Baghdad and held a disputation with the Muslim theologians, in which he was utterly silenced, the caliph tried to induce him to embrace Islam. But *Yazdanbakht* refused saying, "commander of the faithful, your advice is heard and your words have been listened to: but you are one of those who do not force people to abandon their religion".

It was the same in Eastern Europe where, "The Calvinists of Hungary and Transylvania, and the Unitarians of the latter country, long preferred to submit to the Turks rather than fall into the hands of the fanatical house of Hapsburg; and the Protestants of Silesia looked with longing eyes towards Turkey...." The writer speaks in the same vein of other countries and other lands. "Even in Italy there were men who turned longing eyes towards the Turks in the hope that as their subjects they might enjoy the freedom and the toleration they despaired of enjoying under a Christian government".

As said earlier, this toleration of Muslims, in all the then known lands of the Globe, was the result of magnanimity shown by the Prophet of Islam (Pbuh) when dictating this Document in *Yathrib*, at the time, when the first state of *Yathrib* was coming into existence. The Muslims have honoured the spirit of this Document throughout these fourteen centuries, which is not a mean achievement. In spite of it, and may be because of it and the resulting popularity of Islam, it "inspires perfidy of the *Balkans*, the hate of the Jews, the apprehension of the *Hindus* and the animosity of the Russians".[1] The remarks of *Abbas bin Ubada Ansari* have been referred to above. His prediction continues to come true and may continue much longer. The basic reason for this opposition is the fear of loss of vested interests of the ruling classes and the religious hierarchy, of many faiths which upholds these classes and are a hindrance towards universal equality of man and the resultant justice and fairplay for the masses.

The tenacity with which Muslims have held on to the principle of equality is due to the fact that, they believe staunchly in the Sovereignty of Allah, which is the core and basis of all Islamic teachings. Islam stands for the Sovereignty of Allah alone and of none else. This, in practice, means that the Eternal Laws enjoined by Allah cannot be altered. If this principle was accepted by the ruling classes they would, after that, not be able to frame laws as and when it suited their vested interests. They desire to keep the framing of laws in their own hands and thus they and their institutions set aside for framing and promulgating laws retain Sovereignty in their own hands.

Parliament, Paramount : The law assures that Parliament is omnipotent and paramount. It can make or unmake laws on any matter whatsoever.... The power and jurisdiction of parliaments, says Sir Edward Coke, is so transcendent and absolute, that it cannot be confined, either for causes or persons, within any bounds.... It hath sovereign and uncontrollable authority in making, confirming, enlarging, restraining, abrogating, repealing, reviving and expounding of laws, concerning matters of all possible denominations, ecclesiastical or temporal, civil or military, maritime or criminal. This fact is contained in their Constitutions, whether written or based on practice, precedence and legal judgements. Speaking of the Constitution of England (which included English possessions in Scotland, Ireland and Wales) Dicey, an eminent lawyer, has mentioned "three leading characteristics in the existing Constitution of England; they are now generally designated as the Sovereignty of Parliament, the rule of law and the convention of the constitution"." If a similar analysis was to be made of the Constitutional Charter of Median, its leading characteristics, that would emerge would be firstly, the "Sovereignty of Allah and His Prophet" (Pbuh), secondly, "The Rule of Law" and thirdly, "The Equality of Man." As composed to the Sovereignty of Parliament which means sovereignty of man made laws, and Convention of the Constitution, these characteristics certainly carry more weight. Mankind has, time and again, failed to convince itself that it can successfully conduct its affairs, without Guidance from Allah. Mankind, in nearly every land, "has been the victim of disastrous illusion—the illusion of our ability to emancipate ourselves from natural laws". Whether we call them as Natural Laws, (Revealed to prophets of earlier eras) or openly admit that they are Laws given by Allah who alone is our Creator and Sustainer and Knows our needs far better than us, makes no difference. These are laws which are based on Truth from Him, who has set a destination for mankind which cannot be arrived at except by conducting ourselves in accordance with these Laws. Man has been given knowledge and intelligence, but both these qualities are limited as compared to the knowledge and Power of Allah. "It is evident that human intelligence has not increased simultaneously with the complexity of the problems involved." Today, as much as in the past, civilized humanity has shown itself incapable of directing either its individual or collective affairs. The modern world, like the *Quraish* of Mecca, needs to be bold and pay homage, to the basic principle of the acceptance of the Sovereignty of Allah.

This Document, The Constitutional Charter of Median, laid down, in no uncertain terms, that Allah alone wielded Supreme Power and that the method of invoking that power is Allah Himself and His Prophet (Pbuh) is the interpreter of His Laws. This Document also lays down priorities to be adopted for the security and defence of states established by Muslims. The test of Constitutions whether they are capable of meeting the needs of their respective states has been suggested by a modern American writer as follows:

> "How effective is the constitution in enabling us to come to grips with periodic crises? What are the principal objectives of our national institutions? What service do they render? What are the rights and obligations of American citizenship"?

The Constitutional Charter of Median, as a Document, is fourteen hundred years old. If modern constitutions are examined in the light of the above mentioned questionnaire it would clearly come out that human mind has not made any perceivable advance in this respect. The history of events in Median, subsequent to the issue of this Constitutional Charter, has been recorded in greatest possible detail. We can, as a result of its perusal, say that the periodic crises that occured, in Median, after the promulgation of this Document, were conveniently solved through actions based on it.

There is no doubt about the fact that at the time of its promulgation, the entire population of *Yathrib* had rejoiced about it and had unanimously accepted to live under its protection and abide by its laws.

This Document, "brought into existence a voluntary association of all sections of Medinites-Muslims and non-Muslims, emigrants and locals, principals and clients,..." *Aus* and *Khazraj*, the two Arab tribes, were the only people who could claim that *Yathrib* belonged to them. They had been at war with one another but had settled their differences, lately. An agreement had been reached tentatively that in order to give the place semblance of an organised community they should choose a king. *Abdullah-bin-Ubay*[8] the leader of *Khazraj* was being talked of as the future king of *Yathrib* when *Bayate Aqba Thani* took place. Soon after this, *Muhajirs* started arriving in *Yathrib*. They and the Ansars were a far more organised group, than any tribe could be, and *Abdullah bin Ubay*'s crowning ceremony was soon forgotten.

There were Jews also in *Yathrib*. They were all engaged in trade and commerce and being rich had built themselves strong forts outside the main city of *Yathrib*. The Jews, however, did not either own or belong to the place. A number of theories have been advanced, but the most plausible theory is that they were immigrants from Syria as a result of one of purges that used to be carried out from time to time, to rid the Holy Land, of them. They were living under the protection of various sub-tribes of Aus and *Khazraj*. They did not possess any right other than what the *Haleef*-protecting tribe-cared to allow them.

This Document had completely altered their social and political status. They were being raised to the status of citizens of *Yathrib* like any other person from amongst the tribes of Aus and *Khazraj*. This was a great elevation in their status. They were no more aliens or emancipated slaves. They would, henceforth be able to speak up to the Arabs as equals and the word Jew would soon loose the sense of inferiority which it had, hitherto, carried all the world over. The Prophet (Pbuh) was allowing them a further concession, which would soon make them a political force to be reckoned with. He was, on certain conditions, inviting them to become a part of the *Ummah* of Believers. This invitation happened to be under Divine Guidance and was, therefore, all the more attractive. Although this invitation was also given to the Christians but they were so few in Arabia that the Jews would have been certain to overshadow them always. This invitation, however, had one point which in the end was likely to be unacceptable to them. It was that they had first to accept the Sovereignty of Allah. The invitation being the result of an *Ayah* of Quran must have made them hesitate but they do not seem to have shown any such hesitation in the beginning. The Words of this *Ayah* of Quran, are:

> "Say, O People of the Scripture! Come to an agreement between us and you: that we shall worship none but Allah, and we shall ascribe no partner unto Him, and that none of us shall take others for lords besides Allah. And if they turn away, then say, Bear witness that we are those who have surrendered (unto Him)". (3: 64)

The Prophet (Pbuh) was trying to create a multi-national *Ummah* which was to form a coalition of all those who believed in Allah and thus were being asked to form a united front against the godless. He had advocated an idea, which the West have taken up lately but not with the intention of finding a united platform for all religions, but, to find out means of accelerating Christian Missionary activities in Africa and South East Asia. What would have been the shape of a society, in which, all those who believed in Allah, were to form one *Ummah*, and yet continue calling themselves by their old denominations, would be difficult to imagine.

Hijrah of the Prophet (Pbuh) had brought about a fundamental change in the society of *Yathrib*. There were, in *Yathrib*, Mushrekeen, who were pagan Arabs and did not follow any set rules, which could fall under the heading of Laws of a Religion. There were, as mentioned earlier, Jews, who, at least in principle, followed the law of Moses[9] (May Allah's Blessings be on him). Because of being the followers of a Revealed religion, they considered themselves as superior to the pagan Arabs, although they lived under their protection. There were some Arabs who had adopted the law of Moses but their position was strangely unidentifiable. They lived among their own families and observed Arab customary law but considered themselves as possessing a higher intellectual creed. If they were asked to choose one of the two camps, in case of a quarrel, they would have joined their particular tribe and not gone to the Jewish camp.

The arrival of the Prophet (Pbuh) altered the social structure of *Yathrib* completely. In fact, it had started undergoing a change since the Bayate Aqba Thani. The Prophet (Pbuh) had appointed twelve leaders from among the Medinites who had come to Mecca to embrace Islam. The Prophet (Pbuh) had told the gathering, "Bring out to me twelve leaders that they may take charge of their people's affairs.' They produced nine from al-Khazraj and three from *al-Aus*". This was the beginning of Muslims bringing into existence an organised Islamic Society. "With the appointment of these twelve leaders an organised Islamic Society came into being". On their return to *Yathrib*, these twelve leaders conducted the affairs of Medinite Muslims, until the arrival of the Prophet (Pbuh).

Sovereignty of Allah : The Jews had not been able to set up any communal life with the few Arabs who had accepted the *Shariah* of Prophet Moses. The Prophet (PBUH) of Islam was inviting not only Arabs but Jews, Christians and all others to share with the Believers higher values of the activities of a community organised on the basis of Sovereignty of Allah and equality of man, His most Balanced creation. The result was that, even when the Believers were in a small minority, the social life of *Yathrib*, due to their presence, had started taking its direction from the Muslims and adopted Islamic values in an imperceptible way. The

Prophet (Pbuh) and the small band of his Companions set the pace and texture of social life and thus became the centre of all communal activities. Whenever any issue demanded Allah's commandment for its settlement or the Prophet's own verdict in the matter, the Muslims did make all possible efforts to arrive at the authentic views of Islam on the basis of these two sources. The earlier Revelations of the Quran of Median period are all relating to laws regarding various aspects of life. Many of them resulted from questions asked at these gatherings where the Prophet (Pbuh) invited people to embrace Islam. He is known to have gone to a Jewish school to preach Islam to them. If there passed a group of people, by the road, he would stop and join them to invite them to Islam, even though they disliked it.

A new social structure based on the Sovereignty of Allah and equality of man was taking shape. A new culture was emerging out of this social structure. Man was being given, for the first time in his cultural life, the proper place in the scheme of things, and man's mind was awakening to his place in this universe. One can find no better key to the internal logic of a society than its conception of man and his place in nature. This high position had been bestowed upon man by Allah Himself, in His Eternal Code of Life. The result was that the social and cultural trends of life in *Yathrib*, at a time when the Believers were in a small minority, took a turn towards adoption of Islamic values, and life became centralised around the personality of the Prophet (Pbuh) and his Companions.

Important in More than One Way : As mentioned earlier the Constitutional Charter of Median has importance for more than one reason. It is the earliest written document of the Government and State of Median. Later documents like the Peace Treaty of *Hudaybiya*, the Victory Proclamation of *Khyber*, and the Overlordship Gazette Notification of *Aila* granted to the Christian population of that place, were all of the nature of proclamation of cessation of hostilities due to one or the other reason. This Document stands in a different position. It established a state and a government in order to meet aggression. Invasion by *Quraish* of Mecca had to be stopped. Defence of a society cannot be assured without first organising that society. When a society is organised it takes the shape of a state. The state must have law and it must also lay down as to what was the source of law and who in future would be entitled to amend or add to this law. All these steps were being finalised through the Constitutional Charter of Median. This process has been explained in modern terminology in the following words. "Peace among men and a civilized society, which are one and the same thing, are imaginable only within a legal order equipped with institutions to give effect to principles and norms in the form of law..." The Prophet (Pbuh) was laying down that the final authority in Islam would be Allah, through revelations to him. Arabian society was losely governed by custom. There was no written law. Absence of law was a great hindrance to the establishment of a progressive and stable society. The Charter was removing this imbalance. "Whenever men group together and approve of a given standard morality, they must speak finally in terms of a law. Law permits morality to grow and as it grows the standard of law is elevated and morality is further advanced, for the two have reciprocal influence".

In this case, although hostilities had not started, war had been declared and arrangements had to be made to face the enemy. Allah had also Commanded.

> "O you who believe! Take your precautions, then advance the proven ones, or advance or altogether". (4: 71)

It is beyond doubt that the Document was promulgated to bring into existence the State of Median so that it could be defended against the impending attack by the *Quraish* of Mecca. Discussion leading to the declaration of its contents, if any, are conspicuously absent from both the Seerah and Hadith literature.

Above Doubt : Its authenticity is, however, above doubt of any kind. It cannot be a spurious document. Once Islam and the Muslims had emerged as victorious, not only within Arabia, but had also liquidated the two strongest empires of the then civilized world, there was no need for them to concoct a document of the early period when Muslims were very few and not very strong. In actual fact once they stepped out of Arabia, they paid no particular attention to it. It is genuine both from external evidence and from the inner evidence of its contents. The idea that it is the sum total of a number of agreements arrived at on a number of occasions is so illogical that it should be ignored completely. As is well known, the events which took place after the promulgation of the Charter, developed with such after, and in such an unforseen manner that a situation had arisen where there was no need of fresh terms being issued, or new agreements gone into with any party. The idea that the document in its present shape is the result of numerous agreements is the result of the basic misconception, that it was an agreement. One may ask "agreement between whom, because the Document was being issued with the heading "From Muhammad, The Prophet (PBUH) of Allah." Its contents were Legal Orders and not paragraphs of an agreement. A charter from some one in power can be amended or additions made to it by the authority issuing the original charter. From Badr onwards the Prophet (Pbuh) did not have to issue new instructions to any one in *Yathrib*. The Jews were getting weaker every day and signs of rebellion on their part had developed immediately after *Badr*. They had not "followed the Believers and not fought along with them." They had not, therefore, qualified for any of the concessions granted to them through the Charter. If anything, any fresh document, would have curtailed concessions granted to them from the incidence of rebellious behaviour of the Jewish tribe, *Banu Qainuqa*[10], immediately after *Badr*, the Jews were not in a position to request for a reappraisal of their relations with the ruling party.

The arrival of ultimatum from the *Quraish* of Mecca was a serious affair. They were a powerful tribe and had the influence which leaders of thought possess in a society. They exercised the sole authority of laying down the religious ceremonies and the Arab way of life. They held the monopoly of carrier trade between southern Arabia and the flourishing market of Middle East, and were very rich as compared to the rest of Arabia. An attack by them, against *Yathrib*, would wipe out this small agricultural town of *Najd*. War in any case "is not a pass time. It is a serious means for a serious object".

The Meccan object was very serious. Muhammad (Pbuh) had "mocked their Way of Life," and taken refuge in *Yathrib* to save their Way of Life they had to destroy him completely. They had awoken to the danger from the time of the second *Bayah* of *Aqba*. As already mentioned when some of the Companions started migrating to *Yathrib* they "assembled in their council chamber, the house of *Qusayy-bin-Kilab*[11], where all their important business was conducted, to take counsel what they should do in regard to the Prophet (Pbuh), for they were now in fear of him." It was suggested that "they should put him in irons behind bars." This was objected "on the ground that news would leak out that he was imprisoned, and immediately his followers would attack and snatch him away then their numbers would so grow that they would destroy the authority of the *Quraish* altogether".

After some further discussion *Abu Jehl* came out with a new plan. This was "that each clan should provide a young, powerful, well born, aristocratic warrior; that each of these should be provided with a sharp sword; then that each of them should strike at him and kill him. The *Banu Abde Manaf* could not fight them all and would have to accept blood money which they would all contribute". Having failed to kill him they were not able to liquidate Islam in Mecca. They could not, however, let it prosper in *Yathrib*. They were afraid, as they said that "Their numbers would so grow that they would destroy the authority of *Quraish* altogether". They decided not to permit their numbers to grow and decided to act quickly. They knew of the disappointment of *Abdullah bin Ubay*. His people had made a sort of jewelled diadem to crown him and make him their king, when Allah sent His Prophet (Pbuh) to them; so when his people forsook him in favour of Islam he was filled with enmity realising that the Prophet (Pbuh) had deprived him of his kingship. However, when he realised, that his people were determined to go over to Islam, he went too, but unwillingly, retaining his enmity and dissimulating.

The *Quraish* sent a letter to the people of *Yathrib*, but addressing it to *Abdullah bin Ubay*. The letter was, in fact, a declaration of war. It said, "you have given protection with you, to our men. You should kill these people or turn them out of *Yathrib*. We swear by Allah that if you do not do that, we will all attack you and having destroyed you, will capture your womenfolk". This was a very good excuse for him to use force and turn the Prophet (Pbuh) and his *Muhajir* Companions from *Yathrib*. He was the head of a very powerful tribe, which appears to have been numerically stronger than others. Its members were alive to the needs of religious revival. Out of twelve leaders chosen to look after the affairs of Muslims of *Yathrib*, nine belonged to his tribe. He decided to use force if the occasion demanded to kill the Prophet (Pbuh) and the few *Muhajir* Companions.

The Prophet (Pbuh) heard of his decision and went to him. Very little of the conversation between them is recorded. *Abdullah bin Ubay* was confronted with a new reality. Islam, although a religion of peace, denoted complete submission to the Will of Allah. It meant the acceptance of the Sovereignty of Allah which in practical life was demonstrated by obeying the Laws of Allah. This is what is meant by:-

> "I created the *Jinn* and humankind only that they might worship me". (51: 56)

And one of the Commands of Allah is that He has Ordained fighting for the Believers.

> "Warfare is ordained for you". (2: 216)

The occasion for which this Commandment has been primarily Ordained is when some other group fights against you. It says:

> "Fight in the Way of Allah against those who fight against you, but begin not hostilities". (2: 190)

It has to be remembered that this *Ummah* is One:

> "Verily this *Ummah* of yours is One *Ummah*". (23: 52)

The Prophet (Pbuh) brought home to *Abdullah bin Ubay* in these words:

> Do you realise that if you use force the Muslims from *Yathrib* will fight alongside the *Muhajir* Muslims and you will be shedding blood of your tribe on both sides.

He realised the mistake he was making and decided not to use force against the Prophet (Pbuh) and his Companions. His change of attitude was the result of his fear of being defeated at the hands of determined fighters. History is replete with instances, where people have had recourse to peace for fear of being hurt, in the end. The philosophy of Ahimsa—non-violence—is also the product of such logic, because the same people believe in *Kali Devi*, the goddess, who quenches her thurst from blood of gory murders. Peace accepted by him was of this kind. When we could not use force he resorted to mischief and remained a hypocrite and a tool of the Jews until his death.

History books are silent on further details of the conversations, that took place between the Prophet (Pbuh) and *Abdullah bin Ubay*, it would be correct to assume that the latter must have asked the Prophet (Pbuh) the way *Yathrib* was to be defended against the Meccans. The details of the Charter lead us to the conclusion that the Prophet (Pbuh) must have replied that the Muslims would defend *Yathrib* and if the others would like to share that responsibility the Believers would permit them to join in this great honour. It could also be said that, as a result of the urgent need to defend *Yathrib*, the Prophet (Pbuh) formulated the plan of establishing the state of *Yathrib*, giving it a Constitution, and laying down the responsibility of defence on Believers. *Abdullah bin Ubay* could not help accepting this plan. The next event mentioned in history books is the Constitutional Charter itself.

The Charter was dictated under the shadow of an impending war of extreme intensity. Its defence paragraphs must belong to the same period. The concessions granted to the Jews are linked with defence paragraphs and must belong to the same period. The paragraphs covering general administration were also the demand of the time. There are no further events in the history of *Yathrib*, which could have resulted in the issue of further the documents. The division of the Document of Professor Sergeant in 'A, B, X, Y, etc, amounting to eight different documents can certainly be called a futile effort, made merely to create doubts and with no fruitful object. The war that was visualised when dictating this Document lasted for nine years and had, before ending, embroiled the largest Empire of that period in it, thus initiating the longest war of history— The war between the Crescent and Cross—which is raging even today, fourteen centuries after the Charter came into force, and is nowhere near its end as yet. Islam until then had laid greater stress on the building of character of individuals. The Charter ushered in the collective life of the *Ummah*. The principle that Muslims formed a nation by themselves, even when they lived in surroundings, which were not purely Islamic and it was given prominence by the Charter. The contents of the Charter make it clear that even when living as a numerical minority. Believers take over the administration of the society on condition that the principle of the Sovereignty of Allah is being acted upon. As mentioned earlier, as far as details are concerned, when dictating the Charter, greater emphasis has been paid to matters relating to the defence of the state, than to other matters. The Prophet (Pbuh) as a result of the wisdom and insight granted to him by Allah, kept his mind centered on the period after the war when need would arise for rehabilitation of people. In the words of a modern military thinker, "The true national objective in war lies in the 'after war'. If the civilized world is to be saved from collapse, there is urgent need to produce true grand strategists to replace the blind exponents of mass destruction". He argues that "If you concentrate exclusively on victory, with no thought for the after effect, you may be too exhausted to be profited by the peace, while it is about certain that the peace will be a bad one, containing the germs of another war". The author is speaking from experience of two World Wars. Britain won both of them but lost the peace that followed.

The experience of modern world over the last two centuries has shown that the war to end war has yet to be fought, unless laws of war laid down by Allah are observed in total. The war that was initiated by the *Quraish* of Mecca and won by the Prophet (Pbuh) ended, as far Arabia was concerned, because the Prophet (Pbuh) keeping the after-war period in view had done nothing, during and at the end of war, which could keep alive the hatred generated by war. Modern wars have tended to increase hatred to a point, when, a rapprochement becomes impossible. We need, therefore, to study his life, his teachings, his foreign policy and the manner in which he fought his war and then magnanimously pardoned his enemies. It will show a pattern of human behaviour unparalleled in the annals of human history.

The Prophet (Pbuh) had accepted the responsibility of defending *Yathrib* against the threatened attack, when *Yathrib* had yet no state, no government and no army. He and his Companions were the total force available for this onerous task. There were no armaments, no provisions, no transport animals and no finances to provide all these instruments of war. He had, however, men, who were prepared to lay down their lives on the Path of Allah. He had trained them to such unchartered heights of Belief in Allah, that no weapon could force them to abandon their positions.

He also knew his enemies. They were resourceful. They were rich merchants and could furnish their army with the most sophisticated weapons. They also had the means to last them during a long drawn war. They had friends among Arab tribes.

They could, as a result widen the zone of war and have him surrounded and they had the means and facilities to make the blockade permanent, but his Belief in Allah outweighed those considerations. It is true that "once war begins, no one can tell how it will go. There are some who urge that we should abolish all armaments, and refuse to fight on any pretext. If this view is put forward on religious grounds, I will not deal with it beyond saying that it does not seem to me in accordance with the Bible... If on the other hand, its advocates believe that it would make for peace, it is inconsistent with recent events. China offered little or no resistance to Japan, yet that did not save her from the loss of territories as large as Europe, and the slaughter of some thousands other citizens".

The position of Believers, at the time of declaration of war by Mecca, was far more precarious than any community of peaceful and peace-loving people, who are threatened by a neighbour, who does not approve of their Ideology and their Way of Life. The enemy was the same, who had persecuted them in Mecca, ignoring relation of blood and friendship. A small number, a little over seventy had migrated to *Habsha*, and now less than fifty males had reached *Yathrib* and found a place, where they hoped to live according to Allah's given Way of Life, and they were being threatened with war and possible extermination.

They had no alternative but to accept war. If they decided to avoid war, where could they go. They would have become stateless. The result would have been that the Islamic Society, which was visualised by the Prophet (Pbuh) as a result of Revelations to him, from Allah, would not have been possible to be established. Allah's Promise was that they would be uppermost if they were Believers, was enough for them:-

> "It is a promise from Allah in truth; and who can be more truthful than Allah in utterance"? (4: 122)

And:

> "(It is) a Promise of Allah. Allah faileth not His Promise". (39: 20)

And Allah has promised that:

> "Faint not nor grieve, for ye will overcome them if ye are (indeed) believers". (3: 139)

> "And verily Our word went forth of old unto Our bondmen sent (to warn) that they verily would be helped. And that Our host, they verily would be the victors". (37: 171-173)

They were indeed Believers in its fullest meaning. No group of any *Ummah* of days gone by had reached heights of Belief in Allah which they had proved to have reached, and were yet to prove on many an occasion.

The Pressing Need : Documents of this nature are not issued in a vacuum. There is always a background and a pressing need for them. In fact, pressing necessity, for the execution and enforcement of such documents alone made them acceptable to people. Such documents, whether they are named as agreements, treaties, charters or constitutions, are promulgated because the very existence of those societies depends on bringing into existence means of laying down the pattern of communal life, and such documents provide and guarantee a disciplined life of the community.

Apart from rights and duties of individuals and groups such documents lay down restrictions and penalties for the breach of rules of conduct, expected of those for whose guidance they are issued. Preparations to meet the threat of war are taken in hand, when the danger is real and the entire society recognises it. War cannot be taken lightly because it "is a social phenomenon too complex to be governed by any simple formula". Except the Prophet (Pbuh) himself no one was either qualified nor was there anybody who had the moral strength to accept the responsibility of making the decision to defend .*Yathrib* or when the decision had been taken to take defensive preparations in hand and then conduct the war.

To accept the duty of defending a state and its people is a decision of great moral character. An ill prepared nation is in serious danger of losing its war. To lose a war means to surrender the "right of freedom of thought" and to lose freedom of thought means to lose the right to live according to one's chosen Way of Life, which includes one's mode of worship. The Muslims could not afford to lose the war. They had chosen the Islamic Way of Life of their free will. It was being challenged by the people, who had persecuted them for nearly thirteen years. They were determined that if they could not win the war they would fight to the last man. The battles fought by the Believers for the defence of *Yathrib* were all fought with the determination that they would fight until each one of them had achieved *Shahadah.*

The Prophet (Pbuh) had trained his Companions to wish for *Shahadah* and he was certain that they will come up to his expectations. His historic words, just before the attack of Meccan Army started at the battlefield of *Badr* are a testimony of the Believers having absorbed this philosophy. He had said:

> O Lord!
> If this little band of Believers
> Is wiped out today
> There shall be none left
> To obey your Commandments
> Until the Day of Judgement.

There had been wars before and there were to be wars in future as well, but this war was different both in conception and the manner in which it was expected to terminate. Both sides were fighting to defend their respective Way of Life. It could end in not only the defeat of one army or the nation it belonged to but it was to end with the end of the Way of Life to which the loser belonged. It was a war aimed at the extermination of the Muslim's Ideology and Way of Life. The idea, that all wars are fought for differences, which can be solved peacefully, does not appear to be applicable to this war. Normally it can be said that, "Just how senseless and futile an expedient it really is, can usually best be judged by those who lose rather than by those who have won". In this case it was not applicable because the losers were to forego the freedom of living in accordance with their chosen Way of Life.

This Document had been dictated keeping in mind this Philosophy of War that to remain a Believer in Allah was only possible when Sovereignty of Allah could be proclaimed and life was led in accordance with His Commandments. To achieve that it was essential, that land occupied by Believers had to be defended to the last. It was, therefore, necessary, that *Yathrib* had its Basic Law—its Constitution—promulgated in a manner that its defence preparations could be taken in hand legally and constitutionally. Hence the correct heading of the Document can be "The Constitutional Charter of *Yathrib*... Median".

It was not an agreement with the Jews as *Allama Shibli Nomani*[12] calls it. He says "The Prophet (Pbuh) sent for *Ansars* and Jews and dictated an agreement....which was accepted by both parties". Another eminent writer *Jalal-ud-Din Jafery* writes, "When the Prophet (Pbuh) arrived in Median, he had an agreement written between the *Ansars* and the Jews". *Naeem Siddiqui*[13], the only one out of all *Urdu* writers has shown a different approach to the problem. He writes, "The Prophet (Pbuh) created an organisation for the arming of the State of Median, through which he integrated the Muslims, the Jews and the un-believers, into a new society. He had a written document of the nature of an agreement, prepared. The nature of this document was of a proper constitution and it can be correctly called as the first written constitution".

Nearly all writers of *Seerah* in *Urdu* have called the "Charter" as an "Agreement," between either the Prophet (Pbuh) and the Jews, or between the Believers and the Jews. An eminent learned man like *Syed Abul Hassan Ali Nadvi* has termed it as an agreement of peace with the Jews. Having correctly said that, "The Prophet (Pbuh) on this occasion gave a writing to the *Muhajirs* and *Ansars*, "he adds "which contained an agreement of peace with the Jews". Another eminent historian writes, "On arrival at Median, the Prophet (Pbuh) during the very first year of *Hijrah* considered it appropriate to execute an agreement with all nationalities on the principle of internationalism so that a national solidarity should continue in spite of the ethnic and religious differences". *Khalid Alvi*, referring to the Jews writes, "He (the Prophet PBUH) made an agreement with them".

It could be that the word agreement has crept in because of absence of a proper equivalent of the term "Charter," in *Urdu.* The mistake dates back to *Ibne Hisham*, due to absence of a technical term for "Charter" in that age. He has used the word *Aahadahum* which has been translated as "covenant." The sentence as a result reads " the covenant between the Muslims and the Mediann s and with the Jews".

Muslim and non-Muslim writers of *Seerah* in English, who belong to the present age, have also relied on *Ibne-Ishaq*, in more or less the same manner as *Urdu* writers. *Abu Bakr Sirajuddin*[14] (Martin Ling) who has written with great devotion says, "and the Prophet (Pbuh) now made a covenant of mutual obligations between his followers and the Jews of the *Oasis*".

A non-Muslim writer of Pakistan origin says that before the signing of the agreement a thorough exchange of views had taken place. This may be correct but no work of early period seems to mention a thorough exchange of views. He writes, "After a thorough exchange of views, an agreement was reached and was reduced to writing".

Muir while translating the Document uses the words "Charter of Muhammad the Prophet" instead of "Charter from Muhammad," but in introducing it he writes, "It was natural that Muhammad, holding these sentiments should desire to enter into a close and binding union with the Jews, and this he did in a formal manner shortly after reaching Median. He associated them with himself by a treaty of mutual obligation drawn up in writing,...".

The difference between an agreement and a Charter is very vast. An agreement is between two equals and a Charter is given from one to others. An agreement can be rescinded by either party. A Charter can be altered, amended or cancelled only by the authority which promulgated it. Apart from the heading given to the document its contents alone can guide later researchers to give their verdict on it, whether it was a treaty, an agreement or a Charter. Treaties are between states and usually the heading says so For instance, "Security Treaty between Australia, New Zealand and United States of America". Similarly Pacts are between independent sovereign states. For instance, "Pact of Mutual Cooperation (CENTO)" was signed between a number of states including Pakistan, Turkey and Iran. Recently a new name for mutual treaties has appeared. This is called a "Convention." For instance, "Convention regarding the Regime of the Straits"

Let us, once again, look at Meethaq-e-Median in a little greater detail, particularly its heading. It says:

> "This Document (writing) is from Muhammad, The Prophet of Allah (PBUH.)...."

It is clear that it is neither an agreement nor a treaty because it is not between Muhammad (Pbuh) and some others. It is from him and he is the Prophet (Pbuh) of Allah. Those receiving the Document are being told that the person issuing this Document is doing so in his capacity as the Prophet of Allah. Then it goes on to say that it is being given:

"To"

"Quraish and Yathribite Believers".

Believers whether from Mecca or from *Yathrib* were all his followers known as his Companions. No group of people in the history of mankind have shown their devotion to their leader as was shown by his Companions to Muhammad (Pbuh) the Prophet of Allah. When marching out to the battlefield of Badr, the leader of Ansars of *Yathrib*, Saad bin Muadh said, "We believe in you, we declare your truth, and we witness, that what you have brought is truth, and we have given you our word and agreement to hear and to obey; so go forth where you wish, we are with you, and by Allah, if you were to ask us to cross the sea and you plunged into it, we would plunge into it with you, not a man would stay behind. We do not dislike the idea of meeting your enemy tomorrow. We are experienced in war, trustworthy in combat...."

Whatever else description or name may be given to this Document it cannot be called an agreement between the Prophet (Pbuh) and his followers. It was being given by him to them and they were all included in it, both the Muhajirs from Mecca and the Ansars of *Yathrib*.

There were others as well. They were:

"those who will follow them and fight alongside them."

It would be applicable to others as well, provided these others followed the lead of his followers, the Believers, from Mecca and *Yathrib*. Apart from following the Believers they had to take part in fighting alongside the Believers to qualify themselves as recipients of this august Document.

This heading ends with a brief last remark, "They will form ONE UMMAH to the exclusion of others." It means that if the others qualified as recipients of the Document, then they and the Believers, the Companions of the Last Prophet of Allah, will form an Ummah apart from the rest of humanity. It was a great honour, that was being bestowed on them but the price was also very high. They had to accept the Believers as their leaders and continue to follow them by joining in war with them against their enemies.

Thus the Document was primarily issued as the Basic or Fundamental Law

The Constitution of *Yathrib*, so that defence arrangements could be taken in hand, on behalf of the entire population. The Believers, being the group which had sworn allegiance to him as a result of the *Bayah* formed the manpower of his army. The march to the battlefield of *Badr* proved this fact. None others were prepared to sacrifice themselves for a cause, in which they did not believe.

A Different Charter : History has recorded one more Charter given by the head of a state. This was King John of England. This Charter, however, was taken by force by the barons of the realm, because, "King John was very unwilling to grant it. This was on the 15th of June 1215 A.C., that the Great Charter was sealed with the king's great seal. He agreed that 24 barons shall be appointed to see that he kept the promises which it contained. He agreed only because he was compelled.... He never meant to keep the promises that it contained, and he did not keep them. He sent to France for soldiers and when they came he made war on his own people. He asked his friend the Pope for help and the Pope helped him by ex-communicating all barons, by London under Interdict, and by telling John that he had no need to keep his promises". The surprising part of the whole story is, that, there was not much in the Charter, which an honest ruler of an average society need to have objected to.

It may seem strange that the Pope of all the people, should have advised a Christian ruler to go back on his promises. It was, however, not the first time, nor the last time, that the head of Church had advised a prince to go back on his promises. In one case, "the Pope, who seeing his plans being nullified, by this (peace treaty) initiated the Magyars to break the peace; oaths sworn to infidels not being binding".

The Charter given at *Yathrib* was in the spirit of Islam, the New Way of Life. It had to be in accordance with all ethical, moral and legal principles laid down by Allah, for Believers in Him and His Prophet (Pbuh). The time of its issue was the most critical period in the history of Islam—a time when the threat against Islam and Muslims was the greatest. This fact must be kept in mind while studying the Clauses of the Charter.

The position in which the Muslims were placed at this time has been misrepresented by some Western writers. Preparations for defence of *Yathrib* have been interpreted as aggressive designs against the Meccans. A well known British historian writes that "Muhammad had now, as it were, thrown down the gauntlet, which the Meccans could not but pick it up. He had effectively challenged them to a full scale trial of strength". It appears that after writing a few more sentences he remembered that it was the Meccans who had declared war. He adds; "The Meccan belief thought Muhammad would avoid them rested on a misappraisal of the relative strength and fighting qualities of the two parties". He has avoided to give the source on which he has based the superior strength of the Muslim Army.

Condition of Muslims

The historic chapter deals with the Laws which affect Believers only. For practical purposes the whole Charter concerns the Believers. However, there are some Clauses whose subject matter concerns Believers only, while there are others which affect those people who have not accepted Islam but will be working under the leadership of Believers. The heading of the Document, which also forms Clause I deals primarily with Believers clears all doubts about its nature and also that they are the people forming the Government of the state.

One of the significant points to note is that the Charter is addressed primarily to the people; the common man; the Believer whether a free man, a freed man or not free till then.

"This is a Document from Muhammad the Prophet (Pbuh) between the Believers, Muslims of *Quraish* and *Yathrib* and those who followed them and fought with them. They form one *Ummah* to the exclusion of others."

It includes others with a condition, otherwise the Believers *Quraish* from Mecca and from *Yathrib* form One *Ummah* to the exclusion of the rest. This formation of *Ummah* was not to be confined to the Believers of these two places. Whosoever voluntarily Believed in Allah and Muhammad (Pbuh) as a Prophet (PBUH) which in practice meant that he lived in accordance with the Laws of the Quran and *Sunnah*, became a member of this *Ummah*.

Similar Charters : There may have been similar Charters in other parts of the world. We have already referred to a Charter issued by a king of England in 1215 A.C., which is known as the Great Charter— Magna Carta. There are many differences but the first difference lies in the people to whom the Charter is being given. While the Constitutional Charter of Median is given to the common man, the Magna Carta is given:

> "To the archbishops, bishops, abbots, earls, barons, justiciars, foresters, sheriffs, stewards, servants, and to all his bailiffs and faithful subjects."

The subjects also formed categories and were at the mercy of the bishops and sheriffs and in practice held no social status unless they happened to be retainers of the categories enumerated above. The common man, the man in the street had no voice or weight until centuries later, when contacts with Islam is Spain and the Holy Land had brought about a certain amount of awakening among the Europeans, returning from Muslim lands.

The promulgation of a Constitution or Fundamental Law by a people or to them by the ruler signifies the commencement of organised life of that *Millah*. Organised collective life alone is most important characteristic of a human group from a herd of animals. Meccan life was the life of individual Muslims placed amidst unfriendly surroundings. Such a life could not last for ever. It cannot last even in the twentieth century. There are a number of countries today where Muslims find it impossible to live as Muslims. Hijrah of the Prophet (Pbuh) was inevitable. Hijrah and the declaration of war by Quraish created the situation where a Fundamental Law became essential to be promulgated. Islam became a living organisation with the Charter controlling the collective communal life of those who had accepted Sovereignty of Allah and His Prophet (Pbuh). Allah's Sovereignty was to control and direct the life of these individuals from hearth to the farm or the shop and would include the behaviour and inner feelings from the Mosques to the Battlefield.

It must be remembered that the Charter is being issued and promulgated by Muhammad (Pbuh) The Prophet of Allah and not by Allah, although it is primarily for the people who have accepted Allah's Sovereignty. This fact reminds a Believer that he has accepted the Sovereignty of Allah, because, Muhammad (Pbuh) has said so and the individual has accepted his Prophethood. It is the character, the conduct and the life of Muhammad (Pbuh) although regulated, controlled and directed on the Right Path by Allah, which has made men believe in him, when he said, "Allah is the Creator, the Sustainer and Master of the Day of Resurrection." It is his statement that Allah the Merciful, the Loving, the Compassionate and Who has appointed him as His Last Prophet. Therefore, be it understood and remembered that when a Believer accepts the Sovereignty of Allah, he does not relegate the Prophet (Pbuh) to a position of no consequence. It is the acceptance of his Prophethood which has prompted the Believer to Believe and have Faith (*Iman*) in Allah. Therefore, as Law Givers, they both remain side by side. This is the explanation of repeated reminder of Allah regarding the position of Muhammad as a Law Giver and not one who as a result of applying himself to a problem, at hand, does Ijtihad and deduces supplementary law, under certain given conditions. Allah has repeatedly Commanded:

"Say: Obey Allah and the messenger". (3: 32)

The preceding Verse is worth noting:

"Say: If ye love Allah, follow me".

Whereever the Command to "Obey Allah" occurs it is followed by "Obey the Messenger." Obedience to Him is given singly only in one Verse, where it is said "Obey My Command" (20: 90) and not the usual Word, "Obey Allah."

The Law Giver : The position of Muhammad (Pbuh) as a Law Giver in accordance with Allah's Own Commands is direct. His Commands take the place of Law directly and independently. Any reported Command of his, which does not fully support the Words of the Quran, can be rejected as Maudhu-Spurious, concocted and coined by some one and not merely as of a secondary nature, which, may or may not be applicable in all cases. He knew the place he held. He could not give an Order which would be contrary to the Dictates of Allah. Allah has said about him:-

> "By the Star when it setteth your comrade erreth not, nor is deceived, nor doth he speak of (his own desire)". (53: 1-3)

The Quran and the *Sunnah* are complementary to one another. Neither can be understood except by studying the other. If Allah Himself has, in a dozen places bracketed His *Rasul* with Obedience to Himself then we must also give to his Commands an equally important position. It is Muhammad (Pbuh) who has had to say that the Quran is not the result of his authorship. Who, except Allah and his own Conscience, was there to stop him from crediting himself with the authorship of the Quran Who was there, except Allah, his Creator and his own truthfulness to stop him from declaring himself as God in human garb? After all, there were many in Arabia, who, by the queer theory of Trinity, then prevalent, gave to Jesus Christ the position of the Son of God, and of the God who came to earth to be crucified for the sins of humanity. The Quran is the Word of Allah because, apart from the Quran itself, Muhammad (Pbuh) has said so. Muhammad's command, therefore, must be believed and acted upon as eternal commands, in the same spirit as Commands of Allah.

The Clauses of the Charter dealing with Believers only are very few. As the Charter was addressed to the Believers initially the clauses dealing with Believers only precede all others. We have already dealt with Clauses I including the few words given above.

Clause 2: "*Quraish Muhajirin* will continue to pay blood-money among themselves in accordance with the existing custom."

This Clause has thus laid down:

1. The Principle of payment of blood-money will continue.
2. Its amount and manner of payment can be in accordance with the tribal custom.
3. Uniformity in the amount etc. is not demanded.

Quraish Believers had migrated to a new place, the city of *Yathrib*, where there must have been local customs regarding the payment of blood-money. It was neither advisable nor in accordance with the Spirit of Islam, which was meant to cover the whole of the Globe, to lay down permanent laws regarding matters which should, preferably, be decided in accordance with local customs, conditions and requirements. Within Arabia itself there were different standards of payment of blood-money, in view of this it was decided and proclaimed that local and tribal practice, in the case of blood-money would continue to be followed in future.

Last Revealed Way of Life : Islam is the Last Revealed Way of Life. It has lasted for fourteen centuries and has to remain during the coming one thousand or one million centuries that will take this universe to reach its destination in the immeasurable void. A Way of Life which has to last for ever, and, to be applicable in all places at all times, cannot have eternal laws for situations which must undergo changes with change in time and place. Allah alone possesses the knowledge and the Wisdom and knows what aspects suffer change. He has, as a result, not Laws for problems, situations and matters which are likely to undergo changes. Those matters, which are of lasting nature, have been the subject of Laws given by Allah and His *Rasul.*

If the problem had been posed to a man, it would have been impossible to bring the permanent and the temporary, to reconcile. The permanence of Islamic Laws has been possible only because Allah and His Prophet (Pbuh) have meticulously avoided to give Laws, for aspects of human life, which are of changing nature.

All men are equal. They will always remain equal. Hence Equality of man has been brought under Law. And yet the question of electing, selecting, nominating or appointing a leader of society. *Khalifa* or *Imam* has not even been touched because this is a purely social problem, the solution of which is subject to change with time and place. Uniformity is advisable but only where it is possible. Where uniformity is likely to create hardships Allah and His *Rasul* have left it to the Believers to come to a decision through discussion. The Prophet (Pbuh) himself was Commanded to decide problems after consulting his Companions. But once a decision has been taken then all have to see to it, that it is suitably carried out.

Clause 3: "They will redeem their prisoners with kindness and justice common among Believers."

The word "they" cannot refer to anyone else but those to whom the Charter was being issued. It was a state of Muslims in which laws of Islam were to be administered. The Fundamental Law had included "those who followed them," but that was to be seen as to who were prepared to follow them and defend *Yathrib* along with them. Muslims of *Quraish* and *Yathrib* were being given the Document and as such this Clause referred to them jointly. The subject is the redeeming of prisoners, which could be tackled at the level of the Federal Government of *Yathrib* and none else.

It must be noted that the, "redeeming of prisoners of war is being made a collective responsibility," of the *Ummah*. It is also worthnoting that the standard of sentiments involved in redeeming prisoners of war is "the kindness and justice common among Believers." The kindness and justice of Believers cannot be of any other kind than that of Allah Who is Most Merciful, and His Prophet (Pbuh) who has come as "Mercy to Mankind."

Prophet's Command : This Command of Allah's Messenger was not confined to the Believers of *Yathrib* only. It was the first Muslim state, which expanded within a century to cover two continents and had started influencing the third as well. This order did not merely apply to the subjects of the state of *Yathrib*. Although the Charter was given to the then existing *Ummah*, this order was and is applicable to the *Ummah* of Islam for ever. The present writer has no knowledge of this Order being amended, deleted, cancelled or replaced by any Quranic Injunction or an order by the Prophet (Pbuh). The question arises as to what has the world of Islam done to redeem the Muslim prisoners of war in the hands of various victorious nations, who during the last three centuries have availed themselves of the weakness of Muslim peoples and while occupying Muslim lands have taken millions of Muslims as prisoners of war. These Muslims are kept as prisoners jointly and singly in these territories known as European colonies. Generation after generation has grown up and lived as slaves and the Muslim World elsewhere has not moved a finger even to redeem them. We have to admit that a greater part of Muslim World was, until few years ago, under the domination of one or the other Christian power, but nothing has been said regarding the redeeming of millions who, though in majority, in their homelands, are living as slaves and leading a life worse than the life of ethnic minorities. This Clause of The Constitutional Charter of Median is still operative and I, as, an humble individual, and a student of Muslim history, would submit, that, it needs further thought by the intellectuals of Muslim World.

Until the issue of this Charter there was no question of redeeming prisoners of war. The armies in those days did not belong to the nation. There was no notion of an *Ummah*. They used to belong to the kings and when a king was killed in war and was defeated the personnel of that Army had no one else to look to. If they were taken prisoners they were made slaves. If they escaped they became robbers and highwaymen. Very few managed to reach their homes. *Yathrib* was not a country or a state in the normal sense of the word. It was a place, a piece of land, where the Muslim *Ummah*, the Believers in Allah and His *Rasul* (Pbuh) had commenced a communal life and were beginning to demonstrate the New Way of Life granted by Allah. *Ummah* which was then coming into existence was completely new. Those who were to fight the battles of this *Ummah* were the Army of the *Ummah* and not of the land comprising the territories of *Yathrib*. Hence he Ordered that the *Ummah* will redeem their prisoners of war, and not only that, but they will do so with love and justice which is a hall-mark of Believers in Allah and His Prophet (Pbuh) and Mercy to Mankind.

This order was so new and unique, that, the moment the Prophet (Pbuh) had dictated it and the scribe had written it, there must have been a demand from "The others", who were present, that this Law should be applied to all. Hence Clause 5. There were some who were not even satisfied with the words "all parties will redeem their prisoners with kindness and justice common among Believers." Their names had to be inserted that such and such tribe and so and so group, "will be governed on the above lines." The demand was placed a second time and names of four more tribes had to be included for the fulfilment of this humane responsibility which was to take ten centuries for other parts of the world like Europe to emulate.

Clause 8: "Believers will not fail to redeem their prisoners or fail to pay blood-money on behalf of one of them."

This Clause is to emphasize Clauses 2 and 3. It has been brought in particularly because Clause 2 had mentioned *Quraish* only. This Clause emphasizes the contents of both Clauses mentioned earlier and reminds the Believers of today that contrary to the expectations of the Prophet (PBUH) of Allah, they have failed to redeem their prisoners for centuries.

Clause 9: "A Believer will not make the freedman of another Believer as his ally against the wishes of the other Believer."

The relations between the master and slave are of personal nature. When a master frees a slave new relations are formed. The trust or lack of trust a person places on his freedman is known only to him. His good points, his weaknesses and his idiosyncrasies are also known to a freedman. Relations of allies are on a different level. A Believer giving protection to a freedman is undertaking certain responsibilities in respect of a person not really intimately known to him while Believers are like brothers to one another. Therefore, when a Believer takes a freedman of another Believer as ally, and gives him protection, it is in their common interest to have the blessings of the other Believer. This order was being given to maintain internal peace of the community.

Clause 10: "The Believers who fear Allah, will oppose the rebellious elements and those that encourage injustice or sin or enmity or lack of cooperation among Believers."

It has to be kept in mind that the Believers were to defend *Yathrib*. It was, therefore, essential that the best of relations existed among them. There were people within *Yathrib* who were likely to create mischief and create situations detrimental to internal security. The factor which had to be kept in mind was that every Believer had, until then, persons closely related to him, who had not yet embraced Islam. It was possible that some such person was found guilty of injustice, sin, or enmity to Islam or of creating trouble between Believers. On such occasions. Believers were being told that their duty lay with law and order and their loyalty lay with High Command's policy and decision and not with the kindred, however dear they may have been. It was a very delicate situation and the *Ansars* deserve all the credit for having come out of this very severe test successfully.

The leadership provided by the Prophet (Pbuh) and the minor circle of his Companions deserve equal praise for steering the *Millah* with patience, love and tact, through this most difficult period. "Believers who fear Allah", is the key factor in the shaping of an Islamic society. Love of family ties can over-ride all other situations, except that of men and women, who fear Allah, and as a result of fear of Allah are prepared to sacrifice family interests and affiliations. When the object is to create a flawless Muslim society in which no Believer can be thought of committing a sin, rebellion, injustice or create dissension, then every Muslim is expected to oppose such sinful elements even though they may be his close relations. A country or a state can be defended only if there is peace and harmony within the boundaries of that state.

Such a society can only come about if individuals fear Allah and have firm belief that they will have to answer for their actions on the Day of Judgement.

Clause 11: "If anyone is guilty of any such act all Believers will oppose him, even, if he be the son of any one of them."

This Clause is more or less a corollary to the foregoing Clause. It was being laid down firmly and without any ambiguity that injustice, sin and rebellious acts would not be permitted in that society, which was being created in accordance with the Code of Law Revealed by Allah. This was after centuries that a society was taking shape on the principle of Sovereignty of Allah. This society was to prove to humanity, for all times, that a people, a nation, an *Ummah*, observing in their day to day life, the Sovereignty of Allah prove in actual practice that their objective was to achieve three things:

(a) A happy and contented individual who has patience, for-bearance and steadfastness and these individuals show love for each other in their normal day to day dealings.

(b) These happy and contented individuals bring into existence a happy and loving society.

(c) They do not fall prey to the temptation of committing aggression or transgression against other nations even though as a result of being a happy, contented and united people they have gained strength and have the capacity of over-running their neighbours. In addition such an *Ummah* does not engage in any war unless they are attacked first. But whenever they are attacked they punish the aggressor to an extent, that he does not repeat it again.

Such a happy and strong society can come into existence only if its individuals observe law for themselves and for all who may be near and dear to them. This Clause draws the attention of Believers to the injunction of the Quran:

> "O you who believe! Be ye staunch injustice, witnesses for Allah, even though it be against yourselves or (your) parents or (your) kindred, whether (the case be of) a rich man or a poor man, for Allah is nearer unto both, (than ye are). So follow not passion".

Clause 12: "A Believer will not kill another Believer for the sake of an un-Believer."

This Clause was a further explanation and an illustration of Clause 11.

Family ties held strong loyalties in Arabia as in all tribal societies. If a member of a family was killed, his kith and kin were expected to avenge that death or be satisfied with the usual blood-money. These prejudices were very deep rooted. The Prophet (Pbuh), however, was creating an *Ummah*, the members of which were to be above all such ties, prejudices and loyalties. He was stressing on Believers and un-Believers alike that the only loyalty in Islam is loyalty to Allah and this is exhibited by obedience to His Laws. The Law of Allah is clear on the subject that a Believer cannot kill another Believer unless by mistake. He ceases to be a Believer if he kills another Believer wilfully.

> "Whose slayeth a believer of set purpose, his reward is Hell for ever".
> (4: 93)

The society was, as yet, a mixed society but laws had to be promulgated, which would gradually develop the society into a society of love, peace and justice all round. This could only be achieved by having strict laws and meticulous observance of those laws. Believers and their un-Believers relations were being told categorically, that no Believer, should be expected to avenge the death of a relative killed accidentally or otherwise by another Believer.

Islam had to step out of Arabia and spread to far off lands. It was to declare, from the beginning, as to where did the loyalties of new-Muslims lie immediately after becoming Muslims. The Code was strict, unusually difficult to observe but the choice of observance of loyalty was between the Sovereignty of Allah and worldly ties. Allah had to be given preference by those who claimed to have accepted Him as their Lord and Master.

Clause 13: "No Believer will help an un-Believer against a Believer."

This Clause in conjunction the foregoing sets a standard of behaviour for Believers in a mixed society where Believers are placed in a non-Believer majority, even though general relation may be on the best of terms. Believers must remain united among themselves, if they desire to possess weight, as an Ummah, however small their number may be.

This Clause could be used as precedent and for relations between Muslim states, so that inter-state relations between Muslim states are kept at friendly level and instances of acute differences between them do not arise. It would then coincide with the directions given in the Verse quoted below:

> "Let not the believers take disbelievers for their friends in preference to believers." (3: 28)

Disobedience of Clause 13 and the Verse quoted above have brought about the situation, that vast areas populated entirely by Believers have fallen prey to un-Believers and millions of Muslims are forced to live as atheists. It is punishment for having rebelled against both the letter and spirit of the Quran and the Charter.

Condition of Non-Muslims

The Jewish tribes of *Yathrib* were rich and had fairly large number of members prominent in business. They, however, had no political or social status among the Arab population. They appear to have migrated from Syria during one of their exodus resulting from *Assyrian* invasion. Some writers are of the opinion that they were settled in *Yathrib* even before the Arabs. This does not appear likely. The theory, that they were Arabs who had been converted to *Judaism* also does not appear plausible. They were, at the time of Prophet's *Hijrah*, adherents of one or the other of these Arab tribes (*Aus* and *Khazraj*). They had, however, preserved a sort of intellectual ascendency, owing to their being in possession of the Scriptures and their fame for the occult sciences, the pagan Arabs consulting their rabbies on occasions and paying heed to what they said."

Privileged Position : The Prophet (Pbuh) gave them a privileged position in the Constitutional Charter, provided they followed the Believers loyally and fought alongside with them. They possessed strong forts just outside the main city of

Yathrib and each tribe was independent in every respect, each having a separate fort. They had all the weapons of the period and boasted of their prowess as fighters. When the *Quraish* were defeated at *Badr*, one of their tribes, *Banu Qainuqa*, in reply to the Prophet's advice of good behaviour, they boasted of their strength and rebelled. They are a people of the Book. The way in which the Prophet (Pbuh) was laying the foundations of bringing humanity on one platform would have benefited the Jews in the long run, but they were short sighted and did not avail of the special position, they could have enjoyed under the terms of the Charter. In spite of the behaviour of leading Jews of *Yathrib* the Prophet (Pbuh) continued treating them with kindness and until a Jewish tribe did not commit an act of treason or outright rebellion he did not take any action against them. He pardoned two of the rebellious tribes, when they surrendered.

Those terms of the Charter, which were of general nature and those in connection with defence of the state, were applicable to Jews as well. There were, however, some Clauses which referred to the Jews only. The Clauses of general nature included the heading (Clause 1) in which it was laid down that those who followed the Believers and fought alongside with them will form one *Ummah* with them. This was a great attraction for the Jews. They were being elevated to the status of equality with Arabs and in some respects they were becoming superior to them, because, they were becoming equals of the ruling party of *Yathrib*, the Believers. Clauses like Clause 5, which laid down that "All parties will redeem their prisoners with kindness and justice according to practice among Believers," are being studied elsewhere. In this Chapter only those Clauses will be brought under discussion, which pertain to Jews exclusively.

Clause 16: "Those Jews who follow us, will be helped and will be treated with equality."

We have touched on this Clause very briefly, under Laws pertaining to defence. As the Clause mentions Jews particularly, we feel that it must be due to some special reason, that the question cropped up again, although it had been touched upon in Clause 1, where it referred to "those who," followed them. The only reason, for the mention of Jews specifically, could be that they had, during the dictation of the Charter, asked a direct question about the subject.

Clause 15 had spoken of "Believers are all friends to each other to the exclusion of all others." The Jews and 'the others' were being denied the friendship and equality with Muslims, which had been promised in Clause 1. The Jews must have felt that their position, in respect of equality with Muslims, needed to be clarified. They must have asked a specific question, "What about us." The answer came in the form of Clause 16 that "Those Jews who follow us will be helped and will be treated with equality."

This Clause shows their keenness to gain an equal socio-political status with the Believers. As yet they knew very little about Islam. They may have been still under the impression that the Prophet (Pbuh) will announce himself as a sect of Judaism, and not as final shape of Islam, the Way of Life, preached by Ibrahim and Musa (*Alaihi-ssalam*). The Prophet (PBUH) having sensed the worries of Jews dictated the next Clause.

Clause 17: "No Jew will be wronged."

Jews had been persecuted all the world over to such an extent that it was rare to find a place where they could live an honourable life. It may have been, that the Jews themselves have followed a policy of persecution in respect of communities which happened to be weaker than them. It could also be that wherever they happened to be in a minority, they took recourse to mischief and intrigue, which invited persecution against them. Centuries of such mischievous and selfish behaviour gave them a reputation that they attracted hatred merely by the mention of the word Jew, whereever they went. The only person in authority, throughout history, who has shown compassion and kindness to them through the enactment of a Law is Muhammad (Pbuh) the Prophet (PBUH) of Allah. This historical Clause placed the Jews on a pedestal of honour, respect and safety which they had not enjoyed under their own kings. This assurance of safe and respectful life was independent of the Clause giving them equality with Believers if they fought alongside them on the Path of Allah.

It is clear that the Clause governing their status of equality must have been the result of their volunteering to take part in the defence of *Yathrib* against an attack by the *Quraish* of Mecca. It could be because according to *Yaqubi*, the famous geographist, they were from an Arab stock. He says that "Jews of Median were basically local Arabs and were Judaised by immigrants who fled from Palestine after the Roman invasion. It could also be through Jews who migrated earlier. In any case, they had not only adopted the Law brought by Moses but had also imbibed the universally adopted national character of Jews based on miserliness, cheating and mischief mongering, and had, as a result lost their status as honest citizens, as in other parts of the world." The history of the scattered tribes of Jews has been a history of fraud, criminality and cunning; sabotage and destruction", but he being "Mercy to Mankind." could not refuse a request of a down-trodden people even though they may have deserved such a behaviour in the past.

The Jews, however take their roaming around the world as a boon from above. They call it, "A beneficent protection, which God has instituted in the life of the Jews is, that He has dispersed them all over the world".

The Prophet (Pbuh) was giving them equality because they were a part of mankind, created and fashioned by Allah. To a Muslim, equality has become a second nature, as a result. "A barefooted Beduin, in a ragged cloak, would walk upto a king, shake him by the hand and wish him good morning, completely disregarding horror of the whispering courtiers".

It may appear strange that the Jews were accepting to live under Laws of the Quran and the Commands of the Last Prophet of Allah as loyal citizens and fight for the safety of the New Deen in a chance, for receiving the status of free citizens of *Yathrib*. It may be because in this way they were becoming co-rulers along with Arabs, as their equals. It speaks of their urge for living an honourable life of equality with the high born in Arabia and be subject to Laws, which gave equal status to men, irrespective of their ethnic or geographical origin. They were proving the dictum that, "The most obvious and recognised characteristic of just laws is that they are equal", for all concerned. Justice has been recognised as the central theme of Islam. It is based on the principle of equality of men in the eyes of Allah. When human beings, irrespective of the colour of their skins, the language that they speak and the creed they prefer to follow, are treated as equals before law, there is no possibility of injustice prevailing. "Injustice arises when equals are treated unequally and also when unequals are treated equally". This was the first time, that Jews were being treated as equals, and were to enjoy complete freedom. "Closely related to the value of equality is that of freedom. These two values are often defined in terms of the other. Freedom is most often defined, in terms of absence of restrictions, which we see as one way of defining equality.

Freedom as a value calling for absence of restrictions or restraints is laden with contradictions. Society can exist only if human behaviour is predictable and controllable to some extent....Unconditional freedom could result only in chaos in all areas of activity".

It appears that Jewish mind has always wanted uncontrolled freedom. Movements like Socialism and Communism have been supported by Jewish intellectuals with greater zeal than thinkers of other schools of thought. The treacherous behaviour of Jews in different parts of the world, at various periods of history is the result of unbridled thought of their thinkers and intellectuals. They have a history which abounds in rebellious conduct even under their own rulers.

The number of occasions, when anti-Jewish communal disturbances have taken place are too numerous to be mentioned in an essay of this nature. A few instances may, however, be mentioned.

Jews massacred in Alexandria (216 B.C.)

Antiochus killed 40,000 Jews in Jerusalem (170 B.C.)

Titus killed 11,00,000 Jews and destroys the Temple (70 A.C.)

Desolation of Judea (135 A.C.). Rebellion of Jews. Romans killed 580,000. (136 A.C.)

Rebellion of Jews at Alexandria. Jews massacred (415 A.C.)

Umar took over Jerusalem not a single person was killed(655 A.C.)

No more Jews killed in the Middle East. Jews banished from England (1020 A.C.). Jews returned to England (1060 A.C.). Jews massacred in London on Coronation day of Richard I.

Christian priests joined in the massacre. (1189 A.C.)

Jews besieged in the castle of York. (1190 A.C.)

They cut each others throats. Hunderds killed.

Jews of both sexes imprisoned in England.

Their eyes and teeth pulled out.

A large number butchered by king John. (1204 A.C.)

700 Jews slain in London (1262 A.C.)

Statute that no Jew should enjoy a freehold (1269 A.C.)

Jew moneylenders forced to hang a plate on their breast or quit England. (1274 A.C.)

267 Jews hanged, accused of clipping coins. (1278 A.C.)

All Jews 16511 banished from England. (1290 A.C.)

Jewish fate in France and other countries of Europe during 14th and 15th centuries is a grim story.

Several hundred thousand banished from Spain. (1492-1494 A.C.)

Addicts against Jews rescinded by Pope Sixtus V Cromwell permitted them to return to England. (1650 A.C.)

These instances of persecution of Jews speak of the manner they have been hunted from place to place. Their own laws of war and peace are primarily responsible for introducing cruelty during and after war.

According to their own history books, the behaviour of Jewish personalities of note has not been praiseworthy either. "Edom and Jeshurun were rivals and great were the cruelty of the Hebrew arms in their countries. When David[15] was king, his sister's son Jacob went down and killed Adonites in the Ghrov twelve thousand men and Jacob's brother *Abishai* killed eighteen thousand of them... Other ten thousand taken captives, he brought to the top of the rock, and there he made them the king's tumblers, casting them headlong down together, by the sharp rocks, that they were all broken in pieces".

There have been numerous occasions during 20th century in Europe and particularly in Germany when great atrocities have been committed against Jews because they had captured the economic life of these countries. Efforts have been made to get rid of them. Israel has been created for this purpose, but the Jews have not left either Europe or America. Christianity appears poised to start a fresh campaign to annihilate them during the 21st century of the Christian Era, while Muhammad (Pbuh), gave *Yathrib* a Charter in 7th century, which said:-"No Jew will be wronged."

Professor Sergeant has tried to prove, that the Charter is not one Document but a collection of eight different documents. He, however, admits the authenticity of the Document, and does not deny the existence of the Clause "No Jew will be wronged." This guarantee of safety was being given to a people, who did not hold the status of nationals of that city and were living at the mercy of the tribes, which had given them protection.

Muslims have always shown magnanimity to the Jews. When they were banished from Spain between the years 1492 and 1494 A.C., "it was to Turkey that the persecuted Spanish Jews fled for refuge in enormous numbers." The persecution of Jews by Christians appears to he natural justice, after a lapse of centuries. They persecuted, in their time, those who fell into their hands. "The Jews used to bum their prisoners alive and most barbarously mutilate the slain".

Yathrib was witnessing a change. A new order was being established by Muhammad (Pbuh) who has been sent by Allah, as "Mercy to mankind." All barbarities, all prosecutions, all wrongs to humanity were being made as illegal. All men were being declared as equal. Even the Jews, the downtrodden of East and West were being promised, that no harm will come to them as long as they committed no sin or crime. They were being given a place in the Charter, which was being offered without any pressure. Centuries later king John of England gave a Charter, at a time when "The capital was in rebel hands, the whole administration was at a stand still. Without his exchequer, John had no revenues. He had to yield. The king agreed to meet the barons on the meadows of *Runnymede*, between

Staines and Windsor, and there signed the Great Charter". It would be interesting to read the Great Charter and compare it the Charter of Median and see which Charter gives more freedom, equality, justice and human rights.

Jews have had a chequered career throughout history. They have invited this fate because of their internecine warfare. They butchered one another, whenever and whoever had the upper hand. Their final self-inflicted blow came when, "After the defeat of Bar *Cochba*, in A.C. 135, much of Judea was left a desert and some towns of *Galilee* were also ravaged".

They seem to have a rebellious nature. If they were not quarrelling among themselves, they would rebel against authority, however benign it may have been. They rebelled against *Nebuchadnessar* and "resolving to settle the Jewish problem once for all, as he thought, he recaptured Jerusalem, burned it to the ground, destroyed the temple of Solomon[16], drew *Zedekia*'s sons before his face, gauged out their eyes, and carried practically all the population of the city into captivity in *Babylonia*."

During one of their marches in captivity and when their women were ordered by their guards to sing for them, they are supposed to have composed a song, bemoaning of their separation from Jerusalem. The words are:

"By the river of *Babylon*, there we sat down,
Yes, we wept, when we remembered *Zion*,
We hanged our harps upon the willows in the midst thereof.
For there, they that carried us away captives, required of us a song.
And they that worked us required of us mirth.
Saying, sing us a song of Zion.
How shall we sing the Lord's song in a strange land"

In later days, Jews have suffered only at the hands of Christians because of their having had a hand in the supposed Crucification of Jesus[17] Christ. We have given a list of well known instances of persecution of Jews but did not include the migration of Jews to Babylon during the sixth century when Justinian withdrew citizenship from all those who were not members of Orthodox Church. Jews, as a result, chose the kindlier atmosphere of Babylon, which, at that time was under the Iranians. When the Iranians reconquered Syria, at the beginning of the 7th century, the Jews, who had been left behind, sided with the invaders. They paid heavily for this when Emperor *Heraclius* reconquered the country. During the "early period of Arab rule they prospered....The Jewish towns and villages remained Jewish, paying taxes to Muslims, instead of Christian rulers, but otherwise continuing their normal life". This kind of treatment by Muslim rulers was in the spirit of the Constitutional Charter of Median, which had categorically made it highly illegal to do any wrong to the Jews. The only other people who have been kind to the Jews are the Iranians. *Yazdgard* I was most kind to them. His "married to a Jewess, was so well disposed to them, that they called him "The Christian King".

The Prophet (Pbuh) was so kind to the Jews that, he, made it illegal for everybody to harm the Jews, unless they were guilty of a crime. Also he laid down that —

Clause 18: "The enemies of Jews will not be helped."

Both these Clauses were independent of the Jews following the leadership of Believers otherwise. These concessions were given to them as ordinary citizens of *Yathrib*. This was a great step forward towards freedom, equality and basic human rights of man considering that this legal Document was being dictated verbatum in the year 622 A.C.

In the normal course of events, this is not much of a concession to a group accepted as free citizens of a state. It becomes a great concession when no civic duties are imposed on that group. It gives the impression that although their Arab Haleefs were giving them protection yet they were on friendly terms with the enemies of the Jews previously. They were now being told that their enemies will not be befriended.

Good Treatment to Minorities : These two Clauses give a clue to the consistently good treatment of minorities by Muslim rulers. These two Clauses have served as a *Sunnah* of the Prophet (Pbuh) indicating the manner in which, minorities living under Muslim rule should be treated, Muslim rulers have never persecuted people on whom they may have had to rule. Persecution of the weak appears to be a part of the European race and Muslim, in their earlier period, were fortunate to have escaped European influence. Even during the present civilised century Europeans have prided themselves on their superior strength to dominate other people. A German writer of early twentieth century, *Ludwig Welliman*[18], "affirmed as early as 1903, that, the race is called upon to dominate the earth, to exploit nations' treasures, and the physical strength of man, to make the passive races simple subaltern organisations for the evolution of its nation".

When Germany overran France, during the Second World War, it set about to depopulate France, so that France was not able to provide itself with adequate manpower during any future war. "The annual total of French births which did not exceed six hundred thousand in 1939, would be halted or worse, since there would also be economic difficulties and privations skilfully organised and maintained by the victor".

Jews, though a mislead people, have been unfortunate throughout history. They have been persecuted in all lands except where Islam reigned. We know how they suffered in the Middle East and England. Their fate in Germany during twentieth century has been worse. To persecute them for having particular religious views has been highly unjust. It appears, that Europeans are too narrow minded, to permit others to hold views, which differ with their own views, and yet nearly all European nations pretend to be secular. One of those who have suffered at the altar of their Secular Christianity writes, "Christian Missionaries, who came from secular states of Europe, with public funds, introduced education on the Western pattern, which spread all over the country. Admission to these Christian schools was conditional on accepting Christianity". In some cases and particularly after independence "they were baptised forcefully, at the Victory College Chapel". The writer goes on to say, "What is most essential for the dignity of man and social progress is freedom of thought, the very freedom, which the Churches have striven for, through centuries of religious wars and persecution to destroy". The Last Way of Life, sent to mankind, through Muhammad (Pbuh), happens to be the only Way of Life, with the school of thought that there will be complete freedom of thought and has forbidden use of force in "Deen."

"There is no compulsion in religion." (2: 256)

Clause 29: "The Jews will contribute towards the war when fighting alongside the Believers."

The last Clause dealing with the subject of Jews was in relation to their enemies not being helped. Immediately after that Clause matters of defence were taken up. As a result the Jews must have asked about contribution towards the war, in case they also took part in it. It was logical for them to come forward and share the expenses of the war. This, however, was a general statement and Jews under the protection of Arab tribes must have wanted, that their names be specifically mentioned in the Charter. It had been dictated earlier that those Jews who fought alongside the Believers will be considered as part of the *Ummah*. When they had accepted to share at the cost of war at the time of joining in *Jihad* on the Path of Allah, they were entitled to become a part of the *Ummah* on by the Jews would have gradually brought humanity on to the same platform. Mankind is destined to become one *Ummah* eventually, when they will be following the same Law. Clause 28 already dictated says, "When you differ on anything the matter will be referred to Allah and Muhammad (Pbuh)." Reference to Allah means the Dictates of the Quran and reference to Muhammad (Pbuh) signifies his *Sunnah*. It meant that the mode of worship was to remain separate but the Law governing the society was to be that of Islam. Orientalists have failed to comprehend the significance of Prophet's approach to forge an *Ummah* in which all People of the Book, should live as One *Ummah.* Muir accepts that "No expression regarding either the Jewish or Christian Scriptures ever escaped the lips of Muhammad (Pbuh) other than of implicit reverence". And yet on the same page he writes:

> "In his later years Islam diverged rapidly from all sympathy with the Bible". He has given no proof of this divergence. He, however, has realised that, "It was the opposition of the Jews, and the martial superiority of Islam that imperceptibly led to the exclusive authority of Muhammad (Pbuh) and the Quran".

If *Muir* had read the Charter carefully, he would have realised that exclusive authority of Muhammad (Pbuh) and the Quran had been established from the beginning of Islam in Median. The Jews failed to perceive, and so has Muir missed the point that unity of human race was the object of the Final Way of Life being Revealed to Muhammad (Pbuh). It was the Jews who sabotaged it and it is Christian Missionaries and the Zionists who are still on the path of war with Islam the Deen of Peace. Allah has said:

> "Mankind were one community". (2: 213)

Differences arose and people forgot the true Faith. Messengers were sent to guide them back to the right path. Some listened and some did not. Although many Messengers were sent the main theme remained, as the Sovereignty of Allah. When the Last Messenger came, he tried to bring people on to the same platform. A beginning was made, but when people of the Book laid stress on their own separate identity and ignored the Sovereignty of Allah, the experiment failed. The present writer feels that, the result was that for the future the order came, that, who ever accepts Islam must submit completely.

> "O you who believe Come, all of you, into submission (unto Him)".
> (2: 208)

Clause 31: "The same applies to Jews of *Bani Al-Najjar, Bani Al- Harith, Bani Saeeda, Bani Josham, Bani Al-Aus*, *Thaliba* and the *Jafar* and the *Bani Al-Shuraiha*".

Clause 34: "Those in alliance with the Jews will be given the same treatment as the Jews." The Jews were accepting the responsibility of joining in the defence of the state. They had allies abroad. As the Jews had promised to become a part of the *Ummah*, it was only fair to consider and treat their allies in the same manner as the Jews.

Clause 37: "The Jews bear their own expenses and the Believers bear their expenses."

The subject matter of defence continues. The question of payment has arisen again. This refers to expenses connected with each ethnic contingent of the Army. Each was to pay for its own contingent.

Clause 43: "The Jews must pay with the Believers."

This was to refer to expenses of general nature like blood money or other damages, in which both parties had to share the expenses.

Clause 47: "The Jews of *al-Aus*, including their freedom have the same standing as other parties to the Charter."

This Clause speaks for itself. Late-comers were being accommodated.

These were Clauses in respect of Laws binding and giving rights to Jews. Irrespective of what status they had possessed prior to the *Hijrah* of the Prophet (Pbuh), they were to be governed and treated in accordance with the dictates of this Document. It is incumbent on all students of Seerah and early history of Islam to bear in their minds the contents of the Charter. Without reference to this important Document no opinion can he formed on the behaviour of one or the other party.

Defending Law

As we know *Yathrib* had no organisation, which could be called a state or any institution in the nature of an organ of a state to run its collective affairs, normally known as a government. The result was that there was no arrangement or an organisation to defend it. The tribes had been fighting among themselves, but they had never been involved in war with outsiders. Hence lack of arrangements for defence. As a result of absence of an institution to look after their collective affairs, there was no arrangement for internal security either. The Constitutional Charter of Median had to cater for both of these requirements. We have already studied the background of the Charter and the declaration of war by the *Quraish* of Mecca and as a consequence, the Prophet's undertaking, that Believers will defend *Yathrib* and "The others," will be welcome to join in this common cause, provided they worked under the leadership of Believers. This decision resulted in the issue of the charter and it gave to all governmental and defence activities a legal framework in which defence preparation, training and contacts with neighbouring tribes and treaty obligations could be looked after. Preparations for war take a great deal of time and planned efforts. "It is not merely the number of able-bodied men who could be thrown into the battle line, but their training the quality and the numbers of experienced officers and equipment", that count in war.

Those who do not take adequate precautions and remain unprepared are forced in the end to follow a policy, which ends in the surrender of their independence. Believers in *Yathrib* were new to the environment. They had sought protection, in a place, which did not have a unified defence policy, because that city, in the past, had no occasion to do so. With the arrival of Islam and *Muhajir* Believers, the situation, both in *Yathrib* and in relation to the Meccans, had altered. War had been declared and as explained earlier, the threat of the invasion, and eventually the invasion itself demanded action. Allah had commanded, apart from other instruction that, defence and internal security arrangements were vital to the existence of *Ummah*.

"O you who believe! Take your precautions". (4: 71)

Vast Application : The original word has so vast application that it includes all aspects of defence, internal security, foreign relations, defence production, educational policy and planning the entire life of *Ummah* in a manner that it can guarantee its future Islamic Way of Life. The *Ummah*, at that time, was confined to *Yathrib*. Therefore the Commandment at that time meant the defence and internal security of *Yathrib*. Believers had accepted the responsibility but their strength was inadequate. It was not yet known if the others, would join in defending *Yathrib* or not. Shortage of manpower demanded excellence of training and morale. Training demands time.

Readiness for war, therefore, posed very serious problems. The issuing of the Charter was, in this respect, the first step. It gave legal base to all future activities towards defence and internal security. We would now like to proceed with the clauses dealing with defence.

Clause 1: We have so far, looked at it from the angle that it also forms the heading of the Charter. In view of the fact that it mentions 'War' and 'fighting' we feel that it very appropriately opens the Charter with the purpose for which it was being issued. It says:

" Those" (others) who followed them (the Believers) and fought with them".

Defence is guaranteed only when a people are prepared to fight and accept losses in men, money and equipment. When a nation is threatened with invasion by a stronger power, the only honourable course open to them is to accept the challenge like free men who fear none but Allah. Weakness, both physical and moral invites aggression. Philosophies, which advocate peace at any cost soon disappear. It has been rightly said that "War is perhaps the most searching test of national worthiness.... nor has any nation kept its place when martial spirit died away".

The Meccans, although, at the time of the issue of the Charter, do not appear to have started hostilities, but because of the declaration of war by Mecca, a state of war had come into existence. State of war permits both adversaries to take defensive measures as though hostilities had commenced. It has been accepted at international level that, "being at war refers to a state or condition of affairs and not merely acts of force ...."

Mecca having declared war, was automatically, in a "State of War," with *Yathrib* and the same was being reciprocated by *Yathrib*, by initiating defensive measures. The issue of the Charter was the first step. Through it the rights, duties, responsibilities of various types of residents of *Yathrib* were being announced and established by law. Events occurring after the issuing of the Charter have to be viewed and judged in the light of this Document. All previous undertakings between parties mentioned in this Document, and hence governed by it, stand cancelled, unless reiterated in it in some form or other.

Historians have been referring to the conditions agreed upon during *Bayah of Aqba Thani*, between the Prophet (Pbuh) and men of *Yathrib*. This Charter does not mention the Bayah, or conditions agreed upon at that time. The Charter being a later document, cancels all previous undertakings between the parties. In any case, they being Believers and having sworn allegiance to him would only too willingly have given assent to any decision he was pleased to take on the issue of defence of the abode of the *Ummah*. The fact that a state of war had arisen and they had sworn to defend him further strengthened the contents of the Charter. We feel, that in view of this "state of war" all future events should be judged keeping the contents of the Charter in view. As mentioned elsewhere this Charter announced the existence of an *Ummah*, which had existed but had not been recognised. This Document gave an official international recognition to Muslim *Ummah*, which has never been challenged, though efforts have been made to give it a nomenclature of religion like dozens of others in the world. It was to differ from all other denominations, which, had hitherto existed, whether ethnical, linguistic, religious or geographically based nationality. It was global, universal, and beyond the boundaries set by time. It would last until time would last. Having been based on the acceptance of the principle of Sovereignty of Allah it would last until there was a single individual, who believed in His Sovereignty.

A nation has been defined as "a separate society of individuals, who possess a common government, common laws, rights, institutions, interests, common history and glory, common defences and security of the rights, riches and lives, constitute one body free and independent."

In order, eventually, to bring about unity of mankind, this Document, which was being bestowed by Muhammad (Pbuh) to *Yathrib*, was inviting others to live and endeavour alongside the Believers, to bring into existence a society of individuals whose readiness for sacrifice, in the name of Allah was of a standard not achieved by any human group before, with the object of bringing mankind under one flag and on one platform. This alone could put an end to perpetual wars which had plagued mankind throughout the ages.

It will be admitted that-it is an unusual Document. It is, therefore, important that every phrase, every sentence and every word of it must be studied with great care. For instance this very first Clause of the Document says, "Those who followed them and fought with them, they form one *Ummah* to the exclusion of the others."

It means, that those who fight alongside one another and maintain discipline by following those who had set up and established the central core of *Ummah* are entitled to become One *Ummah* to the exclusion of the rest of the world. It means that those who are prepared to lay down their lives for a cause form part of one *Ummah*. There is no geographical, ethnic or linguistic barrier to their forming one *Ummah* — nation in the modern terminology. It also would mean that those who deny the principle of fighting to safeguard the basic principles on which an *Ummah* is based would surrender their right to be a part of the *Ummah*. Being outside the pale of *Ummah* they should be excluded from all assignments of trust, in the defence and administrative departments. Quran has laid down:

"O you who believe take not for intimate others than your own folk".
(3: 118)

This Clause, which establishes the basis of a universal *Ummah* also lays down the disqualification for being bestowed the honour of belonging to a universal brotherhood spread out along the entire surface of the globe.

The use of the phrase "making utmost effort," has been used for "fighting on the Path of Allah." This new meaning has vast application. It covers total war in which fighting in the front lines and supporting those involved in fighting are all included. The notion of National War and Total War are special ingredients of the term *Jihad*, particularly in view of the involvement of the entire *Ummah* in it.

The opening Clause of the Charter speaks of war. To start a Document with mention of war was the requirement of the situation because the Document was the result of declaration of war by Mecca. It was, therefore, appropriate that the first Clause which also formed the heading of the Document should refer to war. The matter does not end with Clause 1 but subsequent eight clauses also deal with one or the other aspects of the problems of war. It also shows the stress and strain under which Believers must have been living during this early period after Hijrah. The war, however, was not the result of their choice. It had been forced on them. This war was the result of vested interests as it had been in bygone ages, "for century after century war was the recognised method of settling international disputes. Not only was it legal, but it was the authorised court of last resort.

Trial of Right : Francis Bacon called it the highest trial of right. As long as war was recognised as legal, there was no punishment for those responsible for it. Islam, however, holds these mischief makers responsible. The Quran has laid down that if these guilty persons who wage war but are in the end regretful, then they may be pardoned. If, however, they break their promises then:

> "And if they break their pledges after their treaty (hath been made with you) and assail your religion, then fight the heads of disbelief- Lo! they have no binding oaths -in order that they may desist". (9: 12)

People guilty of dragging mankind into uncalled for slaughter must be punished.

Highest Test : The Prophet (Pbuh) had to prepare Believers for the "Highest Test of Right," to establish the principle that those who believe in the Sovereignty of Allah, prefer to lay down their lives rather than live under any other sovereign and laws promulgated by it. He was a man of peace. His whole life had been spent in peaceful activities, but he was now placed in a position, where he had to prepare a peace loving people to stand for "the highest trial of right," and prove, that Allah is with the righteous, provided they prepare themselves for the task. He has ordered:

> "Make ready for them all thou caust of (armed) forces and of horses tathered that there by ye may dismay the enemy of Allah and your enemy, and others beside them ye know not. Allah knoweth them. Whatsoever ye spend in the way of Allah it will be repaid to you in full, and ye will not be wronged". (8: 60)

Modern military writers have accepted this truth. A well known authority on naval matters of modern times has echoed these thoughts very aptly, when he says, "It behaves countries whose genius is essentially not military, whose people, like all free people, object to pay for large military establishments, to see to it that they are at least strong enough to gain time necessary to turn the spirit and capacity of their subjects into the new activities which war calls for."

War brings all human beings on the same platform. A general and soldier of rank and file are made of the same flesh and blood. The sword and the arrow or a bullet and a missile treat them alike. This was a document, which was the product of state of war. It had to bring home to mankind that those who face danger as equals must be treated as equals in day to day life as well. Islam has given to every man the same status. All are equal. All are free born. All must, therefore enjoy equality and freedom. This is the first written piece of paper which has declared that those who followed them and fought alongside them would be equal to them, because they would have become members of this "the best of all *Ummahs*. "

> "Ye are the best Community that hath been raised up for mankind. Ye enjoin right conduct and forbid indecency; and you believe in Allah".
>
> (3: 110)

Borrowed from Islam : The world has borrowed the terms of equality, liberty and justice from Islam but have not yet been able to understand the full meaning of these qualities, when adopted by an *Ummah* as a whole. Europe has failed to achieve equality and liberty because they have divorced day to day life from the faith they acknowledge as their guiding principle. The result is that all ethical standards fall outside the realm of daily life. That is why such statements are heard. "The two great ideas of liberty and equality are often mentioned together, but the right relation between them is far from simple.... We give the strong members of the community to have the liberty to dominate the others as they like to acquire wealth as they like and to keep it as they like. Such a system is bound to be so ruthless that equality, in any meaningful sense, is impossible."

Clause 3: "They will redeem their prisoners with kindness and justice common among Believers."

Clause 1 had spoken of fighting *Jihad.* Prisoners of war is a natural consequence of war. In the past and for a long time afterwards redeeming of prisoners was not thought of. As explained elsewhere a defeated army and its nation could not look after its prisoners of war or ask for their being returned to their home country. Armies used to belong to the rulers. When a ruler was defeated each soldier had to look after himself, if he was not taken prisoner. Slavery resulted from the fact that prisoners of war had to be fed, clothed and provided with other necessities, because their governments could not pay or did not care to pay war indemnities. Modern states have shown interest in their men who have been taken prisoners of war, but it is rarely thought of to redeem them with kindness and justice. It was during the later part of eighteenth century that consideration started being given to prisoners of war. Matters, however, stood still and after the First World War, when the League of Nations came into being steps were taken to see that nations did not maltreat each other's prisoners of war. The Hague Convention is the official document to which most nations have shown agreement and it governs the manner, in which prisoners of war have to be treated. Inclusion of this Clause in a Document executed during the first year of *Hijrah*, corresponding to 622 A.C. should not surprise readers. It was in line with the spirit of Islam and in conformity with other laws promulgated for Believers. A point to note is, that during nine years of war fought by the Prophet (Pbuh) the enemy, including the Byzantine Imperial Army, did not capture a single Believer to make him a prisoner of war. It was a fight until *Shahadah*, that the Believers believed in. In spite of it, the Prophet (Pbuh) included this clause in the Charter, mainly because his Commands had to last for ever.

It is after fourteen centuries of the promulgation of the Charter, that we read in Article 118, para 1 of the report of International Committee of the Red Cross that:

> "prisoners of war have an inalienable right to be repatriated once hostilities have ceased...."

Islam has laid great stress on alleviating hardships of prisoners of war and redeeming them. *Zakat*, which is official collection of 2½% of one year old savings of every Believer has to be spent on specific needs of the *Ummah*. One of the needs specified in Quran is the freeing of prisoners. These naturally could be no other than the prisoners of war in enemy's hands. Today, they would be the persecuted Muslims under foreign domination. The manner in which they can be helped through *Zakat* is a point, which should be thrashed out by the learned and the intellectuals of the *Ummah*.

If redeeming of prisoners is given the importance envisaged in this Clause, early discussions will have to be initiated so that prisoners do not have to remain in enemy hands too long. War is not undertaken with kindness, for the enemy, "War is a contention between two or more states through their armed forces for the purpose of overpowering each other and imposing such conditions of peace as the victor pleases."

The army which is keen to see that its personnel, which has fallen into the hands of the enemy, should be treated well and repatriated speedily, will necessarily look after enemy prisoners of war with kindness. A year after this Document was promulgated a number of the enemy fell into the hands of Believers. They were treated kindly and permitted to be repatriated gracefully. Those, who could not pay ransom but could teach others to read and write they were asked to teach ten people each and were allowed to return to Mecca.

The words "with kindness and justice common among Believers," could only be used if in the short time that Islam had been introduced in *Yathrib*, these qualities of Believers had been so noticeable that they were being appreciated by all who came in contact with them. These national characteristics of the Believers had made them respected in *Yathrib* and had resulted in *Abdullah bin Ubay* to give up the idea of using force against Believers from Mecca.

Well-knit nations both individually and collectively behave in a certain manner under certain conditions. It is difficult to analyse or define as to how a certain National Character comes into being, but the fact that National Character does exist, is a fact, which cannot be denied. "What is National Character and how shall we define its nature." The author then asks "Is it a natural and inherent datum, or is it a growing product, which is being shaped by historic revolutions and the ongoing and pressing mind of man. If it has within itself both of these elements, how, and by what combination of nature and human art, has it been made? By what influences and in what direction it is now being shaped. What forecast we shall make of its future turns and trends."

The answer to these questions, with reference to the National Character of Believers in Allah and His *Rasul* (Pbuh) is given in Clause 24 of this Charter, which says, "The Believers, because they fear Allah, they are better in showing steadfastness..." Thus it can be said that reading clauses 3 and 24 together, to the National Character of Believers is that they are kind and just in peace and steadfast in war. This would be a reflection of the Quranic Verse which reads':

> "Muhammad (PBUH) is the messenger of Allah. And those with him are hard against the disbelievers and merciful among themselves". (48: 29)

It was the result of training given by the Prophet (Pbuh) to his Companions and their Faith in Allah that they developed the characteristics of kindness Justice, bravery and steadfastness to such an extent that they surpassed those around them in these and other similar qualities.

It is said that:

> " National Character being the common traits in a million or more members of a nation, it is difficult to analyse the process by which sympathetic feelings connect the working of the minds of innumerable individuals. It is said, that "The superstructure is a mental organisation connecting the minds of all the members of national community by ties

and connections as fine as silk and as firm as steel. It is a subtle spiritual cobweb of threads which are spun from mind to mind."

Focal Point : The focal point of the National Character of Believers, however centred in their belief in Allah, "When a man joins the brotherhood of Islam...... it is as an association of self-effacing individuals, that the community can come into being." Belief in Allah, the Creator of Universe, "not only permeates and encompasses universe, but also His Domains beyond. He is the unique Other Self, that transcends and encompasses the private personality of the finite individual self."

Training is an integral part of preparation for defence. It was entirely in the hands of the Prophet (Pbuh) himself. Thirteen years spent in Mecca moulded the character qualities of this small band of devoted Companions, which were based on belief in Allah the Creator of this entire Universe. To realise the source of moral strength of these few devoted Believers, it is necessary to study minutely the Verses of Quran Revealed at Mecca. The deep impression of the Might and Glory, Mercy and Benevolence, Wisdom and Knowledge, Absolute and Complete resulted in moulding their character.

If He be the Lord of man, so insignificant to look at, but so far-reaching in his comprehension of Him, Who has no second, then what difference if I, a Muslim, His humble servant lived in this world or while giving evidence of His Omnipotence, was to step into the next world and was granted His Audience. The sooner the entrance into His Grace the better.

Experts tell us that defence preparations cannot be completed in a short time. This is a long and tedious task, which is accomplished with great care and patience, on the part of both the trainer and the trainee, but the time at the disposal of the Prophet (Pbuh) was not only short, it did not exist, and yet, when hostilities started he was ready for them. The course of the "Battles of the Prophet (Pbuh) is outside the scope of this essay, but the manner in which he fought these battles is a refreshing story, worthy of being narrated again and again.

No nation can defend itself unless it has a well thought out defence policy. Based on that policy a defence organisation is brought into existence. Without a defence organisation no worthwhile achievement can be expected. A successful general of Second World War having won the severest and most expensive war of human history desired to create a more efficient organisation for his nation. He says, "We will build a national military team that will make it unavoidably clear that anybody who endangers our Way of Life, will risk destroying himself." The Prophet (Pbuh) in the short time at his disposal, created a Military Machine which destroyed the enemy, which wished to destroy the Islamic Way of Life. One of the lessons learnt from the successes of this machine was that they were the most respected individuals of the society. *Abu Bakr* saying good-bye to the commander of the Army proceeding to the north was walking beside him while the commander, the son of a former freedman, was riding at the head of the Army. The Germans lost Second World War because German Army in and around 1930, "felt that they were regarded as something less than the respectable members of a modern society."

Clause 5: "All parties will redeem their prisoners with kindness and justice according to practice among Believers."

A soldier who is sure of being looked after if he is wounded and redeemed if he is taken prisoner will fight better than otherwise. The Prophet (Pbuh) had dictated the Law that Believers must as an *Ummah* redeem their prisoner with kindness and justice common among Believers. This must have, at first, surprised the listeners. It was something new, which had not even been heard of. On second thought people must have felt that this responsibility must be accepted by other parties as well. They, therefore, must have requested that their parties must also be ordered to redeem their prisoners in exactly the same manner as the Believers were ordered to do.

This request was accepted and it became legally binding on "the others" as well to redeem their prisoners "with kindness and justice according to practice among Believers." It was felt, or it appears so that the redeeming of prisoners of all parties was not being made the responsibility of the Central Government because of two factors. One, that a certain amount of autonomy was advisable in a new Federal set up. Second reason was that, as yet, no central treasury had been established. It was, therefore, more suitable if all parties bore their own expenses.

The term, "kindness and justice common among Believers," needs being paid special attention to by the leaders and intellectuals of the *Ummah*. How is it that a small group of early Believers was able to have it accepted by all concerned, that kindness and justice were part of the National Character of Believers. We feel that the learned *Ulema* of *Ummah* owe it to themselves and the *Ummah* to examine, if they can say that these qualities can still be included in the National Character of Believers. If this is not so, what factors of collective life need reform so as to inculcate these qualities once more.

Could it not be that Islam, which is a Way of Life, has been equated with religion in which the basic principle is that it is a personal matter and has no place in directing collective morality. Islam has been Revealed to guide human life in this world so that its followers by conducting their lives in accordance with it, win the place of being the heirs to Viceroyalty of Allah in this world, and be near to Him, in the next. If, Islam becomes a matter of personal relations between man and Allah, and in disassociation from the conduct of its followers in public and international life, then humanity will never achieve peace and unity on the global scale.

Clause 6: "The *Banu Saeeda*, the *Banu Harith*, the *Banu Joshan*, and the *Banu Najjar* will be governed on the above lines."

The importance of being redeemed was so great that although Clause 5 had made it statutory duty of all parties that they would redeem their prisoners in the same manner as the Believers were duty bound to do, but all those tribes, wanted that an order should be specifically given that those tribes should also redeem their prisoners in the same manner.

This Clause confirms our view that the Document was being dictated in the presence of members of all parties. The moment a duty or a concession was dictated for the Believers or any other party, those not included would speak out, if they also desired to be governed by the same enactment.

Inclusion of some tribes in a separate Clause does not mean that they were governed by a separate document, which, at a later date, got joined up with one or all other similar - documents If this was so the words "on the above lines," would not have been there and the whole text would have been repeated and not in the same workings but in a totally new context.

Clause 7: "The *Banu Amr*[19], *Banu Auf*[20], *Bani Al-Nabeet*[21], and *Banu Al-Aas*[22] will be governed on the same lines."

Once again, a few more tribes make up their mind to join in. Tribal habits are strange. They take time to make up their mind, in matters which are new and they have no previous experience. They, as a result of centuries of hard life are afraid of pitfalls. The tribes joining in the redeeming of prisoners of war confirms our view that although this was not the custom previously, the inclusion of this responsibility on the High Command of Believers opened the door to the acceptance of this responsibility by elders of other parties as well. It is possible that the little hesitation shown by the late-comers may have been due to the consideration whether they would be able to raise funds for the purpose or not. Second thought, however, would have prompted them not to be left out of this social service to the common man of the tribe.

Modern world has risen to this need rather late. "The axioms of international law exerted an undeniable influence on the mode and manner of warfare, before the close of the seventeenth century." One of these was the treatment and disposal of enemy prisoners of war.

The first Geneva Convention was held in 1899 and the first Geneva Conference was held in 1929. It says, "Each of these fundamental international agreements is inspired by respect for human personality and dignity." It has been proudly announced that, "whereas the 1929 text demanded respect and protection only for the wounded. Article 12, which is new gives a list of prohibited acts, attempts on life, torture.... etc."

Clause 8: "Believers will not fail to redeem their prisoners or fail to pay blood money on behalf of one of them."

This clause and its wording clearly show that the Document was not an agreement, but a statutory and constitutional document in the form of an order and no less. The words, "will not fail," is a firm order, a legal binding which cannot be evaded under any circumstances. The importance of redeeming the prisoners can be judged by the number of clauses which cover the subject. It was a new subject but extremely important from the point of view of the fighting men. Prisoners of war, until then, as mentioned earlier, remained slaves for the rest of their lives. This could not be permitted in case of a Muslim soldier, because, as a slave he could not continue to observe his duties to Allah and thus lost freedom of action to submit to the Laws of Allah. He had, therefore, to be redeemed so that he could continue to observe all the functions of a free Believer. Slaves cannot continue to remain Believers in Allah and His *Rasul* (Pbuh). We see that even in the twentieth century, there are countries where they are forcibly prevented from observing Islamic practices or even to give their children Muslim names. Has not the *Ummah* forgotten to redeem them or free them. This question has to be answered by every one of us, more so, leaders of the *Ummah*.

Redeeming of prisoners becomes all the more important, when it is realised, that military service during Jihad is obligatory on all able bodied Muslim males, wherever they may be. The order, quoted as under has been addressed to all Believers.

"Fight in the way of Allah against those who fight against you".
(2: 190)

It has been addressed to all Believers. Believers are one *Ummah*, both according to this Document and according to the Quran. When any part of the World of Islam is attacked, *Jihad* becomes obligatory on the entire *Ummah*. Those nearest to the area attacked have to face the enemy first. But that does not absolve the others. The World of Islam, today, should find it much easier to coordinate an integrated defence of the entire area occupied by them. Lack of plans, however, is no excuse for not redeeming those Believers, who due to ignorance or other reasons are under the domination of others and leading lives of slaves or prisoners of war. It is said that, "From the earliest records of man, war has been his dominant preoccupation." It is, therefore, more than likely that war will be resorted to for a long time to come. It is a proper time for Muslim World to start thinking of organising coordinated defence. Believers, have, for a long time, ignored opposition to them from various quarters. As in the case of *Quraish* of Mecca, the world at large does not approve the Islamic Way of Life, because of the equality and freedom it allows to poor and rich alike which is the result of belief in the Sovereignty of Allah. War against Believers will, as a result, continue until such time as they remain weak, disorganised and an easy target. The only solution to this is unity. As the Quran says:

"And lo! this your religion is one religion". (23: 52)

Muslim can lead an honourable life if they live as one Ummah.

Clause 14: "Protection in the name of Allah will be common. The weakest among Believers may give protection and it will be binding on all Believers".

Protection to Strangers : Protection used to be given to strangers by powerful individuals. The practical effect of such protection depended on the power and prestige of the person giving protection. Islam had, however, changed the very concept of power held by individuals and the society or organisation, in which an individual lived. Believers, irrespective of their numbers, living in a place and forming a society are an *Ummah*, apart from any other group of human beings. Each individual Believer is equal to all others in his status as a Believer. The task he performs in the society, the job he holds, the wealth he possesses or the rank he has achieved in the hierarchy formed for the purposes of conducting affairs of the *Ummah* do not infringe on or enhance his status as a Believer and member of the society. "An individual who belongs to an organisation of equals is an integral part of that organisation- This is specially so, where the organisation is based on a particular mode of thought, a distinct Philosophy of life and a Way of Life distinct from all other ways of life."

In such a society, if protection can be given to individuals or groups of people who are not Believers then it stands to reason that any one of the Believers should possess the right to give protection. As far as Believers of other towns or areas were concerned, they were brothers in faith. They were, as Believers, part of the *Ummah*. They needed no protection. On the contrary, as members of brotherhood of Islam, they could themselves promise protection and that would have been honoured. It was to un-Believers that the Clause applied. Any Believer, however humble, poor or weak he may be, he was entitled to give protection and this protection was valid from the point of view of the state and government of *Yathrib*. The protection could not be in the name of the person giving it or in the name of the *Ummah*, but it had to be in the name of Allah.

Most societies, however primitive they may be, assign certain human rights to the individual as long as he has the status of a freeman and is not a slave. Islam had given human rights to all individuals, whether free or otherwise. He had to believe in Allah in order to benefit from some of those rights. The right to offer freedom in the name of Allah, demanded his belief in Allah. This was logical. He enjoyed all other rights; rights of equality, justice and freedom to hold any views, but to give protection to a sworn enemy in the name of Allah, he had to be a Believer in the Sovereignty of Allah.

In this right, he held the same position as the head of state himself. This greatness of the status of an individual in society was the greatest factor which attracted masses towards Islam. It has been remarked by a modern writer that "one can find no better key to the internal logic of a society than its conception of man and his place in nature." In Islam all men are equal. The Prophet's last address, at his Last Hajj is very clear. Its words still ring from millions of pulpits around the Globe. He has said, "All men are descended from Adam and Adam was created from clay...." As far as man's position is concerned he is Allah's viceroy on earth (2: 30) and the most balanced creation of Allah.

"Surely we created man of the best stature". (95: 4)

Total Equality : It is due to this equality in socio-economic fields, political matters and before the law that the frontiers of Islam have been expanding throughout these fourteen centuries. European literature, whether dealing with social development, philosophical treatises or political movements in the West, have lauded the pre-Revolution philosophers of France, for having given to Europe the principle of equality of man. If French Revolution was the result of the preaching of principle of equality by French philosophers then the streams of blood which flowed as a result, show that it has not achieved much. America is said to have been affected by this French movement. One of the critics of unchecked principle of equality says, "I attribute so many different aspects to the principle of equality; it might be inferred, that I consider this principle as the only cause of everything that has taken place in our day ... many persons would take it upon themselves to inform men of the benefits which they might hope to receive from the establishment of equality, while very few would venture to point out from afar the dangers with which it would be attended." This fear of equality appears to be premature because, as yet, America has not been able to introduce equality in its society. When this happens many white Americans may decide to migrate to some other part of the Globe.

Clause 16: "Those Jews who follow us will be helped and will be treated with equality."

The Clause deals with Jews. The reason for including this Clause under Laws Concerning Defence is that the Heading of the Charter had said, "Those who followed the Believers and took part in *Jihad* with them, were to form one *Ummah* with them." The act of following was to be supplemented by taking part in *Jihad* alongside the Believers. The words, "those Jews, signifies that the concession were to be restricted to those "who will follow," in future. Therefore, there was no question of having gone through the procedure of having an agreement, with the Jews, as has been suggested by certain writers.

The fact that they never took part in *Jihad* means that the situation did not arise, where they could be treated with equality and be included as a part of the *Ummah*.

Clause 19: "The peace of Believers cannot be divided."

Leading to Peace : Islam, submission to the Will of Allah, leads to peace from the level of individual man and woman to peace among entire humanity. Islam signifies absence of tensions within man and within the society of men and women, who have discarded love of all things, which take away from the Path of Allah. This gives them further contentment and determination to abide by the Commandments of Allah. He has conveyed the greatest secret of success to Believers that they are one people - One *Ummah* (21: 92 and 23: 52) and must remain united. That is the only way in which they can fulfil their duty of guiding mankind along the Right Path.

Allah has also Commanded Believers to take all precautions so that they can avoid splitting themselves into factions, sects and parties. Allah has warned:

> "Lo! As for those who sunder their religion and become schismatics, no concern at all hast thou with them. Their case will go to Allah, Who then 'will tell of what they used to do." (6: 160)

He has clearly told Believers the result of dividing Deen into factions:

> "There is no altering (the laws of) Allah's creation. That is the right religion, but most people know not. Turn unto Him (only); and be careful of your duty unto Him, and establish worship and be not one

> of those who ascribe partners (unto Him) of those who split up their religion and become schismatic each sect exulting in its tenets. And when harm touched men they cry unto their Lord turning to Him in repentance." (30: 30-33)

When having divided themselves, they suffer and then cry for the Mercy of their Lord. Even when He gives them respite, they go back and divide themselves again and again, until they are overpowered by others who deprive them of even the right to cry for the forgiveness of their Lord. About them the order is:

> "Say, He is able to send punishment upon you from above you or from beneath your feet, or to bewilder you with dissensions and make you taste the tyranny of one another." (6: 65)

The world of Islam has tasted enough of the tyranny of one another and have been punished a great deal because Allah and His Messenger had Commanded them to remain united and they arrayed themselves after their nominees and were thus guilty of Shirk. (30: 30-32). They had refused to obey His Prophet's Command, that:

> "The peace of Believers can not be divided."

In their arrogance, they dared to show, that it can be divided. They divided it and they are being punished by being denied the power and freedom to proclaim the Sovereignty of Allah. How many are the lands, where they cannot call Muslims to their mosques through *Adaan* and how many are the lands where their mosques have been turned into clubs for drinking wine and ....

The Commandments of Allah and the Command of the Prophet (Pbuh) have been disobeyed so flagrantly that one wonders if they really believed in Allah and His Prophet (Pbuh). The punishment has been equally severe. Dissension among Believers has been responsible for inviting comparatively small European nations to invade lands held by Believers and rule over them for nearly two centuries.

Peace not Divided : The Command that "Peace of Believers cannot be divided," demands that states controlled by Believers must bring into existence an organisation which acts as an advisory and supervisory body, so that such situations do not arise, which lead to the breach of peace between Muslim states. If, however, inspite of it, two countries of Muslims go to war then this body can act according to Quranic Injunction in *Surah Al-Hujuraat*, Verse 9. If the World of Islam was united for such an action other nations will not dare to fan such internecine warfare. The basis of weakness is disobedience of the Quran and Constitutional Charter issued under the seal of the Prophet of Allah (Pbuh).

There are other aspects of this Clause as well. Fighting among themselves is the worst form of breach of this Clause of the Constitution of Median. The other form is that when one part of the *Ummah* is invaded or attacked, some other part commits breach of peace, between Muslims, by either having friendly relations with the aggressor or taking a neutral posture. It must be remembered that at the time of second Bayah of *Uqba*, the Prophet (Pbuh) had replied to one of the questions of a member of new Believers from *Yathrib*. The question was:

> "When Allah will have given you victory, you will return to your people and leave us?"

The Prophet (Pbuh) had replied:

> "No! blood is blood. And blood not to be paid for is blood not to be paid for. I am of you and you are of me. I will war against them that war against you, and be at peace with those at peace with you."

This is exactly, what is meant by "Peace of Believers cannot be divided." They are either all at war with a third power or all at peace. Their peace and war are indivisible.

Unity of the Muslim World in time of *Jihad* has so great an importance, that even when a Muslim country, which has been attacked by a non-Muslim country, and it can cope with the attack single handed, the rest of the *Ummah* is not absolved from considering it a common cause. In such cases it is necessary for them to send token forces, or observer groups. Allah has Commanded:

> "And the believers should not all go out to fight. Of every troop of them, a party only should go forth, that they (who are left behind) many gain sound knowledge in religion, and that they may warn their folk when they return to them, so that they may beware. O you who believe! Fight those of the disbelievers who are near to you, and let them find harshness in you, and know that Allah is with those who keep their duty (unto Him)." (9: 122-123)

The nearest to the enemy is the one, who is attacked. He engages the enemy with determination and harshness so that it gives time to the others to go to his help. If the country attacked can defend itself then the others send token forces only as in Verse 122 above.

Unity in Peace and War : Importance given to the unity of Muslim *Ummah* in peace and war is so great, that even when the part of *Ummah*, which is attacked is capable of defending itself the other parts have all to send token forces. These token forces and their main body gain experience of war, learn new methods and tactics and get acquainted with new weapon used on such occasions. When they return home, they acquaint their home-forces of new defence techniques. The advantage of unity and strength being the main object and advantage in such undertakings and the satisfaction that they have obeyed Commands of Allah and His Prophet (Pbuh).

The greatest tragedy in the annals of any *Ummah* is that Muslims have been dividing their peace, particularly during the last few centuries and thus enslaving themselves and their future generations. An Englishman, by the name of Colonel Lawrence, who for years remained active in dividing the peace of Muslims, writes, "Some Englishmen of whom Kitchner was chief believed that a rebellion of Arabs against Turks, would enable England, while fighting Germany, simultaneously to defeat her ally Turkey—so they allowed it (rebellion) to begin, having first obtained formal assurance of help for it from the British Government."

Abdullah, the eldest son of *Shareef Hussain of Mecca*, who probably was the only person, who could influence his father to embark on the path of betrayal of brother Muslims, has not been honoured by his benefactors, the British in their writings. The same Englishman writes about him, "The Arabs thought *Abdullah* a far seeing statesman and an astute politician. Astute he certainly was, but not generally enough to coerce us always of his sincerity. His ambition was potent. Rumours made him the brain of his father and of Arab revolt, but he seemed too easy for that. His objective was, of course, the winning of Arab independence and the building of Arab nations, but he meant to keep the direction of the new states in the family. So he watched us, and played through us to the British gallery."

It is lack of belief in Islam and its Commandments which result in breach of peace among Muslim states. Reasons have been various and they date back to the early period. When the masses in Syria, Egypt, Iran and Central Asia, were attracted to Islam due to liberty, equality and freedom offered by it to them. The upper classes and rich Jews, also accepted Islam, in order to retain their privileged positions in the society. As a result, these states and their provinces and districts remained family properties of the previous owners. During subsequent centuries families, changed ownership passed into new hands but traditions of personal and family interests being superior to the interest of *Ummah* remained. Rulers like *Shah Abbas*[23], *Taimur*[24], *Nadir Shah*[25] have been appearing and disappearing, but the passage of every one of them has been strewn with the corpses of Muslims. In most cases there are names of foreign advisers encouraging them in their follies. It is said that Shah Abbas had two Englishmen Sir Anthony and Sir Robert Shirly at his court who, "enabled him with the help of a cannon caster accompanying them," to provide the Persian Army with artillery to attack Turkey while the Turks were busy defending themselves from the European side.

In 1612 *Shah Abbas*, had broken off war with Turkey, but in the next year he wrote letters which reached Spain in 1614, offering to renew it if the Christian powers would fulfil their promises, adding that, it was long since the Christians had taken up arms against the common enemy..... At that time a great plan was afoot for a Crusade....." It is said of him that by 1618, he "was growing weary of the insincere and dilatory princes of Christendom." *Shah Abbas* died in 1628, amazed to the last, it would seem, at Christian neglect of opportunities. The habit of Europe to divide the peace of Muslims has been a constant affair. The same writer says, "It should be added here that Persia was not the only Islamic power whose aid was invoked by Christendom against the Turks, at this time. Morroco was also approached." In the nineteenth and twentieth centuries selfishness on the part of Muslim rulers has led them to seek the help of foreign powers quite frequently. A well known Englishman writes, "It is true that all the chiefs concerned were genuinely desirous of cooperation with the English in their struggle with the Turks."

Many an Instance : Instances of breach of peace among Muslims are so many that it would be impossible to enumerate them in an essay of this nature. The numerous Muslim states of Central Asia fell into the hands of Russia because of the internecine warfare, that had been waged by them for centuries and weakened them all. The surprising part is that the rulers of these states, their nobles and their learned did not see through the game which the invaders were playing. One of the despatches of Russian court issued on 21st of November, 1864 gives out the policy followed by Russia. It says, "Of late years people have been pleased to assign to Russia the mission of civilising the countries which are her neighbours in the continent of Asia. The advancement of civilization has no agent more efficient than commercial relations. The last to become developed, require order and stability, but in Asia this necessitates a complete change of customs. Asiatics must be made to understand that it is more to their interest to favour and insure the trade of caravans than to pillage them. These elementary notions can only penetrate the public conscience, when there is an organised society and a government to direct and represent it. We accomplish the first part of this task in advancing our frontiers to the limit where these indispensable conditions are to be found. We accomplish the second by endeavouring henceforth to prove to the neighbouring states by a firm system, so far as the suppression of their ill dealings is concerned, but at the same time by moderation and justice in the employment of force..... In consecrating itself to this task the Imperial Cabinet is inspired by Russian interests....."

Prince Gortschnakoff's excellent logic reminds of the story of the wolf and the lamb. When the above mentioned policy was put into practice in Central Asia, Colgnel Venukoff, the Russian commander of Orenburg area, wrote down the way he and his compatriots had been acting on the policy formed by the benign Russian Cabinet. He writes, "In Central Asia, that is to say, where it is easy to apply the principle, divide et imperial (and rule), by making use of rival antagonism of the Bashkirs, Kirghiz and Kalmucks; the Orenburg and Siberian Governors have taken for their guidance the rule to weaken each one of these troublesome nations by the means of the others."

Nearly all leading Eubopean nations have tried to weaken Islam by dividing Muslim countries. "To preserve its authority the Church managed to urge the Christian princes to fight Islam in the name of religion; it was able to diffuse the spirit of exaggerated fanaticism and religious zeal in Christian societies for long ages..."

The rulers were, at times, keener than even the Church. "The policy of Charlemagne towards Islam was one of the most important elements of Prankish diplomacy. The policy was contradictory in appears. While Charlemagne was planning to crush the Muslim state in Spain, he was, as the Prankish chronicle records, in correspondence with the *Abbaside* Caliph and sent his envoys to strengthen the bonds of friendship and alliance with him.... His relations with the *Abbaside* Caliph were, from his point of view, nothing but the means to facilitate his mission to fight Islam in Spain and to protect Christianity in the East. The fault, however, lies with the Muslim ruler who disobeyed the Prophet's order, and divided the peace of Believers.

This principle of divide and rule, which had been successfully applied by the British in the subcontinent of India, proved very useful to the Russians in Central Asia. Ever since the time that the Russians had taken on the role of Saviors of Christendom, they had developed an inborn hatred for the Muslims. Travellers heard remarks pertaining to Muslims as if they were the very incarnation of Satan. One Russian talking to another was heard saying, "I would give anything to drive out those....Mussalmans....."

The Russians had started their eastward move against Central Asia about the end of sixteenth century. By the middle of nineteenth century they had nearly accomplished their object. *Khiva*[26] had put up a fairly stiff resistance. Their advance had been very calculated. They always waited for the weakest moment of the defenders. In one instance, "After crossing *Oxus* they attacked the *Khivan* town *Urgench*. The *Khan* and his force were absent. Little resistance was made and the town was destroyed, the Cossacks carrying off thousands of women, besides many carts laden with rich booty. When the *Khan* returned, they were given a chase and were overtaken and surrounded by the *Khivans*. They had to flee leaving behind the prisoners and the loot."

The peace of Believers has remained divided for centuries in Central Asia, as in other parts of the world. *Brave Khivans* were eventually defeated by the Imperial Russian forces, "The *Khan*, Said *Muhammad Rahim Bahadur Khan*, had fled, the Russians were in possession of his palace and harem, and so fell Khiva, the greatest stronghold of Islamism in Central Asia, after a succession of disastrous expeditions extending over 200 years."

The disobedience of the Law promulgated by Prophet Muhammad (Pbuh) has been repeated again and again by those, who proclaim him as the Last Prophet (PBUH) of Allah. British gold must have attracted a great number of leaders of Muslim masses, because an Englishman has said, "The people of the *Hejaz* and large number of tribes in the Arabian desert were openly for the allied cause."

In order to profit by the folly of Muslims in dividing their peace the author puts forward an excuse. He says, "Steps had to be taken on our side to protect British interest. Accordingly when Shariff Hussain[27], *Amir* of Mecca, showed a desire to throw off Turkish sovereignty, he was strongly encouraged and given promises of material assistance by the British Government."

A Sordid, Long Story : The story of Believers, breaking peace among themselves is both sordid and long. It is also painful but it has to be referred to, if not the whole of it, at least some of the instances, where it has been broken to get a little richer or for satisfying feelings of hatred of some inconsequential belief of a ruler. *Nadir Shah* of Iran invaded India, for no apparent reason and weakened the already decaying power of a Muslim dynasty. When in occupation of the capital, as a victor, he, a believer, or so he maintained, without verifying the report of death of three of his soldiers, he, "remained in the mosque, his sword by his side, while the work of death and destruction went on..... How many persons, the vast majority of whom were guiltless of any crime against the Persians, lost their lives on this troubled occasion, will never be known."

As a result of Believers dividing their peace for such earthly benefits, the Christian writers get an occasion to say, "Are we to say, that the reality of Islam is purely subjective — that it is defined strictly by the feeling of belonging to it? This would be evading the problem, which is to know to what degree belonging to Islam involves an actual solidity, a will to mutual aid, a community of custom, of interests, of aspirations...." We know that the feelings of oneness are present among the people but history points in the other direction. Is it not time, that the intellectuals of Muslim countries put their heads together to find out if political leadership of Muslim lands is voicing the wishes of the masses or not?

A New Way of Dividing Peace : The present century has introduced a new form of dividing peace of Muslim societies. This happens to be on the ideological level. The generation of Muslims educated on European lines, immediately after the Second World War, had started discussing, whether Islam was suited to the demands of this Atomic age. When asked as to which were the demands of the present atomic age, which could not be met, it did not bring out any clear-cut answer. These were the very people, who due to their having received modern European education were entrusted with the reins of the Muslim lands by their outgoing colonial mentors. The Muslims have been loyal to their erstwhile "masters, but have betrayed the trust of their brothers and sisters. They have not been able to secularise the thinking of their masses but they have succeeded in producing confused minds among the present generation, who having seen through the trap have turned to religion, but they find that the secularised education, society, culture, and law do not permit them to coordinate their activities in this atmosphere of contradictions. If efforts had been made to acquaint the youth with Shariah and the fact that they are the part of an Ummah, this confusion would not have arisen. "The two essential and primary ingredients of the Islamic political theory are the *Ummah* and the *Shariah.* " It is difficult to get a clear picture of Islamic polity, without first understanding the impact of belief in the Sovereignty of Allah and Prophethood of Muhammad (Pbuh). This belief automatically leads to the acceptance and application of *Shariah.* The application of *Shariah* starts with the Command "This *Ummah* of yours is One *Ummah,* " and therefore, "The peace of Believers cannot be divided."

It is a matter of time alone, because as soon as the generation left behind by colonial masters and their immediate successors have relinquished authority, Muslim lands will discard secularism. Some neutral observers feel the same. It has been remarked that, "We can be sure, despite all the secularisation, all the economic, legal and social explosions, Islam will be able, in the course of time, somehow, to recreate its active specificity and to manifest once again the power as a common primordial factor." This resurgence of Islam is frightening Europe, because its economic colonialism is still dominating the Muslim world. The Muslim lands are quite likely to go over to Islamic social and economic system on the pattern established during the Prophet's (Pbuh) lifetime and followed in later periods, which is quite likely to free them from western capitalistic economic domination.

It is felt by some that, "All Muslim countries, are fated, one might say, to do one of two things: to deny the Laws of Islam and opt for a secular state; or persist with the arduous task of trying to produce an Islamic state, or even more difficult, an Islamic order." The ultimate goals can be nothing else, but an Islamic Order, because an Islamic state, by itself is unimaginable and if efforts are made to bring in *Shariah* without the support of an Islamic Order, its Laws will be broken like any other secular laws. The fight is uphill. As we know, the Europeanised minority now firmly established in power in these countries will not abdicate easily. A civil war will be worse. The extremists of both camps should learn a lesson from the failure of secularists in Turkey and the revolutionaries of Iran. It is, as yet, difficult to lay down the details of the middle course but it will have to include equal opportunities for all in all walks of life. The basis, however, should be a sincere effort coupled with knowledge of both the word and spirit of Islam and the needs of the time and place.

It is correct to say that "the question of accession to the seat of authority has unquestionably been the most controversial subject of Muslim politics," but if the solutions found by the Companions of the Prophet (Pbuh) had been kept in view this question need not have been controversial. The first *Khalifa*[28] of the Prophet (Pbuh) was elected by common consent according to the custom of the time and place. The appointment of the second was indicated by the first *Khalifa* and accepted by the people. The third was elected by a nominated council, as is done in the case of a Pope in Christendom, and the fourth was elected according to the custom of the time, keeping in view the urgency of the occasion. The question thus devolves to the conclusion that the wishes of the people of the time and place should be the final judge of how the question of succession should be solved. The decision whether to have Islamic Law or continue with borrowed and out of place secular laws should also be left at the will of the people who have time and again demanded introduction of Shariah. "If the interpretation of the law ultimately depends on popular consensus, correct interpretation and good government are best obtained by consulting the people."

Westernised Minority : At the present moment, the reins of government in nearly all Muslim lands, except in Saudi Arabia, Libya and Iran, are held by a small westernised minority, who incidentally are ignorant of both the Islamic and Western political thought and philosophy. They are not even pseudo-intellectuals. They were trained either as clerks or soldiers and have little inclination to develop into statesmen. If they had been sincere Muslims then if not the Islamic Order, at least Islamic states would have come into existence. "Islam is the state, or should be, if those in charge of the state were true Muslims." Islam was a Way of Life in Mecca and Median. It still is, but those who wish it to be a religion only, and a private affair, would like it to be kept out of the Houses of Parliament of Muslim States and thus maintain the division and fragmentation of the Believers. It is this class which is at the root of trouble in all Muslim lands. A young writer of Pakistan has said, "The so-called educated class of Pakistan is creating intellectual anarchy..... Laws of logic and systems of reasoning are abandoned .... overcharged emotionism replaces the strength of calm conviction." If it is the majority that will eventually win the battle then the hurdles placed in the way of Islamic Order are not only a mere waste of time, but are a cause of creating confusion. We all agree that "Muslims generally do not look at social and economic issues from, what we call, a purely secular angle. Their perception of such issues is usually faith oriented."

This perception is bound to remain faith oriented as long as they claim to be Muslims. The modernist, under the influence of occidental free thinking, is like the pre-Islamic Arab, when every individual had his own little god and the idea of state or society being subject to ethical and moral restraints, was completely absent. The opposition to the implementation of *Shariah* is purely on the basis of supposed freedom, otherwise, "The regulations of the Shariah do not go contrary to most of the Natural Laws."

Delay in Development : The result of these inner tensions is delay in the development of the various sectors of collective life of the *Ummah* and its peace remains divided. The conflict created by ideas borrowed from abroad and efforts to reorientate life on so-called conservative patterns has held up intellectual progress unnecessarily. These foreign oriented intellectuals forget that, "In all great movements of the human intellect the force of progression or delay should be looked for mainly from within, not from without."

It is difficult to convey the sense of one discipline in the terminology of another and more so when the phrases used have been coined after an internal of centuries. "Islam is a comprehensive phenomenon, making no distinction between sacred and secular: all creation is suffused with the ineffable oneness of God. This inseparability of sacred and secular is not simply pantheism, it is argued, because nature is decidedly created and God uncreated...." Islam is religion, social behaviour and statecraft all at the same time. It also cannot be denied that, "Muslims in all parts have become more devout..... concerned with social, economic and political application of Islamic values..... all the people believe that, Islam, not a secular ideology, increasingly shapes the attitudes of their actions." It is this trend towards Islam, particularly among the young generation and those living as minorities amidst non-Islamic societies, that has created the hope that time will soon come when it will be difficult for the ruling classes to keep the peace of Believers divided, Muslims who have come in contact with the free thinking Western society are keen to get organised so that they find it easier to live by their Islamic values. One report says, "Finally there are those, who are highly organised, with international connections and specific identifications of what constitutes right practice. They are committed to an Islamic vision, striving to realise an Islamic Order and an Islamic state where religious laws are implemented and where a just government rules equitably."

This may be due to having been exposed to unbearable pressures in the middle of an alien surrounding. It has been generally observed that once a Muslim finds himself in a non-Muslim environment it becomes his Islamic duty to get organised with other Muslims. Inspite of these observations it is important that Muslim intellectuals get together and try to chalk out a programme for bringing about concerted efforts against forces trying to create ideological confusion amongst them. This is the only way to see that the *Ummah* itself is no more guilty of dividing the peace of *Ummah*.

It would not be out of place to lay a part of blame of "dividing the peace of Believers," on the intellectuals and learned men of the *Ummah*. They equally share this blame with the rulers and courtiers of the rulers. "*Nasiruddin Toosi*[29], who after having served the Assassins, then acted as counsellor to Hulaku[30], on the Baghdad campaign, and ended up happily in the observatory built with funds furnished by his new protectors.

Such a flexibility allowed the Persians to come through many trials, but it has not been without its effect on national character." His ability in Mathematics and Astronomy cannot be denied but it was *Nasiruddin Toosi*, the great mathematician, "who continuously urged him (*Hulaku*), to march against Baghdad, and to accept the invitation of *Mohiuddin bin Abdul Malik Alkami*, who as *Wazir*, administered the affairs of the Caliphate with unlimited power and by the blackest treachery, caused its fall, is stigmatised ignominously as traitor throughout the whole world." Their sectarian prejudices were so intense that they invited non-Muslim against a Muslim ruler who had placed his trust in them.

> "Say, He is able to send punishment upon you from above you or from beneath your feet, or to bewilder you with dissensions and make you taste the tyranny of one another." (6: 65)
>
> "So learn a lesson, O you who have eyes". (59: 2)

Clause 20: "No separate peace will be made when Believers are fighting in the Path of Allah."

Wide Implications : This Clause has wide implications. The proceeding Clause has laid down that the peace of Believers is indivisible. It follows that Believers, who are fighting a common enemy have to remain at war with that enemy until the end. One of the parties from among the Believers, cannot make a separate peace treaty and get out of the war, thus in a way stabbing its Believer allies in the back. This Clause had very little significance, as far as the Believers, of that period, were concerned, but, like Clause 19 it has a great significance under the present state of affairs. The Commandment obey Allah and obey His Prophet (Pbuh), still stands and when Believer states go to the aid of another state of Believers which has been attacked, one of them, under pressure from the enemy, cannot sign a separate peace treaty with the enemy. Such a treaty will be rejected by all Muslim states and the people of that state will be justified in demanding the abrogation of such a separate peace treaty.

As far as the situation, that existed in *Yathrib* itself the Clause had a certain amount of possible application, if it was assumed, that those who "would follow the Believers and would fight alongside them," did avail of the status of equality and become a part of the *Ummah.* In that case any separate peace agreed by them with the enemy would have been considered as null and void, in view of this Clause.

The others did not decide to help the Believers in the defence of *Yathrib.* In case of their joining, there was the danger of their losing heart and trying to make a separate peace treaty with the *Quraish* or one of their numerous allies. It is just as well that "the others," thinking that the Believers were weak, as compared to the *Quraish,* remained aloof and did not opt to benefit by the offer of becoming a part of the *Ummah.*

Information about the general contents of the Document must have reached the *Quraish.* Throughout the period of nine years, that the war lasted, there is no evidence of a friendly document being signed between "the others" and the *Quraish.* The *Quraish,* the Jews, and even the Hypocrites are known to have been in touch with the *Quraish.* Before the battle of *Ahzab* the Jews of *Khyber,* including men who had left *Yathrib* are known to have sent a delegation to Mecca to persuade them to join the confederacy and attack Median but there is no evidence of a proper offensive or defensive treaty between "the others" and the *Quraish.* The links between the Jews of *Yathrib* like *Kaab bin Ashraf,* the poet, and the *Quraish* existed until the end. Similarly the leader of Hypocrites, *Abdullah bin Ubay* kept in constant touch with the *Quraish,* but no proper treaty of friendship has come to light. It appears that although the Jews lived and led their lives according to Arab tribal pattern of life they had inter-tribal rivalries and never thought of putting up a joint opposition to Believers. From the remarks of *Banu Qainuqa* after the battle of Badr, it is certain that, due to the small number of Believers the Jews did not think, that the *Quraish* will be beaten by the Believers.

This Clause, as explained in foregoing paragraphs needs to be kept in mind by the statesmen of Muslim states of today, when signing defensive pacts among themselves. They need to insert words to the effect that no separate peace will be made by any of the signatories.

Clause 21: "Conditions must be fair and equitable to all alike."

War has peculiar effects on the ruling party and its administration. Security measures have to be adopted. The Prophet (Pbuh), for instance, did not give out the destination of the Army, marching out of Median, on numerous occasions. The patrol sent to *Nakhla* had been ordered to open its orders after three days march from Median. Such security arrangements and the desire to be watchful about the elements, whose loyalty is doubtful, sometimes results in unfair and inequitable conditions for a part of the population. The Prophet (Pbuh), who was always just and kind, according to the principle of "justice tempered with benevolence," made it a point through this Clause, that whether a person or a party took part in defence or not, the whole population must be made to realise that justice was being done to them.

Pre-Islamic conditions were not equitable to all. It was, therefore, vital that equality and freedom given to mankind by Allah had to be practised with special care in this very first state brought into existence by the Prophet of Allah and his devoted Companions.

The Prophet (Pbuh) had undertaken the defence of *Yathrib*. Fighting men and armament were given a secondary position and a low priority. His first concern was a willing, happy and free society. Apart from the fact that free soldiers are better soldiers, he desires to infuse the spirit of equality in the society he was creating. He planned to win the war and achieve peace at home and abroad by infusing new ideas in the population of *Yathrib*. "The major hope of peace lies not in armament, however important they are, but rather in ideas." There could have been no better idea than the idea of equality and conditions being fair and equitable for all.

It has to be kept in mind that Islam was being made the state religion for the first time. This period was to remain as the Ideal Period for all times. The Prophet (Pbuh) has said that his period is the best of all periods. Equity, justice, kindness, compassion and forgiveness are the hall-mark of this period. Allah is the Creator of Believers and un-Believers all alike. The Law of Allah must, therefore, be applied with the same spirit of equity for all. If this did not happen and injustice prevailed or the followers of other ways of Life were denied the good things of life, how could Believers maintain their distinction as slaves of Allah? Conditions, therefore, had to be "fair and equitable to all."

Even most modern societies cannot claim to have given to their nations such conditions as can be called "fair and equitable" as mentioned in this clause. "The leadership in England is drawn from a narrow class base....especially educated in England for the task."

Clause 22: "On expeditions a rider must take another behind him."

There was a shortage of all material resources, suitable for defence, with the Prophet (Pbuh) and his Companions. He had accepted to defend *Yathrib*, not because he had the means to defend it. He undertook the task and responsibility to defend *Yathrib* because he had been ordered to do so. Allah's orders had to be obeyed. Allah alone knew, what would be the outcome. It was not for the Prophet (Pbuh) to question; Why? Although the number of men available to go on expeditions was small, the number of transport animals was inadequate even for the few men available to go out on expeditions. It was essential, that there should be "Standing Orders" that men who possessed camels, must take another behind them.

The number of camels available to the first large expedition of 313 men which moved out of Median, was only seventy. There was less than one mount per four people. Even the Prophet (Pbuh) had to share a camel with three other Companions. If two could ride a camel at a time, then every one had to walk half the distance. The Prophet (Pbuh), who was over fifty years of age at that time had to walk at least forty miles to the battlefield. It was his habit to share the vicissitudes of life with his Companions. During the early days at *Yathrib*, when there was constant fear of Meccan night attacks, he used to perform sentry duties taking his turn along with his Companions.

The word, 'expedition,' signifies conditions, then prevailing in *Yathrib*, as a result of the certainty that it will be attacked by Meccans. The transport needs of future are being brought within the legal frame work of a Constitutional Document. The problem was being viewed from a long term point of view. The *Ummah* was to fight many wars in future and it had to be brought home to the leaders of *Ummah* of the future, that they would need to remain on the look out, whether they could transport their fighting forces to the areas of selected battle-fields. The numerous lands that the Muslims were to inhabit around the Globe would certainly find that they were short of war material.

Here was a precedent for mutual help and pooling of resources by them. The principles laid down by him in this Document, need to be studied afresh and acted upon in planning the Defence of the World of Islam.

Clause 23: "The Believers must avenge the blood of one another, when fighting in the Path of Allah."

The war with Meccan, which was the basis of this Constitutional Charter, was, as yet on a scale, that the blood of one another would have been avenged, when fighting in the Path of Allah, without an order of this nature having been issued. He was the Supreme Commander and he could have ordered any action felt necessary. The Charter was, however, meant to be for all times. The problems being faced by the *Ummah* today are such, that, their correct and certain solution is possible only if the *Ummah* observes the Commands given in this Document. The history of the Battles of the Prophet (Pbuh) show, that the blood of Believers was avenged every time. It is regretted that it ceased to be avenged soon after.

The Muslims are being persecuted in more than dozen lands today. Those who are persecuting the Muslims happen to be on the friendliest of relations with other Muslim state. We are thus guilty of breaking at least two Commands is possible only if the *Ummah* observes the Commands given in the Document. The history of the Battles of the Prophet (Pbuh) show, that the blood of Believers was avenged every time. It is regretted that it ceased to be avenged soon after.

The Muslims are being persecuted in more than dozen lands today. Those who are persecuting the Muslims happen to be on the friendliest of relations with other Muslim state. We are thus guilty of breaking at least two Commands of the Document. We are dividing the peace of Believers and at the same time not avenging the blood of other Believers, who, risk their lives even if they demand humane treatment at the hand of ungodly regimes.

The main problem appears to be, that no one can tell the reason why the Muslim countries find it difficult to act unanimously in international affairs. What lies at the bottom of joining different camps. What benefits do Muslim countries derive by developing relations with the so-called super powers which result in their estrangement with neighbouring Muslim countries. It is time that some studies were undertaken to analyse the events of last hundred years to determine the cause of conflicts between members of *Ummah* of Islam, an *Ummai* which came into being to bring mankind on to one platform. It because the majority of us wish, like, the *Quraish* of Mecca to protect our vested interests and will not step on to the same platform unless forced to do so.

Zakat has to be spent according to the formula laid down in the Quran. One of the lawful subjects given is to free prisoners. Muslims who are held by non-Muslim regimes as virtual prisoners would seem to deserve help under this Clause. The subject, however, needs further study and the present writer feels that such questions need to be studied at a mud higher level.

War, if it is fought with an objective in view, must be multi-dimensional, because life itself is such. Believers, which ever part of the world they may be inhabiting, share the same purpose in life; to help mankind in acting and achieving good and to discourage and prevent evil to the best of their ability. This would be the only way to declare Sovereignty of Allah in a practical manner. War aims of entire Muslim *Ummah* would thus be identical. Their political aim thus becomes the unity of the *Ummah* for purposes of establishing good and discouraging evil. Any war fought with this in view would be in the words of an eminent military thinker, "War thus becomes a political instrument as much as it is a political act." He arrives at this conclusion by arguing that "War starts from a political condition and is called forth by a political motive. It is, therefore, a political act." This reasoning, however, does not apply to the war declared by Mecca against the Believers.

The war that had been forced upon the Believers was because of the fear of *Quraish* of Mecca, who thought that the New Way of Life would eclipse them and they would not be able to maintain their social and economic supremacy. They did not hold any political power which could have been usurped by the Believers. They were the leaders of the existing Way of Life in Arabia. They were confident of the entire support of Arab tribes, who each, in its own tribal area, held sovereign power. This power had not been challenged by the Prophet (Pbuh), except through the Islamic Belief that Sovereignty belongs to Allah alone and that obedience of the Laws given by Allah was the symbol and token of accepting His Sovereignty.

Man made laws had created a Way of Life within a society, which denied equality and justice to a greater part of humanity. The Believers in defending the New Way of Life were, in actual fact, fighting a war on behalf of the present and future generations of humanity, which were being denied their birthright of freedom. This war was in support of the weak and downtrodden of the world and not for political supremacy over the *Quraish* of Mecca. If the Prophet (Pbuh) had desired political power he had been offered it but under the old Way of Life, and he had rejected the offer.

The war, as far as the Believers were concerned, was for the freedom of the downtrodden of entire humanity, which was the creation of Allah. It was, therefore, termed as "Fighting in the Path of Allah," by Allah Himself. Being a war in the Path of Allah, the Believers had to continue it to the end and as such be ready to "avenge the blood of one another, when fighting in the Path of Allah." There could be no question of surrendering, when fighting such a war. The spokesman of Western Philosophy of War, Clausewitz, accepts that, "Wars must differ in character according to the nature of the motives and circumstances from which they proceed."

It cannot be denied that the war had resulted from an imaginary fear of losing vested interests, which were not territorial and could be called ideological. The interests, that were being threatened, were in the possession of a particular class, which feared the New Way of Life. As it happens elsewhere, in the case of war, here also, the tribe which held the leadership in socio-cultural field was the one to start the war. As has been said, "The problem of power in international relations would not exist if it was not for the vested interests of the governing classes that created them." In this case vested interests figured on one side only.

The imaginary fear of losing prestige, economic power, religious eminence and threat to monopoly of international carriage trade through the followers of the New Way of Life had initiated this declaration of war. They had hoped that people of *Yathrib* will throw out the handful of Believers from Mecca. Peace among Believers being indivisible and the determination to avenge the blood of other Believers had brought about a solidarity among Believers, which could not be splintered by such threats. They may have hoped that threat of force will achieve what they desired. They, however, did not realise that the threat and eventually the use of force, in this case, will start a war, which will continue for centuries. "Force, or a threat of it, may not settle argument, but it does play a considerable part in determining the structure of the world in which we live."

Commands of Allah and decisions of the Prophet (Pbuh) hold inviolable position. This Clause may not have appeared of great consequence to the observers of that era. Believers were confined mainly to *Yathrib* and as refugees in *Habsha*, in addition to possible individuals scattered about in various parts of Arabia. Except those in *Yathrib*, the other Believers were not in a position to avenge the blood of their brother Muslims. If, however, we look at this Clause to the centuries that PBUH Muslim countries falling a prey to the domination of Christian West, we realise how significant would have been the result, if Muslims had been obeying the Commands of this Document, issued by the Prophet (Pbuh), whose Commands are as inviolable as those of Allah Himself.

"Obey Allah and obey His messenger but if you turn away, then the duty of Our messenger is only to convey (the message) plainly."(64: 12)

He conveyed the message, in the best possible manner. In an age, when written orders were not resorted to, he gave a written Document in as plain words as possible. How numerous, in fact, countless are the occasions, when Muslims have failed to avenge the blood of their brothers, in various corners of the Globe. Muslims have failed to visualise *Jihad* in its correct perspective, because they have failed to comprehend their own identity in circumstances which have been changing constantly. Because they failed to comprehend the meaning and consequence of being One *Ummah*, they have failed to organize their collective affairs in accordance with the dictates of the Quran and Prophet's Orders which in the case of this Document is not merely *Sunnah* of the Prophet (Pbuh) but an outright order and which should not have been disobeyed under any circumstances. Muslims have for centuries ignored their correct standing and as a result could not evolve correct strategy and tactics to defend themselves. "The object which every one, who undertakes war proposes to himself, and the means he calls forth are determined entirely according to the particular details of the position."

When the *Ummah* ceased to exist as one body, its war strategy never attained that position, which alone could fully defend its interests. It has been said that "the objective of military strategy is the creation, by military means, those conditions, under which politics is in a position to achieve the aims it sets for itself." The Prophet (Pbuh), through successful defence of *Yathrib*, had been able to create those conditions where unity of *Ummah* could be guaranteed. Later generations have, one after the other, failed to maintain that condition of *Ummah*, with the result that they have lost the will and the means to defend themselves.

Unity of *Ummah* demands sacrifices by all in an equal measure. Separatist tendencies spring, very often, from hesitating to contribute to the common cause by members of ruling classes. This leads to hesitation on the part of the common man to sacrifice his life and wealth for common defence. When nations are threatened with extermination, as the Muslim *Ummah* has been for centuries, and they do not resolve to put up a fight and are afraid to go to war, they cannot survive as free people. In the words of a modern military thinker, "if a nation is really determined not to fight, ardently desires not to fight, and is prepared to endure anything rather than risk a decisive campaign," then that nation or *Ummah*, ends up as an acquired and conquered territory to be used as a colony by its victor. If Muslim of the present age desire 10 live as free people, then the first step for them is to organize themselves for defence, and act in accordance with the dictates of the Constitutional Charter of Median. Muslims, in the past, may have defended their territories individually. They have not fought as an *Ummah*, for a number of centuries. The result has been that they have all been defeated one after the other. They have wasted their sacrifices for having failed to act as *ONE UMMAH*.

Clause 24: "The Believers, because they fear Allah, they are better in showing steadfastness, and as a result receive Guidance."

This Clause is more of a statement of fact, and a standard set for Believers, which they must maintain in order to continue to receive Guidance from Allah. This is the standard to be achieved by all true Believers. The basis of excellence in showing steadfastness has been established as Fear of Allah. It must be remembered that this Document was being dictated soon after *Hijrah*. The steadfastness, which had been shown by *Quraish Muhajirin* was known to all. The manner in which they had migrated and the hardships endured by them on the way could be imagined. The short period of stay in *Yathrib* was also a period of patience, hard work and facing hardships in an extremely disciplined, coordinated and united manner. The *Ansar* Believers who were although new to Islam, had shown great changes in their moral qualities and had achieved character qualities not found in their other compatriots, who had not yet embraced Islam.

This Clause was a reminder to non-Muslims of that period and the world at large of future generations that Belief in Allah and Muhammad (Pbuh) leads to Fear of Allah, which transforms the very character of men and women who are fortunate enough to see the Light, without staunch Faith and Fear of Allah, it is difficult to remain steadfast and achieve "Calm courage in the midst of tumult and the serenity of soul in danger and cool headedness." The Companions of the Prophet (Pbuh), whether from amongst the *Quraish* of Mecca or the *Ansars* of Median, excelled one another in their devotions to him and Faith in Allah, which had been bestowed to them, through his teachings and personal conduct. It has been said of them that, "these men formed the venerable stock of Islam, from whom one day was to spring the noble band of first jurists, theologians and traditionalists of Muslim society." *Abu Bakr*, the first successor of the Prophet (Pbuh), when advised by *Umar*, Ali, and other brave Companions to postpone the despatch of the Army to threatened Northern Areas, refused to listen to any such advice.

He had said, "I will not revoke any order given by the Prophet (Pbuh). Median may become the prey of wild beasts, but the Army must carry out the wishes of Muhammad (Pbuh)." Such strength of character was the result of faith in the Prophet's Mission and Belief and Fear of Allah, in which he excelled all others, and was known as Siddique for such staunch faith. Faith in Allah leads to the firm belief, that death comes only once and then the eternal life of the hereafter starts for ever. This belief in life after death seems to have been the hall-mark of early Muslims. Chinese Muslims are known as '*Huyee*' by others, which means, "those who believe in life in the hereafter". To a Muslim life continues after death. A Muslim soldier does not go to war merely because he desires to "die in war so that others may live," but he goes to war because he wishes that he dies as a martyr so that he achieves Eternal Life.

> "Think not of those, who are slain on The Way of Allah as dead. Nay, they are living. With their Lord thy have provision". (3: 169)

Belief in the hereafter pre-supposes the Day of Reckoning and Reward from Allàh. Dangers of all kind, thus, fade, into insignificance. Steadfastness, when fighting in the Path of Allah, is the logical outcome.

Proved by History : History was to prove the truth of this Clause in many a battle-field around the surface of the Globe. This fundamental truth was being brought home to those engaged in war, that Belief in Allah and Fear of Him result in ignoring the consequences of the losses and injuries caused in war. As a result it is the quality and not the quantity of human and material sources that influences the issue. Military thinkers of all ages have admitted this truth. A modern writer has to say, "Neither policies nor machines will determine the history of tomorrow. Man is the measure of all things.... This then is the ultimate battlefield: the hearts and minds of men." Life, to the Believers, was one entity. They stepped from this to the next world with clear conscience. Both worlds were subject to the Sovereign Power Allah, the Creator and Sustainer of the entire Universe.

> "Have they not pondered upon themselves? Allah created not the heavens and the earth, and that which is between them, save with truth and for a destined end. But many of the mankind are believers in the meeting with their Lord". (30: 8)

This belief in meeting with Lord of men and all there is between the earth and the heavens, makes all the difference. He who obeys Him here, is happy, and longs to meet Him in the Hereafter.

> "Whoso looketh forward to the meeting with Allah (let him know that) Allah's reckoning is surely high, and He is the Hearer, the Knower". (29: 5)

This high reckoning is measured by the sacrifices on His Path. And the sacrifice of the life. He bestowed on man is, with Him, of the highest reckoning.

His knowledge is Complete. The main thing is, whether a man believes in His Sovereignty both here and in the hereafter.

> "Allah! There is no God save Him. He gathereth you all upon the Day of Resurrection whereof there is no doubt. Who is more true in statement than Allah". (4: 87)

When fear of death is no more, then the fighter does not hesitate to face the most powerful on earth. These Companions of the Prophet (Pbuh) were the most peaceful and lovable people in peaceful surroundings but harsh and firm in battle. Allah has said of them;

> "Muhammad is the messenger of Allah. And those with him are hard against the disbelievers and merciful among themselves". (48: 29)

Thus they were more steadfast than others.

This characteristic of being hard in battle and mercifulness .....with companions and those who came in contact with them under peace condition has been portrayed by a modern writer in these words:

> "War and peace is personified respectively in heroes and saints."

Heroes in War and Saints in Peace : The Companions of the Prophet (Pbuh) were all heroes in war and saints in peace. This was the result of their Faith and Fear of Allah. They knew their proper place in the scheme of things. When man realises this, he feels how close he is to Eternal Truth. As one such person who realised it in the middle of throes of war has remarked, "The discovery—that is discovery for myself that God is Universal, which is not so obvious as it sounds, was, I think, the first great step I made in finding that within that Universal, fear shall be impossible."

In the final analysis, it is the determination and steadfastness of the combatants which decides the issue of war. In this first war between Islam and The Rest, it must be remembered that the *Muhajir* Companions were initially the product of the old Way of Life of Mecca and the *Ansar* Companions had grown up in the same surroundings, background and upbringing, as other residents of *Yathrib*, but both had been transformed into new beings as a result of their Belief in Allah and His Messenger (Pbuh). These two groups of Companions of the Prophet of Allah had shed all their earlier prejudices, fears, and taboos by becoming Believers. Like the word "*Huyee*" in China, the word Believers has a special meaning. It covers steadfastness, patience, forbearance, courage, bravery, and fearlessness apart from benevolence, forgiveness and mercifulness to the weak and persecuted. A modern writer thinks that, "courage is will-power....and when, in war, it is used up (the soldier) is finished..." In actual fact courage and willpower and other allied qualities spring from the same source-Faith. This author was a medical officer, during war, over a very prolonged period. He feels that "Time" exhausts courage. In actual fact, it is courage based on temporary factor, like pride, loyalty to king and country and fear of being called a coward that gets exhausted. "The using up of courage" does not happen to those who crave to become martyrs, as a result of their Belief, that they are fighting in the Path of Allah. He, however, admits that, "Faith is the only thing, which can delay the eating up of courage. Lord Moran, ends up by saying that, "Faith had come into the lives of many men," which saved them, from becoming mental and physical wrecks. Those who lack "Faith," break up. It is such people who are the real victims of war. It has been said that, "War demands its toll of broken men— broken in mind or body or both; to mend these is the function of a medical service." Yes, but only for the repairs needed to the body. The mind needs to be cured by a much higher authority.

Other military writers have also expressed views on courage and similar other qualities. A well known military writer has summed up his views and said, "Courage and self-reliance are principles essential to war. It is a serious undertaking, by a serious man, for a serious object. " We would like to differ by saying that a Believer does not rely on himself. He relies on Allah, who is the Arbiter in all things. One of the successful generals of Second World War has said, "I consider morale the greatest and the only factor in war; without high morale, no success can be achieved, no matter how good the strategic and tactical plans may be." Morale has been translated as *IMAN* by some scholars. Western writers often admit the strong impact of morale on the outcome of war. As has been said that, "The military victories of the Germans were due as much to the demoralisation of the enemy as to their superiority in the field."

As this Clause points out, the Muslims have from the beginning been known to have shown great moral and physical courage as a result of their staunch Belief in Allah. Speaking of the Muslims of the early period one writer has remarked, "The spirit of discipline and contempt of death manifested at the first armed encounter of Islam, proved characteristic of it in all its latter and greater conquests."

Spirit Infused : The spirit, which had been infused into the mind of these Companions of the Prophet (Pbuh) has been commented upon by a modern writer in one brief sentence. He writes, "No others have made practically all their soldiers to actually seek death in battle." This achievement of the Prophet (Pbuh) was the result of his own Faith in Allah and his example, both in mosque and on the field of battle, helped his Companions to reach those unchartered heights of courage, steadfastness and sheer "contempt of death," which had never been reached by men of any nation throughout human history. Liberty and freedom, which was needed to usher in and live in accordance with the New Way of Life dictated by

Allah, through Quran, could only be achieved through steadfastness. No nation has achieved liberty without it. Liberty "is a prestige that must be earned." This was the pre-requisite of free and unfettered obedience of One Allah.

Fear of death and injury can only overpower the minds of those men, who lack Faith. A surgeon who had lived and worked in the trenches with soldiers, in the front line, has said, that officers, who commanded troops in action, often asked him about the influence of religion on troops facing danger. He has summed up his observations by saying, "Often I was asked about the importance of religion. Speaking as if they did not know how to put it, they separately told me how faith had come into the lives of many of their men." The same writer, when speaking about the officers who led their men into attack has to say, "The art of selection is the secret of leadership."

Selection of Leaders : The selection of leaders at all levels, from the Second *Bayah* at *Uqba* to the last, was done by the Prophet (Pbuh) himself. Those Companions, whom he selected to lead other Companions, showed qualities of leadership unsurpassed in human history. The training given to *Abu Bakr, Umar, Ali, Abu Ubaidah*[31], *Saad-bin-Waqqas*[32], *Khalid*[33] and many others produced leaders of unique qualities of head and heart. They turned out to be great military leaders and equally capable statesmen. This clause has expressed their qualities in a modest manner by saying that, "Believers, because they fear Allah, they are better in showing steadfastness and as a result receive Guidance."

Modern thinkers are gradually understanding the influence of faith in Allah; as one writer has said that full freedom and liberty are achieved only as a result of Belief in Allah. "If there is any freedom anywhere it is consummated in God, whose service, for man, is perfect freedom." When man becomes His Slave (*Abd-Hoo*), and not the slave or servant of another man, or even his own earthly desires, he is really free. He can speak the truth, because he is not the slave or servant of any person. "A man to be free is to be in command of his own destiny. When free men freely combine to shape a common destiny, you have a free people." The Believers, because of their Belief in Allah, were a free people. They had combined freely to shape the common destiny of all those existing and future generations, who would choose to be free people. It was this freedom, which gave them steadfastness and earned them Divine Guidance as a present.

We must, constantly, bear in mind the background and the circumstances under which this Document was being dictated. In this assembly of all men of *Yathrib*, some were Believers, and some were "The others," who, were to work under the leadership of Believers, were being given the Charter, which was to remain their Fundamental Law, as long as they remained in *Yathrib*. They all were aware of the fact, that the *Quraish* of Mecca had declared war against them all. They knew of earlier decision of *Abdullah bin Ubay*. They had been told that the Prophet (Pbuh) had undertaken that Believers would defend *Yathrib*. He was through this Clause, bringing home to the others, "that to achieve the steadfastness required to defend a territory, chosen by a people, as its homeland, it was necessary to possess the quality of truthfulness and that this rare and highly valuable quality could be achieved by belief and fear of Allah alone. He was telling them that through belief in Allah, alone, could man achieve such qualities.

Those who deliberate on happenings around them and ponder a little over the sequence of events, come to the realisation of how little power does man possess to channel events on the broader spectrum of this world. Winston Churchill, the undisputed leader of Great Britain, during the time of its greatest struggle, has said, "Let us be contented with what has happened to us and thankful for all we have been spared. Let us accept the natural order in which we move. Let us reconcile ourselves to the mysterious system of our destinies, such as they must be in the world of space and time. Let us treasure our joys but not avail our sorrows. The glory of light cannot exist without its shadows. Life is a whole and good and evil must be accepted together." Those who think and deliberate, sooner or later, come to the conclusion that there exists a power higher than us all. Faith in Him alone enables men to bear hard and harsh moments in life. Discussing happenings during the conduct of the same war another writer has referred to steadfastness in the following words. "Calm courage, in the midst of tumult, that serenity of soul in danger, is the greatest gift of nature for mankind." He appears shy of using the word God or Allah.

One must realise that "The soldier is alone with the terror....", that can grip his heart and mind. He needs support and there is nothing more durable than "inner support," supplied by Faith in Allah. This eminent writer who had personal experience of treating the war wounded adds, "when their self-control was worn thin, they were given to moods, which was the language in which they spoke to us of their distresses."

Steadfastness, a Gift : Steadfastness is a gift from Allah. When his very existence is denied men are deprived of this gift. Speaking of those who had no Divine support to fall back upon, another observer has said, "They have no religious conviction by which to obtain leverage in their struggles. They have no firm philosophy of life on which they or those who could help them can lay hold." Western world seems to be groping in the dark. Another writer on the subject has to say that, "Gradually it began to dawn on the Western world that anticipating this danger was really more dangerous than the danger itself. "

There has to be a Philosophy of Life based on a lasting principle. Islamic Philosophy of Life is based on Sovereignty of Allah. There can be no firmer basis for a Philosophy of Life. This Philosophy is as Eternal as the basis on which it stands. It is immovable and unshakable. It may weaken under certain conditions of immature leadership, but it can be revived and has reappeared with added vigour. Islamic Way of Life is distinct, all pervading and complete in itself. It needs no outside props. It reasserts itself on its pivot—Oneness of Allah and the Finality of Prophethood of Muhammad (Pbuh). It has this philosophy from which springs the Islamic Way of Life. This is what is missing in the West, as one observer has said, "Lacking a way of life, a philosophy, we have had to run before the wind of change and yield in the face of attack by the more dynamic philosophies ranged against us.... our entire military system was based on tactics alone and out of date tactics at that."

This Clause brings out another important aspect of being a Believer. It gives a place of prestige to him and places him on a high pedestal of being a bold and straight-forward person, who is not afraid of telling the truth, and to follow a path free of common evils. As has been observed by a Western scholar," One of the reasons for the warm welcome, which Muhammad (PBUH) received in Median would seem to be that the adoption of Islam appeared, to the more thoughtful, of the citizens to be a remedy for the disorder from which the society was suffering by its orderly discipline of life and bringing the unruly passions of men, under the discipline of laws enumerated by the authority, superior to individual caprice." In other words, the disciplined life, that an individual led, after becoming a Muslim and the Belief in the Supreme being, which strengthened his heart and mind was visible from his conduct and it attracted towards him and Islam, all those, who came in contact with him.

This transformation was the result of the towering personality of the Prophet (Pbuh).

They had become, so to say, new individuals, both within themselves and to the observers. The *Muhajir* Believers were foremost in this respect. They were the result of thirteen years of guidance given by him, in accordance with the dictates of the Quran. "They were the depositories of the Sacred Text of the Quran, which they alone knew by heart; they were the jealous guardians of the memory of every word and bidding of the Prophet (Pbuh), the trustees of the moral heritage of Muhammad (Pbuh). These men formed the venerable stock of Islam from whom one day was to spring the noble band of the first jurists, the theologians, and traditionalists of Muslim society."

The credit for selecting and training of these men of extraordinary sincerity goes to the Prophet (Pbuh) himself. When the Voice directed him to "Recite," and he spoke of his Mission to *Abu Bakr*, who did not hesitate to acknowledge the Prophethood conferred on him to the moment of his departure, *Abu Bakr* had remained closest to him. The soft and benign nature of this most devoted Companion of the Prophet (Pbuh) proved as if it was made of twice tempered steel, when the responsibility of carrying on the torch of Islam fell on him. It has to be admitted that he and others were all the product of guidance given to them by the last Messenger of Allah. Modern writers give great importance to the understanding of human psychology, when selecting men for tasks which carry great responsibility, it has been said that during World War II, "the application of psychology in selecting and training men did more to help win the war than any other single intellectual activity."

The great laurels won by Muslim Armies just after the death of the Prophet (Pbuh) in defending Arabia, against the two supreme powers of that age and the juristic and literary excellence achieved within less than a century, by Muslim scholars was the fruit of the selection and training of his Companions, given by him on the floor of his modest mosque in Median and the battle fields of *Badr*, *Uhud*, *Khyber* and *Hunnain*. When we consider the meagre resources available to him, and his readiness to accept the responsibility of defence, through the promulgation of this Document, his achievements make a new but gigantic picture. He had trained his Companions to such high standard of sacrificing their wealth and their lives that he did not have to hesitate in accepting the responsibility to defend *Yathrib*. In the circumstances that he was placed and the meagre resources he possessed, it needed great courage and faith in Allah to have accepted to launch the entire *Ummah* of Islam in battle. His words which were in fact, prayers to Almighty, has been quoted many a times, but its true implications can only be understood, when it is kept in mind that this was all that Islam possessed. He had said:

> "O Allah! if this little band of Believers is destroyed today, there will be none left to obey your Commands, until the Day of Resurrection."

It depicted the true picture. He was the last Messenger of Allah, with the last Message from Allah, which meant the Last and Final but Perfect *Shariah*, and this small band of Believers was the entire strength of the last *Ummah*. If they were fighting *Jihad*, until *Shahadah*—martyrdom, none would have been left alive, to live in accordance with the Dictates of this Last Shariah sent by Allah.

It is in view of such critical situations that present day military writer has said, "What strength of will and greatness of soul it takes to launch one of those decisive battles, on which the fate of a nation depends." Badr was truly the most rare occasion, when the fate of the entire *Ummah* depended on one battle. When the Believer defending the rights of humanity stands steadfast in battle, he feels that he is performing the most sacred task, ever allotted to mankind.

> He is demonstrating the meaning of: "You are the best community that has been raised up for mankind. You enjoin right conduct and forbid indecency; and you believe in Allah." (3: 110)

Strength of Mind and Body : The Believer gets strength of mind and body from the Conviction of fighting in the Path of Allah. "War is the province of physical exertion and suffering. A certain strength of body and mind is required, which produces indifference to them." Belief in Allah enhances this strength of both body and mind. It is strength of this kind that keeps nations alive. An European travelling through Turkey and observing their morale during the later part of eighteenth century had to remark, "Internal causes are the most immediate in national elevation or decay, as no feeble state was elevated to extraordinary eminence by the mere aid of alliance, however powerful; similarly, on the other hand, scarcely any great nation perished by means of external violence, unless it had something within itself vicious and unsound." Another traveller has also paid tribute to Muslim soldiers. He says, "When a Turk could ride with the Sultan's firman, he was respected all the way, from the banks of Volga to the confines of Morocco — when its armies threatened Vienna, and its fleets blockaded the coasts of Italy it then excited the fears of civilized Europe." This was not so because of the ability of Turkish *Sultans* alone, but because Turkish soldiers believed in Allah.

Speaking of the modern *Turks* and their performance during the First World War, a military historian of repute states, "For the most part they were illiterate conscripts from the country,.... although they were always outgunned and outnumbered, their steadfastness never forsook them......they were very cool and very skilful."

The same writer has mentioned that "When the (British) submarine was first abandoned and the British sailors were struggling in the water the Turkish soldiers, on the shore, jumped in and rescued them..... When the first English submarine prisoners were led into the hospital at Chanak, shivering in their wet clothes, the Turkish wounded called them guests, and insisted on their being given everything new and few such delicacies as they possessed."

Belief of an individual shapes his character. When a people possessing strong belief develop certain common tracts, the sum total of such traits is known as the national character of that people. As a result of Belief in Allah, to remain steadfast, has become a part of the national character of Muslims, all the world over.

Clause 25: "No un-Believer will be permitted to take the property of the *Quraish* under his protection."

The situation as it then existed in *Yathrib* was that there were fewer Believers than the un-Believers in *Yathrib*. The *Quraish* of Mecca, mostly un-Believers had declared war on *Yathrib*. A state of war had come into existence between the two states. It was quite possible that due to past relations some *Yathribite un*-Believers might have decided to take Meccan property, under his or her protection. If the un-Believer were not debarred under Law of the land, they could not be stopped from giving protection to what was legally enemy property and thus liable to be appropriated by the state.

The *Quraish* were a business community. They had always held monopoly of carrier trade of goods arriving at Aden or other ports of the Red Sea to be conveyed to Syria and other market towns in the North. It would be wrong to assert that this monopoly had been the result of war between Byzantium and Iran, as some Orientalists have said. Montgomery Watt, for instance writes, "While the war ran its course and perhaps as a result of making travel difficult between Iraq and southern Syria, the commercial centre of Mecca was experiencing great prosperity. It had gained monopoly control of the trade by the caravan route up the westward of Arabia." The *Quraish* had always held monopoly of this trade.

So far as Montgomery Watt's assumption that, "perhaps as a result of difficulties of travel between Iraq and southern Syria, the commercial centre of Mecca had become prosperous". In case travel between Iraq and Syria had been disrupted as a result of war between the Byzantines and Iran, the *Quraish* would not have sent their caravan to Syria via Iraq. This was the caravan, which was not permitted to proceed to Iraq and its goods had been captured as enemy property, under orders of the Prophet (Pbuh). The Prophet (Pbuh) had inserted in this clause, as a result of his correct enunciation of International Law regarding the method of dealing with enemy property during war. Confiscation of enemy property, during war, is a common practice, in modern times as well. A Gazzette notification of British Government during World War I reads as follows:

> "Any sum which had a state of war not existed, would have been payable and paid to for the benefit of our enemy, by way of Dividend, Interest, or Share of profits, shall be paid by the person, firm or company, by whom it would have been payable, to the Custodian....."

Apart from confiscation of enemy property, the national of the home country are prohibited from carrying on trade activities with the enemy country, as long as the war lasts, or the state of war continues. During the same war a notification of the British Government had laid down:

> "Whereas a state of war exists between us and the German Emperor, and whereas it is contrary to law for any person resident carrying on business, or being in our Dominion to trade or have any commercial intercourse with any person resident, carrying on business, or being in German Empire without our permission...."

Similarly, ships are not allowed to leave for anchor, or communicate with any port situated in enemy territory. It is also customary to prohibit aliens from carrying on business and free movement within territories of the home government during war. This Clause can thus be said to be the first instance of Codification of International Law on the subject.

Quraish of Mecca had declared war against *Yathrib*. A state of war existed from the moment the ultimatum had reached *Yathrib*. Every person of the tribe of *Quraish*, who had not embraced Islam was an enemy of *Yathrib* and all property belonging to or in possession of the enemy had become enemy property, for as long as the state of war was to continue between Mecca and *Yathrib*.

The reason, why, only un-believer had been debarred from taking the property of *Quraish* under their protection was that the Belivers were the direct cause of this war. Protection given by *Ansar* Believers to *Muhajir* Believers had resulted in the declaration of war by the *Quraish*. It was not likely that any Believer would give undue protection to the property particularly caravans belonging to Meccans. The other reason for not including Believers in this restriction was that any property taken hold of by a Believer was to become a part of spoils of war, which was to be handed over to the state, for distribution in the normal manner.

This precautions are normal during war. The present day governments are even more particular in placing restriction on enemy properly finding its way back to the enemy either directly or through neutrals. Hence we find, that this Clause had opened the way to legalising taking over of enemy property.

Clause 26: "No un-Believer will intervene in favour of *Quraish*."

War had been declared by Mecca. All possible precautions had to be taken that the un-Believers could not interfere with war efforts. At a time when the threat of invasion was new, everybody was afraid of the possible severe action being taken by Meccans, if they succeeded in defeating the Believers. There was, however, the possibility that due to old connections between the un-Believers in *Yathrib* and the *Quraish* of Mecca, some of the former may not intervene on behalf of the *Quraish*. There was also the possibility of some individuals from amongst the un-Believers to plead the cause of Meccans and to undertake to supply them with secret military and other vital information from within *Yathrib*. Legal course was the best method of proceeding in such circumstances. The Document laying down the Fundamental Law of the state was the best source to promulgate such security laws. The nature of these laws and the manner in which they were being promulgated were, no doubt, new to that age, but his actions had to remain as precedents and as in this case legal commands for all times.

Clause 29: "The Jews will contribute towards the cost of war when fighting alongside the Believers."

Clause 1 had mentioned that "the others," which meant the un-Believers and Jews, would be considered as part of the *Ummah* if they followed the Believers and fought alongside with them. This Clause clearly mentions the Jews, fighting alongside the Believers. It is possible that the Jews, at this instance, had asked for some sort of clarification and the Prophet (Pbuh) in answer to some query laid down that if they fought alongside the Believers, they would, at the same time, have to contribute towards the cost of war. This refers to general expenses and not those expenses, which are incurred by all armies on the equipment, food and personal equipment of individual soldiers.

Jews may have been more numerous than the Believers, at that time but they did not form the government party and they were living as a minority. They were, therefore, not being coerced to undertake the defence of the state. If, however, they were keen to undertake this arduous duty and become equal members of the *Ummah* they had to defray the cost of war along with the Believers.

This Clause was being written at a time when Jews and other minorities in neighbouring lands were being persecuted or permitted to live as serfs and slaves only. It was a great step forward towards the unity of mankind. The important part of the whole philosophy of equality of man is that it was being written down and proclaimed through a legal Document, which can be termed as a Constitution or Constitutional Charter of Median. The Charter was not being demanded by the citizens or any section of the community. In fact all concessions in it, were being freely given by the Prophet (Pbuh). He realised the importance of "War Potential" of a nation. He knew that internal dissentions weaken war potential and man power is no mean component of it. It has been said that, as far as the war potential of a nation in a modern setting is concerned, "Its principal components are not only its industrial capacity, but the administrative skill, with which it is managed and the morale or motivations of war". To have included the Jews to volunteer to join in the defence of the state amounted to successful efforts towards motivation of a common cause. He was taking the first practical step towards bringing entire mankind on one platform, a duty which now devolves on his *Ummah*.

Clause 32: "Loyalty gives protection against treachery."

This clause deals with internal security and security of defence plans and other defence matters. It has to be in the statute even though there may be no likelihood of war starting in the near future or a state of war being declared soon. In the case of *Yathrib*, a state of war already existed. There could be no more appropriate time for giving a warning of this nature, than the occasion when invasion was imminent.

The Jews had volunteered to join Believers in their against Mecca and thus gain an equal social and political status with the Government Party. They were told that they will have to join in the defraying the cost of the war. They were being warned, that, loyalty to the cause of *Ummah*, they desired to join was most important. After Clause 29, the clause dealing with the cost of war, there were two more clauses referring to the different sections of Jews who wanted the names of the *Haleef* Tribes, to be specifically included, as those who had volunteered to become one *Ummah* with Muslims. It has to be noted here that this request for being allowed to become a part of *Ummah* had been put forward when Clause 28 had already been dictated, which lays down, "When you differ on anything the matter will be referred to Allah and Muhammad (Pbuh)." This meant, that the Law of the Quran and the decisions of the Prophet (Pbuh) were to be Supreme in *Yathrib*. They may not have realised but they were coming in as a part of Muslim *Ummah* and were happy to be governed by Islamic *Shariah*, although they were to retain their separate identity as Jews. How much freedom they were to retain is not known but if they gave a different version to Clauses 30 and 31 or any other Clause, of the Charter, or they differed even on other socio-political or economic matters concerning the collective life of the community, the final decision was to rest with Allah and His Messenger (Pbuh).

To have spoken of loyalty as the best course of conduct and warned them against treachery, when state of war existed, looks very appropriate. Events, which took place after the promulgation of the Charter have to be viewed in the light of this and similar other Clauses of the Charter.

Clause 35: "No one shall go to war except with the permission of Muhammad (Pbuh). If any wrong has been done it may be avenged."

Muhammad (Pbuh), on behalf of Believers had accepted to defend *Yathrib*. Therefore, he was the only person in *Yathrib* who was responsible for the efficient defence of the state and its territories. He, alone, was the person who could decide on defence plans. As such he was the only person who knew, when and in what manner defence movements for defending *Yathrib* were to be made.

Head of the State : Apart from that, he was the head of the Government Party, and as such, he became automatically the head of the state as well. He, alone could therefore, declare war. It has been universal practice, since ancient times, and throughout the world, that war can be declared by the head of state alone. This practice still exists. In modern democracies the parliament may take the decision but the declaration of war has to be made in the name of the head of that state. According to the British custom and law, in a country which claims to possess the oldest parliament, it has followed the same practice. "It has been said, by the law and the constitution of the country that the sovereign alone can declare war......and such a declaration carries with it the force of law. As such it is of equal authority with the Act of Parliament and is judicially taken notice of."

It is worth keeping in mind that this Constitutional Charter was being dictated on the certainty that *Yathrib* was to be invaded soon. The Prophet (Pbuh), who, with the help of Allah and his Companions, had decided to undertake the defence of *Yathrib*, was, from legal point of view promulgating the Constitution of the territories now being declared as the state of *Yathrib*. These territories were later to be known as Median. All parties then living in *Yathrib* were represented in this assembly. In this most representative Assembly, that *Yathrib* had ever witnessed, it was being declared that the prerogative of the head of the state of *Yathrib* would be exercised by Muhammad (Pbuh) alone." No one shall go to war except with the permission of Muhammad (Pbuh)". It meant that they had voluntarily and unanimously accepted him as the factual head of the state and the government of *Yathrib*.

When a state goes to war or is forced to get involved in war, it is governed by the universal practice concerning "state of war," in respect of a country. During the state of war emergency laws are enforced, which are vital for the safety of the state. Orders regarding necessary action against the enemy and property belonging to enemy state or its individuals, is taken. England, which is considered to be a country, which tries to explain all its actions through one or other law, maintains that, "Actual invasion of this country would, of course, create a state of war.... and it may be assumed that common law would be suspended, for the simple reason, that no courts would be able to administer it."

As a result of declaration of war by Mecca a state of war had come into being between Mecca and its allies on the one side and *Yathrib* on the other. This "state of war," lasted between these states until the defeat of various allies of Mecca and Mecca itself, except during the short period of Truce resulting from the Peace Treaty of Hudaybiya[34]. Those, like *Banu Ghatfan* and the Jews of *Khyber*, who did not join the peace treaty, continued to be at war with *Yathrib*. Campaigns against *Banu Ghatfan* and Jews of *Khyber* were under taken because they had first attacked *Yathrib*, as allies of Mecca. These, therefore have to be viewed in the light of Clauses of this Charter and those of the Peace Treaty of *Hudaybiya*.

"State of war," has a special connotation. When state of war is declared, or due to an act on the part of one of the parties, it comes into existence, legal implications of large number of acts and omissions, get new colour and receive enhanced dimensions. Acts aimed at spreading despondency, defeatism, anti-war slogans, or even those movements, which create internal dissensions and undue and malicious criticism of the government and its functionaries, assume a dangerous posture and as a result are declared to be punishable by death or imprisonment according to the severity of the act. As a rule, in England, "if it amounts to wilful defiance of authority it is punishable under section a (1) with death."

Historians have reported the case of *Kaab-bin-Ashraf*[35], a member of the tribe of Tay, but was living in *Yathrib* because of having married a local Jewish lady went away to Mecca and was guilty of inciting the *Quraish* against Median. He returned to Median, under dubious conditions and continued his anti-state activities. A sentence of death was passed against him by the head of the state and he was killed in such a way that his death did not create any internal disturbance. Critics of the judgement passed against him have failed to realise that when he was punished the war had been going on for a considerable period and a state of war existed. His crimes were too many and too serious not to be taken notice of.

Practical Reasons : It is a common practice among countries with parliaments that the person or the office, where the authority to declare war lies, in addition to being the head of state, is not necessarily the head of the government as well. Under Imperial and Presidential systems, however, he functions as head of state and head of the government also. In addition he is the Commander-in-Chief of the Armed Forces of the nation as well. The Prophet (Pbuh) held these three positions in addition to having been accepted as the Prophet (PBUH) of Allah.

He was, however, the head of the Government of *Yathrib* and Commander-in-Chief of its Army due to another and a practical reason. He was the only person who could undertake the responsibilities of these two very important functions of the state. He was unlettered; but he had received training of the Highest Order from Allah Himself. He could and did undertake these responsibilities and carried them out successfully. It could not be otherwise. Allah the All Knowing has said of him:

> "By the star when it setteth, your comrade erreth not, nor is deceived; nor doth he speak (of) his own desire. It is naught save an inspiration that is inspired, which one of mighty powers hath taught him".
>
> (53: 1-5)

As the legal head of Army it devolved on him to decide on the strength of the Army and the qualifications, training and capabilities of the soldiers and the commanders alike. His battles are a proof of the fact that he recruited, trained and led his army in the most efficient and profitable manner. The way he selected different commanders for each campaign, the way he gradually increased their responsibilities and the clarity with which he briefed them, when they were despatched on special missions, is a miracle, of which there is no explanation except that he had been trained by The Supreme Sovereign of this huge Universe and he received communications from the "Master of The Throne" every second of his life.

He alone knew and understood the *Quraish* and the likely manner of their offensive and the tenacity, with which they were likely to persist in their opposition to The New Way of Life, named Islam. He kept the collection of Military Intelligence also in his own hands. Security arrangements, public dealings both with elements within the state and abroad were retained by him, though, at times he used to have consultations with the inner circle of Companions on such matters. The art of war, if stated in brief words is very simple but it demands the attention of those who know and understand their enemies. "The art of war, which being very simply defined as the art which enables any commander to worst the forces opposed to him. By the time this ended he had worsted over twenty adversaries, which included the Meccans, the *Banu Ghatfan*[36], the Jews of *Khyber*, and the first Army which the Emperor of *Byzantium* had sent to finish Islam, before it became a real threat to the sovereignty of the Eastern Roman Empire.

It has been said that war, "is not the condition of generalised and random violence.... it is on the contrary a highly social activity... as Rousseau has said, war without social organisation is inconceivable''. The Prophet (Pbuh) is the first person in the history of war, who put restraints on War. He had to set up a state and a government to defend himself and the people, who had given him protection. In order to make his actions legal and based on reason and logic, he gave a Constitution to a place and people, who had no organised society and their abode was just a name of a piece of land and a small habitation, which did not have a state — not even a city state like the toddlers in civilization — the Greeks.

This aspect of organising the society in *Yathrib*, through a Constitutional Charter, has not been given proper attention by either early Muslim historians or students of modern history and other social sciences. The impact of thus organising the society on the bases of Islamic Polity and the results achieved in smooth running of the government, resulting in the restrained conduct of war and relations with neighbour rulers from tribal Sheikhs to the rulers of the Empires of *Byzantium* and Iran have not been studied in detail. It is correct that *Ibne-Khaldun* has derived a number of his conclusions from the Socio-political development of Median, but very little, if any, study has been undertaken by a social philosopher keeping the society of Median and its influence on the lands conquered by Muslims.

Modern writers have taken pains to bring out the influence of earlier cultures and neighbouring civilizations on Islam, but they have touched the mere surface of influences and impacts made by the social structure of Median, when its young and vigorous youth occupied first the Fertile Crescent and then lands upto Indus in the East and the shores of Atlantic on the West.

This is not the occasion to go into all the Revelations received by Muhammad (Pbuh) on the steps to be taken for the Defence of the *Ummah*. As we have touched on the preparations he had to undertake in this connection, it would not be out of place to briefly study one Verse of the Quran, on this subject.

"Make ready for them."

This denotes the following:

1. The *Ummah*, which then consisted of mainly *Yathrib* had to raise men and material, for the enemy or enemies.
2. It indirectly hints that Muslims have not to be the first to start war. If aggressive wars of conquest were permitted in Islam the words would have been different. Making ready for them means keeping ready until they come.

All your strength.

This includes:

1. All human resources, each according to the task he can perform best. Under present circumstances obedience to this Command of Allah will have to be on the level of different political entities and finally on the level of the *Ummah*.

2. All material resources of all Muslim countries and within these countries of all individual Muslims. Unless preparations are made on a vast scale, the level of preparations laid down in this Verse cannot be achieved.

And your tethered horses:

The human and material resources mentioned above was in addition to "tethered horses," which means, all the Armed Forces. It would include formations of tanks, armoured carriers, squadrons of bombers, fighters and other types of military aircraft and naval Armadas. It would include all the regular and standing armed forces and reserve echelons. (The phrase "tethered horses" gives authority to standing Armed Forces.)

(So) That the enemies of Allah and your enemies and others beside them, whom you do not know but Allah knows them, are dismayed by it.

1. This wide range of enemies has to be dismayed, which means that the preparation should be to the extent that it acts as a deterrent against known and unknown enemies.
2. Allah's enemies are all those who are enemies of Islam and those who persecute humanity, whether these weak people are Muslim or non-Muslim and the Muslims are expected to help them in getting free from their persecutors. (See Verse 4: 75)
3. This duty falls to the entire Muslim *Ummah*. Let us pray, that we understand our duties according to the Quran as soon as possible. Otherwise even our future generations will fail to fulfil their duties. The Prophet (Pbuh) defended *Yathrib* and eventually freed entire Arabia from persecution and ignorance. (This is only a part of Verse 8: 60)

The Prophet (Pbuh) had to organize the society of *Yathrib*, so that he could utilise in war all human and material resources, that could be made available. It was a difficult task, because the Muslims were still in minority. Students of his life and particularly of his battles with Mecca and its allies will notice that as the enemy's efforts increased, the organisation of society in *Yathrib* accelerated and the Muslims became more integrated. In every battle, the strength of Muslim Army kept increasing.

"An organisation, which will bring every available man.... in the shortest possible time and with utmost possible momentum....." is considered ideal by modern military thinkers. This is what the first Supreme Commander of the Army of *Ummah* was able to accomplish through an efficient organisation of the society. He had seen to it that the enemy did not find him in an unarmed condition because, "The worst condition in which a belligerent can be placed is being completely disarmed."

Thus we find that from every angle and every point of view he was the only person, who was fit and qualified to declare as to when *Yathrib* or any one in *Yathrib* should go to war. To avenge earlier wrongs outside *Yathrib* was being permitted but they were not to involve the state and government of *Yathrib* in war.

As far as the last part of this Clause, regarding the avenging of a wrong is concerned, it happens to have been universally accepted that a wrong may be avenged. "Cicero insists on two elements necessary to the just war: one being a declaration in proper form, the other, a good reason for resort to violence. As good reason to violence he mentions only three: to avenge a wrong to drive off an enemy and to recover what is due."

As the time when Christianity was linked with secular power of the empire, St. Augustine[37], (354-430 A.C.) had to say, "Just wars are those which avenge injuries....," Centuries after St. Augustine, another Christian authority lays down the law for declaring war in a different manner. Jesuit Francisco Suarez[38] (1545-1617) lays down, that "A sovereign may resort to war, in default of obtaining justice from Pope to redeem an injury inflicted, and he may wage war for purposes of defence."

Clause 37: "The Jews must bear their own expenses and the Muslim bear their expenses."

Clause 29 had laid down that when Jews are fighting alongside Believers, they will contribute towards war. This only referred to general expenses like purchase of caterpillars and other weapons used jointly. There can be other expenses like blood money to be paid to an enemy if his men are killed by mistake after they had received proper safe conduct.

Clause 37 is regarding expenditure incurred on personnel, their mounts and personal equipment of fighters. As a rule this was undertaken by the individual himself, but occasions could arise as before *Ghazwae Tabuk*[39], when the state had to provide riding animals to a number of people, although there were some for whom this facility could not be provided and they were left behind. It is interesting to know that the total strength of the Army of *Yathrib* which was 313 at *Badr*, had increased to an army of thirty thousand well equipped and well mounted disciplined soldiers. We are told that one third of this force was equipped by *Uthman*,' who later became the third *Khalifa*.

Clause 38: "If anyone attacks anyone, who is a party to this Charter the others must come to his help."

This is a fair clause, getting an undertaking from all parties to a joint defence. It could be termed as the basis of a Joint Defence arrangement by the head of the state. In a way, this was an indirect way of commenting all parties, through the Command of a central authority, which was superior to all. Primarily this clause would refer to attacks from outside *Yathrib*. It may appear that it could have had reference to a party attacking from within. This does not appear possible because the text of the Charter gives a strong impression that it was the whole of *Yathrib* requesting the Prophet (Pbuh) to defend the city.

Keeping this object in view, he was organising the state, the government and the society. An attack on a group, which was a party to the Charter from within *Yathrib* could not be even thought of, unless it amounted to an outright rebellion. Later events show that there were rebellions, but they being armed rebellions, were dealt with in the proper manner. The first two tribes which rebelled were defeated before the Meccan and *Banu Ghatfan* could come to their help, but were pardoned and permitted to leave *Yathrib* with all their movable possessions.

Clause 39: "They must seek mutual advice and consultation."

This clause is a follow on or it can be called a part of clause 39. All parties were being commanded to come to the help of one another, when attacked from abroad. This clause was laying down that success in joint defence could only be achieved if previous consultation between parties was carried out and advice from one another sought for and given freely.

Differences are possible to arise in any society. An heterogeneous society, being, imperceptably taken towards a well knit unitary society, was bound to go through a certain period of tensions. It was, therefore, appropriate to lay down in clear words that they were all expected to consult one another and seek advice. whenever in doubt. Enough studies have not been undertaken on this earliest period of Muslim 'history. The rebellions of Jewish tribes having taken place, one after the other, and not simultaneously, must have been the result of sobering influence, on those Arab tribes who had been giving them protection prior to this Document. The subject needs further research, which, we hope is undertaken by young scholars, who are conversant with other social sciences also.

Clause 40: "Loyalty gives protection against treachery."

This clause is a continuation of Clauses 38 and 39. It was meant to bring home to the weaker elements, that they should not fall a prey to foreign propaganda in their own interest. In fact, the subject is related to Clause 35, which lays down that "no one shall go to war except with the permission of Muhammad (Pbuh). Clause 36 deals with murder within the society and the subsequent clauses pertain to the question of war. Loyal conduct leads to cooperation and eventually integration is achieved.

Disloyal thoughts lead to disloyal words which are followed by disloyal acts. Enemies of the state are always on the look out and select people, who have wilfully or inadvertently been guilty of disloyalty. They persuade them, coerce them and eventually by the threat of revelation of their misdeeds force them to treacherous acts against the state.

Disloyal acts, in themselves, are a source of mental tensions and unrest. Fear of exposure robs such people of peace of mind and no amount of worldly gain can be a substitute for peace of mind. This warning, in this clause, is being given a second time. Under the circumstances, which were likely to develop as a result of Meccan invasion and subversive propaganda such repetition of the warning was appropriate.

Social structure existed at that time very loosely and was being strengthened by the Prophet (Pbuh), in a gradual manner. It demanded that enough warning was given to likely disruptive elements.

Defence of the State : It was imperative to strengthen the defences of the state, both internally and externally. Man power was not only short, it was not of the best quality also. The Jews were keen to gain equality with Arabs and particularly with Believers, and had requested to be allowed to fight alongside the Believers. Their past was not very encouraging. They had not been very enthusiastic and loyal supporter of their own cause and had not honoured the call of one of their Prophets (PBUH). They had insisted that if they were provided with a king as a leader they would fight, but they eventually backed out.

> "He said: Would ye then refrain from fighting if fighting were prescribed for you? They said: Why should we not fight in the way of Allah when we have been driven from our dwellings with our children. Yet when fighting was prescribed for them, they all turned away all save a few of them." (2: 246)

The story of Jew's reply to *Moses* (*Alayhi-ssalam*) is well known. They had said:

> "So go thou and thy Lord and fight! We will sit here." (5: 24)

Such was the material which he had to mould into men of courage, fearlessness and steadfastness of the standard, he had already inspired into the hearts of Muhajirin and Ansars. He had to point out the importance of loyalty and consequences of treachery. His warnings could not be delayed. Wars have been lost, more often, because of loss of opportunities and timely preparations. A modern statesman has remarked, "The history of failure in war can be summed up in two words, Too late. Too late in comprehending the deadly purpose of the potential enemy, too late in realising the mortal danger, too late in preparedness, too late in uniting all possible forces for resistance, too late in standing with ones friends." There is a great deal of weight, in what this seasoned statesman of twentieth century has said. Conditions then prevailing in *Yathrib* and deadly threat of certain invasion, did not allow any delay to the head of state of *Yathrib* and the supreme commander of its meagre forces. Disloyalty and treachery could not be ruled out and he was justified both in timely warning about it and insistence on bringing it home to all parties, the importance of complete and unalienated loyalty to him.

Clause 43: "The Jews must pay with the Believers."

This Clause lays down, that even when the Jews do not take part in war but the Believers have to incur expenditure as a result of war, they will have to pay part of the expenses. This was in addition to what had been laid down in the earlier two clauses dealing with payments to be made by Jews. Those two occasions were when the Jews were fighting alongside the Believers. This Clause deals with payments of share of war expenses, as citizens of *Yathrib*, even though they may not have sent a contingent into the battle. The words "must pay with Believers," signify a payment, which may have to be made without prior notice. The payment which had to be made after *Beir Mauna*, and which led to the rebellion of the Jewish tribe of *Banu Nadhir*, falls under this Clause.

The Clause is worded as a Standing Order. There is no "if" or "when" about it. The payment has to be made, whenever it is demanded. As it is not an agreement but a part of fundamental law, there is no question of the Jews tribe breaking away from it.

They were to be governed by it as long as they lived in *Yathrib*. It being a legal obligation, mere refusal to make payment would amount to breaking of a law and an open rebellion.

Clause 44: "*Yathrib* shall be sanctuary for the people of the Charter."

Strictly speaking, this Clause does not fall under laws pertaining to the defence of the state of *Yathrib*. The Clause, however, provides safety, continues safe conduct of normal activities of daily life, and complete mental relaxation and peace of mind, which permits loyal citizens to double their defence efforts, so that they and their families can lead a peaceful life. A sanctuary permitted unhindered preparation for war. Hence it can be considered as helping towards war efforts.

A sanctuary precluded internal disorder. The place gets a hollowed status, which people are afraid to disturb. It is, at the same time, mutual. If anyone dares to deprive his homeland of the status of a sanctuary he lays himself open, not only to censure, but a retaliatory attack, which will be more often than not, from more quarters than he can foresee.

Mecca had been a sanctuary for a long time. It was a city possessing enviable status. From now on *Yathrib* was to rival Mecca in this respect. It certainly was a matter of honour and prestige for its inhabitants whether Believers or non-Believers.

Clause 48: "*Quraish* and their allies will not be given protection."

Clause 44 had declared *Yathrib* as sanctuary for those living in *Yathrib*. It was a natural heaven, a place of safety and an abode which promised protection. The next two clauses pertained to protection of different nature, which could be given subject to certain conditions but it had to be clearly laid down that under no circumstances could protection be given to the main enemy, the *Quraish* of Mecca.

People could give protection in the manner given in Clauses 45 and 46. But no member of the enemy clan, unless he proclaimed Islam could enter the area of the sanctuary and claim protection on the strength that it was an area of universal protection, as long as the war lasted. The Jews and other un-Believers could not give protection to a member of the *Quraish*, even otherwise. Clauses 25 and 26, debarred un-Believers from taking the property of *Quraish* under protection or intervening in favour of a member of the *Quraish* tribe. This Clause has been added because of *Yathrib* having been declared as a sanctuary for its inhabitants. A person, who is secure can normally give security to strangers. Here this protection or security could be given to every body except the enemy.

Clause 49: "The parties to this Charter are bound to help one another in the event of an attack on *Yathrib*."

This is clear cut order for joint defence of *Yathrib*. Any attack on any party residing in *Yathrib* was to be considered as an attack on all parties. This reasoning appears natural today, but *Yathrib* had, in the past, no common government, or even an agreement to consider *Yathrib* as a unit apart from all others. The main two Arab tribes had been fighting a war against one another. There had never been any understanding of jointly defending *Yathrib*. A Charter was being given to them all, making them subject to a common Law. It had to be clearly told to them, that if any one of the parties to the Charter was attacked it was to be considered as an attack on every body and Yathrib was to be defended jointly. Although the letter from *Quraish*, declaring war against Yathrib, had made it clear that the attack will be against all, but, from the "point of view of joint defence being made certain, it was essential that the text of the Charter also made it clear.

Clause 50: "If they (the others) are called upon to make and maintain peace they must do so. If a similar demand is made on the Muslims, it must he carried out, except when the Muslims are already engaged in a war in the Path of Allah."

This Clause would not have been needed in normal circumstances where every body knew the position and force of a Fundamental Law of the land. It had been categorically stated that no one will go to war without the permission of Muhammad (Pbuh) (Clause 35). It was, however, possible that one of the parties ignored that order and started a small war of their own with a neighbouring tribe. This Clause lays down that in such an eventuality the call to make and maintain peace will be obeyed at once.

To maintain the semblance of equality it was being stipulated that, if the Believers were also called upon to make and maintain peace, they will also abide by this decision of the others. There was, however, a very important proviso. If the Believers were fighting, in the Path of Allah, they will carry it on till its logical end. The Believers were not going to fight a war except in the Path of Allah. Therefore there was no possibility of such a call being made to them.

It is difficult to imagine the intricate situation, in which the Prophet (Pbuh) was placed. He had to deal with unwilling partners as far as fighting was concerned. The following Verse refers to this very people, when new entrants into the fold of Islam had not yet been inspired with the full meaning of belief in Allah.

> "Warfare is ordained for you, though it is hateful to you, but it may happen that you hate a thing which is good for you and it may happen that ye love a thing which is bad for you. Allah knoweth, you know not." (2: 216)

War had been declared with the object of annihilating him, either through the Yathribites or failing that by a direct attack on *Yathrib*. He had undertaken to defend *Yathrib* and in order to accomplish it he had started organising the society, in a manner that he could pursue the dual responsibility of propagating Islam, while at the same time, defending the territories of *Yathrib*. He had placed every future move of his on legal basis. He had, at the same time to see that his decisions and his actions, particularly when they were submitted to pen and paper, had to have the applicability of a precedent for all ages. On the one hand, there were those, who did not understand, what were the implications of a written Constitutional Law and on the other would be followers, after the lapse of centuries, who will have to read and study them, not as a part of historical document, but as Guidelines from the Last Messenger of Allah. We believe, that although the task appears impossible, to us, he was able to accomplish it, as a result of Guidance from Allah The Exalted. It is reasonable to Believe that if guided by his precepts we will also succeed.

Clause 56: "Whether an individual goes out to fight or remains in his house, he will be safe, unless he has committed a crime or is a sinner."

The state of *Yathrib* was created, apart from the need of setting up a society, for the defence of *Yathrib*, as a model society for future generations, when life would have become far more complicated. A time would come when those, who remained at home, and did not march to the battlefield, would be contributing towards war effort, through their pen, or a number of other tasks, which are performed for the support of men fighting in the trenches, at sea and in the air. The state and its defence were, in this case, complimentary. The enemy had declared war and defensive measures had to be taken.

The question arose, as to, what was to be defended? If the answer was given, that *Yathrib* was to be defended, then the question arose, as to, what exactly was *Yathrib*? If it was a country, then it must have a state and a government to arrange and supervise the defence of this piece of territory. The next question, that could be asked was regarding the extent of the territory. The Prophet (Pbuh) answered this question, in the most practical way by taking out thirty to forty *Muhajir* Companions with him to visit neighbouring tribes and conduct details of treaties of friendship between himself, as head of the state of *Yathrib*, and the chiefs as heads of those tribes.

The area covered by such journeys constituted the territories of the Islamic state of *Yathrib*. Speaking, both, from theoretical and practical point of view, the World of Islam has no fixed boundaries. Boundaries of Islam expand, as the people of adjoining lands embrace Islam or seek protection under the rule of Muslims. The world of Islam diminishes in extent of territory, when Muslims fail to protect them and un-Islamic Laws are proclaimed there. If the population still manages to adhere, even nominally to Islam then those individuals, theoretically at least, continue to belong to the world of Islam.

The citizens of free Islamic states of today, have a duty to continue in their efforts to free such communities according to Verse 177 of *Surah Al-Baqarah*. To "set free people in bondage," is one of the eight headings for spending *Zakat* and *Sadaqat*.

Territory of the State : The initial territories of the state, which had been created through this Document, given by Muhammad (Pbuh) to Believers, and those who followed the Believers had thus been demarcated by these early *Ghazawat*' undertaken by the Prophet (Pbuh) for diplomatic purposes and for training and acquainting his Companions with the area in which they were likely to operate during the forthcoming struggle.

Because of the fact that the state of *Yathrib* had been created as a result of the impending invasion and the Charter was being issued to define and bring to light various aspects of defence requirements, it could create ideas in the minds of some people that absence from taking part in war, in active capacity, may not be considered a crime.

The Prophet (Pbuh) realised that, conscription was not advisable in a mixed society, where a large number had not yet accepted Islam, in spite of the fact that they had accepted the leadership of Muslims and imposition of Muslim *Shariat*.

This concession, however, did not apply to Believers. They were the main target of Meccan fury. They had volunteered to defend *Yathrib*. Commandments for them were to be Revealed from time to time. The Command, "Fighting is Ordained for you" (2: 216) belongs to pre-*Badr* period, but it cannot be said with certainty whether it was Revealed before this document or after.

Humanity has taken recourse to war on countless occasions. This has happened in spite of the contention of followers of every religion that the religion they follow is a religion of peace. It is true that later generations of Muslims transgressed and apart from embarking on conquests, were guilty of internecine warfare as well. The battles of the period of the Prophet (Pbuh) and his successors were the result of aggression against territories of the state of Median which had been acquired as a result of Defensive War or expansion of Islam itself.

The wars between the state of Median and the two adjacent Empires of Byzantium and Iran had been initiated by the rulers of these two Empires. They lost the earlier battles and in retaliation continued to attack Muslim forces again and again. The "state of war", having been brought about by the rulers of these Empires, the blame for subsequent wars lies at the door of Christian Byzantium and Iran.

This Document, the Constitutional Charter of Median, was dictated for the purposes of defending *Yathrib* and yet it does not say a word about attack being mounted against an outsider, It refers to "fighting in the Path of Allah," which prohibits aggressive wars and transgression even when war has been started by the enemy.

The war started by Mecca against Islam was in every respect a war of aggression and yet the Meccans claimed that they were on the right path because they were protecting their interests. This human failing of going to war, under the excuse of the need to protect one's interest, has become common during the last two centuries. "Every generation believed its war to be just, defending values that could not be otherwise protected and that its war would be the last." In spite of it there are thinkers who maintain that mankind knows how to stop war.

"We already know how to stop war. The world has method for preventing these entirely." The remedy suggested by this writer has not yet been developed into an effective force. He says, "When the U.N. has become strong, we will no longer have to waste our time, our money, our thought, blood and in war."

This Clause of the Charter, permitted the non-Believers had to ignore the call to "march to the battlefield," because war in Islam is neither for the fulfilment of individuals glory or collective gain. The only fighting Commanded in Islam is against aggression and persecution and that also to the Believers only. To embark on an offensive war to save imaginary interests is not fighting in the Path of Allah.

Most nations will march into the territories of other people or occupy areas, while contravening the undertakings given in solemn treaties, but there are few nations who would try to restrain other nations from embarking on undertakings contrary to their treaty obligations. The Second World War was the result of *Nazi* Germany marching into many countries and not being checked by others, who merely stood and watched. The beginning was made with the march into Rhineland in which, "Some of the French wanted to march, but did not quite have the nerve. Most of the British wanted to temporize and did....Hitler not only invaded the Rhineland by so doing, he automatically tore up the Treaty of Locarno, which had been a bastion of European peace since 1925."

According to this Document, *Yathrib* was not to march against any other power. Islam believed in universal peace. The Prophet (PBUH) of Islam, as such, could not advocate breach of peace. He, therefore, left it to the conscience of every un-Believer individual to defend, whether he would like to share in the war, which was to be fought in the Path of Allah. The philosophy of "Fighting in the Path of Allah," was new to the world. It was to be only against persecutors of Allah's "Most Balanced Creation," the Man.

The grandeur of the mere thought of lighting for the pleasure of being an obedient servant of Allah is a rare feeling. Those who do not believe in Allah have, as a result, to call defensive war as "fighting for oneself." As a result, Mao Tse ung had to name a justifiable war as fighting for oneself. He writes, "The Red

Army has abolished the mercenary system, making the men feel that they are fighting for themselves, and for the people and not for anyone else.... and they know that they are fighting for themselves for the working class and the peasantry"

Muslims were fighting for Allah and the future of Allah's most balanced creation mankind. Those, who had not had the good fortune to believe in Allah, could not be coerced into a war in the Path of Allah.

If the laws pertaining to defence, promulgated through this Document are compared with laws, issued by modern states during war, it will be found that very few restrictions were being placed on the civil population. The second point of significance is that this Charter was of permanent nature and needed no subsequent documents adding more restrictions for the common man. Curtailment of liberties has become a common feature of modern wartime instructions and notifications. "During the time of war changes in laws have been so far reaching and the laws have been speaking with such multitude of voices that the ordinary citizen has found himself in a state of complete bewilderment. The operation of these war time laws has drastically affected the daily life of the citizens in all its spheres."

Few Restrictions : The war declared against *Yathrib* had the object of annihilating Islam and Muslims and yet restrictions placed on the civil population were so few that it did not disturb the normal pattern of the life of every individual. This was so because the object before the Prophet (Pbuh) was not war, but the establishment of a society, which would give peace to all round them. The establishment of such a society demanded men who could distinguish themselves both in peace and war.

> "Muhammad (PBUH) is the messenger of Allah. And those with him are hard against the disbelievers and merciful among themselves." (48: 29)

The Prophet (Pbuh) and his Companions fought a war, which was forced on them for ten years, during his life-time, but this was not their main pre-occupation. They were establishing a unique society which had been given the task of purging evil and establishing good. Allah has said:

> "You are the best community that hath been raised up for mankind. Ye enjoin right conduct and forbid indecency; and ye believe in Allah."
> (3: 110)

He had to train them for this task. An eminent writer has said, "It would, however, be a serious mistake to imagine that Muhammad's interest and attention during these years were given up solely to politics and war. On the contrary, the centre of all his preoccupations was the training, educating and discipline of his community." His attention remained focused on creating a society of saints, a society of men and women who were devoted to Allah in all their deeds. The individual training of Belief in Allah had been finalised in Mecca. The collective training of creating a model society was accomplished in Median.

References

1. *Old Name of Medina.*
2. *The king of Iran, Perwaiz Khusro.*
3. *The ancient ruler of India.*
4. *People who welcomed the Prophet warmly and helped him most at his arrival at Medina.*
5. *The arch-enemy of Islam and the Prophet (Pbuh).*
6. *The Historic agreement between the Prophet (Pbuh) and the idolaters.*
7. *Prosperous tribe of the Prophet's time, the only claimer of Yathrib.*
8. *Leader of Khazraj tribe, talked of as the probable king of Yathrib.*
9. *Prophet Musa who was given Ten Commandments.*
10. *Jewish tribe who was in the fore for rebellious behaviour.*
11. *The Companion whose house was used for the gathering of the companions for the purposes of counselling.*
12. *A great scholar of Islam.*
13. *A distinguished writer and historian.*
14. *A writer of Islam with great passion and enthusiasm.*
15. *Prophet 'Daud' (Pbuh) as named in the Bible.*
16. *Prophet 'Sulaiman' (Pbuh) as named in the Bible.*
17. *Prophet 'Isa' (Pbuh) as named in the Bible.*
18. *A great writer and historian of the German origin.*

19-22. *Different tribes of Mecca.*

23-25. *Famous Persian rulers of the 17th century.*

26. *Russian army person who demonstrated tough resistance against the Victorian troops.*
27. *A leader of Mecca, who gave his consent to root out the Turkish troops.*
28. *Arabic word for Caliph.*
29. *Counsellor of world-famous ruler, Halaku.*
30. *A great man in the history of tyranny.*

31-33. *Companions of the Holy Prophet (Pbuh).*

34. *A famous peace agreement in the history of Islam.*
35. *An important character who guided the Quraish against Median.*
36. *The army who tried to abolish Islam.*
37. *A renowned figure of the British origin.*
38. *A British historian.*
39. *A famous battle of Islam between the Prophet and the idolaters.*

7

CODIFICATION OF ISLAMIC LAW

METHOD OF LAW

Legal Literalism : *Ibn Arabi* is not specifically pointing to some outwardly 'reformable' defect in the teaching and transmission of the law in his time, nor to the fraudulent pretensions or normal defects of particular individuals. Rather, he is primary alluding here to the fundamental—and in our present circumstances, humanly inescapable—problem that the just, appropriate application and interpretation of the traditional sources concerning the divine commands and their historical application by the Prophet (PBUH) usually require a far deeper understanding of both their ultimate contexts and intentions and the relevant factors in each particular case than can be expected of any but the rarest individuals, those whose every action is divinely inspired and protected from error. As he remarks those truly qualified 'authorities' (the true *wulat)* in any age, whether or not they outwardly rule, are none other than the divinely guided 'saints', i.e., the *awliya* (a term drawn from the same Arabic root as the words translated as 'authority' in these passages, and having explicit connotations of spiritual authority *[wilaya]* that are not readily conveyed by the term 'saint' in Western languages). (*James Winston Morris*, in *Michel Chodkiewicz* (ed.) (1988). *Les Illuminations de La Mecque* (Paris: Sindbad).

Let us examine the methodological basis for *Ibn al-Arabi*'s *fiqh,* and then two cases of that method in practice. *Ibn al-Arabi* describes his colleagues as *ummal,* those entrusted to act, among the *Ulema*, those who know.' As with all the technical words used by *Ibn al-Arabi*, this finds sufficient description in the Arab language, which is not the growing and changing language of Arabic but the language of the Quran. *Ibn Manzur* says about the word *amil,* which is the singular of *ummal,* 'The *amil* is the one who is put in charge [w.l.y., *cf. wilayah* and *awliya*] of someone's affairs, his wealth, his property, and his works.' The actual self of the true *amil is* invisible, because the activity one sees is rather that of the one on whose behalf the *amil* negotiates or contracts or speaks. Hence, the description of the 'people put in charge', the *awliya: When they are seen, Allah is remembered.'*

Another word describing people who give a certain kind of command *is umara (amr, a.m.r.),* where when 'they' command, 'He' commands. The superimposition of commands comes about with literal transmission. They are, Ibn al-Arabi says, *umara* who hear the divine Word and give it back just as they heard it, word by word. He says.

This [reward] does not occur except to one who propagates the revelation from the Quran or *Sunna* with the words which it came in. And this does not happen except for the transmitters of the revelation, among the reciters and transmitters of *Hadith,* and for the legal scholars; but not for the one who transmits the *Hadith* according to meaning (that is, not literally), like Sufyan al-Thawri and others believed in doing.

The problem with such transmission is that what is being transmitted is one's own understanding of a particular *Hadith.* Such a transmitter has, in fact, falsely claimed to be a messenger himself. In great contrast, the *amil* transmits the word directly, without intervention and without adding his own ideas or understandings. The ones who propagate the revelation as they heard it, and give back the message as they heard it, the reciters and transmitters of *Hadith, 'they* will assemble at the row of the messengers, on them peace." Because it is easy to transmit literally and exactly, and because it is difficult to be a prophet and carry the burdens of caring for a community, *Ibn al-Arabi* links the *Hadith, There will be a people on the day* of *judgement the prophets will be jealous of'* to this situation.'

Thus, the importance of literal transmission. Besides this literal transmission which allows one to assemble with the prophets, there is another prophet-like activity. That activity is *ijtihad,* which looks like the creation of Law, while we know and accept as a tenet that the creation of *Shariah* ended with Muhammad (PBUH). Given that the decision of the *mujtahid* (one who does *ijtihad)* is confirmed by the *Shariah*, given that new law is impossible, and given that, *There is no messenger after me, nor prophet, Ibn al-Arabi* categorizes that act of the *mujtahid* as giving him the degree of the prophets but without giving them Law. He says,

Allah honoured His messenger by making his people witnesses to the nations of prophets as He made the prophets witnesses to their nations. Then He made this nation special, meaning its *Ulema*, by making Law for them *ijtihad* of the legal properties *[ahkam,* singular *hukm],* and by determining as the *hukm* what their *ijtihad* leads them to.

Then,

Such a one in this nation would not be a prophet, as he is not a prophet through revelation sent down. But Allah made law for the *Ulema* of this nation their *ijtihad,* just as He said to His Prophet (PBUH), *So that you would judge [h.k.m.] among the people by what Allah showed you [4:105];* the *mujtahid* does not judge except by what Allah shows him in his *ijtihad.*

One characteristic of *ijtihad* is that the right determination gets extra reward and the wrong determination still gets one reward. The standard text for this situation is found in *Subul-al-Salam*[1], from *Amr Ibn al-As*, that 'He heard the messenger of Allah (Pbuh) saying, when the *hakim [h.k.m.]* determines the *hukm,* that is [interjects the author of *Subul al-Salam],* when he wants to determine the *hukm,* based on his word, let him do *ijtihad,* because *ijtihad* is done before the *hukm* [is determined], then if he hits the mark, he gets two rewards, and when he determines the *hukm* and does *ijtihad* and errs, that is not consistent with what the *hukm* is with Allah, then he gets one reward'.

There is also a lesser known *Hadith.* In *Musnad Ibn Hanbal* 2:187, *haddathana* [it was told to us in the form of a *Hadith* by] *Abd-Allah haddathani* [it was told to me in the form of a *Hadith* by] my father [*Ahmad ibn Hanbal*] *haddathana* Hassan *haddathana* Ibn Lehyah *haddathana* Amr Ibn al-As who reported that he said, 'I he [...] and the messenger of Allah came and he said, when the *Qadi* judges [q.d.y.] and does *ijtihad,* and hits the mark, he has ten rewards; and when he does *ijtihad* and errs, he has one or two rewards.'

One of the ways *Ibn al-Arabi* explains this characteristic is found in his *fiqh* discussion of the prayer during the eclipse. He crosses over from the outward legal positions to the inward truths to show that if 'the *mujtahid* errs, he is at the level of the one who is in the concealed area of the eclipsed area. There is no burden on him; he is given one reward.' But there are those who, in full daylight, still refuse the light. About them, he says,

But if the revealed text appears to him, and he leaves it in favour of his own opinion *[ray]* of his *qiyas* [deduction], manifesting his false allegation, there is no excuse for him before Allah, and he has offended.

Continuing, he says,

Most of this comes about with the legal scholars following those who said to them, 'Do not follow us blindly, but follow the *Hadith* which comes to you, if it opposes what we have determined as *hukm* [legal property], because the *Hadith is* our *madhhab* [way, school]. We do not determine anything except by the evidence which appears to us, and which appears to us to be evidence; we do not make requisite anything other than that. We have not made requisite on you all following us, but we have made requisite on you to be petitioners of us.

These eclipsed legal scholars refuse the text itself. They do not appreciate that as the moment changes, the situation changes, and the legal properties change accordingly. *Ibn al-Arabi says,*

During every moment, during a single event, the *hukm* [legal property] alters according to the *mujtahid.* Because of this, [*Imam*] *Malik* used to say, when someone asked him [for a legal decision] about an event, 'Did it occur?' If he said, 'No', he would say 'I will not give a *fatwa* [legal opinion].' If he said, 'Yes', he would give a *fatwa* at that moment according to what his evidence gave him. The blind follower [q.l.d.] of the legal scholars of our times has decided that he has fulfilled the duty of his following his leader by following the *Hadith* which his *Imam* commanded him, and his blind following of the *hukm,* despite finding something which opposes.

So he disobeys Allah, in His word, *So take what the messenger gives you, and adhere to it [59:7],* and he disobeys the messenger, in his word, *So obey him,* because he [Muhammad] did not say anything except from a command of his Lord. And he disobeys his *Imam*, in his word, 'Take the *Hadith* when it is sent to you, and scorn my word.'

They 'are in eclipse perpetually, endless for them until the day of judgement. They are not with Allah, nor are they with His messenger, nor with their *Imam*. Of them Allah and His messenger and their *Imams* have washed their hands and they have no proof in respect to Allah. So let them see who gathers with these!

First Case : Respect for the literal words and phrases of the revelation involves respect for the silences as well. *Ibn al-Arabi* condemns the silences of the revelation being filled in with arrogant noise, often justified as *qiyas* (analogical deduction). There are two kinds of *mujtahids,* he says at one point. One predominates declaring taboo and the other predominates lifting difficulties (where the word is *haraj,* about which *Ibn Manzur* says, 'You are in *haraj,* that is, in tightness and constriction', and based on the verse, *We did not make any haraj on you all in the religion [22:28], by adhering to the verses and by returning to the root [asl]."*

The latter 'is according to Allah closer to Allah and greater in level than the one who predominates declaring taboo, as taboo is an accidental thing which occurs randomly on the *asl*.'

Given this, in the absence of taboo declared by the revealed text, one should return to the root. The first issue is about purification for the circumambulation of the Kaaba." *Ibn al-Arabi*'s position is, 'The circumambulation is permitted without *wudu* [a form of purification] for the man and the woman, unless the woman is a menstruant, based on the mention of the revealed text about it."' The restriction is only on the menstruant, 'and not every worship makes as a precondition for it this outward purification [of *wudu*].' So, in the absence of a text for non-menstruants, men and women, *Ibn al-Arabi*'s position is to return to the root; then, we find that everything in existence has a face towards Allah, and in this respect, it is pure.

> There is not in existence, according to the real determination, anything but The Pure, because the name *al-quddus* [The Holy] *is* associated with existence, and this is confirmed by His statement, 'To Him returns the entirety of the affair, so worship Him and rely on Him; your Lord is not Unaware of what you are doing.' [11:123]

Here, *Ibn al-Arabi* glosses the Quranic phrase 'what you are doing'. He says it refers to 'your interference between Allah and His creatures'. The word he uses, *tafriq (f.r.q.),* carries negative connotations, where *Ibn Manzur* says, *farraqa* (differentiation) for something good *is farq* (difference), and *farraqa* for something bad is *tafriq* (interference). Therefore, *Ibn al-Arabi* says, 'It is not appropriate to intervene between the creature and his Master except to enter in between the creature and the Master for good *[khayr].'* The negative intervention he is talking about is our speaking unfavourably about creation; the only proper intervention is interference for the good. He tells the following anecdote to demonstrate this. *Ibn al-Arabi* says,

'I met one of the Itinerants on the seashore, between *Murcia* and *Manarah* [in *Tunis*], and he said to me, I met in this place some one of the Truthful Substitutes when he was walking along the edge of the ocean; I greeted him and he returned the greeting. In the country was a great oppressive tyrant. I said to him, O you, have you seen what oppression there *is* in the country? He looked at me very angrily, and said to me: Do not say anything but the Good.'

Ibn al-Arabi explains, 'Because of this, Allah has made intercession Law and accepts legal excuses'. This is then linked to impurity. 'Impurity is an accidental thing, designated with Law-property; but purity is an essential thing'. Therefore, if there is an accidental property which emerges at some moment, then every other moment remains in its root property, which is purity.

Unfortunately, 'the legal scholars have been heedless of this, flailing at it, but they do not get it. We have already explained that one does not get into a disobedience completely, if one is a believer'. *Ibn al-Arabi* explains that the situation of the believer who does something bad is described as, *One who mixed a wholesome act with another which was bad [9:102].* The bad is the bad but the wholesome act is the faith of the believer (the *iman* of the *mumin),* because there is no disobedience by the believer except faith that accompanies it, which tells the believer that it is something disobedient. Hence, the 'faith which knows it is a disobedience is actually an obedience to Allah'.

This conclusion combines with *Ibn al-Arabi*'s *fiqh* position on praying behind a bad-doing leader, which focuses on the standard legal question which is based on the paradigmatic case of the Muslims praying behind *al-Hajjaj* and whether their prayers would be accepted. *Ibn al-Arabi* says that, of course, one cannot pray behind a bad-doing leader; but let us look at the legal facts. When *al-Hajjaj*[2] does *wudu* for the *salah* and follows every condition for the validity of the *salah,* how can the name 'bad-doer' apply at that moment? Furthermore, '*al-Hajjaj* and others in the context of their bad-doing are believers obeying their faith' that what bad they are doing is disobedience.

Ibn al-Arabi sums up the situation as follows.

> The most amazing thing about this issue is that we are commanded to have a fine impression of people, forbidden to have a bad impression of people. We saw one whom we knew to be a bad-doer, who did *wudu,* and did the *salah,* so how could we apply to him the name of bad-doer during the moment of his worship? And how much more is the fine impression than the bad impression of him in doing it? We have no knowledge of the future for him, and we do not see what Allah did in the past with him, and the *hukm* [determinative property] belongs to the *waqt* [moment] of obedience which he is upon, being involved [right then] in obedience. So the fine impression is prior.

Then, *Ibn al-Arabi* tells a story which is a warning to smug piety. He mentioned that someone 'firm in his religion told me about a man who was a legal scholar and a theologian who was a profligate of *nafs* [self].' This is a clue to the audience that this man struggled with his self (cf. *mujahidah),* and it is the terms of the struggle, not the discreet outcomes, which is of significance.

He said to me, 'I came upon him in a gathering where wine was being circulated, and he was drinking with the rest. The drink was finished, and it was said to him, "Send someone to fetch us some drink". He said to them, "I shall not to do it! I have not decided upon disobedience completely. For me between the cups there is a turning for forgiveness, and I do not wait for the next cup, so when the cup gets in my hands, I wait and ask whether my Lord will give me success and I will leave it, or He will desert me and I will drink it".' Like this are the Ulema, may Allah have mercy on them! This knowledgeable man died while there was in his heart a disappointment that he did not meet me, but he did meet me, but he did not recognize me, and he asked me about myself, and he had love for me, may Allah have mercy on him. That was in *Murcia* in the year 585.

Concluding this section, *Ibn al-Arabi* tells another anecdote about a spiritual encounter' he had. He says,

I witnessed the Real in my innermost being during a *waqiah* [spiritual encounter], and He said to me, 'Tell My worshippers what I designated as My generosity to the believer: the good rewarded with ten like it up to seven hundred as many, and the bad with only one like it. The bad act does not oppose faith in its being a bad act. So why would My worshipper despair of My mercy? *My mercy pervades everything* [7:156], and *I am according to the impression of My worshipper of Me, so let the impression of Me be Good!*'

Second Case : The particular spiritual position of the believer presents certain legal, *fiqh* consequences. One of them is examined in the issue of praying over a person who has committed suicide. 'Should the one who killed himself be prayed over or not? There is one who said he should be prayed over, and there is one who said he should not be prayed over. For the first I argue.'

To support this position, *Ibn al-Arabi* addresses the background situation of intercession. As usual, he finishes his enumeration of the Ulema's outward legal positions with their inward complement, which he calls *itibar,* a crossover. He says here, 'A crossover for this section is that as Allah has permitted intercession in the *salah* over the dead, we know that Allah approves of that, and that the petition for him is accepted.' But we have the seemingly obvious *Hadith* which at first glance seems to refute that background. It is reported that *The one who kills himself abides in the fire, abiding therein ever,* and that *The Garden is forbidden him.* People take that to mean that *salah* over the suicide should not be done, but *Ibn al-Arabi* works from another text which will challenge that first glance understanding.

One key text precedes the text above and has the phrase, *My worshipper rushes to me on his own,* where 'rushes', *Ibn al-Arabi* says, is an allusion to other texts, which are always taken positively. He says, 'The wisdom alluded to, here in this issue, is the word of Allah, *My worshipper [abd] rushes to Me by himself; I forbid him the Garden.* There is an allusion here and a reality, and the allusion is to *They race* [to the Good, 3:114] and *They are foremost* [in seeking forgiveness, 57:21] and *Who approaches Me an inch, I approach him a yard*—all positive images. The root word 'rushes' includes the concept of taking one's own initiative. This contrasts with the usual situation, where Allah 'makes for him a specific limit [of lifespan]. But [the suicide] tries to hasten the meeting and *rushes* to Him before having come to that limit'.

Now, this entire text, with rushing and with being forbidden the Garden, is in a differentiated mode *(tafsil),* and for that reason, it is possible—in the *fiqh* sense—to return to the undifferentiated mode, which is the root, the *asl* or *usul* (plural, roots). It can, he says, 'be brought toward the face which is best for the believer, for helping him out, with the *usul*,' and that 'is a priority'."

When the text is differentiated, that is, made specific and detailed, such as, 'As for His statement about the one who killed himself by iron, or poison, or throwing himself from a mountain', then one can argue that, it is not said in the *Hadith* whether they are believers or something else [and this leaves the way open for debate], so one may advance a likelihood; and if the likely is going to be introduced, we return to the *usul* [basic, general, undifferentiated] texts, where we see that faith has dominion of power which, because of it, the ever-abiding without end in the fire is not possible. So we know, certainly, that the revelation must be reporting that about those who associate partners with Allah *[mushriks]*, is designated that they will be punished forever, so he said, *Who kills himself with iron, among the mushriks, his iron in his hand will take him to the innermost fire of Jahannam, everlastingly, abiding therein everlastingly.* That is, this type of punishment is his determination in the fire. Like that, *Who drinks poison, and kills himself, sips it in the fire of Jahannam everlastingly, abiding therein everlastingly,* that is, that is the kind of punishment he is punished with, this *kafir* [ingrate]. And it is reported that *Who kills himself with something is punished with it.*

Now, since we know that the believer's faith cannot be ultimately opposed, so we know that the text above must apply to the *mushrik,* 'even if the revelation did not specify, in this report, the sort [of person] itself, yet because the *Shariah* proofs are taken from many different perspectives, one of them coming together with another, in order to strengthen one by another, as *the believer is to the believers like the brick* wall, so one strengthens another.'

Also differentiated is the vision of the divine. We know that 'the folk of the Garden see their Lord with a blessed vision, after they have entered the garden, as the report says about the calling to the garden—*When the people take their places in the Garden they are called to a vision.'*

Ibn al-Arabi is going to separate the two events, the taking of their places in the Garden and their being called to a vision. He argues, then that it is possible that, Allah has specified that, for this one who rushes to Him himself by killing himself, His word *I have forbidden him the Garden* may be before meeting Him; the blessed vision preceded the suicide meeting of Allah, and *then* he would enter the Garden, because the suicide saw that Allah was more merciful than the situation he was in, the circumstances which were the cause for him of this rushing. Otherwise, he would not have imagined that the repose with Allah would be better than the punishment which he was in when he rushes *to Him.*

To back up this argument, *Ibn al-Arabi* recalls the *Hadith* we just saw: *I am according to the impression of My worshipper of Me; so let the impression of Me be Good.*

Allah says, *ana inda zann abdi bi, fa-l-yazunna bi khayr [I am according to the impression of My worshipper of Me; so let the impression of Me be Good],* and the suicide, if he is a believer, has a Good impression of his Lord. It was the Good impression of his Lord that made him kill himself. This is more suitable, that one attribute to him the phrasing of this divine report. Well, there is no revealed text which clearly states a contradiction to this *tawil* [interpretation], even if it seems far-fetched; may the observer in his observation keep far away from the stipulated roots which would contradict this *tawil* with eternal wretchedness [for him]! So if he is present in it and balances it, he will recognize what we say about it. In the authentic report, there is *They will exit who have in their hearts the least, least of a grain of mustard of faith,* and nothing else remains except what we said about it. Allah did not say in this report anything but that he *forbade him the Garden,* only.

In effect, it is the job of the legal scholar (the observer above) to argue the best possible case, in this case, for the suicide. *Ibn al-Arabi* admits that his interpretation is far-fetched, but the argument is nevertheless logical and complies with the technical rules of the *fiqh.*

So if we argue for the chastisement, then the Garden is something forbidden to him that he enters without chastisement, like with the person of great sins. The report is a text for the suicide and others, among the people of great sins—they are upon the *hukm* [property] of [divine] volition, because *the man written down in the scrolls will not enter the fire,* even though he is one of the ones of great sins, if there was nothing with him but *la ilaha* in all his Islam in his period of life in the world.

The reason for the [extreme threat] is so that one would realize that the carrying out of the threat against the suicide is for before entering into the Garden, that he will not be forgiven suicide. But Allah is more Generous than that the carrying out the threat be imputed to Him; rather imputed to Him should be His volition and the preponderance of Generosity. It is as one of the Arabs (desert Arabs) described it:

inna idha awad-tu-hu (IV) aw wa d-tu-hu (I)

la-akhlifu iadi

wa unjizu mawidi

When I vow or swear

I may go against my threat

But I would carry out my promise.

There is no mention in the revealed text about the threat *[iad,* root w.d.], but there is a mention about the promise *[wad w.d.]: Never think that Allah would go against His promise [to His messengers] [14:47].* The *iad* is specifically used for bad [e.g., a threat], but *wad* may be either good or bad. This argument is entirely justified linguistically. *Ibn Manzur* says about the root *w.d.*

Al-Azhari[3] said, In the *Arab* discourse, *wad-tu [I* promised] the man good, and *wada-tu (I* threatened) him bad. If they do not want to mention good, they say, *wad-tu* and do not insert the *a,* and when they do not want to mention bad, they say, *awad-tu* and do not omit the *a.* There is a verse from *Amir ibn Tufayl*:

inna in awad-tu-hu aw wad-tu-hu

la-akhlifu iadi

was unjizu mawidi.

There are many who may object to *Ibn al-Arabi*'s legal discourse, but it is not because he is not literal or firmly grounded in the revealed texts or does not follow the rules of legal discourse. But instead there seems to be another reason. *Ibn al-Arabi*'s extreme literalism in the first case served to restore the essential quality of creation-purity. In the second case, he pushed literalism to the extreme and forced interpretations which he admitted were far-fetched. Why? To intercede positively for the eternal soul of a believer. We have quite the opposite legal discourse (if one can even use this term) today: a number of Islamicists who will identify impurity and pollution as essential and general traits of creation. Far-fetched interpretations are used to serve that purpose, but none are profferred to help out the believers.

Perennial Situation : That such a situation is perennial is suggested by *Ibn al-Arabi*'s discussion of the addition during the prayer call of the morning *salah,*

'The *salah* is better than sleeping!' Some legal scholars argued that it was something introduced by *Umar*, so it is not strictly speaking *Sunna* (normative prophetic practice). But *Ibn al-Arabi* says, 'as for our position, we ourselves argue for it as being *Shariah*, even though it is an act of *Umar*, because the revelation determined it in his word, Who *practises a practice [Sunna] which is fine, [and it is practised after him, he gets its reward and the like of the reward of theirs, without diminishing their rewards at all]*, and we have no doubt that it is a fine *Sunna* [practice], so it is appropriate to express it as the *Shariah*'. And then, 'Anyone who dislikes it, dislikes it only from fanaticism *[taassub]*. Who argues that, does not to do justice to it. We take refuge in Allah from the havoc of the egos!'

THE ADMINISTRATION

Ibn al-Arabi and Ijtihad . Frank E. Vogel remarked that Western studies of Islamic law have 'often omitted, justifiably or not, any consideration of the law's application'. This has led to confusion about concepts such as the 'closed gates of *ijtihad'*, where, as *Wael B. Hallaq* noted, we get 'the oddity that scholars should declare *ijtihad* non-existent, while they at the very same time acclaim certain *fuqaha* of their own age as *mujtahids,* exercising *ijtihad.'* Although *Vogel* gives an intriguing outline of an approach which should be used to address this and other issues, I believe there is much more than what meets the historical eye.

Discussions about *ijtihad* are in fact indications of deeply held political positions. Solving the question of *ijtihad* is, therefore, beyond the scope of a narrowly conceived historicity.

Vogel lists three 'peculiar tenets associated with the theory of *qada',* which make the application of law problematic, but which also more deeply evince a radical and uncompromising world-view. First is the tenet that the *Qadi* be a *mujtahid,* one able to do *ijtihad.* Second is that 'nothing but the revealed texts and the concrete facts of the case ought to constrain the *Qadi's* conscience.

And third that there can be no reversals or appeals of decisions based on *ijtihad* of the *Qadi.* Vogel's notes that *Ibn al-Muqaffa* and others must have perceived that if 'this conception of *qada*—so idealistic, individualistic, multifarious, and unpredictable—were given full scope, Islamic legal systems would face great practical difficulty'. Vogel, and a great number of legal scholars over the centuries, favour an 'Islamic legal system' over idealising conceptions. There are thinkers, however, who do not do so, particularly *Ibn al-Arabi*, and it is their concept of *ijtihad* which we examine here.

Vogel correctly links this idealising conception of *qada* to an endemic tension between the sultan and the state, which wants a standardised, centralised, and codified system of law that can be practiced universally and then I would propagate it to every city of the cities of the Muslims, and I would command them to practice it, and they would not refer to anything else.' *Imam Malik* said, 'Do not do so, O *Amir* of the believers, because the people have had handed over to them positions, and they heard *Hadith* and they examined reports, and each people takes what was handed over to them, and they yield to Allah with it, so leave the people alone and what they choose for themselves in every country.'

The desire of the ruler is to codify laws. The kind of application of *Shariah* which *Malik* conceived is impossible for emerging states. The state is interested in one answer not multiplicity, in one mass not diversity, in efficiency and not variance. One tentative contact between those scholars who would aid the state in codification occurred within two centuries of the death of the Prophet (PBUH). Vogel describes it as follows:

[*Ibn al-Muqaffa*] recommended to the caliph that the latter examine all of the conflicting rulings on each issue, select among them, and then codify his choices into a written law. This proposal was defeated, and with it a bid that the ruler—wielding the authority *of siyasah* [political power] with its breadth, flexibility, responsiveness to utility, and, above all, powers of compulsion—should seize control of legislation and thereby replace the *Ulema* and their rigorously individualistic and conscience-based *ijtihad.*

However, other contacts succeeded a thousand years ago and the superstructure of *fiqh* became autonomous and fixed. The contact was genuine compromise. The sultans wanted a codified law which would place all the authority and legitimacy of Islam at their disposal, creating a system of law which would be efficient and centralised, maximising of utility and concentrating all discipline and punishment under the sultan's or state's hand. The *Ulema* wanted a *fiqh* which could be responsive to the highly diverse cultures and situations the Muslims found themselves in; a system which would maintain a hierarchy of knowledge, not a hierarchy of property or be subjugated to demands of efficiency over appropriateness; and a place in a community which sought their knowledge, tradition, and authority. The compromise reached was the 'closed door of *ijtihad'*.

The *Ulema* severely constricted their massive *fiqh* superstructure until it was reduced to 589 issues.' They agreed that for these 589 issues they will proffer one position, which would be the representative position of their *madhhab,* school of jurisprudence. No one would be able to switch from one school to another and no one would be able to reopen the legal discourse first set by the founding *Imams*, even on evidence. They got the door shut on flagrant abuse of legal power by the sultan, while the latter got a codified law and a large degree of *siyasah.*

But it is my argument that many of the *Ulema*, and especially the *Sufi* scholars," were quite conscious of the sultan's and later the state's designs on Islamic law, and that they supported a conception of *qada* which, while causing great practical difficulty, was nevertheless essential to the meaningful life exhorted in Islam. They struggled explicitly to keep the authority of practising *ijtihad* located indigenously, and away from state power.

What is at stake in this debate? For *Ibn al-Arabi*, the denial of *ijtihad* amounts to nothing less than the denial of Allah's continuing, living solicitude and the mission of the Prophet (PBUH) as a mercy to the worlds. In one passage where *Ibn al-Arabi* talks about what we are calling the closed doors of *ijtihad,* he draws out in the starkest terms imaginable, the true location of *hukm,* which means property, ruling, and decision. The *hukm,* he says, belongs to Allah, not the intellect. When we do not know the property of a thing, we must rely on Allah. This act of relying on Allah is *ijtihad,* and entails becoming 'like the corpse in the hands of the washer', which is a definition of being an *abd* (a bondsman or slave) to Allah. When the *abd* achieves this radical passivity, it is as when Muhammad (PBUH) believed that he threw the sand, at the Battle of Badr, but it was Allah who throws—You *did not throw, when you threw, but Allah threw (8:17),* a verse which negates one thing, affirms one thing, and then affirms another thing.

Let us examine one of *Ibn al-Arabi*'s discussions on this issue, found in his chapter on mysteries of *taharah* (purity), when he discusses wiping the shoes for *wudu,* when travelling, but with the added situation that there is a hole in the shoe. *Ibn al-Arabi* is going to use this particular *fiqh* issue (one of the *589)* to demonstrate, again thematically, that it is Allah who Acts, something which orthodox and conventional *Ulema* would entirely endorse, but in a way, which if they perceive, they would find highly dangerous. In particular, Allah Acts; the *Shariah* has confirmed the *hukm* of the one who does *ijtihad;* so h/He a/Acts.

As with all of *Ibn al-Arabi*'s works, the original, fixed and transcendentalised Arab language is used; this is not the living language of Arabic. I use *Ibn Manzur*'s (d. *711/1311) Lisan al-Arab* to access this language. The first word we need is *khuff. Ibn Manzur* says, 'A person's *khuff is* what touches the ground from the *batin* [bottom] of one's *qadam'.* About *khafa (kh.f.y.),* a word that will be crucial for this passage, *Ibn Manzur* says, 'The *khafa* of the lightning is its sparks. And to kh.f.y. something is to make it *zahir* [topside, outward, manifest], appear [z.h.r] and to bring it out. One says the downpour [kh.f.y.] the mice, when it brought them out from their burrows. *Imru al-qays* said, describing horses [racing across the desert], *khafa-hunna [the horses] brought them out [the mice] from their burrows).'* And al-Lahyani said, 'If you keep the secret, we will not kh.f.y. it'. His word, *We will not kh.f.y. it* is, 'We will not make it *zahir'.* And the recitation of His word, *'Verily the Hour is coming, but I shall kh.f.y. it' (20:15),* means, 'I shall make it *zahir',* which *al-Lahyani* related from *al-Kasai*, *Muhammad Ibn Sahl*, and from *Saiyd Ibn Zubayr*. And kh.f.y. something is to keep it concealed; kh.f.y. also means to make it *zahir,* and the two are opposites. And *akhfaytu* (kh.f.y. 'I concealed') something means *satartu-hu (s.t.r.,* 'I veiled it').

Ibn al-Arabi says,

As for the *hukm* in the *batin* [inwardness], we call shoes *khuff* because of *khafa,* as the shoes completely veils [s.t.r.] the foot. So when the shoe is torn, and something of the foot becomes *zahir* [exposed], then wipe that part of the foot which is *zahir,* and wipe the shoe. And that only as long as it can be called a shoe-inevitably with this condition. Here is a strange mystery for the one with sharp understanding. The *khafa is* also the *zahir! Imru al-Qays* says, *khafa-hunna out of their tunnels,* that is, they brought them out and they made them *zahir.*

So in this passage we have the shoe connected to the word *khafa,* which includes the meaning of veiling something, with its act of veiling being the same definition used by *al-Layth* in *Ibn Manzur*'s dictionary. We then have some part of the foot emerging, with the verb here being *zahara,* which is related linguistically to *zahir,* which is the antonym of *batin,* meaning contextually top and bottom or outward and inward. *Ibn al-Arabi* then noted the mysterious—but linguistically-based—connection *of khafy* and *zahir.*

Continuing, we find this:

> We argue for wiping what emerges, because we were commanded in the Book of Allah to wipe the feet, so when something of the foot emerges, we wipe it.

As for the inward realm, the outwardness of the Shariah is a veil *[sitr]* over a reality of the *hukm* of unity *[Tauhid],* in relating everything to Allah. So, if everything is related to Allah, who is then left to be charged with performing the *Shariah*? *Ibn al-Arabi* has a series of answers to this question which he explores throughout the *Futuhat,* but the fact is that certain kinds of descriptions of *Tauhid* (oneness of God) are offensive, requiring an *adab* (courtesy) which attributes all good to Allah and all bad to oneself.

Then, *Ibn al-Arabi* says:

> So the *taharah* concerning the *Shariah* is connected and it is that you associate the *Tauhid* of it with the fact, that you see it as a *hukm* of Allah in His creation, not a *hukm* of the things which belong to creation, like administrative wisdom. We saw that the outwardness of the *Shariah*

> veils the reality of *Tauhid.* This reality of *Tauhid* is related to the 'radical ambiguity of existence'. William Chittick writes that, 'the Quranic verse that *Ibn al-Arabi* cites more often than any other to show the radical ambiguity of existence was revealed after the battle of *Badr*, which turned in favour of the Muslims when the Prophet (PBUH) picked up a handful of sand and threw it in the direction of the enemy. Concerning the Prophet's (PBUH) throwing of this sand, the Quran says *You did not throw when you threw, but God threw [8:17].'* What this means in this passage is that the *taharah* of wiping of the shoe proceeds whether the veil is purified, the shoes or the foot recalling the authentic *Hadith* of Allah that *Verily I become the foot of the abd [worshipper] with which he walks."*

The word *abd* here is crucial, because it is the same station of *abd* which characterised Muhammad and which is recited in one version of the testimony: 'I testify that Muhammad is His *abd* and His messenger'. The station of this kind of *abd* is one which negates any semblance of independence and Lordship, and which consequently affirms that the speech *(kalam)* is Allah's, not Muhammad's.

Another instance of this is the *abd* in this verse: *So they found one of Our abds [abdan min ibadina] on whom We had bestowed a Mercy from Us, and We taught him knowledge from Our presence [ladunna], (18:66),* where the *abd* is characterised as having knowledge not acquired by his own efforts, but as having knowledge directly and immediately bestowed on him by Allah.

So, now we have a situation where the act of *taharah* on this shoe/foot discloses a radical ambiguity of existence. Now we come to *ijtihad.* So, the *shar* is a *hukm* of Allah, not a *hukm* of the *aql* [intellect], as some of them believe. Therefore, the vision [Cyj of *taharah* of the Shariah is based on Allah, One, Real. Because of this, it is not appropriate to contest the *hukm* of the *mujtahid,* as the *shar* [Law], which is a *hukm* of Allah, has already affirmed that *hukm* of the *mujtahid:* it is the *shar* of Allah to affirm whomever. This *[ijtihad]* is an issue in which all the experts of the schools of jurisprudence are falling into the forbidding, without calling to mind what we have pointed out, despite their knowing it. But they have been heedless of calling it to mind, so they have offended proper courtesy toward Allah in that, while the courteous among the worshippers of Allah succeed. So the one who faulted the *mujtahid* himself has in fact faulted the Real in what He affirmed as *hukm.*

The tearing of the shoe, which is outward, corresponds to the tearing of the *Shariah*, which is also outward. Hence;

If the *shar is* torn, it becomes *zahir* in some issue as one of the properties of unity which would remove a property of the *shar* completely, transferring the *hukm* to a *taharah* of that unity which is effecting a removal of a *hukm* of the *Shariah,* just as one who relates all acts to Allah, from every perspective, does not concern himself with what becomes *zahir* as a consequence, whether contradictory or harmonious.

What is needed is purification from this problem; the *Shariah* becomes torn and at some point ceases to be called *Shariah,* as happens with torn shoes. But as long as the name 'shoe' does apply, wipe over the part which emerges. *Ibn al-Arabi* says,

That is explicated, for that unity designated for this issue, is the perspective made *shar,* and this is that one say, *But Allah has created you and what you know.* So the practices of the creation belong to Allah, despite the fact that they are related to us. But they are not related to Allah from every perspective, so they do not affect the wiping. The *hukm* about that would be as we have determined it. In what preceded, the contours of *Ibn al-Arabi*'s opposition to the use of *qiyas* (analogy)" also appear which we will consider briefly below. Simply stated, the interpretation and the application of the *shar* can never admit of purely human intervention, such as logic and analogy.

This is Ibn *al-Arabi*'s discussion of *ijtihad,* and it is found even today. But one need not demand the entirety of this conception of *ijtihad* to still see a lively tradition of *ijtihad* in the face of the state of Islam. If we focus less on the state and the official proclamations of its *Ulema* and more on the lived reality of Muslims, we see a different situation with *ijtihad.*

Jurisprudence : From one perspective of application of Law, the concept of there being closed gates of *ijtihad* is indeed odd. By relying on stultifying descriptions of a static legal discourse, Western scholars have missed the actual function of Islam in communities. The enumeration of the 'sources of legal injunctions' (usul *al-ahkam),* or 'sources of legal discourse' (usul *al fiqh)* was the conventional series of four: Quran, *Sunna,* scholarly consensus, and analogy *(qiyas).* The process of legal reasoning was the conventional one of searching the Quran for an explicit reading, then looking at the *Sunna* if there was nothing in the Quran, and then falling 'back on scholarly consensus, and if no consensus existed, then resorting to the extension of an explicit command by analogy.

This process is a methodology reached after the fact. In fact, the entire enterprise of the *usul al fiqh is* highly contentious. As with most *post hoc* histories, it is difficult to re-evaluate the early history of the development of *fiqh* without the received version colouring our views. There was, and still is, no clear and obvious hierarchy in the first two sources. The *Sunna* gives stoning for adultery, the Quran whipping. The Quran makes circumambulation of the *Kaaba* merely permissible, the *Sunna* seems to make it obligatory. The Quran seems to have the feet wiped for wudu, as we shall see, but the *Sunna* is for washing. The list goes on: it is simply not obvious how the Quran and Sunna are to be taken, harmonised, or ranked. Adding the next two sources, consensus (*ujma*)—(whose consensus? when and where?)—and analogy, only adds to the confusion.

This *post hoc* method, tortuous in its implications, was obviously in dire need of personal interpretations, but the gates of *ijtihad* had been closed centuries before, so the hapless Muslim is constrained. I was startled to realize that the same description of the process of Islamic law which I had learned and absorbed years ago, after four years of direct study of the books of *fiqh,* simply looked bizarre. But putting aside the received histories and the powerfully argued *al-Risalah* of the founding father *Imam Shafii*, and concentrating on the actual case by case debates, I was able to re-evaluate the history. It did take me a while to determine why that conventional description was so jarring: it is because the phenomenon being described is two-fold, but the description is one-sided. As Vogel pointed out, Western studies of Islam often omitted the law's application, possibly because of the linkages with the state of Islam and *Ulema*, to the exclusion of the masses and unofficial, underground expressions of faith (such as Sufi shrine activity).

Islamic law has two sides. There is the *fiqh,* which is the superstructure of interpretation erected on the revealed text. This superstructure sorts and classifies the determinative properties *(ahkam,* singular *hukm)* of the revealed text into categories such as lawful/unlawful; obligatory, recommended, neutral, disliked, and forbidden; generally addressed and specifically addressed, abrogated and abrogating; and so on.

And then there *is qada,* the 'settling of affairs', as we saw described by Lawrence Rosen. The *fiqh* and *qada* are two separate activities. *Ijtihad* is done everywhere and always, despite talk of its closed gates. The establishment of the *qibla,* the direction of the *Kaaba* in Mecca, is a process of *ijtihad,* as the legal scholars always said. Accepting the *qibla* of a particular mosque without personally assessing the *qibla* on one's own is following another's authority *(taqlid).* Many mosques have an old architectural *qibla* which those doing the *salah* today may ignore, turning instead in a direction perceived by *ijtihad* to be more truly the *qibla.* In this example, the requirement to establish the *qibla is* absolute: there is no room for *ijtihad* here to determine whether or not you must establish a *qibla.* But the actual process of establishing the *qibla is ijtihad.* Put these two together—the *fiqh* of the *qibla* and the *qada* of determining it—and one can see why statements about there being no *ijtihad,* or a need for more, sound strange. There are two sides to Islamic law, and there are two types of *ijtihad:* there is the *ijtihad* of the *fiqh,* which has been severely restricted, and there is the *ijtihad* of the *qada,* which is constant in practice (at least in healthy communities).

This misunderstanding arises from not recognising *fiqh* and *qada as* two different things and stems from not appreciating the concept of *hukm,* (a thing's property). The way to see how Islamic law operates is to focus on *hukm.* This word means property, with related meanings of ruling, decision, judgement. But the value of seeing *hukm* as property, and not as ruling or judgement is this: the divine name *hakim is* the 'one who establishes the property' of something; and *Allah says al-haqq (33;4),* meaning the truth of a matter is what Allah says about it. So the key process of *fiqh* is understanding the *din,* religion, which recalls its Quranic derivation—*tafaqquh fil-din* (cf. 9:122)—and that is examining the entirety of novel things and issues and circumstances and assigning them their name," which means giving things their *hukm.*

Naming : What the *Qadi,* who Rosen describes, does is help disputants put names and properties on to their concerns. He is helping them to create a 'metasystem which creates order in a universe that is often experienced in a more disorderly way.

'Knowledge in this scheme is knowing the *hukm* of a thing. And knowing the *hukm* first requires knowing names. In a preceding passage, *Ibn al-Arabi* said, 'And that only as long as it can be called a shoe inevitably with this condition.' *Shariah* refrains run throughout the *Futuhat,* with *Ibn al-Arabi* always insisting on careful definition of names. As long as you have a shoe, the *taharah* of wiping over them is possible. *Ibn al-Arabi* does not propound the more stringent rules relating to tattered shoes—whether the holes involved are one or three inches wide, and so on.

Ibn al-Arabi propounds the easiest position, which is as long as you can call the thing a shoe, it is possible to wipe it. When what is seen is not a shoe but tattered rags, for example, then the *hukm* of wiping it is no longer possible. The importance of names is described by Chodkiewicz in this way:

In the *Futuhat, Ibn al-Arabi* casually recounts an anecdote that might conceivably serve as an exergue to the remarks that follow. The hero of the anecdote is *Malik*, the *Imam* founder of one of the four principal schools of *Sunni* jurisprudence.

Malik b. Anas was asked: 'What is your opinion about the lawfulness of the flesh of the water pig *[khinzir al-ma:* an expression that refers to cetaceans in general, but dolphins in particular]?' He replied, *'[fa-afta:* a judicial consultation, not a simple exchange of words] that it was illegal'. An objection was made: 'Does this animal not belong to the family of marine animals [literally, 'fish', whose flesh is lawful]?' 'Certainly', he said, 'but you called it a pig *[khinzir].'*

Some might be tempted to class this ambiguous cetacean among the taxonomic fantasies of a maniacal casuistry. But *Ibn al-Arabi*'s mention of it on two different occasions shows it to be something completely different for him. What is in question here is the authority of the name *[hukm al-ism]* and the secret of naming *[tasmiya],* which leads us to the very heart of *Ibn al-Arabi*'s hermeneutics.

Most of the application of Law is getting definitions straight. As we saw above, the foundation of interpretation is language, and specifically the language of the Arab. Ironically enough, it is remarkable how liberating a literal reading of the textual tradition is. The *fiqh* approaches each issue with a thorough and exhaustive examination of every relevant piece of information. Was the command made specific for a particular audience, or a particular situation? Are there preconditions? What is the entire range of the key word in question? When did the command appear, and in what context? Debate and discussion fill pages upon pages for each detail. The liberating aspect is that the entire discursive system is designed to answer quite simply this question: What minimum does this command of Allah's require of us?

As we saw, the *hakim* is the one who determines the *hukm* or property of a thing. Today in South and Southeast Asia, the word *hakim* is used for a traditional doctor. The word still retains its meaning, however, where the *hakim* as doctor seeks to determine the property of a person, to identify the constitution *(mizaj)* and to prescribe the medicine/food needed to restore the balance *(mizan).* That this is not a closed system is clear from the fact that historically, the *hakims* did not restrict themselves to the paucity of prophetic statements about explicitly health-related matters, described as 'Prophetic Medicine' *(tibb al-nabawi),* but instead incorporated Greek *(Yunani)* medicine into an Islamic discourse on health and disease.

If we note that the word 'information' may be glossed as `data put information', we can see how the *hakim* operates. The data is data, but the information is the way that data is filed and put into forms, and it is that process that is 'Islamic'.' So the important part is identifying novel things, *(hukm);* the central practice is taking new people with new problems and identifying the *hukm* over them and prescribing accordingly. Once the *hukm* is discovered, the remedy is indicated. Once the *qibla is* determined, the direction one faces is indicated.

The reason then why the *Ulema* (at least some of them) resisted the *sultan* and state is precisely because the state wants to seize the identification process by codifying and standardising highly diverse human behaviour into narrowly defined and static categories. The *Qadi* who insists that each case is unique, is not efficient, and the state can have none of that. The entire project of the Ulema does not fit ideas of progress and efficiency which pervade typical development and social change paradigms.

Also, as opposed to a precedent and adversarial-based legal system, fairness and justice are not seen as predictable outcomes based on repeatable events nor as the result of a dialectical process, but rather as the process of arriving at a unique description of a situation which restores a universe of harmony for the disputants, the *Qadi's* role being that of facilitator.

This is, too, a system which resists efficiency, as does the constant use of *shura* (consultation) for explicitly political affairs. No one could say that the *Quaker* or *Amish* systems of *shura* are efficient: but they are remarkably effective.

Another indication that the project of the *Ulema* resists centralisation and state power is found in its rejection of 'one-man Islam' which involves a denigration of the slow, gradual, and cumulative nature of the *Ulema* project and its substitution with a single perspective of reform that will solve all problems. *Nuh Ha Mim* Keller, the translator of *Umdat al Salik,* remarks that 'each school [of jurisprudence] does not merely comprise the work of a single *Imam*, but rather represents a large collectivity of scholars whose research in sacred Law and its ancillary disciplines has been characterised by considerable division of labour and specialisation over a very long period of time. . . . The result of this division of labour has been a body of legal texts that are arguably superior in evidence, detail, range, and in sheer usefulness to virtually any recent attempt to present Islam as a unified system of human life.'

The basic methodology of *Ibn al-Arabi* and the non-state Ulema stems from a concern with the literal, linguistic meaning of the text. *Ibn al-Arabi* goes further, being more literal and more keyed into linguistic possibilities than most of the Ulema. Chodkiewicz[4] notes *Ibn al-Arabi*'s 'concern for considering each of God's words and silences', but understands that this 'is certainly not sufficient to convince his adversaries of his orthodoxy'. In fact, 'Nothing better illustrates the impossibility of satisfying the *Ulema al-zahir*[5] by rigorous fidelity to the *zahir* or Quranic text than the reading that *Ibn al-Arabi* does of the famous verse [42:11] *Laysa ka-mithlihi shayun.'* This verse, which means 'There is nothing which is H/his similar', has *ka* which must be explained. Chodkiewicz comments that *Qushayri* and *al-Razi*, among others, take the particle *ka* as *li-l-mubalagha* (having an intensifying function), something like, 'There is nothing at all which is His similar'.

But while *Ibn al-Arabi* takes this meaning throughout the *Futuhat,* he also reads another linguistic possibility of this verse. Chodkiewicz says, '*Ibn al-Arabi* completes it by another one, which is its exact opposite. God does not speak to say nothing: the particle *ka* can thus also preserve all the force of its normal meaning. And the verse thus means: "There is nothing like His similar"—an interpretation that, for the *fuqaha, is* supremely blasphemous.'

In his commentary on this verse (42:11), al-Razi affirms the 'problem' of accepting the Quran literally. He says, 'The *zahir* [obvious, literal] meaning of this verse has different modes; one says the intent of verse is to reject something similar to Allah, but the *zahir* requires the affirmation of something similar to Allah, because the *zahir* necessitates rejecting something similar to His similar, not something similar to Him.' *Al-Razi, Ibn Hisham* in *Mughni al-Labib,* and *Ibn Aqil* respond to this problem by citing the Arab usage of *ka* in the statement *ka-mithlika la yabkhulu,* that is, the likes of you would not be miserly, so we deny miserliness by your similar, and the Arab means denying miserliness by you, as *al-Razi* says it. *Ibn Manzur* sums up the problem by saying, *Laysa ka-mithlihi shayun* means *laysa mithlahu,* and it could mean nothing but that, because if it is not said like that, this verse would affirm that He has a similar.

The Ulema who promoted particular meanings of this verse did so for well-documented reasons. *Al-Razi*, for example, was concerned with the *Jahmiyyah* or *Jabriyyah* school of theology which over-abstracted divine attributes and tailored his argument to refute them. But the intellectual rigour of the Ulema is such that ideas, even ideas the author is utterly opposed to, are presented straightforwardly. For example, in the long discussion of the issue of washing or wiping the feet during *wudu* presented by *al-Razi*, one could not discern which of the many arguments he presents would be approved of and which would be disapproved of, until he inserts his own comments directly onto the argument.

Another example of this is with the issue of a woman leading the *salah* when there are men present. There are arguments for and against. *Abu Thawr*, for example, takes the positive argument that the revealed text, 'Let him lead who is best at reciting *[aqra]* the Quran' is general, not specific to men. *Ibn al-Arabi*, as another example, takes the positive argument that leading a *salah is imamah* (leadership) and that *imamah is* a sub-set of being *kamal* (complete) (such that all complete people can be *Imams*, but not all Imams are complete), and since we know from an authentic *Hadith* that among the complete people are *Maryam*[6] and *Asiyah*[7] (the wife of *Pharoah*), we know that *imamah* of women is permitted.

The only against argument proffered is that the Prophet (Pbuh) *is* supposed to have said, 'Woman shall not lead man'. Now the majority of legal scholars through the ages have not accepted the *imamah* of women over men. When they argue, they generally leave aside the for arguments for this case. As for the against argument, scholars like *al-Nawawi*[8], *Ibn Hajar*[9], and *al-Bayhaqi*[10] admit the *Hadith,* 'Woman shall not lead men', is weak (and therefore cannot be used as evidence), but then say, 'But we [still] do not permit the *imamah* of woman over men'.

Added to the for arguments is the case of *Umm Waraqah*, who was commanded by the Prophet (PBUH) himself to be the Imam of her household in which there were men. *Al-Darqutni*, in an effort to divert this argument, goes to great lengths to fabricate a scenario where the men run out to the mosque before *Umm Waraqah* starts leading the prayer. *Al-Bayhaqi* tries to divert the argument by saying that the best rows for women are the back ones; this is a non-argument, because the woman may as well lead from the back rows or between the men's and the women's rows.

Ibn al-Arabi's acceptance of the position of those Ulema who permit the woman leading men is based on the literal, outward, *fiqh* evidence. This is the basis of accepting one or another position. He is also able to delve into the inward or spiritual explanations for the outward truth. The inward affirmation of the outward position is found in crossing over from the outward to the inward. This he does by crossing over Man to *aql* and Woman to *nafs*," explaining that it is permissible for the *nafs* to lead the *aql* (but that is not permissible for *hawan-caprice,* which is crossed over to the *kafir*—to lead the *salah*). In this context, gender is inwardly determined; a female gender inwardly may exist in a male sex outwardly. More accurately, genders operate in a yin-yang mode.

One wonders what Muslim communities would look like if they took some of the positions held over the ages by the *Ulema*, especially those not linked into state power. One can imagine far-reaching corrections and readjustments which could be made without extensive *ijtihad.*

Logic and Analogy : One of the ways in which positions such as this one, which forbids the leadership of women over men, gain sway, is by a storming of culture (paternalistic) over the legal text. The flexibility of opinion and cultural input into the legal discourse meant that the strict textual approach to *fiqh* and contextual approach to *qada* succumbed to sultanic forces. The kind of legal reasoning that emerges, then, seeks to cut off what Allah pronounced *(mantiq)* and fill in what Allah was silent about (*maskut*). In his strict rejection of all *qiyas* which is not explicitly *ijtihad, Ibn al-Arabi* recognizes the dangers of extending, through analogy, explicit commands into realms of silence.

There is a firm boundary separating the *mantiq* and the *maskut*, and to breach the line is to take Lordship on oneself. To silence what was spoken and to vocalize what was silent is to assume Lordship. The *abd,* in complete contrast, seeks to be utterly passive and receptive to Allah's command, like the corpse in the washer's hands.

One of Ibn *al-Arabi*'s arguments against *qiyas* is found in his discussion of *tayammum* (preparing for *salah* by dusting the hands and face). To understand how *qiyas* is related to the issues surrounding *tayammum,* we need to understand how *Ibn al-Arabi* crosses over (cf. *itibar)* a *hukm* from the outwardness to the inwardness. The most felicitous folk, *Ibn al-Arabi* says, are those who follow the *hukm* of Allah in the outwardness and also in the inwardness. For *Ibn al-Arabi*, each *hukm* has an outer and one or more corresponding inner dimensions. First, the linguistic base. About *itibar* and *ibrah (b.r.), Ibn Manzur* says, 'The *ibr* [crossing] of the arroyo.' And 'in the *Hadith* of Abu Dharr there is, What were the *suhufu Musa* [books of Moses]? He said, They were all *ibarahs.* That is, they were like admonishments which people would heed and would put into practice.' Also `in the *Hadith* of *Ibn Sirin*, he said, I do *[itibar]* of *Hadith,* the meaning of which is that he crosses over (b.r.) the perspective of the *Hadith* as he crosses it over with the Quran by its interpretation; for example, "the crow" is crossed over to the *fasiq* [bad man], and the rib to the woman, because the Prophet (PBUH) called the crow *fasiq* and declared the woman like the rib. The likes of that is done with allusions and nouns.' (The word *itibar* is the thing crossed over, in the Greek sense of metaphor.)

Ibn al-Arabi says,

A taharah of sight for example, for the inwardness, is considering things through the eye of *itibar,* so one's eyes will not chase after distractions. The likes of this are not for any but the one who has realised the performance of the *taharah* set down by revelation in [different] places, each one of them. Allah said, *In this is an ibrah for the ones having sight [3:13].* He made the *ibrah* with 'sight' because it is the secondary cause that leads to the inward, which is that to which the eye of insight crosses over. It is like this for each of the bodily parts.

Receptivity to divine speech *and* silence are necessary. This makes most kinds of analogical deduction, *(qiyas)* illegitimate.

One of *Ibn al-Arabi*'s discussions about *qiyas* is found in his justification for taking the position that *tayammum is* not a substitute for purification. In this case of *tayammum,* the key properties in his discussion are water, dust, earth, knowledge, and *taqlid.* Water is crossed over to knowledge for those with insight, and if one examines the Quran, the water which animates dry earth and causes plants to grow is fluidly crossed over to knowledge which inspires the hard heart and causes good fruit to be produced. Dust and earth are humble, reminding the one with insight that we are dust to dust, and that the earth was made humble. Then, the *hukm* of *tayammum* is crossed over to situations where water—knowledge—is not found, or cannot be used.

For *Ibn al-Arabi*, *tayammum* is not a substitute for *wudu* or *ghusl,* as the Ulema believe, but a *taharah* set down in the Shariah in its own right. For *Ibn al-Arabi*, the only way to approach Allah in the *munajah* with Him," which is the *salah,* is to do *taharah* with water or with dust. Because each is set down by the *shar* (Law-giver), there is no question of denigrating *taharah* with dust simply because dust is not a linguistic or rational form of purification.

Therefore, in the absence of knowledge, *taqlid* is required. For *Ibn al-Arabi* *taqlid* is certainly not following the authority of one of the experts of opinion, but of one of the 'people of remembrance' or *ahl dhikr,* which means the one who can tell the person without knowledge that this or that is indeed the *hukm* of Allah, or of His messenger. *Ibn al-Arabi* says this:

> Our position is that *tayammum is* not a substitute but rather a *taharah* set down by *shar,* specified and designated for a specific state; the One who revealed it revealed the use of water for this specified worship, and it is Allah, and his Messenger, so it is not a substitute. Rather, it is based on an extraction of the property for this issue, from a revealed text mentioned in the Book or *Sunna*, encompassing the property for this issue in a synopsis of that discourse. It is the *fiqh* of the *din.* He said, *Let a contingent from every expedition remain behind to apply themselves* [cf. *tafaqquh] to the din and admonish the people when they return to them that thus they may learn to guard themselves [against evil]* 19:122]-and we do not need *qiyas* for that!

Taking a standard argument, that we have no revealed text regulating beating one's father with a stick, and that we need to extend the 'Say not *uff* to them' (17:23) to cover beating with a stick, *Ibn al-Arabi* says this:

> We say that we do not have the exercise of declaring the property over the *shar* [Law-giver] concerning anything, even among the things it is permitted that we be responsible for—no declaring of the property, especially not in the likes of this. If there had not been mentioned explicitly in the revelation something other than this [saying of *uff]* *qiyas* would not have been made required of us, and we do not augment it by the saying of *uff.* Rather we make as *hukm* what He mentioned, and it is His statement, *treat with kindness your parents [17:23]—so* the address is undifferentiated; we extract from this synopsis the *hukm* about everything which is not a kindness. Beating with a stick is not one of the kindness which has been commanded by the revelation in

our relationships with our parents. So we did not make as *hukm* anything but the revealed text, and we do not need *qiyas*.

The *din* is perfected, and it is not permitted to add to it, just as subtracting from it is not permitted. So the one who beat his father with a stick has not treated him kindly, and the one who did not treat kindly his parents has rejected what Allah commanded of him, that he practise kindness toward his parents. And the one who opposed the word of his parents, and did what his parents do not approve of, something which is permissible for him to leave off, has in fact been disrespectful to them both. And it has been established that disrespect to parents is one of the great sins. Because of this, we argued that the *taharah* with dust—and it *is tayammum*—is not a substitute. Rather it is set down by *shar*, just as *taharah* with water was made *shar*.

Besides the peril one places oneself in with breaching boundaries between what Allah has stated explicitly and what He has not stated, between the *mantiq* and the *maskut*, societies yield to pressures to make Islam a culture. Thus, the patriarchy and racism found in culture is extended analogically to Islam.

The contest over *ijtihad* revolves around the role the intellect will play in determining rulings. For *Ibn al-Arabi*, *ijtihad* requires an *abd* who is so effaced that in effect the *hukm* discovered is the *hukm* of Allah. Novelty does not faze the *abd*, because in fact 'Every moment He is upon some task' *(kulla yawmin huwa fi shanin, 55:29)*, nor the *Qadi* who sees each case as novel and unique. Whether desire for standardisation and codification is natural or state-induced, the fact remains that the complacency this produces is antithetical to the perpetual receptivity—even confusion—required by the radical ambiguity of existence.

Spirituality and Components

The attack on the *fiqh* by modern movements, such as fundamentalism, includes an attack on spiritual things as well. Western scholarship on Islam is beginning to recognize that traditionally, the majority of the Ulema participated in one or more *Sufi* paths.' For them, the concept of *ilm*, of sapiential knowledge, meant an integration between virtue, praxis, knowledge, and sanctity, just as it meant the integration of law and spirituality. One problem which disturbs contemporary Muslim life, is that of the separation of law from spirituality and *vice versa*. There are Muslims who elevate their spiritual life beyond the concerns of their daily lives and discard law as an essentially mundane, rigid, and trivialising discipline. Then there are Muslims who have reified the law, taking a static and arid lump of rulings as the last word on a dead revelation. I would like to explore here the world-view which maintained an integration of law and spirituality and offer encouragement to those who work for a reintegration of *Shariah*, *fiqh*, and spirituality. The world-view which sustained the traditional *Sufi* scholars posited the following scenario. The essence of Islam is the *Shariah.*

The messenger of Allah, Muhammad (PBUH), was sent as a mercy to the worlds and a demonstrator of the *Shariah.* The *fiqh* is the application of the *Shariah* to different times and places based on deeply and vigorously debated rules and methodologies (e.g., *the usul al fiqh).* Spirituality is sought and expressed within the confines of the *Shariah* boundaries. This world-view maintained Islamic communities through hundreds of years. It is my hope that by engaging the areas of law and spirituality, once again, in an integrated discursive system like the *fiqh* we may achieve some degree of integration, where our physical and worldly lives are perfected through our imaginal and spiritual lives; or to say it another way, our spiritual lives are perfected through our physical lives.

Divine Guidance : The classical Ulema have a very clear idea of how divine guidance is to be applied and realised in communities. The importance of knowledge of language is seen in such works as the fourteenth century *Ibn Manzur*'s *Lisan al-Arab,* where he creates, *Nuh*-like, an ark to contain the words in circulation during the time of the Prophet (PBUH) and massive works identifying his Companions. In it, as many details of their lives as possible are assembled to enable the *Hadith* scholar to evaluate chains of transmission which testify to a very particular structure of knowing—developed and maintained by an amorphous knowledge elite, the *Ulema*. Their vision is by no means the only possible vision—its formal structure did not appear until three or more generations after the death of the Prophet (PBUH). So while that vision is often either assumed as obvious, or rejected equally out of hand, I prefer to identify its implicit values and its normative force. Once we recognize its normative position, we immediately begin to identify its challengers. Three groups especially have been seen by the Ulema as threatening and illegitimate.

The Khawarij, Batiniyyah, and Ibahiyyah Types : These three groups are present today, so one may speak of types. First is the *Khawarij* challenge. Historically, this is the group which sought a radical Islam, shorn of its cultural, linguistic, and human accoutrements. It is this group which could contemplate the murder of *Uthman*, draw a definition of 'Muslim' so tight as to wage war on slackers or Muslims not up to their standards. This group in its later incarnations could destroy the tombs of the Prophet (PBUH) and companions, as the *Wahhabis* did. Their orientation towards the future and their vision of movement and progress make this type peculiarly modern. Their ideology makes it desirable to erase centuries of learning and tradition (going directly to Quran and *Sunna*, they ignore and denigrate centuries of Muslim scholarship). This type, as it manifests itself in modern fundamentalism, creates clear lines of battle, quickly and surely defining its enemies (Jews, tradition-bound Muslims, Americans), seeks rapid development and success (throwing derision at the traditional responses of *sabr* [patience], and the other worldliness of *Sufis*), and mocks the sacred, whether in art, attire, housing, or occupation.

Ibn Manzur emphasizes their tendency to restrict and make the religion hard and harsh. Among the *Khawarij*, there is another group called *Hurrayrah*—a name based on their locale. *Ibn Manzur* says, '*al-Harura* is a place outside of *Kufa* to which is related the *Hurrayrah*, belonging to the *Khawarij*, because *al-Harura* was the first place they founded their community, and the place where they declared their authority after they opposed *Ali*.' He then goes on to describe how the word is adjectivally used:

> 'The linguistic extension is, "Someone is *Harurawi*." ' He then quotes *al-Jawhari*, who said, 'al-Harura is a name of a village.' The word also appears in a *Hadith* from *Aishah* when she was questioned about the menstruant making up the *salah*. *Ibn Manzur* says, 'She replied, "Are you a *Hurrayrah*?" They are the Hurrayrah belonging to the *Khawarij* who fought against *Ali*. On their part they used to make harsh that which in the religion was an easing, so when Aishah saw this woman making the affairs of menstruation harsher, she compared her to the *Hurrayrah*. They make their affairs harsher in many of their issues, and they torment themselves with them. It is said they want to oppose the *Surma* and leave the [local] community just as they left the [larger] community of the believers.'

Groups which make their religion more difficult and demanding in order to distinguish themselves from the larger body of Muslims fit this type.

A second group are the *Batiniyyah*, a word based on *batin,* the inward, who denigrate the body and the material. *Ibn al-Arabi* describes their error in this passage:

> Know that Allah addressed humankind in his totality and did not honour his outwardness over his inwardness, nor his inwardness over his outwardness. They are dedicated, the ones who invite people [to the religion], most of them, to knowledge of the *ahkam* [legal properties] of the *shar* (cf. *Shariah*) in their outwardness, but are heedless of the *ahkam* set down by revelation in their inwardness, except for the few, and they are folk on Allah's path. They investigate that, outwardly and inwardly. There is no *hukm* [legal property] which they determine according to the revelation, for their outwardnesses, except they see

> that that *hukm* has a relationship to their inwardnesses. They take, in that way, the entirety of the *ahkam* of the revealed religions. They worship Allah with that which He made *shar* for them, outwardly and inwardly, and they succeed where the majority fail.

Continuing, *Ibn al-Arabi* says,

Three groups arose, one misled and another making others misled. One takes the *ahkam* of the *Shariah* and discharges them for their inwardnesses, and they leave nothing of the *ahkam* of the *Shariah* for their outwardnesses. They are called *Batiniyyah*, and they are, in that, in different schools. *Imam Abu Hamid* [*al-Ghazzali*] indicated, in his book *Kitab al-Mustazhiri* refuting them, something of their schools and explained their errors therein.

Summing up, *Ibn al-Arabi* says,

Felicity is with outward folk. They are diametrically opposite inward folk. But felicity, all felicity, is with the group who combine the outward and inward; they are Ulema (knowers) of Allah and His *ahkam.'*

Although there is a historical identification by *Sunnis* of the *Ismailis* as the *Batiniyyahs*, this tendency is found among many scholarly and progressive Muslims, who have intellectualised, abstracted, and made philosophical and symbolic, their approach to the sacred text.

A third group may be called the *Ibahiyyah*, the ones who make everything permissible, denying divine punishment, and relativising all actions.

The *Khawarij* voice is the fundamentalist voice which commands a great audience, and not just because of the Western media. The secularist or liberal voice, which has elements of *Batiniyyah* and *Ibahiyyah*, gets its amplification from a cosy relationship with liberalist yearnings in the West and political power in the East.

Since one could hardly imagine a Muslim who claimed not to believe in the fundamentals of Islam, fundamentalist is not a very apt description. Let me introduce the term 'technist' for the *Khawarij* tendency as it appears today.

A technist is a Muslim who believes fervently that the historical decline of Muslims is due to a problem of technique: if only Muslims had correctly applied such and such a technique, they would not be suffering today in Bosnia, Somalia, Palestine, and elsewhere. And if only Muslims would apply another technique (e.g., 'be as brothers unto one another', or apply the *hijab,* or the *hudud* as in the *Hudud* Ordinances in Pakistan), we would be as successful as the Israelis or Americans or Japanese. The ultimate in technist thinking is the notion that the

Quran is a constitution, reducing, as only technists can do, a sacred text into a tremendously unidimensional and flat document.

One consequence of the text produced by the technists is that they have in effect co-opted the revelation and the *fiqh,* Well-meaning Muslims, *Sufis* and spiritualists, lay and non-academically trained Muslims alike, tend to accept the technist arrogation of the texts without challenge. Believing themselves bereft of *Hadith* and the Quran, they forsake the text and search elsewhere for solutions to the problems facing their communities. The contemporary *Batiniyyah* and *Ibahiyyah* viewpoints have accepted the primacy of the modern world-view. Now, in order to live in this world, they must derive a means of handling the Islamic text. The means derived often revolve around a rejection of literal and narrow-minded interpretations and an emphasis on a moral and ethical Islam distanced from its historical roots.

Views of Technists : The views of technists concerning man and caliphate, for example, are utterly modern. For centuries the Quranic commentaries restricted the entire caliphate complex, described in the Quran, to Adam and the other prophets. Suddenly, due to the attractiveness of an all-powerful modern Western man, technists were saying that we are all supposed to assume caliphate. This ultra-modern sleight of hand allows technical Islamicists to paint an Islamic facade over newly industrialising countries' efforts to gain power and prestige, to treat nuclear weapons as a simple Islamic progression from swords and arrows, and to explain why modern Muslims are wielding such power over environments and peoples whereas traditional Muslims were wallowing in passive and unaggressive relationships with others and with nature.

Nation States : If their nation-states are caught in neo-colonial nets, then it must be because the leaders are not ideal. Logically, if you could install ideal leaders, you would avoid all problems. So the search for a caliph who will forcefully implement the *Shariah*—whose politics must be absolute because they are linked to absolute religion—preoccupies the technists.

Ironically, the traditional view is that caliphate is preceded by absolute servanthood to the divine, such that the only person qualified to lead is the one who is so effaced that the divine rules through him as a marionette is led by the puppeteer. One recalls the admonishment to His messenger in the Quran, It is *not you who killed them: it was Allah who killed them; and you did not throw when you threw, but Allah threw (8:17). Ibn al-Arabi*'s metaphor for this is the *Hadith qudsi,* that is, a *Hadith* of Allah's words, '...I am his ear with which he hears...'

For centuries the scholars of commentary have interpreted (13:11) *Verily Allah does not change what is with a people until they change themselves* as meaning, 'Verily Allah does not change what is with a people [by way of good] [to bad] until they change themselves [by doing bad, and so become deserving of punishment]'. For example, *al-Razi*'s commentary on this part of the verse is as follows:

> As for His statement, may He be exalted, *Verily Allah does not change what is with a people until they change what is with themselves,* the word of all the commentators indicates that the meaning of *will not change is* what *is* with them by way of good fortune to the descent of vengenance, unless there are among them people of disobedience and wickedness. *Al-Qadi* said, there is no other possible meaning except this one ... since He, may He be exalted, begins with good fortune in *din* [religious matters] and *dunya* [worldly matters], and then blesses in that whom He will ... *Al-Qadi* [also] raises the issue that He does not visit punishment on the children of the polytheists due their fathers since they have yet not changed what is with themselves by way of good fortune.
>
> Today, of course, the interpretation is quite the opposite, implying that if only we will change ourselves—become punctual, brotherly, and technically correct—God will make us successful, like the Americans or the Japanese.

These modern technical interpreters are not literal, nor do they have any special claims to authencity. They entirely dispense with the connecting chain *(silsilah)* which links ourselves to the prophetic period, seeking to tear out the revealed data onto their supposed *tabula rasa.* In fact, by claiming to consider only the Quran and *Sunna*—which they do not do literally nor very well—they ignore the inevitable cultural baggage they bring. And this baggage, quite clearly, was packed in the West. By sweeping away centuries of Islamic civilization, they claim to approach the texts literally. They reject previous scholarships, legal schools, and spiritual paths.

They claim to take just from the Quran and *Sunna*, effectively denying the interpretive process and so erect for themselves an unassailable stance. The way to challenge this stance is to demonstrate that they do indeed, bring with them their modern baggage, their televisions and computers, their ache for industrial power and prestige, and their frustration with female suffrage and universal education, thereby coming to conclusions utterly at odds with a thousand years and more of commentary on the Quran.

It is impossible to give credence to someone who takes a Quranic verse, especially in translation, and says 'so and so' is what it means. To be authentic, a discussion of a verse or a *Hadith* must be prefaced by references to classical commentaries. This does not necessarily preclude novel interpretations, but it discourages the arrogance of believing that fourteen centuries of devoted Muslim scholarship missed something we only now see.

The answer of how Quranic verses have to be understood and interpreted is that it is all contextual and interpretive. It is the Muslims who are striving to respond to the divine commands, to live a life of sacred obedience, to produce on earth-as much as He wills—a just society. The way we accomplish what is good, is by engaging at every step our understanding of the divine revelation. *Fiqh,* then, is one of the means we have of following, of engaging, the guidance of the Quran and *Sunna.* The *fiqh* has its rules of engagement, its courtesies, and protocols for disagreement, its systems of logic and demonstration; it has its rules of citation and chains of authority which are evaluated intellectually, not charismatically.

The Islamic life is not a technique. Nor is it an abstract ethics, a vague desire to 'do good'. It is rather the manifestation of guidance, the strides we take for ourselves and in society to follow the straight path. One beauty of Islamic civilization is that so many scholars have expressed a number of positions and interpretations. While this dismays the technist, it emboldens those who wish to realize the general divine command for their particular situation.

One example of a *fiqh* discussion which rejects the reifying and reductionist machinations of technists can be found in the following case. For this issue, the imamah (prayer leadership) of a child, *Ibn al-Arabi* examines three different positions and gives a metaphor for each position.' There is quite clearly no one position which is absolutely better than the others. The issue is not one of the right answer, but one of delving more deeply into the case in order to find appreciation at the higher levels, instead of moving down to a least common denominator. In fact, in order to quiet inevitable conflicts in Muslim communities, some suggest we ignore the details of Islam and hold firmly to the bigger picture. *Frithj* of *Schuon* denounces this kind of exoteric ecumenism, writing that :

> When a man seeks to escape from 'dogmatic narrowness' it is essential that it should be 'upwards' and not 'downwards': dogmatic form is transcended by fathoming its depths and contemplating its universal content, and not by denying it in the name of a pretentious and iconoclastic 'ideal' of 'pure truth'.

Or worse, as *James Cutsinger* adds, 'in the name of a tolerance whose chief objective is of a strictly social or political sort'. *Schuon*'s metaphor is the false ecumenism where, 'to reconcile two adversaries, one strangles them both, which is certainly the best way to make peace.'

Ibn al-Arabi's discussion follows:

> The [scholars of the *fiqh]* disagree about the leadership of the child, *sabiy [s.b.y.]* who is not mature, even though he is a reciter of the Quran. Some people permit that absolutely, and some people forbid that absolutely, and some people permit it for the supererogatory prayers, but not for the required *salah.*

The crossover [from the outward ritual to the inward truth, but not vice versa] of the matter for that is, that one says, 'So and so childishly tends [s.b.y.] to something' when he inclines to it, and since the child inclines toward the property of Nature, and is swayed by his individual desires, he is called a child; meaning, he is inclined to his cravings. He is without maturity in respect to intellect, which is required for the prescription of the Law.

Nature, in its standing, is without the intellect, so it is not correct for Nature to have priority, nor for the one who inclines to Nature to have priority, even if he is inclining to Nature by rights, so in fact Nature has the position of the one behind, and indeed [the one who inclines to Nature] is behind, and the one who is behind shall not be a leader standing in front: it is the opposite of what the property of leadership is about.

So the one who considered *this* crossover did not permit the leadership of the child even if he is a reciter. And the one who considered the fact of his having memorised *hamil [h.m.l.]* the Quran, understood the leadership to be that of the Quran, not of the child-leadership to be subject to being followed on account of the Quran, so he permitted the leadership of the child. He said, 'We gave him jurisdiction as a child' [19:12]—i.e., jurisdiction of leadership—and They said" 'How shall we talk to one who is in the cradle, as a child'? [The newborn infant Jesus] said, 'I am a slave of Allah; He gave me the Book and made me a prophet [19:29-30]—and Prophethood is the position of leadership, despite his being called a child.

And the one who saw the worship of the child to be a free—will worship in the absence of a prescription of the Law requiring him to do it—and who saw that the supererogatory prayers are a freely-willed act of worship, he permitted the *salah* of the child as the leader for the supererogatory prayers, but not the required prayer, due to the supererogatory prayers' relation to free-will.

Thus, without seeking to create a new position, *Ibn al-Arabi* instead examines previous decisions and describes what Allah had disclosed for him about the truths behind the different positions. In fact, in the thousands of pages of text expounding *Ibn al-Arabi*'s special understanding of the *fiqh* positions, he enumerates the various positions held historically by the *Ulema* but usually indicates which of those positions he himself prefers and then illuminates the 'crossover' (from outward ritual to inward truth) involved in each case.

As a result, one gains from this kind of study of the *fiqh* a deep understanding of the physical manifestation of following the commands, and at the same time bridges the inward and outward aspects of the revelation, affirming at once the necessity and value of strict obedience to the outward realm of ritual while grounding and authenticating the inward spirituality of the believer.

References

1. *A famous book of Islamic literature.*
2. *A famous name for his extraordinary contribution to the Holy Quran.*
3. *An important Islamic Scholar.*
4. *Western Philosopher and Historian, Writing esp. on Islamic Issues.*
5. *Experts of the Quranic Text and Meanings.*

6-7. *Wives of the Egyptian king Pharaoh (Fir'on).*

8-10. *Famous Commentators and Traditionalists.*

8

RELIGIOUS FOUNDATION

Shariah: Valuation of Need : The obligation of a believer to the Islamic Law is a derivative of the truism that Islam is a code of life. From another viewpoint, definition of a civilized society, or the social organisation of high order, is the prestige accorded to law in it. The Islamic Law can be envisaged to attain a high degree of prestige in society and, hence, can become a factor for its civilization. Unlike the Canon Law which was not intended for the actual organisation of society, Islamic Law's orientation is particularly focused upon this objective. The Gospel confirmed the validity of secular principles by its famous allusion to Caesar, the Islamic Scripture extolled the requirement of benefiting from the original sources of law. The religious duty towards the obedience of law plays an important role in establishing the authority of the law and ensuring its observance. A particular type of human undertaking, religious law offers rewards in morality of aspiration and excellence in social life.

Shatibi distinguished between two intentions of the Lawgiver: Creational predestined intention in which human will was not assigned any role, and imperative legal intention wherein Divine Will did not impose itself upon human volition. The response to the query, why has the law to have a religious basis, by *Fazlur Rahman*, was that the concept of Lawgiver denoted an excellence of the knowledge of deducing the conditions of practical intelligibles and of actualising them in peoples and states. Additionally, the theoretical excellence available in, and the interests of public weal served by, religious law are the other attributes. In the opinion of *Ibn Taymiyya*, revelation of laws through Prophets (PBUH) was an expression of Divine religious, moral and legal intention or will, and the revelation of laws by instituting them in nature comprised the Divine scheme of physical laws, social habits and human natural instincts and capacities."

As an important deduction then, the rules of *Shariah* should conform to the laws of human nature and social behaviour. This logically leads to the conclusion that for the religion to continue to be a reflection of the real world, the factor of human ingenuity is indispensable. If this perspective is cogently suited to the continuity of the Islamic juristic principle of *Ijtihad*, then, the critical differentiation between an evolved religion and the religion that is situated at a low rung of evolution is marked by that reflection. With this in view, the long-standing pursuits of the science of law, devoted to discovering the principles of just law for many centuries, are appreciable, so that, such principles conform to the Will of God, to nature and to reason." The fact that such a criteria has already been demonstrated for the Islamic religious law does not represent a simple coincidence. On similar, if not the same, grounds the some what daunting and seemingly unresolvable problems faced by humankind, as a consequence of socio-political complexities in the present age, the adherence to the legal positivism is yielding to the enthusiasm in the revival of natural law.

Religious Law-Advantages : Multiple advantages that accrue from the religious law should emphasize the significance of Islamic legal system. Theoretical excellence as an attribute and the interest of public weal as the accompaniment of the law with religious basis have been already observed. In support of these benefits emanating from religious law, and the fact not well recognised, that *Aristotle* and *Plato* formulated actual theories of state and law on the basis of religion, is citable. On other occasions, the search for the maximisation of the efficiency of law has pointed to religious and moral codes. In religious laws the association of obligatory aspect of legal rules with feelings of obligation exists, which is not the situation in legislated laws otherwise. And in order to achieve the excellence of respective capabilities among the observers of a law, the assistance of religion is always complementary.

Morality : Religion is incomplete without a moral code and it is a matter of general agreement, but not without contention, that between law and morality, there is a "necessary" connection. Law and morality are not synonymous, and Hart has isolated four features of morality which distinguish it from law, however, according to his concept of law, morality constitutes an indispensable component of necessary and sufficient conditions for the existence of a legal system." The explanation for this connection resides in the commonness of purpose that exists between the two, for proximate nexus of actual human weal is discernible in both instances. On this basis, the viewpoint appears valid that an interaction between the two is recognised, with the implication of effecting the contents mutually. For law to be founded upon a sense of moral obligation, or on the conviction of the moral value of the system, is a matter of general consent, since this proves exclusive of the personal arbitrariness. The superior criteria of legal validity have come to rely upon the scrupulous conformity with justice and substantive moral values. From a practical standpoint, a legal synthesis of law and morality, and such an opportunity is available in religion, is achievable, so that, moral obligations are transformable into positive legal requirements.

Morality and Society : In view of the determinants of the fundamental moral outlook of a society, not unlike those of an individual, and the correlation that exists between law and society in terms of the former being the reflection of its soul, religion occupies a prominent place. Ideals and morality in a society perform a recognised role in the development of law, and religion functions as their rich source. The concept of Islamic morality resides in the upper reaches of human excellence and in the highly dedicatory ideas of duties, such as are epitomised by the religious notions of "inwardness of sin" and "martyrdom," respectively.

The subject of justice is universal as a centrepiece of invariably all major legal systems, however, the duty to be just in personal sense is identifiable with sublime moral and religious codes. Similarly, the legal notion of liberty may be enshrined in many a political constitution, but the aspiration to individual freedom is not fully subscribed without the impact of the systematised belief system of an evolved religion. Understandably then the view of "good life" remains essentially incomplete without a moral basis, which is regularly available in an evolved religion. This concept of the morality of *excellence,* translatable in the complete realisation of human potentials, as suggested by the Islamic scriptural idea of the "best community," cannot remain without leaving its desirable impact upon the law. It is appropriate to quote a modern legist in this respect: "As sound laws cannot be in contravention of the moral dictates in a social set-up, therefore, the legal validity of laws necessarily requires the criterion of consonance with moral reference and, as its extrapolation, the legal system is in need of conformity with moral precepts being adhered to in society."

DIFFERENT ADVANTAGES

The aspect of religious obligation to support a "comparable" legal system notwithstanding, various benefits that accrue from the Islamic legal system to the society, underscore the necessity for its institution. The *sine* qua *non* of an authentic political society in the present-day world is the exercise of its own law. Any society which has entertained aspiration in order to make manifest its separate identity as a paradigm of socio-political organisation, or even to maintain its independent distinction, for it to lay claim to its legal personality is an indispensable requirement. The set of rights and the legal apparatus for their satisfactory fulfilment, more than the complex of duties, are regarded as a distinctive feature of a society.

Within the meanings of Islam being a code of life, religion as the source of Islamic Law, and the latter-day legal concept of fundamental rights, it is apparent that Islam is a "nomocracy" and the "rule of law" is the foremost fundamental right. This legal notion of "rule of law," in the context of Islamic fundamental right, is definable as the political rule in the society according to the requirements of Islamic Law as an antecedent to the securing of public interest from the infringement of political authority, and it is typified in a pivotal Quranic verse. Realisation is due to the observation of critical legal significance that the freedom of individual is absolute within the confines of "rule of law."

The Islamic legal system, to apprehend its significance in the organisation of a society, or in the political life of a civilization, cannot reliably be introduced without entertaining the vision of the "unity of purpose" as embodied in the Quranic concept of "best community." In this perspective, the legal system cannot remain without undergoing a transformation to become scientific, realistic and ascendant. For the development of the science of law or jurisprudence, rather than allowing the system to simply function as the means of legal dispensation, the retention and enhancement of the capacity for legal adaptability according to the evolved methodology, and divising of juristic means for the system to enter the ranks of major legal systems in the world, are a necessity.

The lessons offered by history are fecund with invaluable instructions concerning the preeminence of Islam in the past, and the role played in it by the legal acumen of Muslim jurists in the framing of legal system. And from a more proximate age, the considerations, in opting for a particular type of legal system by another society, proffer inferences which can find analogous application in the Muslim society. During the eighteenth century, with improvement in colonial living conditions and changes in the economy and political ideas in North America, the need was felt for a more developed law.

The negative orientation towards the viewpoint of Common Law, to have been made by and for a feudal society, underwent change and gradually the law was seen in a different light. To use it as a bulwark to protect civil liberties against royal absolutism was realised, and its utility as a link between all that was English in America, in the façe of the menace constituted by Louisiana and French Canada, was recognised. On the other hand, due to the natural orientation toward methods out of favour with colonial jurists, the increasingly popular idea of an autonomous national law was in harmony with the new American political independence. These political determinants, in the wake of lessons furnished by the French Revolution, were to result in the American constitutional document. The distinguishing features of this constitution were the indissoluble association of the idea of liberty with the natural law, and the inclusion of the natural rights of the citizens as the subject of legal guarantees, with the granting of special legal priority to their adjudication.

The present internal as well as external imperatives concerning the security of society, and to repose aspirations in the future, are some of the more important factors that constitute convincing reasons for the adoption of Islamic legal system, especially when viewed in the light of preceding outlines of historical occurrences. In more specific terms, the American constitutional document as the basis of future legal system was adopted primarily due to political considerations, which were the product of concern for the national security, in opposition to natural tendencies. This was notwithstanding of the fact that the political identity of the society remained at the time in want of completion without a distinguishing legal dimension. The subsequent success of the constitutional document is explainable on the basis of the observation regarding the importance of human agency in the building of political institutions, and the selection of a particular system of law then acquires a subsidiary significance.

According to the Marxian theory of dialectical materialism, the material productive forces of society conditions the progress of social, political and spiritual life. The social foundational basis or "infrastructure," according to Marx, was constituted by the material production and, hence, superiority of the principles of political economy was established over those of private law, a view also subscribed by Saint Simon. The material foundation was assigned the role of acting as the determinant of social classes, institutions and political power in the society. The "superstructure" of society, in contrast, comprised of non-material entities and included law as well as religion, and it was viewed to be contingent upon the material production.

Now, on this analogy of economic determinism, Islamic legal system is the foundational entity in the society with a preponderant role over other social entities, including economic production. The Marxist argument, that without control of wealth and the pattern of its distribution, the genuine scope for equality and individual initiative remains extremely limited, is a profound observation, no doubt. However, with the facility of Islamic legal system in a Muslim society, the social benefits and the desirable economic objectives mentioned in the Marxist idea, are significantly enhanced and credibly facilitated in attainment, respectively. The development of fundamental principles relating to economics in primary Islamic source of law carries the potential of providing wide scope to the fulfilment of socio-economic ideals in Islam. The prospects for the formation of original systems, as a consequence of the organisation of Islamic Legal System, should be to the equal satisfaction of an ideologue or a jurist, and a reformer or a statesman, for the political rewards of ideological originality are attainable in the form of ascendant social order.

The Threats

The concept of law is not separable from its sound ideological character, for it partially at least is determinant of the world-view and the interrelationship of man with the society in all its important manifestations. The religion is of recognised value in the definition of these parameters and in accordance with this viewpoint, it maintains ideological character. Any law, with its foundations upon religious principles, can be deemed to fulfill these ideological requirements more suitably, and Islamic Law is no exception in this respect. In this view, the law is not just the means of resolving disputes, but it is the proper instrument for creating a distinct society. The primary function of the Marxist Law was not the expression of a certain concept of justice based upon tradition, but the organisation of the national economic forces, and the transformation of the behaviour and attitude of its citizens. Antedating the Marxist revolution, the law in the Russian society was not considered to be the basis of social order.

It is an ideological imperative to consider law as the basis of social order and the transformation of society is held to necessitate the change in law. This description of the dynamic nature of the functions of law is eminently suited to the law developed with a religious framework. Islamic Law, with a precedent to its distinction in the past and with an original formulation of a legal methodology for the future, has the capacity for the reconciliation of superior requirements of religious legal doctrines and existential realities to an ascendant outcome. According to the ramifications of the material dialecticism, the infrastructure comprising the means of production, retained a primary significance in relation to law and consequently the Marxist Law maintained an economic pre-occupation, while "bourgeoise" law was viewed to concern itself with order and morality. Now any law in its ideological sense is describable as the means of guiding and transforming a society towards its adopted ideals, but this observation is nowhere more naturally applicable than upon Muslim law in relation to the Islamic ideals.

On the other hand, Common Law which has come to establish itself as one of the major law system in the world, in the opinion of C. S. Wade[1], et al it does not ensure the social and economic well-being of the citizen, nor the effective legal remedies or legal limits upon the legislator's power to infringe upon human rights are secured, and Common Law is subject to modification by the legislature. In comparison, the legal principles available in the original source of Islamic Law are distinctly oriented towards the socio-economic weal of the individual in specific, and the law, as the instrument for the completion of Islamic socio-political ideal of "best community," is legitimately concerned with that well-being of the individual in society, in general. Further, these fundamental Islamic legal principles are deemed immune from legislative modifications under any pretext. And, finally, law is acknowledged to exercise a guiding influence upon the way of thinking in a society, and in conjunction with the historical observation that law is a reflection of a civilization, the Islamic legal system remains an antecedent of Islamic identity of the society.

The philosophy of Islamic Law had the objectives of law as its basic doctrine. This doctrine is a continuation and development of the concept of "*Masla*" as expounded in pre-*Shatibi* period. The legal thought in that era centred upon the concept of the unity of Islamic Law, a subject which was, perhaps, the natural consequence of independent schools of law. Aside from being the unity in its origin, the unity of Islamic Law had a more emphatic implication of the unity of the intent of law, whose establishment necessitated the expounding of the doctrine of the end of law to be the good and welfare of human-beings. In the modern legal terminology, the juristic assertion of "law is not what it is, but what it does shifts the emphasis about law from its nature and reallocates it upon the functional results of law.

With this in view, then, and an insight into the object of religion as the purpose for its revelation, which is none other than the "*falah*" or success of mankind, the object of revealed law in Islam is definable as the organisation of the "best community," in the language of the Quranic ideal, through comprehensive network of acts, rights and obligations. At this juncture, recognition is due to the fact that a position of fundamental significance is reserved for Islamic Law in the scheme of socio-political order, and this treatise propounds a formulation for the establishment of Islamic legal system as an essential initial measure for the law in the attainment of its objective. In this perspective, a comparison with the objective of Marxist Law is meaningful in the instance of Islamic Law.

Justice : The definition of justice notwithstanding, justice in the Islamic sense is a religious value, that is, a stipulated purpose or aim for the attainment of success ("*falah*"). A religious value may either function as means or an end itself, on the analogy of the values in the utilitarian concept wherein liberty is considered to function towards the garnering of happiness as an end. In the classification of various values, a hierarchical arrangement appears necessary, for some values function as means to the attainment of higher values which contribute to the ultimate value. In the "attainment system" of Islam, the concept of "success" as an ultimate value at the individual level corresponds to the idea of "best community" at the level of society. Realisation is due to the inference that the notion of ultimate value has the important implication of subordination of all other values. The Platonic conception of justice involved the best of abilities in each sphere of life and as a value it was assigned a place at the summit of the moral realm. Hobbes has sought to treat all laws as just by definition, but this view proved untenable in the light of legal empiricism.

Subscription to the view that every legal system represents a set of values which the law comes to reflect, is of assistance in the delineation of certain Islamic values in relation to the concept of justice. The Islamic conception of justice represents a constellation of values and, hence, its description is multifaceted. Justin known in history as the "lawgiver," defined justice as "giving to each man his due," and the referred verses from the Quranic revelation convey the same idea. Moreover, the attainment of equality is treated by the moral and legal philosophers as the vital function of justice. The values reflected from the Quranic verse, dealing with the subject of polygamy, substantiate this particular notion of justice. But, more importantly, the same revealed verse is illustrative of the "equality of treatment for those in the same category according to a classification," and is describable as "result-oriented," in distinction from "process-oriented" type of, equality.

This vital Islamic notion of equality is intellectually apprehensible by keeping the comparison between the formal and substantial categories of justice in view. The categorisation of justice in its formal and substantial types relies upon the criteria of the existence of rules, their generality and impartial application for the identification of the former type, and the justness of the content of law is the attribute of the latter. This particular concept of equality in practical legal terms is translatable as "equality before law." Application of law in all situations and upon all persons, in present juristic terms, is considered to be the embodiment of justice. On the other hand, equality before law shares several legal features in common with supremacy of law. The last legal value is the practical essence of Islam; it is an evident truth which is as evidently forgotten, and this vital legal notion is conveyed in the revealed verse of central significance that typifies this connotation of Islam, wherein the ruler is directed to uphold the revealed law.

Added features of the legal value of justice are illuminated if viewed in the light of its opposite. Application of a law in want of just content, or the partial application of a law in contrariness to the requirements of its just content, produce the same end-result of legal injustice. Now, as an important issue related to the evaluation of legal history and to the higher consideration of juristic values, imperfect legal development in the constitutional definition of the political authority in Islam, as a result of the misapplication of "just content of the law" in relation to the supremacy of law, is noticeworthy.

Similarly, misunderstandings regarding the Islamic social values were caused as well as perpetuated due to the omission in the legal application of the provision related to the "equality of treatment" in connection with polygamy, which is an instructive instance of the "misapplication" or "partial application" of the "just content of law." Not without a grave sense of historical irony, it is indicated that, more due to unwillingness for the convenience of social customs than due to inability for the reasons of judicial acumen, the omission in the fine understanding of this value and, hence, in the incorporation of the corresponding interpretation of the legal rule in Islamic Law, not only legitimised but also identified polygamy with the sublime name of Islam.

Thus, even for the reasons of the legal values that Islamic Law represents, as exemplified by the value of justice provided in the revealed law, a persuasive viewpoint in support of the development of Islamic legal system is available. And the legal formulation, described in this monograph, outlines an approach towards the attainment of this objective.

Social Functions : Due to the religious origin of Islamic Law, it is viewed as a suitable instrument to regulate the most varied aspects of social relations. In contrast with the law in other societies, it is assigned the primal position in the social order. The conceptual necessities related to Islamic Law allow it to maintain a unity with religion, which affords a delineation of universal principles underlying all the relevant rules. Such principles exercise harmonising influence upon the legal rules and religious precepts.

Islam is essentially a religion of law and *Gibb*, the famous orientalist, observed that Islamic Law was the most far-reaching and effective agent in moulding the social order and community life of the Muslim peoples and it held the social fabric of Islam compact and secure through all periods of political fluctuations. And it was further maintained by the same author that the influence of the Islamic Law was felt in almost all aspects of social and economic life. According to Bergstrasser, the Islamic Law is the epitome of true Muslim spirit and the most decisive expression of Islamic thought. The needs of society that Islamic Law tends to satisfy are pointed out by *Shatibi* in the enumeration of five objectives of its protection: *Din, aql, mal, nafs* and *nasl*. In the language of present day knowledge, the protective functions of the law in relation to social needs are translatable as the interests of the Faith, the Quranic attitude of reason and rationality in Islam, economic resourcefulness, social identity, and propagation of civilization. This approach accords a preference to the functions of Islamic Law rather than to its consideration as an entity. For it is only in this way, that the law can genuinely reflect the aspirations of a society.

Special Needs of Society : A society having no fundamental basis or higher ideals is normally caught in a state of flux by being at the demands of mundane motives and exigencies. It tends to ignore the demands of morality and justice and creates mutually contradictory systems which are in need of frequent adjustments and replacements.

This background provides the justification for ideological pursuit and socio-political systems to be based upon compatible ideals. Without an Islamic Legal System, such an objective of the compatibility of ideals pertaining to various social systems in a Muslim society is unrealizable. Advent of a society founded upon systems with harmonious ideals is then essentially a matter of methodology for the expeditious organization and implementation of a meritorious Islamic Legal System. In the modern nation-states, efforts have been successfully made to organize and reform societies through law, as law is no longer considered simply a means of resolving disputes, but increasingly as the instrument for creating differentiable type of society." The limited perspective notwithstanding, the significance of an Islamic Legal System in the consideration of national security, definable as the capabilities to safeguard the *national sovereignty,* is then obvious.

The *raison detre* of state within the meanings of the universalism of Islam is none other than to provide creative expression to the fundamental principles of Islam, which otherwise would prove elusive. For the principles of Islam as religio-legal paradigms necessitate the framework of political state for their practical expression, which is essentially an explanation of the Divine intent underlying the revelation of law. The Islamic concept of "good life" within an Islamic state structure is epitomised in the symbolic meanings of the Garden, which represents an existence of independence in conformity with sublime principles.

The Islamic constitutional theory, to propose the political authority in such setting, will envision the ruler as the custodian of the trust reposed voluntarily by the believers in exchange for the maintenance of the supremacy of the Islamic Law and the safeguarding of the Islamic norms of life. The Islamic legal system, as an indispensable instrument for the promulgation and legal integrity of these principles and a repository of the provisions of the Islamic constitutional theory, serves as the primary guarantee. In this background, the Islamic system of law, necessarily inclusive of its instruments for the impartial adjudication, becomes a political precondition for an Islamic society.

Morality in Society

The implication of the designation, the "code of life," that Islam is characterised with, is the claim to a universal value-system. Such a system should be comprehensive in order to accommodate the attainment of multifarious objectives. Religion and philosophy, according to Boyles, are traditionally considered to be the fountain-head of values, but their shortcoming is reflected from the inability of their proponents in making those values operational. This inability, in specific, resides in the lack of elucidation of means in order to provide political expression to those paradigms, which makes these values meaningless from a practical standpoint. By the same token, it makes the systemic potentialities immanent in an evolved religion, as a reflection of its comprehensiveness in essential values, irrelevant.

The lessons of history in respect of the translation of philosophical theories into ideological systematisations are illuminating. As a proximately allied issue, altering of values in the face of demands made by new realism, such as those emanating from Islamic resurgence, is the re-standardisation of the acquired and operational values. The extent of this alteration may be of wide scope in which a transformation from fatalism to meritocracy, from ascetism to self-reliance and from mysticism to rationalism are involved. Implicit in the act of choice from among the alternatives is preference, which is contingent upon values. Accordingly, a preference for a legal system will entail the subscription either to tradition, that is, a static situation definable as status quo, or to the essentials of the value-system corresponding to the legal system, that is, an aspiration to improvement, which is expressible as reformation. Now a "consummate value" is so designated because it lays claim to a consensus in preference, and it can also function as a standard for the assessment of all other values in terms of implementation. The Islamic preference of "best community," comprising of human, political and religious excellence, relies upon the value premise of Islamic ascendancy. Without Islamic Legal System, moral and social ideals of Islam, which is essentially a religion of norms, will be de-Islamised due to shift in the emphasis upon value-premises.

Nation and Law

The mandatory nature of the Islamic legal system is a requirement of the Islamic Law, which in the latter day legal parlance is denotable as the rule of law. A matter of remarkable legal history, this "obligation" for the observance of law that exists in Islam is a "supraconstitutional" guarantee provided for the rule of law, which is comprehensible according to the modern terminology of the hierarchical view of law.

According to Dicey, a constitutionalist of repute, in Common Law the rights of individuals were secured not by guarantees set down in the formal document, but by the ordinary remedies of private law available against those who unlawfully interfered with his liberty. The law extended protection against the interference of private citizens or officials. The citizens, whose freedoms were infringed thus, did not need to rely upon formal constitutional guarantees before seeking remedies. In this view, Common Law offered a better protection to the citizen than a written constitution and, moreover, these remedies were preserved in the event of suspension of the constitution.

The Islamic obligation to the observance of law is of fundamental value. This Supreme Fundamental Islamic Principle has the following salient features:

(1) Absolute supremacy or predominance of the law as a fundamental Islamic right, whereby the political necessity would not become a justification for a departure from the law.

(2) Equality before the law, as a simple deduction from this fundamental principle, in consonance with the term and obligation of the trust of political rule, should have a vital legal ramification of the power of one man over another not to be substitutive of law.

(3) The political constitution is not the source of this essential Islamic legal principle but its consequence, as the legal validity, in general, of the primary sources of Islamic Law is not dependent upon its constitutional ratification.

(4) The legal principles available from the primary sources of law are extendable to determine the requirements of the political constitution relevant to the powers of state and political authority.

(5) As a derivative of the Islamic legal concept of fundamental right to the rule of law, where such a right is definable is not accessible to abridgement, temporary suspension or abrogation, and the right is availed equally by all, hence, all laws shall advance the welfare of all individuals alike.

(6) The religious law and moral principles are coter-minus, with the implication of any legal obligation not existing in the instance of morally condemnable law.

The absolute supremacy of law is an issue intricately related to the possession by the state of coercive powers that may be used to oppress individuals and it presents fundamental problem both for legal and political theory. Since the age of Greek Civilization, law was thought as a means of extending judicious control over governmental powers, and Aristotle upheld the superiority of government by laws as compared with men. In Islam, state or ruler is not of equal rank with the law which exists as a preponderant entity and is not dependent on either for its existence or legal validity. The Islamic conception of the rule of law furnishes a replacement for the constitutional notion of political sovereignty. Legal development, related to this particular area of Islamic Law, is identifiable as the historic factor in the unsatisfactory making of Islamic Constitutional Law and political theory of state and society. Concurrence with Plato is due in respect of the supremacy of law, that success or failure of a state hinges on this point more than on anything else.

The occasion deserves that the eminent Greek thinker should be quoted on this point at some length: "Where the law is subject to some other authority and has none of its own, the collapse of the state, in my view, is not far off; but if law is the master of the government and the government is its slave, then the situation is full of promise and men enjoy all the blessings that the gods shower on a state. As a matter of coincidence, the suitability of this observation is singularly assignable to Islamic Law. The Islamic conception of the rule of law as a broad political doctrine, and the moral contribution towards the role of law, are compromised once the legal prerogatives are made available to the political authority, for then personal arbitrariness becomes inexcludable.

As a matter of comparative legal evaluation, the political and economic systems under Islamic set-up exist within the context of Islamic legal system, for the Islamic rule of law also incorporates the political and socio-economic aspects, which provide contrast with other constitutions." The consideration of the afore-outlined essential requirements for the Islamic rule of law in the light of Ihring's famous definition of law—the form of the guarantee of the conditions of the life of society, assured by the state's power of constraint—emphasizes the necessity for Islamic legal system in a Muslim society, provided "the state's power of constraint" is meant as requirements of the Islamic rule of law.

Functional Factors

Ideology and Theory : The substantive issue of the practicability of Islamic legal system entails the consideration for ascendant social order and, as a proximately related issue, the comparability of the envisaged Islamic legal system with the other major legal systems functioning in the world. In Islamic legal theory, revelational precepts determine the philosophical and political outlook. Religion is from among the sources, such as ethics, economics and science, which have served as the determinants of a particular legal theory. Ethical principles were formative in the *Kantian*[2] legal philosophy, economics was the underpinning in the Marxian legal thought and scientific facts inspired the functional approach of the realist movement. Islamic response to Man's reflection on his position in the universe furnishes the seminal elements of philosophy, and the Islamic ideas entertained on the best form of society nourish the political outlook, in the Islamic legal theory. In the opinion of Friedmann as well, all the systematic thinking about legal theory is linked at one end with philosophy and on the other end with political theory. The preponderating influence of one or the other in a legal theory is its characteristic feature. As can be seen, the reallocation of requisite emphasis in Islamic legal theory will exercise a critical influence upon the envisioned legal system. The ordaining of Islam as the "best community" entails a political outlook that requires for its benefit the comparative evaluation of the political constitutions from the historical past.

Is Islamic Law a Legal System? : According to Fuller, law is the enterprise of subjecting human conduct to the governance of rules. Unlike most modern theories of law, this view treats law as the product of a sustained purposive effort. In another view, a law constitutes a system if it satisfied certain requirements of a criterion. The use of a vocabulary to express concepts, the arrangement of rules into categories, techniques for the expression and interpretation of rules are such requirements. But the most important of all these requirements is the linkage of the law to a view of the social order itself, which determines the way in which the law is applied and shapes the very function of the law in that society. In Hart's concept of law, a combination of the union of primary and secondary rules, minimal content of natural law, and four special features of morality constitute a set of necessary and sufficient conditions for the existence of a legal system.

The characteristics of a system, Rene David[3] maintains, are the fundamental elements through which the rules to be applied are themselves discovered, interpreted and evaluated. In this perspective, all the outlined legal attributes are demonstrably contained in the Islamic Law to an extent as to be considered a legal system. The view of the universe, man and society, entertained in the original source of Islamic Law, produces a characteristic vision of a social order in which law performs a preeminent role. However, from an internal viewpoint, the antecedents of the Islamic legal system are its comparable attributes with other leading legal systems in the world, and the potential immanent in the legal system to become the instrument of an ascendant society. Confession is due to the fact that these features represent a futuristic view of the legal system, with the inference that such a system does not exist at the present. Therefore, notwithstanding the existence of original sources of Islamic Law, a formulation comprising of legal methodology for the founding and development of futuristic Islamic legal system essentially remains an invaluable quest, which indeed is the onerous task of this discourse.

The issue of the basis of *Shariah* notwithstanding, as in the opinion of Gibb it is ethical and not legal, the juristic acumen of the Muslim legists will reflect from the legal edifice constructed upon it. Although *Shariah* is based upon revelation, however, the actual law is not the text of the communication, but it is framed according to the underlying legal values in *Shariah*. These legal values can be established directly or indirectly from the revealed communication as an indication of acts, rights and obligations of mankind.

The criterion of public interest or "*Masla*".was emphasised by Shatibi as the objective underlying *Shariah* and this is a prominent constituent of his legal thought which imparts legal theory the dimension of consideration for society. This view was an indication of significant development in Muslim legal thought and, as its derivative, legal obligation acquired the important new aspect of social obligation as well. An inference became available that, ensuing from the individual contribution towards the common interest, the overall community, as a requirement of the societal obligation, is to pay attention to the weal of individual.

Marked material deprivation posing a threat to individual sustenance and survival, so as to become a cause of moral depravity and to result in a possible incitement to theft, does not fall within the Islamic meanings of legal offence. The principle that offers itself for evolvement through the method of induction from the preceding legal situation is none other than the contingencies of legal obligation, so that, the adjunct consideration of social obligation has its dual aspects. The obligation of the society towards the individual is an undeveloped legal concept even in otherwise evolved laws. This particular aspect of social obligation is in need of juristic recognition as a part of public interest. Convenience in the administration of law should not become an impediment in the development of law and dispensation of justice, and not to forget that law itself is a means to social reformation. To say that the socio-political benefits in this legal notion are still vagrant is a testimony to *Shatibi*'s legal genius.

The legal connotation of the principle of "public interest" or "*Masla*" included its usefulness as a doctrine of adaptability in law, while its revelational justification resided in the injunction concerning with the revealed purpose of Prophethood in Islam, which is none other than the welfare of mankind. In an intimate relationship to the doctrine was the problem of legal change in Shariah. According to its demands, the universal principles functioning as the basis of *Shariah*, included in the Meccan part of the revelation, and viewed as its objectives, are external to the considerations of adaptability. At the same time, the juristic tradition had established that the more specific and concrete rules of revealed law did not accommodate alterations. However, the vital legal issue of the contradiction between the universal principles and concrete rules arises and, without its satisfactory resolution, the important jurisprudential consideration of the interrelationship of rules related to the uniformity of law, as a criterion of a legal system, remains without a legal resolution.

The fore-mentioned issue of public interest as the objective of the doctrine of adaptability in *Shariah* is translatable in the terms of modern knowledge as the needs of social institutions. This interrelationship between *Shariah* and the social institutions, that can function according to selective conformity, imparts *Shariah* the possibility of legal continuity, and lasting usage. This responsiveness of *Shariah* to social change ensures the stability of law and that of the social system, and *Shariah* furnishes general guidelines in this respect. As its logical deduction, any legal formulation which equips *Shariah* law with the capability of responding to the emerging needs of social institutions in a far more comprehensive way than *Shatibi*'s conception of *Masla*, is a proposition for adoption. The realisation is due that elaborate conceptions of social and legal systems can be derived from the analysis of *Shariah*, and this treatise provides the direction.

The Importance

Rational principles are emphasised in the revelation, particularly in its portion which corresponds with the advent of Islam. Observation made by Robinson is then appreciable that the Quran accords a much larger place to reason than do the sacred books of Judaism and Christianity. On the other hand, reason and law have intimate correlation, to the extent that one has been designated as the life of the other. The common denominator of reason that exists between Islam and law, thus, should provide compatibility and complementarity between the two.

There are constant elements in the life of every system, which is a maxim that finds equal pertinence in the instance of Islamic Law. Among these constant elements are ideals which include the rational spirit of Islam. But viewed in the light of history, this particular maxim appears to be less of a poignant fact than a theoretical enunciation. Irrespective of the explanation for this divergence, to quote Gibb provides an insight in this regard: "Islam being an autonomous expression of religious thought and experience, must be viewed in and through itself and its own principles and standards, and that an exposition of Islam should lay more emphasis on its ideals rather than the failings of its followers." The ideal of freedom is evolved from the conviction of monotheism. As its testimonial, notwithstanding that Quran is a code of life, the Scripture omits to provide any guidelines in the event of loss of political independence for believing community. The ideal of "best community" constitutes the purpose and substance of law in its original source of revelation while, for the sake of comparison, the substance of law in other legal systems is based upon the vision of justice and makes its evident impact upon the Common Law and Romano-Germanic families of law.

Availability of legal and moral ideals, fundamental principles and values in the primary sources of Islamic Law, contain a framework sufficient for the development of a self-reliant and ascendant legal system. The giving of institutional form to Islam is an aspiring enterprise whose attainment is an illusion without the instrumentality of legal system. It is obvious, the expression of the source of law into the formal law is an activity dependent upon the techniques of law-making, a fact which is in want of full appreciation due to its conceptual and practical significance, and it substantiates Fuller's definition of law. In legal parlance, the concept of law embodies the will of the sovereign to create conditions of social order and progress among other things, as also the conditions of the individual and social liberties. Aristotle described law as the enactment of the ruling part of the state, while Aquinas viewed it as an ordinance of reason for the common good. Among other definitions of law, "good as defined by reason" by Hooker, "sum total of conditions for the reconcilement of personal wishes" by Kant, "system of rights and obligations as enforced by state" according to Green are noticeworthy.

But some other descriptions like "the definition and limitation of the security and freedom of individuals" in the opinion of Savigny, "rules of action" in the view of Blackstone, "formulated public opinion or that of the ruling body" in the assessment of Holland, "a binding rule of conduct" in the definition by Pollock are illuminating. And yet some more definitions of law such as "set of rules for the conduct of social and political relations" in the words of Holland, "body of principles in the administration of justice" in the judgment of Salmond and "a system of hierarchy of norms as a prescription for necessary outcome in given circumstances" in the analysis of Kelsen are insightful. These varieties of juristic definitions are indicative of the attempts to encompass the concept of law in a befitting manner. The Islamic concept of law is the enactment of the revealed precepts according to the dictates of reason for the "success" of individual in a social setting of "best community". This description of law offers the prospects of overcoming the inconveniences in the way of embodying suitable concept of law, against the preceding perspective and that of the history of legal development.

Overall penal policy of Islamic Law is corrective and reformatory, and less often it is deterrent and retributive. Material compensation, offered to the relations of the deceased in a capital case, is an illustrative instance. An extrapolation of this legal principle of compensation for the loss in Islamic Law brings into limelight the issue at the centre of justice as a legal conception. In no instance of loss the state takes upon itself to duly compensate the aggrieved party. It is within the scope of Islamic jurisprudence to redefine the legal concept of justice within the meanings of the legal axiom of "giving due to the deserving" as exemplified by the cases of violent offences or illicit loss of property. A human issue of moral improvement after the legal penalty engages the intellect, and Islamic jurisprudence, due to its religious origin, has the antecedents for the successful acceptance of such a juristic challenge.

As a distinguishing attribute of Muslim Law, sexual immorality is held in extreme censor and no compensation is available in contrast with capital offences. However, the fact remains, the deterrent penalty is only reserved for criminal sexual offence of public indecency. In this particular legal setting alone, sexual offences are weighed in the scales of justice without compensation. The standard of proof in such an offence is exceptionally high, because no less than four eye-witnesses, adult Muslims of established integrity of character, are a legal prerequisite for establishing the offence. Anyone with a functional knowledge of the subtleties involved in law, will not fail to appreciate the due recognition granted and proper value attached to the legal notions of defamation, human dignity and right to privacy in the particular instance of Islamic laws concerning sexual offences, and the juridical development of the indicated legal notions provides a noticeable source of law in the relevant and allied areas.

Functional Morality

Adoption of the definition of law as the prescriptions for the social coexistence of individuals would necessitate common subscription to certain set of values for the code of conduct. And law in order to secure its objectives of maintaining order and justice, and to provide maximum welfare, requires a delicate synthesis of legal and moral principles. A relationship of "existential interdependence" is viewed to exist between law and morals. The Muslim scholar *Fazl-ur-Rahman* maintained that Avicenna's account of the moral order in the society is based on the conception of the kind of social contract which is operative in it. It then is a matter of inference that the moral order is directly related to the vision of a society it entertains about itself. Law and morals in this sense have come to share the common attribute of normative propositions which refer to standards of conduct. The differentiation between the two is ascertainable, for the morals have the connotation of individual conscience as the underlying principle in their observance, but in distinction with morals, law contains a certain measure for the regularity of its observance.

The search for a standard to provide the means of judging between right and wrong, as a substitute for natural law, led Kant to the identification of "categorical imperative" which was held to contain the absolute rule of morality. Describable as the state of desirable perfection in accordance with rational assessment, the *Kantian* principle was not considered to be devoid of difficulties in its proof and as an effective test for the actual solution of particular problems.

These difficulties in relation to the principle are likely to be observable in association with the "functional view" of law which, in the opinion of *Allen*, pays less attention to the ethical content and aim of law than the actual sociological circumstances. In this consideration, view about individual as the rational being is superseded with the notion of human being as a component part of totality inspired by a common purpose. However, "interests" were viewed as the chief subject-matter of law by Roscoe Pound whose contribution towards the development of legal institutions cannot be underestimated. In the legal history, accepted morality of the dominant group has been utilised as the standard to conform law on innumerable instances. On the contrary, Islamic Law has the standards available that can best be described as belonging to "high morality." And it is for this simple reason that law in Islamic society is always deemed to be in advance of accepted morality. Islamic code of morality accepts all human beings as entitled to equal consideration and respect. The legal expression of the standard of morality is reflected in a legal system which extends equal treatment to all human beings within its scope, as entitled to the equal protection and obligation in the observance of law. This fundamental right of all human beings, without any exception, to equal consideration of law has constitutional merits whose legal sinews can lend socio-political stability to the society.

End to Problems

In describing eight ways in failing to make law, Fuller mentions that a total failure in anyone of these directions not only results in a defective system of law, but it also results in something that is not properly called a legal system. The failure of congruence between rules as announced and their administration, and the enactment of contradictory rules are two such ways. The implications of the former way are the misinterpretation or misapplication of law. A modality for the evaluation of these faulty implications can be the empirical results of law. As a matter of general acknowledgment, Islamic Law of divorce or repudiation leads to appalling lack of security in marital life. In recent past, an attempt at improved lawmaking in the relevant area was undertaken by the Syrian jurists. In order to discourage a capricious and unjustifiable repudiation of wife, and giving concession to public weal, in the event of repudiation without "reasonable" cause whereby the wife has suffered material damage, the provision in law was made available to demand a compensation from the husband. From the viewpoint of those not acquainted with the subject of law-making, noticeworthy is the making use of the original provisions in the Quran whereby the option of repudiation is to be exercised "with consideration" along with the making of a "fair provision" for the spouse so repudiated.

The elegance in law-making in this instance is reflected from the contextual reliance upon the original source, nonliteral or logical interpretation of law and the proper focus upon the objectives of law. The exercise of "*Ijtihad*" in comparison with the retention of, and, in this respect, the assimilation of the empirical results of, the traditional Islamic Law, is also evident. In the Tunisian Law of Personal Status 1957, repudiation was declared a judicial process whereby it became devoid of any legal effect if transpired outside the court of law. The reliance was placed upon the authority of the revealed verse wherein the arbitration is advised in case of the surfacing of discord between spouses. The requirement of arbitration was adopted as the basis for judicial evaluation, and discord as a wide-meaning term was specifically interpreted to include repudiation. And, importantly, the parity of legal status was granted to both spouses in the matter of repudiation, and the authority of the revealed verse wherein the equality of "rights" between men and women is stipulated, was relied upon.

Against the afore-outlined perspective, it evokes surprise to consider traditional Islamic Law of repudiation that prevailed over the last many centuries and indeed holds legal sway in the present time in many a Muslim society.

At once an exemplification of misconceptions about, and an instance of erroneous, law-making in Islam, the law of repudiation should serve as a prototypical example for the "reinterpretation" of the original sources of law in Islam. The philosophy of the Islamic Law of repudiation is the availability of divorce in the face of breakdown of marriage. The revealed provisions for the placement of authoritative reliance would include the juristic values of the use of "consideration" in the matter of repudiation, the apportioning of "fair provision" for the female spouse after repudiation, the equality of legal status in the exercise of "right" to repudiation between both the spouses, and the exercise of judicial "arbitration" to attempt reconciliation or, in the event of no other alternative, to impart legal effect to repudiation.

The revealed injunctions concerning the repudiation are thus numerous, and in conjunction with the rules related to the general subject of women, are in consonance with the general objectives of the revealed law for the improvement of women's status. This general objective, effected in the original source of

Islamic Law, represents some of the most revolutionary reformation of the Arabian customary law prevalent prior to the advent of Islam.

The Scriptural legal concept of "waiting period" or "*idda*," after the formal repudiation and before it takes effect, is essentially meant for the purpose of bringing about social justice and reconciliation during the stipulated period. Thus, it is an evidence of the typical misconception that ironically persists concerning the Islamic laws whereby the repudiation of marriage in Islam is held to be of instantaneous effect.

The repeated injunction to "retain wives honourably or release them with kindness," ought to find its practical implementation in the legal corpus. Therein the rules should be designed for women in general, keeping in view their "honour" as spouses, which is surely unattainable without the acquisition of a corresponding or dignifying social status, and the granting of recourse in the attainment of "equal rights" for women, in society.

An intimately related area in Islamic Law, which had proximate bearing upon the subject of "honourable" status, or equality of rights of women in society, is the general perception of polygamy being expressly permitted according to traditional Islamic Law. Now there is nothing more contrary to the readily ascertainable facts than this long-standing misapplication of law, derived from its original source. The unwholesome impact this particular law left upon the status of women in Islamic society, and the misperceptions it created about the Muslim culture in the view of other civilization, were ironically avoidable for being baseless. To leave the issue of "unattainable equality" of treatment for plural wives, according to the revealed injunction, to the conscience of individual husband, without transforming it into legal condition in Islamic Law, was an obvious misinterpretation of the relevant primary source of law.

This becomes manifest from the perusal of the revealed verse even to those who are not initiated into the subtle demands of law-making. Islamic Law about polygamy is amply instructive; it is also demonstrative of the continuing force of the customary law. Wise nature reserves ridicule for erring in religious laws, besides exacting a retribution of sorts. In the final analysis, the epithet of polygamy is incorrect for being unsustainable on legal grounds and, literally it is the mistaken substitute of polygyny.

The Islamic penal policy is censured for prescribing amputation of hands as a legal penalty for the crime of theft. Astonishingly, no period in Islamic history is recognizable for the adoption of this legal punishment. The explanation resides in the immediately next revealed verse wherein the essential Islamic principle of repentance is invoked for the mitigation of the penalty under review......

The inductive reasoning discloses the invaluable principle of equity, described by Aristotle as a superior form of justice. Distinctions are an indispensable function of law and the making of distinctions between retribution and deterrent penalties in Islamic Law is its salient legal feature.

The participation in holy defensive war in Islam is composite of the twin "rights of God and man." The latter is an individual "obligation" towards the preparedness of society for an Islamic defensive war." The right of God ensues from the requirement of participation in defensive war in the event of general proclamation of *Jihad*, as a religious obligation enunciated in several revealed injunctions. Islam is a religion of peace and the title itself is its indication, but due to the fact that Islamic religious precepts emphasize life as a constant striving or *Jihad*, Islamic philosophy of war is a natural culmination of this ideological view. The characteristic universality of Islam, according to which the gamut of rights and responsibilities are in principle availed and borne equally by all the faith-abiding individuals, is an additional foundational principle of that philosophy. Another such principle is derived from the title Islam in its sense of peace, and the essentially "defensive" outlook of the religious war is its resultant. However, the intricateness of the science of war prescribes deterrent and preemptive considerations as inalienable components of the defensive outlook.

The evident advantages accruing from this Islamic philosophy of self-defence are axiomatic in latter-day literature concerning military defence, such as the concepts of national war, total preparedness and ensured peace. The benefits of individualism are combined with those of disciplined formations, as a distinction of Islamic defensive organisation. The bane of idolisation of armaments, the self-destructive proportions of economic expenditure on national scale, incurred on present-day defence preparations, will be mitigated by the adoption of Islamic philosophy of war. Noticeworthy is the fact, legal obligation has intimate correlation with the vital issue of individual capacity in its fulfilment and, therefore, obligations and corresponding rights have indissoluble linkage. The obligation of holy defensive war earns the individual a right to the ownership of firearm, whose detail comes within the jurisdiction of national consensus, as well as right of the access to a framework of defensive training, available at the national level.

An irony of history, inability or unwillingness to transform religious obligations into legal relationships in the sphere of holy defensive war or *Jihad* must have transfigured itself into sin incurred in religious terms, into missing the contribution towards excellence of ideas in ideological terms, and into neglecting the ascendancy of society in political terms. Censure is assignable either to the benign piety of religious scholars, or to the law-making genius of the jurists, that the obligation of *Jihad* is not included in the five proverbial pillars or obligations of Islam. The invaluable instruction deducible from the allegory of Fall as a part of the Islamic Scripture or from the versified description provided by Milton, howsoever the incident is viewed, it is the lamentable outcome of the disobedience to "high injunction. The foremost task in relation to "Islamic Nomocracy" is the translation of religious and ethical duties in terms of legal relationships. In order to retain its ascendancy, the great belief-system lays obligation of expertise in the framing and formulation of laws, founded upon its primary sources. The "retribution for sin" and the telling disadvantage due to erroneous law-making are nowhere else more evident, perhaps, than in the area of the doctrine of the separation of powers, to describe it in current terminology, and emphasised by Montesquieu.

The ideological translation for the religion of Islam is Nomocracy, with the understanding of the term ideology in the easily apprehensible meanings of the systematisation of ideals for the organisation of social systems and institutions. The common denominator in both is law; in the one it is constituted by the revealed tenets, and in the other, it is derived through the exercise and exertion of juristic acumen from the original sources of Islamic Law. A matter of common appreciation, involvement of rules necessitates arbitration, which is effective to the extent it is judicious and impartial-prerequisites which can be illusive unless the process is uninfluenced and uninterfered. A rational justification for the scriptural requirement of upholding justice during adjudication is available, if any is needed, whereby the justness is conscientious adherence to the revealed law." The judicial independence in Islam would have reflected from the development of constitutional law, or in more specific terms, from the definition and limitation of political authority in traditional Islam. This key-measure would have gone a long way in harnessing the benefits of ample juristic genius that existed in traditional Islam, and a remarkably evolved polity with an original constitution would have been its rewards.

Study in Comparison

The socialist laws adopted a revolutionary character in order to accommodate the objectives of overturning the society and creating the conditions of a new social order in which the concepts of state and law would cease to exist. However, the law was considered secondary to the purpose of creating new economic structure, which was an explanation for the collectivisation of all means of production. Economic infrastructure was deemed to condition and determine the legal system, thus, the framing of rules by the legislature, as its sole means, was of subsidiary significance as a source. The Civil Code of Egypt 1949 represented a compromise between traditional Islamic Law and adopted Western Systems, wherein the elements drawn from other contemporary codes were selected on the basis of their general consonance with Shariah Law. A brief comparison among Islamic Law, Common Law and Romano-Germanic Law is provided in other parts of this discourse.

The Islamic Law will be identified with evolutionary character in its objective of organising the "best community." Social control will be effected with the purpose of facilitating the individual attainment of success ("*falah*"). From the fundamental legal concept of the sovereignty of law, the definition and limitation of political authority, the fundamental individual right to the rule of Islamic Law, and socio-political system with the designation of nomocracy will be the natural derivations. For the reasons of comparison solely, the obvious is reiterated that due to the primal status of law in the Islamic social order, the political and economic systems are to be determined by the legal system. Due to the universalism of Islam, in the sense of being the evolutionary culmination representing the long duration of time in the memorable history of mankind, an expanded base can be envisaged for the source of its law. The comparability with the prominent systems of law in the contemporary era is a consideration in which the issues of the practicability and originality of the system are necessarily implicit, and it is a prerequisite for the organisation of Islamic legal system, which cannot be left unheeded.

Law and Religion

The value of legal concepts in law-making is of basic importance, which serve as the means of interpretation, legal reasoning and grounds for legal decisions. Moreover, adherence to law is facilitated as the reverence for law in society is enhanced. Besides, those concepts become the source of actual and derived principles for social organisation. As vital considerations for the legal relationships involving interpersonal relations, and association between the state and citizens, are the added functions of the legal concepts.

In religion reliance is reposed in various ideas, while several of them are synonymous with legal conception and others can find ready accommodation and legal utilisation in that category. As a matter of common knowledge, Islam is the result of religious evolutionary process, wherein evolutionary change is not to be understood as a necessary deviation from the immutable ideal standards, but as an improvement upon the previous stage of existence. A natural requirement of monotheism, the fundamental belief in the unity of God is a fecund source for the logical derivation of the legal concepts such as human equality, freedom from another source of submission, and social cohesion.

The objectives of *Shariah* law coincide with the legal ideas of public interest, justice and equity. Implicit in the religious concept of the vicegerency of man are the deductible legal concepts of human equality, dignity of man, and recognition of individual's status in society. The importance accorded to the "right of man" in Islam, is a testimonial to these legal values, which acts as an additional dimension of social obligation to the basic concept of legal obligation, which has already been dwelt upon. The religious requirements for the participation in religious defensive war or *Jihad* explicitly accord precedence to individual self-determination over any external imposition upon the option to fulfill the obligation. This revealed value is exclusive of any impelling interference in the decision for participation in *Jihad*, and allows complete freedom to individual conscience. The legal development of this value has immanent ideological benefits to impart the society an ascendant and distinctive institutional attribute.

The essential Islamic doctrine of accountability as a prelude to the reward and retribution is the practical expression of the underlying functional idea of the independence and right of informed choice. Without the exercise of this individual prerogative, justification for religious responsibility and availability of moral code does not arise.

The adoption of this fundamental Islamic doctrine of accountability as a legal conception has the capacity to impart new dimensions to the political constitution. To hold the political authority accountable, any time in future for the decisions which adversely influenced the social order, will be a positive step towards the development of constitutional law and towards tangible improvement in the quality of statesmanship as well as public service.

A religion in which conversion to Islamic faith is dependent upon an affirmation, the simplest in its prerequisites and ceremony among all such requirements of other faiths in the world, and wherein the followers of other revealed religions are described as "people of the Book," and their prophets are accorded utmost reverence as a matter of religious belief, cannot but lay claim to the distinction of religious tolerance. In relation to this vital truth that lends identity to the universality of Islam-the revealed tenet of the "unity of revelation" has been left unheeded and unavailed—Kalam Azad[4] made this laconic observation: "In fact no other truth of the Quran has been kept so deliberately out of sight." Hence, the legal conception of religious freedom as an individual right is likely to influence the substantive legal issues of political and economical emancipation within the meanings of that right, which will also serve as a test of the legal expression of the conception.

This rewarding and chaffenging subject, which affords new vistas in the sphere of law-making, is concluded with the suggestion that several other religious and humanitarian principles are available for adoption as legal conceptions to benefit the legal development immeasurably.

Alteration and Betterment

Islamic Jurisprudence : The Quranic legislation is not a legal code nor there is an attempt to deal with any legal topic comprehensively. Within the meanings of the code of life, however, the revelation contains certain universal principles, doctrines and injunctions utilizable in the making of law. The fact of remarkable value nevertheless remains, the Quran as the source of law is of much profounder legal import than it has so far been realised, and this point has already been elucidated.

In this perspective, the extraordinary belief in the Scripture, to contain the principles and guidelines to resolve the practical issues in life, appears to be suited to the genius of a master mind in law-making in order to fathom its juristic value and harness its legal potentials.

Islamic jurisprudence is to be defined as the science of law, or systematised knowledge, that concerns with the fundamental principles underlying the revealed precepts of legal value, and their use in the interpretation and development of law. Its additional function is to consider the ultimate effect which would be produced if each rule is applied to an indefinite number of similar cases, and to provide such selectivity in that application as to produce the greatest advantages to the society and to the Islamic objectives of law. Hence, it can be viewed as the science of ascertaining, understanding and systematic application of the fundamental principles of law towards the completion of the outlined jurisprudential functions.

It is a part of the evolvement of systematic approach to the "finding" of laws, consistent with the demands of its original sources and, therefore, to establish a consistency of principles and methodology, in contrast with juristic convenience. Its concern naturally then devolves upon the "ought" of law signifying an obligation towards the Islamic "rightness" of law. In this context, the past of traditional Islamic Law or "*fiqh*" is relevant to the extent of drawing valuable lessons in the legal development, as a possible source of law, and in the ascertainment of causative factors involved in the coming of "*fiqh*" to a disuse. In addition, the definition, elucidation and further development of the legal concepts and values in relation to the Quranic concept of "best community" is a function of Islamic jurisprudence.

In comparison, according to Coulson, Islamic jurisprudence in the past was the science of understanding and ascertaining the preordained law of Shariah. On the other hand, Kelsen's definition of jurisprudence reflected his theoretical concern with the legal task of rational reconstruction in the distinction of law and jurisprudence. In this regard, the following observation made by Kelsen is pertinent: "It is the task of the science of law to represent the law of a community, that is, the material produced by the legal authority in the law-making procedure, in the form of statements to the effect that if such and such conditions are fulfilled, then such and such sanction shall follow." The term "represent" is a substitute for rational reconstruction, and to construct the representation of the legal material produced by the law-making authority is the function of jurisprudence or the science of law.

The Rules : Legal rules are not accepted as a determinant factor in the characterisation of a law, and constitute an inappropriate criteria in the ascertaining of essentially salient features of identification for a legal system. However, rules in themselves have their own significance, and they are not to be viewed as merely legal measures appropriate to the solution of concrete cases. The orientation of society towards certain aims is facilitated by legal rules through the formation of public opinion. Within the meanings of the function of law, rule acts as a model of social organisation and, therefore, it is considered of assistance in the building of a new society. With these properties of legal rule in view, in the opinion of Rene David, it should be the product of reflection based upon the consideration of justice, morality, policy and consonance of the system. The rules, as an expression of law which is to be deemed as the main instrument for the realisation of Islamic objectives, are means for the organisation of a society with distinguishable characteristics. The significance of the legal techniques, to develop or define rules, as a source of law is self-evident. Thus the method for the deduction of rules from the revealed sources, in particular, such as would evaluate the text in account with the whole context, and the principles distinctly guiding the policy of the revealed injunction to impart it the real meanings, has its fundamental importance in Islamic legal system.

Vision, World-view and Law : In the understanding of life and universe resides the solution to the "practical problems of existence." Hence, the comprehension of the sublime wisdom and substantive practical meanings of the scriptural precept about the revelation actually intended for those in possession of "understanding" is facilitated. The adoption of that view as a guiding principle for the resolution of practical Islamic issues has rational justification. Such a coherent understanding comprises the world-view, the rationale of being, and man's place in the universe, for these are the partial constituents of the purpose underlying the creation of universe and life. Indeed, the vision that is nurtured by that understanding is the reason for the existence of Islamic society, and the warning of the Hebrew sage that without a vision the people perish, has its historical and revelational basis. Any philosophy of the law, that does not take into account these vital considerations, cannot become the sound foundation of a universal legal system. The establishment of such a system will prove elusive without the intellectual apprehension of the attitude of original Muslim jurists. The vision and clarity of legal perception attributable to *Shafii* and the juristic originality ascribable to *Hanifa* can serve as the paradigms for the evolution of Islamic Law in its new age.

Fundamental Elements in Islamic Law : The view of social order determines the way in which the law is applied and shapes the very functions of the law in that society. The Islamic social context conforms to the characteristic scriptural conception of the Muslim community and serves as a "given factor" in law, which must be operative in the construction and the definition of its function. The realisation of the significance of this observation is a vital factor in the formulation of legal methodology founded upon the Supreme Fundamental Islamic Principles, described in the ensuing sections of this treatise.

Such an approach desirably maintains the distinction between law and legal concepts and it provides full expression to law in the administration of justice, as an Islamic legal distinction. The need to reconcile the various functions of the state with the cherished principles derived from the Islamic fundamental of monotheism, or "*Tauhid*," is also fulfilled. The Supreme Fundamental Principle of the beneficence of mankind as the underlying purpose of the institution of Prophethood in Islam is translatable in juristic terms to be the public interest, with the added meanings of public welfare, and associated legal concept of equity. Augmentation of the judicial independence as a prerequisite for the citizenship-characterised by "equal" citizens and not subjects-is in accordance with the essential requirements of the Quranic rule of law.

This accords the benefit of Islamic Law within the meanings of essential Islamic right, with the important implication of adjudication under the provisions of Islamic Law and, in the present circumstances, it becomes a judicial responsibility. A juristic formulation, that provides satisfactory expression to the fulfilment of these legal requirements ensuing from the fundamental Islamic principles, ensures the practicability of law according to actual Islamic demands.

The Legal Formulation : In Islam the opportunistic proclivities of society cannot be the exclusive determinant of law which only operates within the boundaries of the norms and principles, irrevocably established in the revelation. The justification for legal reforms on the grounds of social necessity *per se* demands the furnishing of a juristic basis in, and sustenance from, the revealed principles in order for the reforms to retain the verifiable validity of Islamic Law. Therefore, a formulation for the purpose of definition and limitation of the juristic basis is indicated. For such a framework to function as a formative instrument of the law, and as the enabling means for the juristic expression of legal concepts which are pivotal in the performance of social functions, assignable to the legal system, is meritorious.

The legal emphasis upon the humanitarian principles, enshrined in the Islamic sources of law, and to impart the juristic direction to the "ought" of law with the Islamic connotations, will be desirable features of such a legal formulation. The non-repugnancy to the injunctions of the original sources of law as a constitutional provision is not adequate as a feasible legal formulation for the reasons of giving full expression to Islamic Law, for it neither provides full expression to Islamic Law, nor it is a convincing schematic plan for the organisation of a comparable Islamic legal system suited to the contemporary requirements. The denouement of such a constitutional requirement is law that only accepts the adjudication of its violation, and the evolved belief-system of Islam is expected to be a precursor of any, but an artless law suited to its genius.

References

1. *An Islamic historian and writer.*
2. *A Marxist philosopher of Economy.*
3. *An economic critic and analyst.*
4. *A great freedom fighter and historian of India.*

BIBLIOGRAPHY

Aghanides, N.P. : *Mohammedan Theories of Finance,* Oxford, New York, 1916.

Ahmad, K. N. : *Muslim Law of Divorce,* Kitab Bhavan, New Delhi, 1988.

Ahmad, M.M.Z. : *Mystical Tendencies in Islam in the Light of the Quran and Traditions*, Daya Publishing House, Delhi, 1986.

Ahmed, Hasanuddin : *Principles of Islamic Culture,* Goodword Books Pvt. Ltd., New Delhi, 1989.

Ali, A. Yusuf : *Message of Islam,* Kitab Bhavan, New Delhi, 2000.

Ali, S. Ameer : *Muhammadan Law,* Kitab Bhavan, New Delhi, 1986.

Amini, Mualana Taqi : *Fundamentals of Ijtihad,* Idaara-I-Adabiyat, Delhi, 1986.

Anwarullah : *The Islamic Law of Evidence,* Kitab Bhavan, New Delhi, 2000.

Arnold, T. W. : *Preaching of Islam*, Luzac & Co., London, 1913.

Asad, Muhammad : *The Principles of State and Government in Islam*, University of California Press, California, 1961.

Asborn, Eide : *Human Rights in World Society,* New Millennium Pub., Oslo, 1977.

Asghar Ali, E. : *Islam : Challenge in Twenty-first Century,* Gyan Books Pvt. Ltd., New Delhi, 2004.

———— : *Islam : Women and Gender Justice,* Gyan Books Pvt. Ltd., New Delhi, 2001.

Azad, G. Murtaza : *Judicial System of Islam,* Kitab Bhavan, New Delhi, 1994.

Aziz, Noomi Kurtha : *Prisoners of War and War Crimes,* Deep Publications, Lacknow, 1980.

Azmi, Majaz : *Muslim Wife,* Idara Ishaat-e-Diniyat Pvt. Ltd, New Delhi, 1991.

Baksh, S. K. : *Politics in Islam,* Kitab Bhavan, New Delhi, 2003.

Basil, King : *The Conquest of Fearm,* Illias Pub., Islamabad, 2000.

Bernard, L. : *Islam,* Oxford, New York, 1974.

Beverly Milton, E. : *Islam and Politics in the Contemporary World*, Blackwell, New York, 1987.

Bhatia, H. S. : *Studies in Islamic Law, Religion and Society*, Deep & Deep Publications, New Delhi, 1997.

Briffault, Robert : *The Making of Humanity,* Islamic Book Foundation, Lahore, 1980.

Brow, John R. : *Islam, Law, and Equality in Indonesia : an Anthropology of Public,* Cambridge University Press, New Delhi, 1997.

Calverley, Edwin Elliot : *Worship in Islam*, University of Madras, Madras, 1925.

Cassese, A. : *The Self-determination of Peoples,* Columbia University, Columbia, 1981.

Chiragh, Ali : *The Proposed Political Legal and Social Reform under Muslim Rule,* Popular Prakashan, Bombay, 1883.

Cook, Michael : *Forbiding Wrong in Islam : an Introduction*, Cambridge University Press, New Delhi, 1985.

Corbin, H. : *Avicenna and the Visionary Recital,* MacMillan, London, 1960.

De, Laet : *The Political Systems of Empire,* Oxford, New York, 1963.

Emil, Brunner : *Justice and the Social Order,* Oxford, New York, 2000.

Enayat, H. : *Islam in the Political Process,* Cambridge University Press, Cambridge, 1993.

Engineer, Asghar Ali : *A Rational Approach to Islam,* Gyan Books Pvt. Ltd., New Delhi, 2001.

———— : *The Islamic State,* Vikas Publishing House, New Delhi, 1987.

Faris, Nabith A. : *The Book of Knowledge*, Feroz Pub., Lahore, 1962.

Fatima, T. : *Islamic Law and Judiciary,* Deep & Deep Publications, New Delhi, 2001.

Fauzi, M. : *The Islamic State : a Study in Traditional Politics,* Oxford, New York, 1967.

Frederic, G. : *Political Islam in the Indian Subcontinent : the Jannat-i-Islam,* Manohar Publishers, New Delhi, 2001.

Gellner, E. : *Post-Traditional Forms in Islam : the Turf and Trade*, Oxford, New York, 1982.

Gerges : *American and Political Islam : Clash of Cultures or Claush of Interest?,* New Academic Publishers, New Delhi, 1992.

Gibb, H.A.R : *Islamic Society and the West,* Luzac & Co., London, 1960.

Gins Berg, M. : *Evolution and Progress,* William Heinemann Ltd., London, 1982.

Grunebaum, G.E. : *Islam : Essays in the Nature and Growth of a Cultural Tradition,* American Anthropological Association, 1955.

Grunebaum, Gustave Edmund Von : *Modern Islam,* University Press, Los Angeles, 1952.

Guillaume, A. : *The Legacy of Islam,* Oxford University Press, London, 1949.

———— : *The Traditions of Islam,* Khayats, Beirut, 1966.

Gustav, E. Von Grunebaum : *Unity and Variety in Muslim World,* Oxford, New York, 2003.

Harun, Yahya : *Islam : the Religion of Ease,* Goodword Books Pvt. Ltd., New Delhi, 1993.

Hasan, A. : *Islami Reassertion : a Socio Political Study,* Progressive Publishers, Lahore, 1981.

Hasan, Ehteshamul : *Fundamentals of Islam,* Idara Ishaat-e-Diniyat Pvt. Ltd, New Delhi, 1990.

Hasanuddin, A. : *Islamic Economics,* Goodword Books Pvt. Ltd., New Delhi, 1991.

———— : *Social Justice in Islam,* Goodword Books Pvt. Ltd., New Delhi, 1990.

Henderson, J.J. Craik : *Parliament : a Survey,* George Allen & Unwin, London, 1965.

Heyworth-Dunne : *Religious and Political Trends in Modern Egypt,* Washington,1950.

Hourani, Albert : *Thought in the Liberal Age*, Oxford, New York, 1962.

Houtsma, T. and Others : *Encyclopaedia of Islam*, MacMillan, London, 1934.

Hughes, T.P. : *Dictionary of Islam,* Allen & Co., London, 1935,

Husaini, Waqar : *Islamic Thought,* Goodword Books Pvt. Ltd., New Delhi, 1999.

Hussain, S. Saukat, : *Human Rights in Islam,* Kitab Bhavan, New Delhi, 2001.

Ilyas, A. : *Social Contract and the Islamic State,* Urdu Publishing House, Allahabad, 1940.

Imtiaz, A. : *Divorce and Remarriage among Muslims in India,* Manohar Publishers, New Delhi, 2003.

Iqbal, Muhammad : *Six Lectures on the Reconstruction of Religious Thought in Islam*, Royal Pub., Lahore, 1930.

Jafar, Sharif : *Islam in India,* Oxford, New Delhi, 1972.

Jansen, G.H. : *Militant Islam,* Pan Books, London, 1979.

John L. Esposite : *Islam in Transition,* Oxford, New York, 1969.

Joseph, and Bosworth, C.E. : *The Legacy of Islam,* Oxford University Press, New York, 1979.

Karnal, A. Faruqui : *Islam : Today and Tomorrow,* Deep & Deep Pub., New Delhi, 1989.

Khab, Qamaruddin : *The Political Thought of Ibn Taimiyah,* Islamic Book Foundation, Lahore, 1983.

Khaduri, M. : *War and Peace in the Law of Islam,* Hopkins Press, Baltimore, 1955.

Khalifa, Abdul Hakim : *The Islamic Ideology,* Fortune Books,London, 1993.

Khan, N. M. Yamin : *God Soul and Universe in Science and Islam,* Kitab Bhavan, New Delhi, 1993.

Khan, Qamaruddin : *Political Concepts in the Quran,* Islamic Book Foundation, Lahore, 1982.

———— : *The Methodology of Islamic Research,* Institute of Islamic Studies, Karachi, 1973.

Khan, Wahiduddin : *Islam and Peace,* Goodword Books Pvt. Ltd., New Delhi, 1996.

———— : *Polygamy and Islam,* Goodword Books Pvt. Ltd., New Delhi, 1996.

Khurshid, A. : *Islam : its Meaning and Message,* Islamic Council of Europe, London, 1976.

Lewin, Roger : *In the Age of Mankind,* Simithsonian Books, Washington, D.C., 1956.

Lewis, Richards : *Universe,* Harmony Books, New York, 1973.

Lok Raj, B. : *Regional Migrations : Ethnicity and Security,* Popular Prakashan, Bombay, 1995.

MacDonald, D.B. : *Development of Muslim Theology*, New Century Pub., London, 1993.

———— : *The Religious Attitude and Life in Islam*, Modern Pub., Beirut, 1965.

Manzuruddin, Ahmad : *Islamic Political System,* Kitab Bhavan, New Delhi, 1991.

Margery Milne : *The Nature of Life,* Crown Publishers, New York, 1995.

Mathew, Thomas : *Political Economy of Etimic Conflict,* School of International Studies, Jawaharlal Nehru University, New Delhi, 2003.

Maurice, B. : *The Bibal, Quran and Science,* Kitab Bhavan, New Delhi, 2004.

McIver, R.M. : *The Community,* MacMillan & Co., London, 1978.

Mole, Marigan : *Les Mystiques Musulmans*, MacMillan & Co., Paris, 1965.

Morgan : *War its Conduct and Legal Results,* Feroz Pub., Lahore, 2000.

Morgenthu, H. : *Politics : Among Nations,* Oxford New York, 1984.

Mortimer, E. : *Faith and Power, the Politics of Islam,* Oxford, New York, 2002.

Muhammad, Asad : *Islam at the Crossroads,* Kitab Bhavan, New Delhi, 2003.

Muhammad, Ayub : *The Politics of Islamic Revolution,* Royal Pub., Lahore, 1991.

Muhammad, M. : *The Political Theory of Ibn Khaldun,* MacMillan & Co., London, 1967.

Murata, S. : *The Vision of Islam,* Ashish Publishing House, New Delhi, 1991.

Murthy, T.S. : *Muslim : the Difficult Years,* Himalayan Books, Chandigarh, 1983.

Muslehuddin, M. : *Banking and Islamic Law,* Idara Ishaat-e-Diniyat Pvt. Ltd, New Delhi, 1990.

———— : *Islam : its Political System,* Kitab Bhavan, New Delhi, 1999.

Nabith, A. F. : *The Foundations of the Articles of Faith,* Feroz Pub., Lahore, 1993.

Naseem, A. : *Liberation of Muslim Women*, Gyan Books Pvt., Ltd., New Delhi, 2001.

Nasr, Seyyed H. : *Science and Civilization in Islam*, Cambridge, New York, 1996.

Nicholson, R.A. : *Tales of Mystic Meaning*, MacMillan & Co., London, 1981.

———— : *The Mysteries of Islam*, MacMillan & Co., London, 1974.

Noorani, A.G. : *Islam and Jihad,* Manohar Publishers, New Delhi, 2002.

Oage, Charles H. : *The Society,* MacMillan & Co., London, 1959.

Oudha, Abdul Qadir : *Criminal Law of Islam,* Kitab Bhavan, New Delhi, 1999.

Palamer, E.H. : *The Quran,* Atlantic Publishers, New Delhi, 1996.

Philips, E.C. : *Politics and Society in India,* MacMillan & Co., London, 1963.

Phillips, O. Hood : *Reform of the Constitution,* MacMillan & Co., London, 1970.

Pickthall, M. M. : *Islamic Culture,* Feroz Sons Publishers, Lahore, 1992.

Qazi A. Qadir : *The Changing World of Islam,* Royal Pub., Lahore, 1992.

Qureshi, A. Iqbal : *Islam and the Theory of Interest,* Kitab Bhavan, New Delhi, 1994.

Rabnson, Chave F. : *Islamic Histroriography,* Cambridge University Press, New York, 1990.

Rahbar, D. : *God of Justice*, Mac & Jac Pub., Leiden, 1960.

Rahim, Abdur : *Principles of Islamic Jurisprudence,* Kitab Bhavan, New Delhi, 1994.

Ray, Samirendra : *Judicial Review and Fundamantal Rights,* Eastern Law House, Kolkata, 2002.

Rodinson, M. : *Islam and Capitalism,* Penguin, London, 1974.

Rosenthal, E.I.J. : *Political Thought in Medieval Islam,* Cambridge, New York, 1962.

Rumi, Jalåludin : *The Masnavi,* Gyan Books Pvt. Ltd., New Delhi, 2000.

Ruthven, Malise : *Islam : a Very Short Introduction*, Oxford, New York, 1990.

Sabiruddin : *Muslim Husband and Wife : Right and Duties,* Kitab Bhavan, New Delhi, 2000.

Said, Edward W. : *Orientalism,* Pantheon Books, New York, 1978.

Saran, P. : *Mystical Dimensions of Islam*, Chape Hill, New York, 1975.

Saxena, K.P. : *Human Rights: Perspective and Challenges,* Lancers Books, New Delhi, 1996.

Scarfe, K. : *Perception of the Islamic Word,* Cambridge University Press, New Delhi, 1992.

Scarman, Leslie : *Law : the New Dimensions,* Stevens and Sons, London, 1974.

Schacht, J. : *The Origins of Muhammadan Jurisprudence,* Clarendon Press, Oxford, 1963.

Schwartz, E. : *Science and Civilization in Islam,* Cambridge, London, 1966.

Seervai, H. : *Constitutional Law of India,* N.M. Tripathi & Co., Bombay, 1967.

Seyyed, H. : *An Introduction to Islamic Cosmological Doctrines*, Cambridge, 1964.

Shad, A. R. : *Duties of an Imam,* Idara Ishaat-e-Diniyat Pvt. Ltd, New Delhi, 1990.

Shaheed, A. Q. A. : *Islamic System of Justice,* Kitab Bhavan, New Delhi, 1994.

Shaikh, N. M. : *Women in Muslim Society,* Kitab Bhavan, New Delhi, 1991.

Sharif, M. Raihan : *Islamic Social Framework,* Islamic Book Foundation, Dacca, 1980.

Shaukat, Ali : *Masters of Muslim Thought,* Deep & Deep Pub., New Delhi, 1992.

Shemesh, A.B. : *Taxation in Islam*, MacMillan & Co., London, 1965.

Sherwani, H.K. : *Cultural Trends in Medieval India*, Popular Prakashan, Bombay, 1968.

———— : *Studies in Muslim Thought and Administration,* University of Hyderbad, Hyderabad, 1975.

Singh, Nagendar : *Human Rights and International Cooperation,* S. Chand & Co., New Delhi, 1969.

Smith, M. : *Readings from the Mystics of Islam*, MacMillan & Co., London, 1950.

Stanton, S. : *Teaching of the Quran*, Discovery Publishing House, New Delhi, 1989.

Stobart, J.W. H. : *Islam and its Founders*, Uppal Publishing House, New Dlehi, 1974.

Syed, Amir Ali : *The Spirit of Islam*, Royal Pub., Lahore, 1979.

Syed, M. H. : *Human Rights in Islam*, Anmol Publications, New Delhi, 2004.

——————— : *Impact of Islam*, Anmol Publications, New Delhi, 2003.

——————— : *Islam and Science*, Anmol Publications, New Delhi, 2003.

——————— : *Islam and the Modern Age*, Anmol Publications, New Delhi, 2003.

——————— : *Islamic Terrorism : Myth or Reality*, Gyan Books Pvt. Ltd., New Delhi, 2002.

——————— : *Status of Women in Islamic Society*, Anmol Publications, New Delhi, 2003.

Tarachand : *Influence of Islam on Indian Culture*, Adam Pub., Allahabad, 1963.

Thomas, A. : *The Legacy of Islam*, Oxford University Press, New York, 2000.

Titus, M. : *Indian Islam*, Milford, New Delhi, 1979.

Tripathi, R.P. : *Some Aspects of Muslim Administration*, Vora Pub., Allahabad, 1959.

Ulama, Majlisul : *Islamic Hijaab*, Idara Ishaat-e-Diniyat Pvt. Ltd, New Delhi, 1997.

Ullah, M. : *Administration of Justice in Islam*, Kitab Bhavan, New Delhi, 1990.

Usmani, J.M. Tariq : *The Authority of Sunnah*, Kitab Bhavan, New Delhi, 1998.

——————— : *An Introduction to Islamic Finance*, Idara Ishaat-e-Diniyat Pvt. Ltd., New Delhi, 1999.

Valliuddin, Mir : *The Quranic Sufism*, Motilal Banarsi Das Publishers, New Delhi, 1989.

Vasudha, D. : *Law, Power and Justice : Protection of Personal Rights under Islam*, Popular Prakashan, Bombay, 2001.

Wahed, H. : *Administration of Justice during the Muslim Rule in India*, Kitab Ghar, New Delhi, 1977.

——————— : *Administration of Justice during the Muslim Rule in India*, Ashish Publishing House, New Delhi, 1977.

Waheed, Akhtar : *The Early Imamiya Shiite Thinkers*, Ashish Publishing House, New Delhi, 1995.

Wahiduddin, K. : *Islam Activism*, Goodword Books Pvt. Ltd., New Delhi, 1994.

——————— : *The True Jihad*, Goodword Books Pvt. Ltd., New Delhi, 1995.

Waines, Davids : *A Introduction to Islam,* Cambridge University Press, New Delhi, 1995.

Wasiti, Hakim Nayyar : *Muslim Contribution to Medicine,* Deep & Deep Pub., New Delhi, 1993.

Watt, W.M. : *Islam and the Integration of Society,* Routledge, London, 1961.

——————— : *Islamic Surveys,* Edinburgh University Press, Edinburgh, 1999.

Wazir, A. : *Economics in Islamic Law,* Kitab Bhavan, New Delhi, 1992.

Weeramanthy, G. G.: *Islamic Jurisprudence—an International Perspective*, Vishwa Lekha, Culcutta, 1980.

Wilfred, Seamen Blunt : *The Future of Islam,* MacMillan, London, 1991.

Willoughby, W. : *Principles of the Constitutional Law of the United States,* Baker Voorthis & Company, New York, 1938.

Yahanan, F. : *Tolerance and Coercion in Islam : Interfaith Relations in the Muslims Traditions*, Cambridge, New York, 1990.

Yusuf, S.M. : *Economic Justice in Islam,* Kitab Bhavan, New Delhi, 1988.

Zafeeruddin, M.M. : *System of Modesty and Chastity in Islam,* Idara Ishaat-e-Diniyat Pvt. Ltd, New Delhi, 1995.

Zahid, Malik : *Subjects of Quran,* Kitab Bhavan, New Delhi, 1998.

Zartman, I.W. : *Man, State and Society in the Contemporary Muslim World,* Lozac & Co., London, 1973.

Ziadah, N.A. : *Sanusiyah : a Study of a Revivalist Movement in Islam,* Poul & Co., Leiden, 1958.

INDEX

B

C

D

J

N

O

P

R

S

Y

Z

❑❑❑